KU-135-326

26 Aug 02

FARADAY

By the same author

Arthur Rackham: A Life with Illustration
William Heath Robinson
Wood Engraving and the Woodcut in Britain c.1890–1990
The Sculpture of Austin Wright
Turner: A Life
Turner and the Scientists
Fields of Influence: Conjunctions of Artists and Scientists 1815–60 (editor)

FARADAY

The Life

James Hamilton

HarperCollins*Publishers*

HarperCollins*Publishers*
77–85 Fulham Palace Road,
Hammersmith, London W6 8JB
www.**fire**and**water**.com

Published by HarperCollins*Publishers* 2002

Copyright © James Hamilton 2002

1 3 5 7 9 8 6 4 2

The author asserts the moral right to
be identified as the author of this work

Decorative illustrations by Michael Faraday

A catalogue record for this book
is available from the British Library

ISBN 0 00 257082 3

Set in Minion by Rowland Phototypesetting Limited,
Bury St Edmunds, Suffolk

Printed and bound in Great Britain by
Clays Ltd, St Ives plc

All rights reserved. No part of this publication may be
reproduced, stored in a retrieval system, or transmitted,
in any form or by any means, electronic, mechanical,
photocopying, recording or otherwise, without the prior
permission of the publishers.

For my family

CONTENTS

ILLUSTRATIONS

Michael and Sarah Faraday. A pair of silhouettes cut in 1821, the year of their marriage.

Sarah Barnard. A pencil drawing, c.1820, of Faraday's fiancée. *(© The Royal Institution, London)*

Michael Faraday in his late thirties. Engraving by Samuel Cousins after a portrait by H.W. Pickersgill, 1829.

Faraday aged forty. Pencil drawing by William Brockendon, 1831. *(Reproduced courtesy of National Portrait Gallery, London)*

Faraday in his early fifties. *(Reproduced courtesy of Museum of the History of Science, Oxford)*

Faraday with John Frederic Daniell in the early 1840s. *(© The Royal Institution, London/The Bridgeman Art Library, London)*

Faraday with William Brande at the Royal Institution, late 1850s. *(© The Royal Institution, London)*

Faraday lecturing at the Royal Institution in 1855. *(© Hulton Archive)*

Michael and Sarah Faraday in the mid-to-late 1840s. *(© The Royal Institution, London/The Bridgeman Art Library, London)*

A cartoon published in *Punch* in 1855, at the height of the public controversy over the filthy state of London's River Thames. *(© Punch)*

Punch cartoon published in 1891, the centenary of Faraday's birth. *(© Punch)*

Faraday's niece Margery Ann Reid. Pencil drawing, mid-1830s, by George Barnard. *(© The Royal Institution, London/The Bridgeman Art Library, London)*

Faraday's lifelong friend Edward Magrath. *(© The Royal Institution, London)*

Sir Humphry Davy. Portrait by Sir Thomas Lawrence, 1821. *(© Royal Society)*

Faraday's friend Richard Phillips, editor of *Annals of Philosophy*. *(© The Royal Institution, London/The Bridgeman Art Library, London)*

The artist John Martin. *(Reproduced courtesy of National Portrait Gallery, London)*

J.M.W. Turner by John Linnell, 1838. *(Reproduced courtesy of National Portrait Gallery, London)*

Mary Somerville. Marble bust by Sir Francis Chantrey, 1840. *(© Royal Society)*

Ada, Countess of Lovelace. *(© The Royal Institution, London/The Bridgeman Art Library, London)*

C.F. Schoenbein, friend and confidant of Faraday's latter years, in 1858. *(© The Royal Institution, London/The Bridgeman Art Library, London)*

Harriet Moore, 1854. *(© The Royal Institution, London/The Bridgeman Art Library, London)*

Pen-and-ink drawing of a pneumatic apparatus by Michael Faraday in his 'Philosophical Miscellany' (1809–10).

John Tatum's lecture room at 53 Dorset Street. Pen-and-ink drawing by Michael Faraday, 1810. *(© The Royal Institution, London)*

A chemical balance at the Royal Institution. Pencil drawing by Michael Faraday. *(© The Royal Institution, London)*

Bridge and River. Wash drawing by Michael Faraday, 1820s or 1830s. *(© The Royal Institution, London)*

Cottage Among Mountains. Lithograph made jointly by Michael Faraday and George Barnard, dated 25 April 1825. *(© The Royal Institution, London)*

Rest on the Flight to Egypt. Engraving by Claude Lorraine, 1670. Print from Faraday's notebook. *(© The Royal Institution, London)*

The Three Trees. Engraving by Rembrandt, 1643. Print from Faraday's notebook. *(© The Royal Institution, London)*

'Scientific Researches!' Cartoon by James Gillray, 1802. *(© The Royal Institution, London/The Bridgeman Art Library, London)*

The laboratory of the Royal Institution as it was in the late 1810s.

The safety lamp, devised by Davy and Faraday in 1814.

Apparatus devised by Faraday in 1821 to demonstrate electro-magnetic rotations.

Faraday's induction ring. *(© Hulton Archive)*

The electro-magnet made in 1845 at the Royal Institution. *(© Hulton Archive)*

Faraday at work in the Chemical Laboratory. Watercolour by Harriet Moore, 1852. *(© Hulton Archive)*

Faraday's Magnetic Laboratory. Watercolour by Harriet Moore, 1850s.

Faraday's study in his Royal Institution flat. Watercolour by Harriet Moore, 1850s. *(© The Royal Institution, London/The Bridgeman Art Library, London)*

The house on the Green, Hampton Court, where Faraday lived from 1858 until his death.

0   5 miles

Regent's Park

4 ■ ■ 5
   ■ 3

2 ■ ■ 11
      ■ 8
Hyde Park   12 ■ ■

Royal Hospital,
Chelsea
■

The
Green,
Hampton
Court

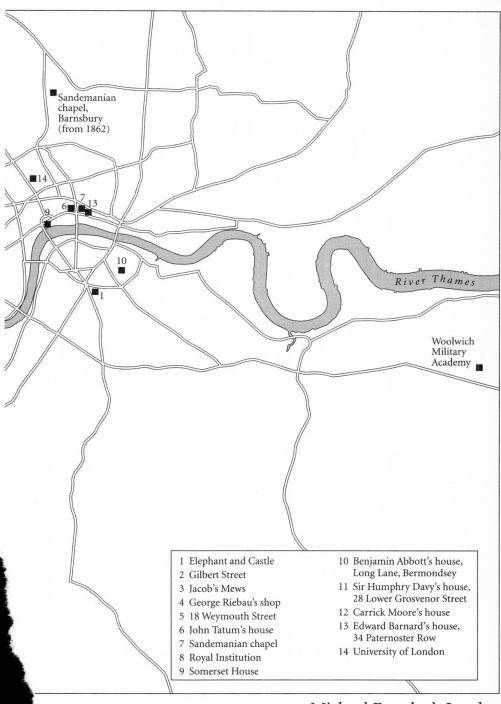

1 Elephant and Castle
2 Gilbert Street
3 Jacob's Mews
4 George Riebau's shop
5 18 Weymouth Street
6 John Tatum's house
7 Sandemanian chapel
8 Royal Institution
9 Somerset House

10 Benjamin Abbott's house,
   Long Lane, Bermondsey
11 Sir Humphry Davy's house,
   28 Lower Grosvenor Street
12 Carrick Moore's house
13 Edward Barnard's house,
   34 Paternoster Row
14 University of London

Sandemanian chapel, Barnsbury (from 1862)

River Thames

Woolwich Military Academy

Michael Faraday's London

ACKNOWLEDGEMENTS

I am very grateful to friends and colleagues including Michael Baker, Geoffrey Cantor, David Knight, Roy Keckwick, the Revd John Reynolds, my father Patrick Hamilton and my wife Kate, who read this book at different evolutionary stages of its writing. They made suggestions, put me straight, urged caution, issued warnings, but above all gave me the encouragement I needed to try to look at Faraday in a way that gives a new and I hope urgent priority to his role as a central figure in the history of western culture.

The earliest glimmerings took flame when Alistair Horne and St Antony's College, Oxford, did me the great honour of giving me the Alistair Horne Fellowship for 1998/99. I am profoundly grateful to Alistair and Sheelin Horne, to Sir Marrack Goulding, the Warden of St Antony's, and to the many friends among staff and students at the college whose encouragement and interest in my undertaking was heartening, particularly at those gloomy times when I wondered why on earth I had taken the subject on; central among them are the late Dr Michael Aris, Geoffrey Best, Alberto Costi, Graham Daniels, Polly Friedhoff, Tim Garton-Ash, Estelle Hussein, Amanda Kaye, Tim Lawrence, Eugene Rogan, Robert Service, Arnold Stockwin, Ann Waswo, and a young man who told me he would be President of Bolivia in 2020, and I daresay he will be.

Other helpful and generous people who gave me guidance through conversation, correspondence, friendship, library assistance or (unbeknownst to some of them) their own writing and teaching include Isabel Armitage, David Beasley, Jim Bennett, Michael Bolik, Thomas Boyd,

Philip Bye, Alan Carter, April Dance, Douglas Davies, Nancy S. Dawson, James Dearden, the late Rowland Eustace, Sophie Forgan, Geoffrey Forster, Robert Fox, Peter W. Girvan, David Gooding, Colin Harris, Jane Hay, Ann Holmes, Giles Hudson, Frank James, Paul Joyner, Reuben Kaufman, Scotford Lawrence, Anne Locker, Irene McCabe, Rusty Mac-Clean, S.W. Massil, Iwan Rhys Morus, Christine Penney, Nicholas Plumley, B.L. Riddle, Richard Rutherford, James Secord, Joanne Shattock, Tony Simcock, Michael Slater, the late Mrs Molly Spiro, Lenore Symons, Diana Thomas and Sir John Meurig Thomas, the late Wynne Thomas, Anne Treneer, Ivone Turnbull, L. Pearce Williams and many colleagues at the University of Birmingham.

Permission to reproduce texts and images in their ownership has been given by the Ashmolean Museum, the Bodleian Library, the Institution of Electrical Engineers, the National Portrait Gallery, the Royal Institution, the Royal Society, the University of Birmingham, Laurence Pollinger Ltd and the Earl of Lytton. Others I have been unable to trace, or wish to remain anonymous.

I cannot tell if the shades of Michael and Sarah Faraday walked beside me while I was writing; but I know that my family did – Kate, Thomas, Elinor and Marie – and to them, with my love and profound thanks, this book is dedicated.

James Hamilton
Oxford, January 2002

INTRODUCTION

Setting off from London in October 1813 to travel on the continent, Michael Faraday found the education of an artist in the company of a scientist. He was twenty-two years old when he left England with Sir Humphry Davy, the most famous and admired scientist of his day, taking with him notebooks in which he wrote a unique diary, perceptive, full of incident and detail, of art and antiquities, of scientific experiments and discovery in the making, and of Europe at a moment of unparalleled change. But he took with him also the affection and good wishes of Richard Cosway, as fashionable and controversial a painter as Davy was a scientist, and of the distinguished and level-headed architect George Dance the Younger, and so had the added opportunity of experiencing the antiquities, landscape and history of Europe with the distant guidance of two senior Royal Academicians. With Davy beside him, and Cosway and Dance at home, Faraday's entourage of mentors was complete.

Faraday's diary of his eighteen-month continental journey, and the many letters home that surround it, reveals the formation of a man whose scientific discoveries would begin within thirty years to affect through gradual change the lives of every person on the planet.

In the twenty-first century, Michael Faraday's discoveries and improvements have become given facts and facilities. Electricity comes out of the plug in the wall; shirts and dresses of every subtle shade of dye hang on the rails of clothes shops; we wear spectacles with precision-made lenses, use steel razors, stir tea with electroplated spoons; we fly in aeroplanes free of harm from lightning strikes; we sail in ships warned off rocks by effective lighthouses; and we swim in pools tinctured by liquid chlorine. But in taking a clear occasional glimpse back at the roots of all these standards of modern life, time and again we see the figure of Michael Faraday standing at the distant crossroads.

If Faraday had not made the scientific discoveries he did, somebody else, or a chain of other people, would quite rapidly have done so. Life now would have been recognisably similar but for one particular: Faraday never patented anything. He built no fences around his discoveries to increase personal gain, nor did he market appliances, such as the electric motor or the dynamo, to exploit them. When his experimental ideas were progressing towards the inevitable practical application he passed them on to others. Faraday saw his role as reading 'the book of nature ... written by the finger of God',[1] determining, through experiment, analysis and deduction, a huge network of interconnected scientific principles which he gave as general knowledge to humanity. In doing so, there were no patent fees to pay to him in the nineteenth century, no 'Faraday and Company' to give dues to for the use of patterned cloth, razor blades or the generation of electrical power; but also, by now (if all had gone well in the twentieth century) no Faraday Foundation to distribute vast profits to speed the pursuit of happiness. We need to see and understand Faraday in the context of his time and cultural influences if we are to come to a fuller knowledge of the underpinnings of contemporary life. If we know where we have been, we may have a clearer idea of where we may be going.

In this biography I am taking a point of view that stands rather off the main track. Modern biographers of Faraday, writing largely as scientists and historians of science, have drawn portraits of the man which centre on his discoveries and their meanings. If Faraday were a seaside town these would be views of the main square, with all its colour, traffic and purpose. In looking at Faraday in his cultural context, and writing as an art historian with some minor, accidental, university experiences in science, the view I am painting is of the town and its landscape setting from the edge of the bay.

The central influence in Faraday's life that set him apart from his contemporaries was his religion. He was a devout member of a small, rigid Christian sect, the Sandemanians, whose members took guidance and inspiration from the Bible, and measured their lives against New Testament teaching. In reading God's book of nature Faraday felt himself to be under direction; Sandemanianism was the rock on which his town was built, keeping him apart from the politics of science, but causing him pain when he strove to reconcile scientific advances with his religious teaching.

Another decisive factor in Faraday's life was his interest in drawing and painting, in methods of making prints, in the development of photography, in the reproduction of images and in artists as people. This tended to have a lateral effect on his vocabulary: when he searched for words or phrases to describe scientific phenomena, he discovered expressions such as 'lines of force', 'magnetic field' or 'crispations', notions that could be drawn as well as written. When he sought to express *to himself* scientific ideas in his laboratory notebook he made marginal pen-and-ink drawings of the physical effect as he conceived it in his mind's eye. Faraday thought in images, would proclaim a successful result 'beautiful', and an understanding of the roots of his imagery and the processes of his image-making may lead to a deeper understanding of him as a man. He had little or no mathematics, and his experimental results were reached not by theory and calculation but by observation of physical and visual effects, using instruments of his own devising.

A third fundamental component of Faraday's personal chemistry was his need to teach people of all kinds and ages, and to lead them to a greater understanding of the natural scientific laws that govern us all. He was the son of a London blacksmith who died young, and of a devout, redoubtable mother. He had himself had a very thin education, of 'the most ordinary description', as he put it in later life. Never having experienced the classical education as fragmentarily delivered by the English public and grammar schools, nor a university grounding in Newtonian science, Faraday had no preconceptions, and was thus uniquely receptive when he first encountered science in London. By the same token, when he came to teach he explained his subject clearly and simply, using graphic illustrations and practical demonstrations which enthralled his audiences and sent them home believing themselves to understand perhaps more than they could fully retain.

Working in his laboratory in the basement of the Royal Institution in London, Faraday preferred solitude. The success of his science, however, depended on his learning from others, on consultation, collective endeavour and prayer. The extent of his correspondence with scientists and other friends reflects the passion with which he wanted to discover, discuss, argue and broadcast. He would not say, 'It is so,' but '*Why* is it so?', and would demonstrate why. With a zeal and enthusiasm that was of a new order entirely, Faraday used newly-evolving modern agencies and techniques, such as the public lecture and the press, to get his work known, and to become a public figure himself. He was a natural preacher; from the lecture theatre to the pulpit, standing up so that he could be clearly seen and heard became second nature. Looking at the way he went about things one might almost be studying the activities of a career administrator from the mid-twentieth century. Faraday worked with his employers to reform the fabric, administration, activities and finances of the Royal Institution so that it was in a fit state to teach science to the world. He took highly detailed and particularised notes of every step of his laboratory experiments. His correspondence bound him firmly to the world outside. He wrote and published in distinct voices for both professional and student readership. In 1826 he instituted the Friday Evening Discourses and subsequently gave children's lectures at the Royal Institution to great public acclaim. In an inspired, trend-setting move, he befriended the journalist William Jerdan and kept Jerdan's *Literary Gazette* regularly supplied with science news from the Royal Institution. In his attention to detail, to systems, to decorum, Faraday was already a Victorian when Princess Victoria herself was a girl playing with her dolls.

The lasting monument of Faraday's mature years is his *Experimental Researches in Electricity* (1832–55), forty-five linked papers which lay down the fundamental laws that guide the natural power of electricity, which Faraday considered to be the highest power known to man. The world's electrical industry is founded on the laws Faraday discovered and tabulated, and, like the Declaration of the Rights of Man, they have been added to but never superseded.

In his old age Faraday's science became increasingly theoretical, flying away from the solid certainties that he formulated in his mature years. In 1862, when he was effectively retired from science through ill-health and the rapidly increasing pace of change, Faraday was invited to give evidence on the teaching of science to the Public Schools Commission.

He accepted the invitation because science education had been the whole purpose of his life; and having emerged as a youth from the bottom of society he felt called in his last years to work to improve education until his breath gave out. But he completely misjudged the narrowness of the Commission's interest, and misunderstood the coded meaning of the words 'Public Schools'. Faraday had come to give his views on science education in all schools for the public of Britain; but the Commission was concerned only with Eton, Harrow, Winchester and six other such. Faraday's anger at being implicated in exclusivity was a late expression of the same passion which had suffused his life, and which drove him across an active career of forty years to reveal, teach and connect.

In writing about Faraday from a background in art history I am only too aware that I may be trying to ride two mettlesome and highly individual horses at the same time. In the 1820s and 1830s, however, the horses pulling the carriage of culture were still at one with each other, still a manageable team, and Faraday held the reins. The divide that began to draw art and science apart in the later nineteenth and twentieth centuries was, then, negotiable. Faraday's driving role in the development of culture in Britain in the nineteenth century is what this book is about.

CHAPTER 1

'The Progress of Genius'

It is clear from the phrasing of his early letters that Michael Faraday spoke at breakneck speed when he wanted to explain something, or to relate his news, fact and reason flooding out of him with excitement and joy in the telling. He lived in London, above a blacksmith's shop, a friendly boy, with an open face and thick brown curls on a head that was a size too big for his body.[1] He was always short, and this made his head seem yet larger; he never grew above about five feet four inches, the height of Napoleon and J.M.W. Turner. His voice had an edge to it, an accent from the streets, and it was perhaps this that betrayed his vulnerability, his apartness, for beyond the accent he was as a boy unable to grip in his mouth words which had a sounding 'r' in them: he had what we now call a soft 'r'. As a result, he could not pronounce his own name. 'Michael Fawaday', he would say;[2] or to avoid misunderstanding or teasing, 'Mike'.

He had had no formal schooling, just a grounding of reading, writing and arithmetic at a day-school near the smithy in the back premises of 16 Jacob's Mews, an alley north of Oxford Street. Faraday's education was blunt – on one occasion when he spoke of his elder brother 'Wobert', the schoolmistress gave Robert a halfpenny to buy a cane to thrash the speech defect out of Michael.[3] Robert refused to do any such thing, threw the coin over a wall and went home to tell his mother who promptly removed both boys from the school. When not at school, which was most of the time, Michael played with his friends in the street, or at home with his parents, elder brother and sisters. Jacob's Mews was, and remains – for while the buildings have changed the building line has not – a wide, deep and bright alley, with plenty of room for blacksmithery and anvils to be set out in the yard, and for waiting horses to assemble. There was no academic learning in the family, and no likelihood of it. Michael's father, James Faraday, had been sick for years, so the family's financial and social future was insecure. Michael's mother, Margaret, had however an instinctive feeling that her younger son, her third child, had a special quality, some rare intelligence and intuition in him that she had no word for. 'My Michael!', she would say.[4]

Both his parents were devout. They had been brought up in the strict, non-conformist Sandemanian church in Westmorland, in the north-west of England. They had met and married in it, and arranged their lives according to its lights and guidance. James Faraday was a plain, practical man, the third son in a large smallholding family of Christians from Clapham in north Yorkshire. The allegiance of his parents, Robert and Elizabeth Faraday, had shifted in the volatile atmosphere of religious dissent of the mid-eighteenth century from one sect, the Inghamites, to the Sandemanians. With a historical perspective these changes are minor twists in the grain, but in their period and parish they could lead to anger, betrayal, family division and exclusion. Robert Faraday preached to Inghamite and Sandemanian congregations in Clapham and surrounding villages, and brought his children up to fear God and support the community. His eldest son, Richard, became an innkeeper and grocer, the second, John, a weaver and later a farmer, and the third, James, a blacksmith. Other sons became tailors and leather workers, while the three daughters remained unmarried.[5]

Michael Faraday's mother was the sixth child of Michael Hastwell, a farmer, and his wife Betty, of Black Scar Farm at Kaber, Westmorland. Having grown up on a farm, Margaret Hastwell brought rural talents such as threshing, winnowing and cheese- and butter-making to the marriage.[6] Like the Faradays, the Hastwells had become Sandemanians, and attended the meeting house in Kirkby Stephen, the small market town on the northern side of the county boundary between Yorkshire and Westmorland. The Clapham and Kirkby Stephen congregations worshipped together from time to time, and it must have been in such sober circumstances that James Faraday and Margaret Hastwell met.[7] He took a smithy opposite the King's Head at Outhgill, five miles south of Kirkby Stephen; she became a maidservant at Deep Gill Farm nearby. They married, aged twenty-five and twenty-two respectively, at Kirkby Stephen parish church in 1786, and their first two children, Elizabeth and Robert, were born in 1787 and 1788.

Outhgill is in Mallerstang, the long, wide, green valley of the River Eden. Coaches travelling to Appleby, Penrith and Carlisle passed along the valley, a northern spur of the only practical route through the hills between Sedbergh to the west and Richmond forty miles over the Pennines to the east. In the year of Robert's birth, life began to change for James and Margaret. There was a long drought in 1788. It had been a beautiful warm spring, but by the summer they were looking and then praying for rain. Their green Eden grew brown, sheep and cattle died, and the coaches came less often because there was not enough hay for the horses. Then came the autumn frosts, and the worst winter anywhere in England for years.[8] For two weeks in December the valley was icy and empty of traffic, and there was no work for the smithy.

The next summer came news of the revolution in France, the mob storming the Bastille, and Louis XVI fleeing Versailles. Then little bands of ill-dressed soldiery marched up and down the valley en route for Carlisle, or Leeds, or London. The prospect of war was frightening, but the presence of poverty was far worse. So, approaching a monumental decision that would change their and their children's lives, James and Margaret Faraday considered moving to a city. They talked and prayed with the Elders of the church in Kirkby Stephen, made their choice, and prepared to move to London. Margaret was pregnant when they left Outhgill. The slow passage from the north to London was Michael's first journey. Conceived in Westmorland, he was born in rented rooms near the Elephant and Castle inn, south of the River Thames, on 22 September 1791.

James and Margaret Faraday brought their children up in the exclusive Sandemanian faith in Christ, keeping themselves to themselves, and walking every Sunday to the neat but severe Sandemanian chapel in Paul's Alley, a dark passage running north from St Paul's Cathedral, and permanently in shadow. The congregation had an unequal struggle to keep their chapel neat and clean, for Paul's Alley, as recalled fifty years later, was 'a narrow, dirty court, surrounded by squalid houses of the poorest of the poor'.[9] When questions of temptation, sin, goodness or example arose in the family, they turned to the Bible for an answer. The family Bible (now in the Livesey Museum, Southwark) was their greatest treasure, and in it they recorded their family's births and deaths. When they opened their Bible, they always found enlightenment and never questioned. Sandemanians followed the lead of the Scottish linen-maker turned divine, Robert Sandeman (1718–71), and dissented from the established churches of England, Wales and Scotland. These they believed were governed against the teachings of the New Testament, were corrupt, and administered as part of the worldly state rather than the kingdom of God.

Sandemanians preached love and hope rather than hellfire and damnation, but it was a tough love. Though they all came together in the aisles to pass the kiss of peace to each other at their services, and washed each other's feet as a sign of humility, they demanded unanimity in church decisions, which was secured by 'excluding' minority dissenters; that is, throwing them out. This was a severe interpretation of 1 Corinthians 1.10, 'Now I beseech you, brethren, by the name of our Lord Jesus Christ, that ye all speak the same thing, and that there be no divisions among you; but that ye be perfectly joined together in the same mind and in the same judgement.' The teachings of the Bible were literally and strictly true in Sandemanian belief, which preached an intellectual rather than an emotional response to scripture. In the passage from 1 Corinthians, 'perfectly joined' was the rub. Any variant interpretation of scripture was forbidden, to the extent that Sandemanians refused to hold communion with any who did not perfectly agree with them.

The Sandemanian faithful dined together in a Love Feast in the chapel's spotless dining room, or at each other's houses on Sundays, between morning and afternoon worship, and would not eat the meat of any creature that had been killed by having its neck wrung, as the blood of the creature had to flow at death: this followed instruction in Acts 15.20. Games of chance were also banned, because to Sandemanians the lot was sacred to God, and property, they believed, was common to all. As a small sect, despised or at best dismissed by the established church, they stuck together, intermarried and assisted each other in welfare, housing and employment.[10]

Sandemanian services, which ran all day, with a break for the Love Feast, followed a strict pattern. They began with a roll-call: all members had to attend on Sundays, or answer for it to the Elders. Study of the Bible took no account of the established church feasts – Christmas, Lent, Easter – but led by the Elders the congregation read the Old Testament through chapter by chapter from Genesis 1 to Malachi 4, and the New Testament from St Matthew 1 to Revelation 22. When they reached the end they started again at the beginning.[11] Under the eyes of their Elders, seated in two raised rows of benches in front of them, the congregation conducted their worship as described by the non-conformist historian Walter Wilson in 1810:

> After singing a hymn [this was voices only; there were no musical instruments], a member of the church prays; these exercises are repeated three or four times; one of the Elders then reads some chapters from the Old or New Testaments; this is followed by singing; another Elder then prays, and either expounds or preaches for about three-quarters of an hour. Singing follows; and the service is concluded by a short prayer and benediction . . . In the afternoon, the former part of the service is curtailed; but after the sermon the church is stayed to receive the Lord's Supper, and contribute to the poor. When this is over, the members of the church are called upon to exercise their gifts by exhortation.[12]

The Faradays cannot have stayed for long at the Elephant and Castle. During their first few years in London they lived in Gilbert Street, south of Oxford Street, and in 1796 moved across Oxford Street to the back premises of 16 Jacob's Mews.[13] The Mews was remarkable for one thing in particular – it ran behind the Spanish Chapel of the Spanish Embassy, the one place in London in which Roman Catholics could worship legally before the Catholic Emancipation Act of 1828. For Sandemanians this was an extreme juxtaposition of faiths; no more extreme could they know. In London, as in Westmorland, the Faradays balanced on the edge of poverty. However hard he worked – and his ill-health was a further handicap – James Faraday found it near impossible to support his family, certainly impossible to get anywhere better to live than rented rooms above his smithy.

[5]

In 1804, when Michael was thirteen or fourteen, he had to put his schooling behind him and begin to earn some money for the family. He found a job as an errand boy for George Riebau, a Huguenot émigré bookbinder and bookseller in Blandford Street, sixty seconds by an errand boy's swift run from the Faraday smithy.[14] As a Huguenot, Riebau was also a member of a Protestant community which, like the Sandemanians, gathered together to protect itself against external aggression. But Riebau was also an activist in radical politics. He published radical religious and political tracts, including translations of the religious writings of Emanuel Swedenborg by Robert Hindmarsh, a founder of the Swedenborgian church in London. He also wrote a memoir, now lost, of Richard Brothers (1757–1824), who claimed to be the Prince of the Hebrews and ruler of the world.[15] Brothers went so far as to demand that King George III give up his crown to him, and this led to his imprisonment as a criminal lunatic. Riebau, who became known on the street as 'Bookseller to the Prince of the Hebrews', and may have been a Swedenborgian himself, was also a member of the subversive London Corresponding Society in the 1790s.[16] So the milieu that Michael Faraday was dropped into was a hotbed of religious dissent and radicalism, an exciting but dangerous place to be, and a place where curious, difficult, intellectual, cranky and dangerous people would gather, discuss and gossip, and where there were always interesting books and pamphlets lying about.

Two contrasting influences on Faraday's early life seem to have met with some force in Riebau's shop: his family Sandemanianism encountered the Swedenborgian beliefs that found sympathy with Riebau. Emanuel Swedenborg (1688–1772) was a world-shaping genius who has been compared to Aristotle. In his earlier career in Sweden he was an eminent and highly influential scientist and inventor who wrote on chemistry, metallurgy, astronomy, natural history, geology and topics ranging wide across the landscape of natural philosophy. Then in middle life his inspiration changed direction, leading him to write profound religious works which created the philosophical foundation of a new church anticipating the second coming of Christ and the building of a New Jerusalem.[17] His writings found fertile soil in England and subsequently America, but the point to be made here is that Swedenborg, who spent some of his latter years in London writing his religious philosophy, had demonstrated how one life could naturally integrate practical science with coherent religion. This would present a potent role model for any young man in the early nineteenth century whose passion for science had to negotiate a firm wall of religious dogma, and Swedenborgian thought may even have revealed to Faraday a doorway through it.

From the start, Michael was known at Riebau's as 'Faraday', a formal courtesy that indicated his low status in the workshop.[18] One of his first duties was to take newspapers round to Riebau's clients early in the morning, and then, later in the day, to collect them again and take them on to somebody else. Thus did news circulate in London in the early nineteenth century. But Faraday was clearly too bright for this sort of work to satisfy him for long, and after a year or so Riebau offered him an apprenticeship as a bookbinder. His indentures were signed on 7 October 1805.[19] Now he had seven years of hard work, training and extraordinary influences to look forward to, but security and companion-ship also, and prospects for the future. Thus his life slipped up a gear, and began to look encouraging, at exactly the same time as the outlook for the nation began to brighten when news of Nelson's victory at Trafalgar on 21 October began to circulate in London by the hands of errand newsboys.

Faraday became a skilful bookbinder under Riebau's tutelage. He learned how to trim the piles of pages sent by the printer, fold them into signatures with a folding stick and beat the folds to make them smooth and open cleanly. Then he learned how to sew the gathered signatures on to their bands – six or seven to a folio book, five to a quarto – and how to flick vermilion and sap-green pigment from a brush in a regular random pattern on the page edges. The covers came next – Riebau taught him how to cut the hides that lay in piles in the yard, and to choose the parts of the leather that were best suited for covering book boards. Faraday learned, too, how to boil wheat flour to make the glue to stick the leather to the board, and how to shave and drill the boards to fit the page bundles. The smells and sounds of the workshop entranced him, so did the tools and paraphernalia, and the heavy wooden benches, worn, bumped and rilled by years of banging and rubbing by bookbinders. The final duty to every well-bound book was to glaze its cover with two coats of beaten white of egg, polish it with a polishing iron passed hot over the glazed cover, and stamp the letters of the title in gold leaf on the spine.[20]

From the beginning of the apprenticeship Riebau spotted something extraordinary in Faraday – his eagerness, his fascination with the books that came for binding, his keenness to study them rather than to treat them merely as bundles of paper to be sewn. Perhaps because of this Riebau gave Faraday just that bit more encouragement than he might give to other apprentices, and gave him too some practical opportunities to follow the directions that his intellect took him. Riebau would have noticed Faraday's exceptional physical dexterity, the nimbleness of his fingers, how he could 'strike 1000 blows in succession [with a hammer] without resting', and his respect for these qualities grew early in their years together.[21] By the end of the apprenticeship Riebau was convinced that he had been the master of a genius, and told others so in an 'account of the Progress of Genius in an Apprentice', which he wrote for publication.[22]

Faraday read what he was binding, and having the third volume of the *Encyclopaedia Britannica* come into his hands, was fired with enthusiasm by the 'Electricity' article. This was no secret from Riebau, who encouraged him to make electrical instruments, and gave him the time and the space in the back of the shop to do so. Faraday read Lavoisier's seminal treatise *Elements of Chemistry*, first published in English in 1790, and *Conversations in Chemistry* by Jane Marcet also came in for binding. With jars and cooking pots Faraday followed the experiments described by that popular author, who wrote particularly for the young. Marcet was widely admired in literary and scientific society. The writer Maria Edgeworth described her as someone 'who had so much *accurate* information and who can give it out in narrative so clearly, so much for the pleasure and benefit of others without the least ostentation or mock humility'.[23] Many years later Faraday recalled the impact that Jane Marcet's writing on chemistry had had on him: '[it] gave me my foundation in that science . . . her book came to me as the full light in my mind'.[24]

Books were sold without covers in the early nineteenth century, and there was such a flow of material for binding through Riebau's workshop that Faraday could not have been better placed. He read Ali Baba, saw Hogarth's engravings,[25] studied landscape engravings, portrait prints and satirical engravings by Gillray and Rowlandson. The *Repository of Arts* journal passed through his hands, as did the *Dictionary of Arts and Sciences*. These are some of the few titles that we know he handled: to skip forward a hundred years, it must have been like sitting in the British Museum Reading Room with the whole world of literature passing book by book, day by day, past your eyes. Riebau encouraged him to copy from the books, text and illustrations, and he would settle down to do this at the end of the day when his fellow apprentices went off to mess around: 'I was a very lively, imaginative person,' he would later write, 'and could believe in the Arabian Nights as easily as in the Encyclopedia. But facts were important and saved me. I could trust a fact, but always cross-examined an assertion.'[26]

Riebau also encouraged Faraday to travel about London to see machinery in action, such as at the new pumping stations at Holloway and Hammersmith, where steam engines had been installed, and to see extraordinary feats of construction such as the Highgate Archway. He urged him to look at works of art on exhibition at the Royal Academy at Somerset House or the British Institution in Pall Mall, and asked customers if they would do him the favour of allowing the young man to see works of art in their private collections.

Among Riebau's customers were some of the leading artists of London. One was the miniature painter Richard Cosway, a Swedenborgian who dabbled in alchemy, mysticism and mesmerism;[27] another was the architect and artist George Dance the Younger; both were art collectors and may reasonably have been among those whose collections Riebau wanted Faraday to see. The Dance family, sons and grandsons of the architect and Surveyor to the Corporation of London George Dance the Elder, had an extended family tradition and made their own influential careers variously in the creative and performing arts. George Dance the Younger was the fifth and last of the sons, his father's pupil who became a highly influential architect and Professor of Architecture at the Royal Academy. Among the younger George Dance's buildings were Newgate Prison, Lord Lansdowne's Library in Berkeley Square and the Ionic portico of the College of Surgeons in Lincoln's Inn Fields. Having spent some years in Rome as a young man, Dance the Younger was well versed in the form and function of classical architecture, and interpreted it in his own buildings. George and the other Dances, all men of some power and influence, were variously Proprietors or Life Subscribers to the new Royal Institution in Albemarle Street.

Towards the end of 1809 the Faraday family moved from Jacob's Mews to Weymouth Street, a two-minute run from Riebau's shop. James Faraday's ill-health, and the death of his landlady, which may have brought with it further complications in the tenancy, forced him to give up the blacksmithery, and he and his family appear to have exchanged the smithy for 18 Weymouth Street with another tenant.[28] James died in 1810, and George Riebau took his place as the father figure to lead Michael Faraday and to broaden his outlook. One lifelong friend, the painter and inventor of optical drawing instruments Cornelius Varley, who was also briefly a member of the Sandemanian church, remembered the young Michael Faraday well: 'he was the best bookworm for eating his way to the inside; for hundreds had worked at books only as so much printed paper. Faraday saw a mine of knowledge, and resolved to explore it.'[29]

As an example of the right boy being at the right place at the right time, Michael Faraday is comparable in one aspect of his upbringing with the young J.M.W. Turner. Fifteen years earlier, Turner had been a youthful presence in his father's Covent Garden barber's shop. The flow that energised him was not one of books, but of customers who passed through the shop and were shown watercolours by the barber's son. 'My son is going to be a painter,' Turner the barber said. Equally, George Riebau's response was that Michael Faraday's name 'I am fully persuaded will be well known in a few years hence'.[30]

As a result of Riebau's encouragement, and the effect of the thousands of books that passed through, or near, his hands, Faraday began in 1809 a collection of 'Notices, Occurrences, Events Etc relating to the Arts and Sciences' which he had picked up from newspapers, reviews, magazines and so on. To this collection he gave the title, with its ring of a published collection, 'The Philosophical Miscellany' (its contents are listed in Appendix One). He wrote his material out neatly, illustrated it with careful pen-and-ink drawings, and indexed the whole thing. It is an omnivorous and enthusiastic gathering, a clue to the future.

In 1810, when Faraday was nineteen years old, Riebau encouraged him to go to lectures given by the teacher, philosopher and silversmith John Tatum in his house in Salisbury Court, 53 Dorset Street. Faraday's elder brother Robert found the shilling entry fee for him.[31] Tatum's house was off the eastern end of Fleet Street, a short walk down the hill from the Sandemanian chapel, and thus on one of the Faraday family's well-trodden routes. The lectures took place on Monday evenings in an upper room where diagrams hung on the walls, and a pair of windows stood opposite Tatum's desk. We know this because Faraday made a detailed perspective drawing of the empty lecture room, taking it as far as the loops of string suspending the diagrams. There he made friends with other young men and women who were transfixed by the new experimental science. Some, such as Benjamin Abbott and Edward Magrath – both Quakers – and Richard Phillips, became friends for life.

Tatum's lectures, from which Faraday took notes which he later transcribed and illustrated in detail, covered electricity, galvanism, optics, geology, mechanics, chemistry, astronomy and many other topics, the whole gamut of science, or 'natural philosophy'. Tatum taught most of what was then known: the gap between basic and advanced scientific research was wafer-thin, and heated disagreements between savants fractured this narrow space. Tatum gave due acknowledgement to his fellow natural philosophers, as scientists were then known, including Professor Humphry Davy at the Royal Institution, who had demonstrated how water could be decomposed by an electrical current, and Luigi Galvani, who showed how frogs' legs could be convulsed by an electrical charge. He would demonstrate phenomena with twenty or thirty experiments each evening, all of which Faraday described meticulously in his notes. Some of the experiments went wrong – one evening an electrical charge was too much for a frog, which flew out of its jar and hopped about the room. Other experiments surprised and shocked members of the audience: 'If any Lady or Gentleman wishes to feel the sensation of the galvanic fluid I should be very happy to accommodate them. They must wet their hand in water and hold one ball in each . . . hah hah hah hah ha . . .'.[32]

After the shrieks had subsided, Tatum made some more spectacular experiments – by passing an electrical spark through a specially perforated and twisted worm of silver foil he spelt out the word SCIENCE for all to see as the finale to a lecture on Electricity.[33]

The lectures were often oversubscribed, with the result that Tatum had to repeat the more popular ones. One of these was 'Optics, theory and practice', in which he demonstrated the camera obscura and camera lucida, and showed glass transparencies of landscape and other scenes with a 'magic lantern'. Tatum's teaching was essentially visual and demonstrative – he did not only tell his pupils, he showed them. Perhaps using waxed, and thereby transparent, engravings after Joseph Wright of Derby and others, he projected 'an operation on the air pump ... a chemist with a pneumatic trough ... a view in a mine in Derbyshire ... a gentleman's mansion'.[34] The scientific education that Tatum gave was complete and fascinating, with an emphasis on what would now be called physics; rather less on chemistry. As an offshoot of the lecture series, he invited a group of the men in his audience to meet at his house every Wednesday evening to listen to and give lectures of their own.[35] This became formalised in 1808 as the City Philosophical Society, whose members heard Tatum speak and who took it in turns, every other Wednesday, to lecture to the group on scientific subjects that they had studied.[36]

Some years after he had transcribed them, Faraday collected his notes of Tatum's lectures together and bound them in four volumes with a fond, gracious and revealing dedication to Riebau.[37] 'Sir,' he wrote on the dedication page,

> When first I evinced a predilection for the Sciences but more particularly for that one denominated Electricity you kindly interested yourself in the progress I made in the knowledge of facts relating to the different theories in existence readily permitting me to examine those books in your possession that were any way related to the subjects then occupying my attention. [To] you therefore is to be attributed the rise and existence of that small portion of knowledge relating to the sciences which I possess and accordingly to you are due my acknowledgements.
>
> Unused to the arts of flattery I can only express my obligations in a plain but sincere way. Permit me therefore Sir to return thanks in this manner for the many favours I have received at your hands and by your means, and believe me your grateful and Obedient Servant, M Faraday.

A close look at the way the pen runs reveals that when Faraday wrote his signature he did the 'F' first: thus what he actually wrote was 'F Maraday', the manner of his signature, with its mild form of disguise, that he practised all his life.

But long before they were dedicated and bound Riebau had already shown Faraday's notes to 'Mr Dance Junr. of Manchester St., who . . . requested to let him shew them to his Father, I did so, and the next day Mr. Dance very kindly gave [Michael Faraday] an Admission ticket to the Royal Institution Albemarle St.'[38]

The Royal Institution, 21 Albemarle Street, was set up and initially funded by a group of aristocrats, MPs and philanthropists who in 1799 had met to consider urgently ways of speeding the application of newly-evolving scientific principles to the betterment of life for the general population of Britain. The Institution's mission was put into words by one of the founding fathers, Benjamin Thompson, Count Rumford: 'for diffusing the knowledge and facilitating the general introduction of useful mechanical invention and improvements, and by teaching by courses of philosophical lectures and experiments the application of science to the common purposes of life'.

The ticket Faraday had been given was a pass to attend the remaining lectures in what was to be Humphry Davy's final series there, on 'The Elements of Chemical Philosophy'. The elder 'Mr Dance' has traditionally been taken to be the musician William Dance,[39] but there is no evidence that proves it was he. All the Dances were members of the Royal Institution, and many of them gave 17 Manchester Street as their address in the Institution Managers' Minutes.[40] The Dance who shows the strongest credentials for being the man who first gave Michael Faraday the introduction to the Royal Institution is the architect George Dance the Younger. As we shall see, it was George Dance who had a particular influence on Faraday's understanding of classical art and architecture, fostered during his years as Riebau's apprentice, and as a result Faraday held a lasting gratitude for him. George Dance also had, as did many people of fashion, a continuing interest in electricity, which is first recorded by the diarist Joseph Farington in 1799: 'Hay's Electrical Lecture I went to. – N & G Dance, – [Benjamin] West &c there . . .'.[41] Twenty years later, when his health was ebbing, George Dance retained a faith in the healing powers of electricity. Farington reports: 'Dance I called on. He was gone to Partington's to be electrified. I met Miss Green who gave me a very unfavourable accnt of the state of his spirits.'[42]

Concurrent with his education as a young bookbinder and natural philosopher ran Faraday's religious education. This took place at the Sandemanian chapel, led by a succession of Elders whose teaching is marked by key symbols in the margins of Faraday's Bible.[43] Very many of the pages in most of the books of the Bible, the Apocrypha excepted, are marked by Faraday's pencil, in single, double and heavier lines denoting the relative significance of the passages to him at that time. Thus, there is evidence of detailed study of Leviticus, the book of Jewish laws and ritual, and the exhortation to obedience to God's law in Deuteronomy 4 is well marked. The biblical foundation of Faraday's youthful pursuit of knowledge is indicated in his firm markings in Job 28, where, at verses 1–2 he highlights:

> Surely there is a vein of silver, and a place for gold where they fine it. Iron is taken out of the earth, and brass is molten out of the stone.

This follows the chapter heading: 'There is a knowledge of natural things. But wisdom is an excellent gift of God'. At places where his own Christian name is mentioned, for example in Daniel 12.1 – 'And at that time shall Michael stand up, the great prince which standeth for the children of thy people' – Faraday has marked it clearly.

The world that Michael Faraday was introduced to at Riebau's was wider and more dangerous than the Sandemanian clique. Another of the sophisticated outsiders who seemed to be regulars in the shop was Jean-Jacques Masquerier, who had fled Paris for England in 1792. Masquerier, who like Riebau was of Huguenot descent,[44] had been born in Chelsea of French parents, but the family had returned to Paris a year after his birth. The young man had studied drawing in Paris, and having arrived in England entered the Royal Academy Schools aged fourteen in December 1792, and went on to become a fashionable portrait and history painter.

During Napoleon's rise to power Masquerier returned to Paris where he made some secret studies of the Emperor-to-be which he used and reused in his paintings.[45] He gossiped about French revolutionary politics and personalities, particularly to Joseph Farington, and in 1801 exhibited in Piccadilly a huge picture of Napoleon reviewing the consular troops. This made him £1000 profit, but it led to scandal when William Cobbett accused him of being a French spy.[46] Among Masquerier's friends in the circles around the Royal Academy at this time were the painters Thomas

Girtin and J.M.W. Turner. Years later, however, the poet Thomas Campbell described Masquerier in temperate, even condescending, terms as a 'pleasant little fellow with French vivacity',[47] while the painter John Constable loathed him: 'although he has made a fortune in the Art, he enjoys it only as a thief enjoys the fruits of his robbery – while he is not found out'.[48]

Masquerier's address in the early 1800s, given in correspondence in the Crabbe Robinson Papers,[49] was Edwards Street, Manchester Square. Nevertheless Silvanus Thompson, one of Faraday's early biographers, asserts that Masquerier was at one time Riebau's lodger, and that among Faraday's tasks as Riebau's apprentice was the dusting of the lodgers' rooms and the blacking of their boots.[50] However it was that they met, Masquerier liked Faraday and appreciated his brightness and talent. He lent him books on perspective and, perhaps in response to a request from Faraday and encouragement from Riebau, taught him to draw.[51] The young man rapidly mastered perspective, as the drawings in the Tatum notebooks plainly show. Faraday developed a fluid line which expressed complicated structures of apparatus, wooden stands, glass tubes, connecting wires, brass rods with balls on the ends and so on, all delicate, characterful, rarefied and self-possessed instruments at the beginnings of their own evolution, constructed for particular and discrete scientific purposes.

When Riebau showed Dance the illustrated notes that Faraday had made, he was displaying him as one of his own products, a fine young bookbinder, very well trained, who was now reaching the end of his apprenticeship. He would have shown the work of all his older apprentices to influential patrons in this way, because it was to his advantage as an apprentice master that he should find good situations for his lads. George Dance, the architect of crisp, elegant buildings, and a portrait draughtsman of rare talent, was an ideal person to appreciate Faraday's neat, informed text and illustrations. The clarity and assurance of the illustrations in particular were of such a level that Dance might reasonably have considered their creator to be a potential student of architecture.

Faraday's early education with Riebau, Cosway, George Dance and Masquerier might have led him towards art or architecture as much as to science – the various scientific and artistic influences on him had by 1810 served to introduce him to the great breadth of contemporary culture as the eighteenth century turned into the nineteenth. His brush with Swedenborgianism gave added coloration, though we may never know its extent or tone. His experiences of Tatum's lectures, however, and his responses to them, were such that by the time he first set foot inside the Royal Institution to hear Humphry Davy lecture, Michael Faraday was already as well versed in science as any young man or woman of his generation could possibly be. His weaker points, however, were mathematics, which he found impossible to grasp fully, and chemistry. In Tatum's lectures chemistry was just one of a wide range of scientific topics, and so by going to hear Davy speak on 'The Elements of Chemical Philosophy', Faraday would be taking his scientific knowledge to new levels.

CHAPTER 2

Humphry Davy

Humphry Davy was a star. Buckles flew, stays popped, and the ostrich feathers worn by some of those who came to show themselves off in the crush at the Royal Institution lectures were apt to end the event as bedraggled zigzags. That, at least, is the impression given by Gillray's 1802 engraving of a lecture-demonstration at the Royal Institution. One thousand and more men and women crammed the theatre at 21 Albemarle Street, a converted eighteenth-century townhouse, when Davy was billed to lecture on geology, agriculture or tanning leather.[1] These were exciting subjects – the new knowledge about the nature and material of the earth and how to harvest it efficiently was beginning to broaden people's horizons – and when the young and handsome Humphry Davy took the stand, ladies and gentlemen of society were hot, breathless, early and hushed. Celebrated actors like Young or Kemble had the coveted asterisk printed beside their names on theatre bills, and were Humphry Davy a professional actor – though a distinguished performer he was nonetheless – he too would have merited the star.

Michael Faraday knew all about Davy's reputation. He had written up some of Davy's ideas in his 'Philosophical Miscellany'; Tatum spoke of Davy, and the word on the street would have intrigued a boy so engaged by science. The puzzle is why he left it so long to take steps to attend Davy's lectures. Albemarle Street is much nearer to Weymouth Street than is Fleet Street, so distance was not a factor. The reason may have been financial: Tatum's series at a shilling a time was perhaps all the Faraday family could afford. But more than that, there was a wide social gulf between the apprentice bookbinder and the great and the good who flocked to the Royal Institution, and Faraday may have been reluctant to cross it. Stories emerged about how Davy packed the Royal Institution lecture theatre to the rafters, how the audience hung on his every word and clapped and cheered him when he exploded a model volcano, or filled the theatre with thick, stinking smoke from a bubbling retort, or – best of all – took a man from the audience and gave him the new Laughing Gas, nitrous oxide, from a silk bag and tube and made him chuckle and jump about, and cry with intoxicated pleasure.[2] News of the Laughing Gas had followed Davy from Bristol, where he had first made his name, and where he had carried out vivid experiments with it. The poet Robert Southey had reported that when he breathed a bagful of the gas in the laboratory in Bristol, 'I immediately laughed. The laugh was involuntary but highly pleasurable, accompanied by a thrill all through me; and a tingling in my toes and fingers, a sensation perfectly new and delightful.'[3]

The antiquary Henry Wansey could only compare the sensations he had felt when breathing the gas with 'some of the grand choruses in the Messiah', played on 'the united power of 700 instruments'.[4] Other reports spoke of staggering, running about laughing, happiness, vertigo and a longing for more, so it is no wonder that London audiences were agog to try it, or see it in action. Gillray's engraving *Scientific Researches! – New Discoveries in PNEUMATICKS! . . .* , which shows nitrous oxide being administered, suggests that the gas also made the patient fart spectacularly, but that may just have been Gillray's personal contribution to scientific research.

Davy had youth, simplicity of manner, a natural lilting eloquence with a soft Cornish burr which had been in his voice since his childhood in Penzance. He had a piercing eye that held an audience as if it were one person, and a fresh-faced healthy look about him which charmed his listeners. 'He was generally thought naturally graceful,' wrote the tanner Thomas Poole, who had known Davy in Bristol, 'and the upper part of his face was beautiful.'[5] He had a winning smile, and when off the podium his conversation was buoyant, animated, cheerful, happy; because of this he was eagerly sought for soirées and dinners in town and country.

The portrait painter Martin Archer Shee RA, who was deeply involved in Royal Academy politics, was one of Davy's hosts. Another was Sir George Beaumont, a powerful art patron and arbiter of taste, whose strongly-expressed opinions influenced the policies of the Royal Academy and the Royal Institution. Others who entertained Davy included Lord de Dunstanville, the Cornish mine-owner and patron of art and science, and William Smith, MP for Norwich, a Unitarian and a campaigner for political reform. With hosts at this level of society, Davy had arrived, and despite his provincial background he became so popular that receptions were considered incomplete without him. Joseph Farington, whose social and political connections ran like veins through the establishment, met Davy on the circuit, and in his diary he recreated the ebb and flow of the conversations. Gossip flowed freely. At a dinner with the Beaumonts in November 1806 the host complained of Canon Sydney Smith's 'levity and indifference in his manner'.[6] Sydney Smith, a Canon of St Paul's Cathedral, who lectured on Moral Philosophy at the Royal Institution, made jokes and throwaway remarks which, Beaumont felt, were 'ill-suited'. Beaumont may also have been giving a veiled warning to Davy, encouraging him to adopt a formal, even seemly manner of lecturing, not the wild antics that Gillray had satirised in the widely circulated *Scientific Researches* engraving. Davy responded by further criticising Smith, whose Whig allegiances irked Beaumont's Tory table: 'Smith is not reckoned to have much reading,' Davy offered, 'or extensive information, but [he] has talent and is now well received at Holland House and may probably be a Bishop.' As the subjects changed, Davy went on to chat about Josephine Bonaparte, Empress of France, and her fortune-teller's warning that she would suffer a violent death. Recalling years later Davy's first appearances in London society, the painter Benjamin Robert Haydon reported a feeling that 'High Life' had ruined Davy, and the ambitious young lawyer Henry Brougham remarked that Davy 'had the supreme folly of giving up [his] *original* and *natural* liberal opinions for love of Lords and Ladies'.[7] But this was 1806; the ruination had not yet set in.

Even in the far north of England, at Cockermouth in the Lake District, when Farington stayed with the newly-created Lord Lonsdale, talk turned to that 'ingenious young man' Humphry Davy. The Bishop of Carlisle, Samuel Goodenough, was present, and he, complaining of Richard

Watson, who besides being non-resident Bishop of Llandaff was a Fellow of the Royal Society and had invented an improved type of gunpowder, said that Davy had 'more chemical knowledge in his little finger than Watson had in his whole body'.[8]

Davy careered through accepted wisdom in science in the first ten years of the nineteenth century, and when that decade was out he had transformed human understanding of chemistry and its applications. His first great triumphs were his discoveries in electrolysis, which he expounded to his fellow scientists at the Royal Society in the Bakerian Lecture, the most prestigious annual lecture in science, in November 1806. This caused excitement far afield, and led the Institut de France in Paris to award him the following year its medal, and three thousand francs, for the most progressive work in electricity. The driving force behind this prize, open to scientists of all nations, was the Emperor Napoleon himself; but because of the war with France, Davy could not collect it until 1813. Davy went on to isolate and identify potassium (1807), and to show that chlorine was an element (1810), thus setting two of the foundation stones in chemistry which had to be laid before there could be any semblance of progress into a modern world.

In his late twenties, Davy was naturally considered a young man by all the ancient insiders whom he met at social gatherings, and he became part of their gossip. When he fell seriously ill in 1807 Farington expressed his concern in his diary: 'Davy of the Royal Institution is in a dangerous state, a low fever, pulse 120, drinks a bottle of wine a day. Has lately discovered in Chemistry what oversets Lavoisier's System.'[9]

Concern for Davy's health was also shown by many of the thousands of people who had been led towards enlightenment by his teaching, and to keep them informed the Royal Institution Managers published regular bulletins at 21 Albemarle Street on the progress of the Professor's illness.

Despite his exposed public persona, Davy saw the lectures he gave as a distraction from his main purpose as a researcher into natural philosophy.[10] Nevertheless, he prepared them in great detail, reporting immediately on his latest discoveries and their relevance, and writing each lecture afresh for each occasion. Very little was repeated, so the same audience could attend, season after season, without being wearied. The evening before he was to perform, he would rehearse the lecture to his assistants, prepare the equipment and illustrations he was going to need, mark his text for emphasis and intonation, and go to his room early with a light fish supper.

Davy's rooms on the second floor of the Royal Institution lacked any kind of personal touch in the furniture and furnishings. He had merely moved into them as his predecessor as Professor of Chemistry at the Institution, Thomas Young, had left them, and he fitted himself in around the furniture. He did, however, make the rooms his own in the way he spread his papers about. Tables, chairs and the floor were littered with papers. Open a cupboard and more tumbled out. Open a side door, and there was a pile there too. The only visible object that was truly elegant and certainly Davy's own was a little porcelain figure of Venus, made and given to him by his friend and early collaborator Thomas Wedgwood. Although he was a prolific letter writer, Davy tended to receive more letters than he wrote, and he could not stop them coming. He received compliments, invitations and dedicated verses, one coming with a gift of a fob for his watch chain from an admirer who asked him to wear it at the next lecture as a sign that he had received her poem.[11] The considered female view was that 'those eyes were made for something besides poring over crucibles'.[12]

His brother John, twelve years his junior, who idolised Humphry and studied chemistry with him, lived at the Royal Institution from 1808 to 1811. There he remembered lying in bed listening through the thin partition to Humphry settling down for the night, rustling and shifting, and 'in a loud voice, reciting favourite passages in prose or verse, or declaiming some composition of his own, or humming some angler's song'.[13]

To Davy, as to the Romantics of his generation, science, literature and art were intertwined, part of a creative whole which enveloped the universe. He practised what he believed, and wrote poetry which drew heavily on landscape imagery and romantic travel for its subject matter and inspiration, and echoed in form and ambition the poems of his friends William Wordsworth and Samuel Taylor Coleridge. He was a passionate, even obsessive, fisherman, and made his own tackle and sets of hooks, with thread and bits of highly coloured feather as flies for trout fishing. Hanging in one of his cupboards was the bizarre green cloth fisherman's suit he designed for himself, 'with pockets everywhere for tackle, caoutchouc boots reaching to the knees. A coal heaver's hat dyed green, and studded with artificial flies. He looked not like an inhabitant of the earth, and yet he was on't.'[14] He was a keen shot too: 'For shooting he wore a hat covered in scarlet cloth so he wouldn't be shot at.'[15]

It was not long before Davy, always attracted by the highly-coloured feather, became caught on a hook himself. During the course of 1810 he met Mrs Jane Apreece, a Scottish widow two years younger than him. Jane Apreece was ambitious, sharp-witted, imperious, grand, but sparkling and mysterious, with a hint of a past. There was an unfounded rumour that she was the model for the heroine of Madame de Staël's novel *Corinne* (1807), an allegorical tale of nationalism and female creativity centred on the liberated Corinne, poet, artist and symbol of a united Italy. The book had been an immediate sensation, and upset the comfortable notion of woman as a retiring, domestic creature. Although Jane had met Madame de Staël when she travelled on the continent with her late husband, Shuckburgh Apreece, the connection is unlikely; but Mrs Apreece will have taken the compliment. Apreece was the heir to a baronetcy, but he had died in 1807 before attaining the title that he and his wife had anticipated. Jane, however, took that in her stride. She had plenty of money of her own. She was an only child, and the heiress of her father Charles Kerr, a merchant in Antigua, dealing in sugar and spices, who had himself died in 1796.

Shuckburgh Apreece's death gave his widow a new release. She moved to Edinburgh, where she set up a salon for the intellectual society of the Scottish enlightenment. She was much more widely travelled than her Edinburgh contemporaries, and dazzled them with her sophistication and gossip. Sir Henry Holland, the fashionable doctor, became light-headed at her memory, mysteriously saying that she 'vivified [her circle] with certain usages new to the habits of Edinburgh life . . . The story was current of a venerable professor seen stooping in the street to adjust the lacing of her boot.'[16]

Jane Apreece also kept abreast of London society. Farington discovered that she had an income 'reported to be 3 or £4000 a year',[17] a piece of gossip he had heard from the watercolour painter William Wells, who had himself picked it up at dinner one evening in March 1812 from his host William Blake of Portland Place.[18] Blake's neighbour was Jane Apreece's mother, Mrs Jane Kerr, and the two ladies were fellow guests that evening; also of the party was Humphry Davy. The roundabout of chit-chat gave another turn when Farington added that Davy 'pays much attention to Mrs Apreece who is proud to have him in her train . . . it is not believed that she will marry him'.[19] The relationship gave much amusement. Sydney Smith spoke of a new chemical salt, 'Davite of Apreece', and an anonymous verse, quoted by a gossip who had spent three weeks in Herefordshire with Jane, included the lines:

> To the Institution then she came,
> And set her cap at little Davy;
> He in an instant caught the flame
> Before Sir Harry said an *Ave*;
> Then, quick as turmeric or litmus paper
> An acid takes, begins to vapour;
> And, fast as sparks of fire and tinder,
> Was burned, poor fellow, to a cinder.[20]

Whether or nor Jane Apreece had any effect on it, Humphry Davy's creativity reached new heights in autumn 1811 when he began to set out a history of chemistry, and its progress from ancient Egypt to his own day. This sped on into a full survey of what chemistry is, what the elements are, and how they can be brought into being and manipulated. In a sentence Davy was able to evoke the vast and minuscule, diverse and unified, teeming and vacant, interdependent, entire and bubbling thing that is the planet we live on.

The forms and appearances of the beings and substances of the external world are almost infinitely various, and they are in a state of continued alteration: the whole surface of the earth even undergoes modifications: acted on by moisture and air, it affords the food of plants; an immense number of vegetable productions arise from apparently the same materials; one species of animal matter is converted into another; the most perfect and beautiful of the forms of organised life ultimately decay, and are resolved into inorganic aggregates; and the same elementary substances, differently arranged, are contained in the inert soil, or bloom and emit fragrance in the flower, or become in animals the active organs of mind and intelligence.[21]

This was the language of Davy's lectures, and the language, as it was now flooding out, of his writing. As each chapter was completed he sent it to the printer, who typeset it for publication in days.[22] There was no fair copy, no revision; it was a stream out of the rock. On Saturday, 25 January 1812, to great public acclaim, Davy began a new series of lectures, straight out of this new writing, billed as 'The Elements of Chemical Philosophy'. This was to be his final series at the Royal Institution, and his life was about to change. He had decided that his teaching phase was over, that he would resign as Professor of Chemistry at the Royal Institution, and that from now on he would devote himself to travel, research, fishing, reflective writing, poetry and life as an influential figurehead in the development of science in London.

The first lecture considered the history of chemistry; the second the forms of matter. The audiences crammed into the theatre as word of the lectures spread, and as it became known by talk in coffee houses and drawing rooms that this was to be Humphry Davy's final series. Davy would have been able to recognise people despite the crush, and where they sat as the lectures progressed – George Dance, for example, had a regular seat in the gallery over the clock[23] – and perhaps Jane, smiling at him and slowly waving her fan, was in the ladies' section in the gallery.

By the time he had reached the sixth lecture, on Radiant Matter, 29 February, Leap Year's Day, the audience had become an old friend, a familiar pattern of faces and attitudes spread out with neat variations like a carpet before him. There was a settling hush; the audience breathed, coughed, muttered and moved vaguely, shifting in expectation as Davy came in from the back and stood behind the speaker's desk. He put his hand on a large lens on a brass stand and moved it a few inches to the left. A vacuum pump he moved slightly to the right. At the far end of the bench was a wooden stand about three feet high with an arm holding a bowl of glowing charcoal near the top, an empty pan near the bottom, and enclosing them both a pair of concave mirrors, like cymbals held wide and about to be clashed together by a bandsman. He gazed about the auditorium, took a deep breath and began to speak. The words flew from him – this lecture was about light, its source and radiance, its reflection and refraction, the way prisms and mirrors can transmit, split and reunite it, the discoveries of Newton, Wollaston and William Herschel. The audience was in his hand from his first utterance as his eyes swept over them and he addressed first one section, then another, then a third, and leant this way then that for emphasis.

When Davy looked up to check his time, he probably did not notice, sitting beside George Dance in the balcony above the clock, a young man with curly brown hair, a black worsted suit and a stock at his neck. On his knees the young man had a tall black hat, and on top of the hat some folds of paper and a pencil. He was attending very carefully to what Davy was saying, taking notes and watching the performance with eager interest. This young man was Michael Faraday. He watched carefully as Davy ran beams of rainbow light from one end of the bench to the other. White light came out of a lamp on the speaker's left, was focused into a prism, split into rainbow colours, twisted this way and that by other lenses and prisms, and then back again as white light to illuminate a sheet of card. A stray rainbow beam broke out of this neat arrangement of paraphernalia to strike out across the theatre and land on the wall above Michael Faraday's head. Then Davy turned to the stand with the concave mirrors. An assistant blew on the pan of charcoal with a pair of bellows, and the twigs glowed bright red. Davy adjusted the lower, smaller pan, and sprinkled some black powder into it. He hesitated, and as he did so the lower pan exploded with a flash and a violent hiss, scattering burning debris onto the bench and causing a sudden shriek of surprise from the audience, followed by silence, then embarrassed laughter. Davy paused before addressing the audience: 'It is evident that in this experiment the whole of the effect must take place by the radiated heat for none can descend by other means from the pan of coals to the powder.'[24]

As the lecture series progressed, Davy might have become aware of the young man above the clock. Faraday did not attend all the lectures, just four out of the ten, but not only did he take notes, which he wrote out again at home in the neatest copperplate hand, he also made drawings of the apparatus Davy had used.[25] This will have taken him down to the demonstration table after the lecture had ended to get a closer look, and if Davy had not spoken to the young man there and then, he might at least have been aware of a presence.

Humphry Davy and Jane Apreece justified the gossips, for on 11 April 1812 they were married in Jane's mother's drawing room, by the Bishop of Carlisle himself. 'I am the happiest of men,' Davy wrote to his own mother shortly before the wedding, 'in the hope of union with a woman equally distinguished for virtues, talents and accomplishments ... I believe I should never have married, but for this charming woman, whose views and whose tastes coincide with my own, and who is eminently qualified to promote my best efforts and objects in life.'[26]

The wedding day was the culmination of an extraordinary week. At a levée at St James's Palace on the Wednesday the Prince Regent knighted Humphry Davy; on the Friday Davy gave his final lecture, on Metals, to echoing cheers, and on the Saturday he was married. If either one of the couple echoed the character of Corinne, adored by the Roman throng when she was crowned for her poetry, it was not Jane, but Humphry. Sitting up behind the clock on the evening of 10 April, Michael Faraday heard the newly created Sir Humphry Davy conclude his lectures at the Royal Institution with words which went to the heart of why it was that scientists did what they did, and how, by experiment, they could discover answers from nature. Davy's words also touched on his own personal happiness and fulfilment, and added fire to Faraday's determination to give his life to experimental science:

Experiment is as it were, the chain that binds down the Proteus of nature, and obliges it to confess its real form and divine origin. The laws that govern the phenomena of chemistry, produce invariable results; which may be made the guide of operations in the arts; and which insure the uniformity of the systems of nature, the arrangements of which are marked by creative intelligence, and made constantly subservient to the production of life, and the increase of happiness.[27]

According to John Davy, Sir Humphry was back in his laboratory within days of his marriage.[28] In June he gave a paper to the Royal Society, and in July he and Lady Davy set off for the Highlands of Scotland. Sir Humphry proposed to spend his time there fishing and shooting, but, with his portable chemical apparatus securely stowed in the carriage, he also went prepared to analyse earth or rock samples, or carry out whatever chemical experiments might move him while he and his wife were away. They planned to return to London in December.[29]

CHAPTER 3

A Small Explosion in Tunbridge Wells

In the summer of 1812, cool and wet according to reports,[1] Faraday stayed in London, looking urgently for a job in science. There were six months left of his apprenticeship with George Riebau; two weeks after his twenty-first birthday he would be out on his own – with no job and no money unless he got on with it and found a position. But skilled as he had become over the past seven years with Riebau, Faraday knew that bookbinding would never satisfy him for life. Ever since he had first heard Tatum lecture, had seen the encyclopedias, the books on galvanism, optics, perspective, electricity and all the philosophies that reveal the workings of nature, and yet more since he had witnessed the revelations of fact in Sir Humphry Davy's lectures, he was determined on a life in science.

He wrote to Sir Joseph Banks, the grand, corpulent and omnipotent botanist, President of the Royal Society, to ask for work in science – anything at all, even scrubbing and washing bottles. He walked across London, perhaps on his way to Tatum's or to the Sandemanian chapel, taking the letter to the Royal Society's rooms in Somerset House and leaving it with the porter. Two or three days later he called for a reply; there was none. He called again and again over the following week or ten days, and each time asked the porter if Sir Joseph had an answer for him. There was still silence, and an answer was never handed down.

Word must have got back to Banks's office that a lad was pestering, and when Faraday returned the next time he found that the porter did have a message for him from the President's office. It was: 'Your letter requires no answer.' A memorandum written in 1835 (see Appendix Three) says that this response left Faraday 'almost disconsolate'.[2] We might infer from this that he went round the corner, sat on a stone coping and wept.

In July 1812 an opportunity turned up, and Faraday applied for 'an excellent prospect' in London, perhaps as a tutor or calculator of numerical tables. He seems to have been offered the post, but despite his great talent for sciences, mathematics always evaded him:

> [I] cannot take it up for want of ability. Had I perhaps known as much of Mechanics, Mathematics, Mensuration & Drawing as I do perhaps of some other sciences that is to say had I happened to employ my mind there instead of other sciences I could have obt[aine]d a place an easy place too and that in London at 5.6.7.£800 per Annum. Alas Alas Inability.[3]

Both at home and in the room at the back of Riebau's shop, Faraday continued to work with his own apparatus, building a battery with copper and felt discs, and zinc, then a newly-available metal. Using this long, lightly bubbling trough, he experimented with galvanism, decomposing solutions of magnesium sulphate, copper sulphate and lead acetate with an electrical charge as Davy had done, making sparks, smells, crystals, sudden heats and gases which made the room airless and uncomfortable and forced him to run to the open window for relief. He experimented with oxides of copper and with phosphorus, and tried his hand at analysing the murky drinking water that came intermittently through the tap at Weymouth Street.[4]

Kept indoors as the rain came down, Faraday was obsessively active with science and self-improvement. These were the days in which he wrote up his notes to lectures, both Davy's and Tatum's, following the practice he had established when he first began to transcribe from Tatum. During those lectures he had taken down key words, 'short but important sentences, titles of the experiments, names of what substances came under consideration', and so on. At home, he made a second set of notes, 'more copious, more connected and more legible than the first'. Then came a third draft, using the previous notes to write out the lecture 'in a rough manner. They gave me the order in which the different parts came under consideration and in which the experiments were performed and they called to mind the most important subjects that were discussed.'

Finally, there was a fourth draft:

I then referred to memory for the whole of the lecture. It is not to be supposed that I could write it out in Mr Tatum's own words. I was obliged to compose it myself but in the composing of it I was aided by the ideas raised in my mind at the lecture and I believe I have (from following my pattern as closely as I could) adopted Mr Tatum's style of delivery to a considerable degree (perhaps no great acquisition).[5]

Four drafts to get the flow and the style right seems to reflect an obsession, but an urgency to learn and to improve himself drove Faraday, and led him to develop practices which matched his temperament and sought out his weaknesses. It was an extraordinary achievement for a boy from the back of a blacksmith's shop, who had taken his own steps to improve his rudimentary education, and who desperately wanted to cling on to the coat-tails of hurrying knowledge and to find the key to an understanding of nature.

Over these same days Faraday wrote an appreciation of Humphry Davy which goes to the heart of what it was in Davy that made crowds flock to hear him, and made him a pivotal figure in the history of the public understanding of science. With a light touch of his pen, describing Davy's peroration at the end of his final lecture at the Royal Institution, Faraday also reveals the depths of his own admiration and longing:

Sir H. Davy proceeded to make a few observations on the connections of science with other parts of polished and social life. Here it would be impossible for me to follow him. I should merely injure and destroy the beautiful and sublime observations that fell from his lips. He spoke in the most energetic and luminous manner of the Advancement of the Arts and Sciences. Of the connection that had always existed between them and other parts of a Nation's economy. He noticed the peculiar conjeries [*sic*] of great men in

[29]

all departments of Life that generally appeared together, noticed Anaximander, Anaximene, Socrates, Newton, Bacon, Elizabeth &c, but by an unaccountable omission forgot himself, tho I will venture to say no one else present did. During the whole of these observations his delivery was easy, his diction elegant, his tone good and his sentiments sublime. MF.[6]

By another in the sequence of lucky gusts of wind that were now impelling him, somebody, an unknown gentleman who may have come into Riebau's shop, gave Faraday an idea. He talked about the correspondences he was having, about letters he had received from Sicily and France, and 'within the space of half an hour' affirmed enthusiastically that letter writing was one of the 'purest enjoyments of his life'.[7] This was how Faraday put it in a letter to Benjamin Abbott, one of the young men he had made friends with at Tatum's science lectures, suggesting that they take up a correspondence together, and send each other letters describing their work, interests and discoveries in science. The conversation with the unknown man was, in fact, only one of the prompts that led to the long correspondence with Abbott; it was a practice also advised by Isaac Watts, the author of *The Improvement of the Mind*, a book which Faraday was now beginning to read closely.

Faraday first came across *The Improvement of the Mind* at Riebau's shop: it was one of the best-known and most widely read text books of the late eighteenth and early nineteenth centuries, and over Faraday's years with Riebau many copies must have passed through his hands for binding and selling. Watts's book is a student's guide to study, to the attainment of knowledge, and to the means of learning. Dr Johnson had known the book well, and wrote of it: 'Few books have been perused by me with greater pleasure . . . Whoever has the care of instructing others may be charged with deficience in his duty if this work is not recommended.'[8]

Faraday found a passage in Watts that urged young people to write letters to each other: 'A very effectual method of improving the mind of the person who writes, & the person who receives,' he affirmed to Abbott.[9] 'I have concluded that letter writing improves; first, the hand writing, secondly the –'

At this point Faraday put his pen down with a sigh. Despite his flow of enthusiasm for letter writing, he had had a sudden memory blackout. Such temporary bouts of amnesia would come to afflict him throughout his life, and over the years would bring three unbidden furies to his doorstep: frustration, depression and anger. He paused, thought, and began to write again: 'I have the Idea I wish to express full in my mind, but have forgot the word that expresses it; a word common enough too: I mean the expression, the delivery, the composition, a manner of connecting words.' Then the thread came back to him: 'Thirdly it improves the mind, by the reciprocal exchange of knowledge. Fourthly, the ideas; it tends I conceive to make the ideas clear and distinct . . . Fifthly, it improves the morals . . .'

In this roundabout way Faraday suggested to Abbott that they begin their correspondence. Finally revealing the true reason, and revealing also a single-mindedness that, behind all his scientific and spiritual works, came to drive his life, Faraday adds in terms that read like the logical steps in an experimental process: 'MF is deficient in certain points, that he wants to make up. Epistolary writing is one cure for these deficiencies. Therefore MF should practice Epistolary writing.'

A correspondence now took off in earnest. The young men met during the week to discuss science, and in the evenings wrote to each other with detailed descriptions of what happened when they did this experiment or that. Speeding back and forth between Weymouth Street and Abbott's house in Long Lane, Bermondsey, the letters carried details such as Faraday's observations on 'the peculiar motions of Camphor on water',[10] or Abbott's electrical experiments.[11] Their tone is enthusiastic and breathless, inclusive, engaging and full of good will and enjoyment of the revelations that science was giving to them both. They reflect on conversations at Bermondsey which drew in other members of Abbott's family. Abbott's brother Robert had 'a friendly controversy' with Faraday about Noah's Flood, and whether it had covered the earth entirely. Robert Abbott 'opposed it', but Faraday appears to have wavered – his Sandemanian influences urging him to take the biblical account literally, his instincts as a young natural philosopher, however, keeping him sceptical, rational, scientific: 'I cannot say I maintained it but thought it was so. If your Brother has no objection to lay down his arguments on paper and will transmit them to me by Post I shall not forget the obliging condescension on his side and the gratifying honor on my own . . .'.[12]

Only one side to the correspondence survives, because while Abbott kept the letters he had received from his friend, Faraday, in one of his later bouts of clearing out, destroyed all his letters from Abbott. But Faraday's letters give a clear view of his activities in this formative period of his life, of the way his understanding of science developed, of his feelings and of the chronology of events. They also echo his youthful voice, vibrant with excitement, particular and clear in its expression, and we hear through the text the timbre and pace of his speech. The sentence structure suggests that he spoke at speed, making pauses for breath within his sentences, and placing the emphases at their end. With every paragraph he wants to share what he has discovered, finding it impossible to keep his knowledge to himself. Running home in the rain one Sunday evening in July after a day spent in Bermondsey with the Abbotts, Faraday found ideas and impulses coursing through his mind, and he wrote them all down for Abbott:

> I . . . did not stop until I found myself in the midst of a puddle and quandary of thoughts respecting the heat generated by animal bodies by exercise. The puddle however gave a turn to the affair and I proceeded from thence deeply immersed in thoughts respecting the resistance of fluids to bodies precipitated into them . . . My mind was deeply engaged on this subject . . . when it was suddenly called to take care of the body by a very cordial affectionate & also effectual salute from a spout. This of course gave a new turn to my ideas and from thence to Blackfriars Bridge it was busily bothered amongst Projectiles and Parabolas.[13]

So the letter continues, tracking Faraday's run home to Weymouth Street, with thoughts of inclined planes, slipping and friction (prompted by the sloping pavement), the velocity and momentum of falling bodies (the rain), and the identification and naming of cloud types – cirrus, cumulus, stratus, nimbus, all then newly-coined terms – suggesting that he and Abbott may that very day have been talking about them.

Between the scientific experiments, discussions and letter writing, Faraday and Abbott went to fireworks concerts together at the New Ranelagh Gardens in Millbank, and, in mid-August, on a trip with Robert Faraday to see 'where the Surrey canal passes by locks over the hill'.[14] With

Thomas Huxtable, another friend from scientific discussions, Faraday went 'down the river to the Botanical Gardens at Chelsea belonging to the Company of Apothecaries. I was very pleased with the excursion,' he wrote to Abbott, 'and wished for you two or three times.'[15] On another boating excursion they banged up against Battersea Bridge and nearly sank in a strong tide. Abbott was one of the passengers, and remembered how Faraday had not panicked like the others, and showed 'remarkable presence of mind'.[16]

One subject that exercised Faraday and Abbott in their letters was more metaphysical than the rest. Faraday mused about the development of ideas, and offered proof to Abbott that they were formed in the head.[17] He told a story of how, when he was an errand boy, he had once knocked on the door of a gentleman's house and stuck his head through the railings while waiting for an answer. What was 'that' side of the railings; what was 'this'? He decided that the place where his head was was the place where he and his thoughts were, 'for there was my perception, my senses'. Then the door opened and made him jump, and he banged his nose. From this Faraday learned a lesson: 'it did more in illustrating the case to me than all the arguments I have heard since on the subject or all the affirmations that have been made'. What he understood was that the lesson he learned, and the opinion he had reached, was as the result of direct experience.

The correspondence continued for nearly ten years until it petered out in the early 1820s as Faraday had less and less time to write such letters, and as his successes in science rapidly outstripped Abbott's. Faraday was always the driving force behind the correspondence. He showed a clear desire to control its pace, and he considered his time to be more valuable than Abbott's. 'I wish,' he asserted,

> to make our correspondence a deposit of Philosophical facts & circumstances that will perhaps tend to elucidate to us some of the laws of nature. For this reason I shall insert in the form of Queries or otherwise all the facts I can meet with that I think are as yet unexplained. They will be as subjects for investigation, and if you think fit to chime in with my fancy and will propose such things as you are acquainted with that are yet unresolved, or anything else that your better judgement may choose, it will give a peculiar feature

to our communications and cannot fail of laying under the obligations of your most Obedient ... Do not delay to inform me at all times as early as convenient, and let me caution you not to wait for my answers. Consider the disparity between your time and mine, and then if you do feel inclined to communicate alternately I hope you will give that notion up.[18]

Lack of time, or his perception of its lack, is another *leitmotif* in Faraday's life. Throughout his correspondence he writes of how little time he has, how easily wasted it is, how he regrets he cannot do this or that because he does not have the time, until it becomes a litany. The letter to Abbott of 2 and 3 August 1812 opens with a riddle which examines this lifelong obsession:

What is the longest, and the shortest thing in the world: the swiftest, and the most slow: the most divisible and the most extended: the least valued and the most regretted: without which nothing can be done: which devours all that is small: and gives life and spirits to every thing that is great?

It is that, Good Sir, the want of which has till now delayed my answer to your welcome letter. It is what the Creator has thought of such value as never to bestow on us mortals two of the minutest portions of it at once. It is that which with me is at the instant very pleasingly employed. It is Time.

And so the correspondence continued through the summer of 1812; ten long letters, mostly heavily cross-written, from Faraday to Abbott survive between July and the end of September. Faraday was genuinely fond of Abbott, describing him on one envelope as

An honest man close buttoned to the chin
Broad cloth without, and warm heart within.[19]

In this same period, besides the home-made experiments, the arguing about correspondence procedure, the trips to Ranelagh Gardens, to Chelsea Botanic Gardens and the Surrey Canal, and the differing interpretations of scientific evidence, Faraday gazed at the stars through an astronomical telescope, and

> had a very pleasing view of the Planet Saturn . . . through a refractor with a power of ninety. I saw his ring very distinctly. 'Tis a singular appendage to a planet, to a revolving globe and I should think caused some peculiar phenomenon to the planet within it. I allude to their mutual action with respect to Meteorology and perhaps Electricity.[20]

And the same night he saw Venus, 'amongst your visible planets – tis – a – beautiful – object – certainly'.

This was the end of a wet but golden summer for Faraday, the final weeks before he came of age on 22 September, and, barely a fortnight later, when he came to the end of his apprenticeship with George Riebau. Perhaps preparing for this change of station, and doing a small redecorating job for his mother, he had set to work on 1 October hanging wallpaper at home, when a long letter arrived from Abbott full of scientific questions, which made him put away 'cloths, shears, paper, paste and brush all'. His answers to Abbott reflect light-heartedly on the tone and friendship of the letters, and speak volumes for the quantity of information that passed between them. One by one, Faraday attends to thirteen or so unanswered questions:

> – no – no – no – no – none – right – no Philosophy is not dead yet – no – O no – he knows it – thank you – 'tis impossible – Bravo.
> In the above lines, dear Abbott you have full and explicit answers to the first page of yours dated Septr 28.[21]

By this time, Faraday had finished writing up and binding the fair copy of the notes he had taken from Humphry Davy's lectures in the spring. He had them ready to show Abbott on 12 September,[22] as a prelude and an encouragement before taking the plunge and sending them to Sir Humphry. Riebau had suggested this course of action at the beginning of the summer, and now that Faraday looked at the product, with its half-calf leather binding and gold tooling, riffled through the pages heavy with ink and with his own effort, heard and felt the cover board close with a satisfying flop when he let it fall shut, he rejoiced in his works. Nevertheless, a certain depression and sense of reality began to settle on him. He warned Abbott that he was on a short fuse: 'at present I am in as serious a mood as you can be and would not scruple to speak a truth to any human being, whatever repugnance it might give rise to'.[23]

He wrote to Thomas Huxtable in much the same tone.[24] A reason for this was that his apprenticeship had expired, and he had just taken up a new position as a bookbinder with Henry de la Roche, of King Street, Portman Square, for one and a half guineas a week, that is thirty-one shillings and sixpence.[25] De la Roche had a hot temper, 'a very passionate disposition', as Silvanus Thompson describes it,[26] and Faraday was bitterly unhappy working for him. He wanted to leave 'at the first convenient opportunity', despite the reasonable salary, 'indeed, as long as I stop in my present situation (and I see no chance of getting out of it just yet), I must resign philosophy entirely to those who are more fortunate in the possession of time and means'.[27]

When Faraday wrote this he understood Sir Humphry Davy still to be in Scotland with his wife. The Davys had, indeed, expected to be away from London until December,[28] but the French scientist André-Marie Ampère had written to Sir Humphry from Paris with some astounding news, and this had drawn the Davys home early. Ampère, known now as the pioneer of electricity, told Davy of a new discovery that a compound of chlorine and azote (that is, nitrogen) created a highly explosive material. Indeed, its French discoverer, Pierre Louis Dulong, had already lost an eye and a finger in an explosion. Davy considered chlorine to be *his* gas – he had been the first to show it was an element, in the face of French belief that it was an oxide. He had named it, and he wanted to try to make the explosive himself. So, late in October, working in the laboratory of his fellow scientist John Children at Tunbridge Wells, he brought ammonium nitrate and chlorine into combination. He discovered instantly how dangerous the experiment was. A glass tube containing the chemicals blew up, shattered into tiny pieces, and badly damaged his eye. He was taken home to London immediately.[29] This small explosion in Tunbridge Wells was the beginning of a chain of events that, in late October and early November 1812, caused Michael Faraday's life to change.

Three 'original' sources refer to Davy's accident and the events around it. The fullest is a long, affectionate letter written to an unknown recipient by George Riebau a year after Faraday had left his apprenticeship:

> [Faraday] would occasionally call on me and expressing a wish to be introduced to Sir H. Davy, I advised him to write a letter and take his manuscript books and drawings, and leave them for Sr H.D. to examine, he did so, and next morning the Footman brought a note requesting to see him he attended. Sir H. enquired into his circumstances and told him to attend to the bookbinding and if any opportunity occurred he would think of him. Soon after this Sir H. met with an accident from the bursting some glass part of which flew into his eye, he sent for M. Faraday who transacted some business to his satisfaction . . . [30]

Riebau shows great pride at Faraday's youthful achievements and at his courage and dogged application to the job of finding employment in science. This, however, is the only source that specifically states that he and Davy had met before the accident. This first meeting must have been in the few days in late October 1812 between Davy's return from Scotland and his visit to Tunbridge Wells. It also suggests that Faraday had acted promptly on Riebau's advice to send his manuscript lecture notes to Davy after Abbott had finished reading them by 20 September.[31] In an autobiographical note that Faraday's first biographer Henry Bence Jones reprinted, Faraday corroborated much of Riebau's account, but gave special credit to Mr Dance:

> Under the encouragement of Mr Dance I wrote to Sir Humphry Davy, sending as a proof of my earnestness, the notes I had taken of his last four lectures. The reply was immediate, kind, and favourable. After this I continued to work as a book binder, with the exception of some days during which I was writing as an amanuensis for Sir H. Davy, at the time when the latter was wounded in the eye from an explosion of the chloride of nitrogen.[32]

After Faraday's brief introduction to Davy's working practice, Davy wrote to him on 24 December 1812. Faraday treasured this letter, in which

Davy had wrongly addressed him as 'Mr P. Faraday', and may not have shown it to anybody beyond his immediate family until he sent it to Davy's first biographer John Ayrton Paris in December 1829.[33] Davy wrote:

> I am far from being displeased with the proof you have given me of your confidence & which displays great zeal, power of memory & attention.
>
> I am obliged to go out of Town & shall not be settled in Town till the end of Jany. I will then see you any time you wish. It would gratify me to be of any service to you. I wish it may be in my power.[34]

Davy's assessment of Faraday's competence as an emergency secretary when he was partially blinded and in need of help was a sure foundation for the success of their later collaboration. Despite his resigning from lecturing, the Royal Institution Managers would not let Davy go, and gave him an Honorary Professorship and made him Director of the Laboratory and Mineral Collection, with no salary.[35]

When Faraday first made his way to the laboratory in the basement of the Royal Institution he knew he was entering hallowed ground. He saw the two parts of the room, rows of seats and the lecturer's table on one side, and the top-lit and well-ventilated laboratory on the other. There was a prominent sand bath with a furnace attached to it, a forge, some double leather bellows, an anvil, and a blow-pipe on a table with more bellows. Further, there was a large trough of mercury which gleamed silvery in the light, some water troughs and long battery troughs with plates of copper and zinc emerging from them, and trailing wires. Then, standing about in a jumble on benches, shelves and open cupboards, there was all the romantic and evocative paraphernalia of the dedicated natural philosopher, a collection so redolent of the exploration of the unsteady edges of science that it was to Faraday as thrilling a place to enter as was the robbers' cave to Ali Baba. It was an unruly collection of stuff: gasometers, filtering stands, glass jars and pipes, retorts, bottles and dishes in earthenware and glass, and in cupboards and the room next door delicate instruments for weighing and measuring, air pumps, balances and so on. As John Davy wrote later describing his brother's laboratory, 'there was no finery in it, or fitting up for display; nothing to attract vulgar admiration; no arrangement of apparatus in orderly disposition for lectures, and scarcely any apparatus solely intended for this purpose'.[36]

From 11 October to 7 December there is a pause in the letters Faraday sent to Abbott. He broke his silence on 7 December, apologising that he had six unanswered letters from Abbott in his portfolio. He pleaded 'inability', which covers a multitude of possibilities, but which may suggest that while he was being loaded with bookbinding work by his 'disagreeable master',[37] he was also taking on as much secretarial work as he could for Sir Humphry. His new employer de la Roche evidently got wind of Faraday's ambitions in science, and for that reason perhaps gave him 'so much trouble that he felt he could not remain in his place'.[38] Nevertheless de la Roche, who had no children himself, made Faraday an offer that he thought the young man could not easily refuse. Impressed by Faraday's bookbinding skills, he promised 'on certain conditions' to transfer his business to him, and 'thus to make him a Man of Property'.[39] This Faraday did refuse, despite the risk of immediately running foul of de la Roche's passions, but having been brought up by Sandemanian parents, he would have found it easy to resist becoming a man of property, and thus have the vote, two civic distinctions which Sandemanians treated with disdain.

Faraday now found himself in a very difficult and uncertain personal position. In one corner he had an unpredictable master whom he had unwisely frustrated; in another the teachings of a church which he respected; in a third he faced impending poverty in the all-too-real possibility of losing his bookbinding job; and in a fourth he had to consider the money he gave to his widowed mother, a landlady in straitened circumstances. Colouring all this in a gloomy sweep of pallid grey was his lack of ready patronage, and no sign of permanent work in science, the one sphere which truly attracted him. The only chink of light was his brief employment with Davy, and the mild interest that Sir Humphry was showing in him. But even Davy, who had after all been Faraday's second choice of employer after Sir Joseph Banks, had advised Faraday to stick to the bookbinding in the long run.[40] No correspondence from or to Faraday survives from the first two months of 1813, but on 19 February there was a punch-up at the Royal Institution, and out of this petty but violent incident Michael Faraday got the job in science that he coveted, and the future began.

During the year following Davy's resignation the day-to-day management of the Royal Institution was in the hands of the new Professor of Chemistry, William Thomas Brande. He was an uncharismatic, plodding man, who was described in later years as giving lectures that were 'eminently sound and useful', and, in a remarkable sequence of negatives that give a half-hearted cheer to him as Sir Humphry Davy's successor, 'he was never brilliant or eloquent, but his experiments never failed'.[41] Brande expected his lectures to be set up carefully for him, with all the necessary instruments, chemicals and illustrations in place. The laboratory assistant William Payne seems to have failed to do the job properly on 19 February, and the Institution's instrument-maker John Newman told him so. Payne punched Newman; they shouted and brawled; the superintendent William Harris heard the 'great noise', and came to investigate. Newman complained to Harris that Payne had hit him, Harris rose to his full height and charged Payne with the offence, and Payne went off muttering imprecations. The Royal Institution Managers were told of this at their meeting three days later, and Payne was sacked.[42]

As Honorary Professor of Chemistry, Davy took the initiative for finding somebody to fill the gap, and Michael Faraday came to mind. So, quite late in the evening of 22 February, a gleaming carriage with a footman up on the box beside the driver made its way down Weymouth Street, and stopped outside number 18.[43] The horses pawed and shuddered in the cold evening air, and blew explosively through their nostrils. The footman climbed down carrying a note, and banged hard on the door. Looking down from his room, where he was undressing for bed, Faraday heard somebody in the house open the door, and heard too a muffled conversation. The door closed softly, and the carriage rolled away into the night. 'A letter has come from Sir Humphry Davy for Mike!' somebody said, and ran up with it to Faraday's room. Faraday broke the seal and read that Sir Humphry Davy requested that Mr Michael Faraday call on him at the Royal Institution the following morning. And then, perhaps, Michael Faraday went, as he had planned, to bed.[44]

We know all this from Benjamin Abbott, who will certainly have been told of it in excited tones by Faraday in the days following. Faraday might also have described to Abbott the interview with Davy, which apparently took place in the anteroom to the lecture theatre, by the window nearest to the corridor.[45] Both Davy and Faraday recalled their earlier interview in the same room, by the same window. Davy had warned Faraday then about the dangers of giving up a secure trade, for which there would always be a need, for the insecure profession of science.

'Science is a harsh mistress,' Faraday recalled Davy saying, remembering as he did so that that was a phrase of Sir Isaac Newton's. Davy went on to warn the young man that science 'poorly rewarded those who devoted themselves to her service'.

'But philosophic men,' Faraday rejoined spiritedly, 'learn to cultivate superior moral feelings.'

Davy smiled at this idealism, thinking of some of the charlatans he had met and the priority disputes he had experienced in his years in science. 'I will leave the experience of a few years to set you right on that matter.'[46]

This morning, however, Davy did not try to dissuade Faraday. He urgently needed somebody reliable to replace Payne, and Michael Faraday had the ability and enthusiasm for the task.

'Are you of the same mind as you were when you called on me last year?' he asked.

'I am sir.'

'Then I will offer you the place of assistant in the laboratory of the Royal Institution, in the situation of Mr William Payne, lately employed here. Will you accept?'

Faraday grinned with delight, shook Sir Humphry's hand warmly, and walked briskly out of the Royal Institution into Albemarle Street. At the next meeting of the Managers, on 1 March, Sir Humphry Davy drew attention to the vacancy and said:

I have the honour to inform you that I have found a person who is desirous to occupy the situation in the Institution lately filled by William Payne. His name is Michael Faraday. He is a youth of twenty-two years of age. As far as I have been able to ascertain, he appears well fitted for the situation. His habits seem good, his disposition is active and cheerful, his manner intelligent. He is willing to engage himself on the same terms as those given to Mr Payne at the time of quitting the Institution.

The Managers considered the matter, looked enquiringly at one another, and the chairman, Charles Hatchett, announced: 'We resolve that Michael Faraday be engaged to fill the situation lately occupied by Mr Payne on the same terms.'[47]

That is the brisk report of Faraday's engagement according to the minutes of the Royal Institution. In between the offer and the formal engagement, however, Faraday courageously and sensibly negotiated the terms he would accept. Notwithstanding how rapidly his luck had compounded over the past few days, he pressed Davy for the best deal possible. This led to the final agreement, which echoed the one that Davy himself had reached with the Managers in 1801.[48] Faraday was to be provided with a regular supply of aprons by the Institution, and allowed the use of the laboratory apparatus for his own experiments. Further, he was to be given two attic rooms in 21 Albemarle Street, as much coal and candles as he needed for heat and light, and a salary of one guinea a week. This was a cut from his pay as a young bookbinder, but with accommodation, aprons, candles and heating thrown in it was worth much more.[49] The post that Faraday had been given was later described as 'Fire-Lighter, Sweeper, Apparatus-cleaner and washer', or 'Fag and Scrub'.[50] That is the basic, lowest-of-the-low runabout servant's job that might by one kind of character be considered a dead end, but by another a door opening onto a broad, bright new life of learning and discovery.

Faraday gave his notice to de la Roche, and took up his duties at the Royal Institution straight away. Released from the pressures he had been under with the bookbinder, he immediately felt the illusion of greater leisure. His new master and colleagues may have introduced him gradually to his new responsibilities, but whether or not this was the case, he was now doing what he had longed to do. A week after starting at the Royal Institution he wrote his first letter to Abbott for three months, and looked forward to the pleasures of a 'recommenced & reinvigorated correspondence'.[51] He reread Abbott's past letters – there had been five since December which he had not answered – and mused on what he might have been doing in his old life: 'It is now about 9 o'clock & the thought strikes me that the tongues are going both at Tatum's and at the Lecture in Bedford Street but I fancy myself much better employed than I should have been at the Lecture at either of these places.'

Then he runs through for Abbott a typical day at the Royal Institution: he has assisted John Powell at a thinly-attended Mechanics lecture on rotatory motion – he 'had a finger in it (I can't say an hand for I did very little)', and has been working with Sir Humphry on extracting sugar from beet, an extremely important piece of research, because the threat of French naval blockades still hampered the import of sugar from the West Indies. He and Davy were also 'making a compound of Sulphur & Carbon', that is, carbon disulphide, 'which has lately occupied in considerable degree the attention of chemists'.[52] Johan Berzelius and Alexander Marcet's article on 'sulphuret of carbon' had just been published in the Royal Society's *Philosophical Transactions*, and already Davy was testing the procedure for himself, and giving Faraday further insight into laboratory practice.

Davy had been very specific about Faraday's duties, the times he would be required in attendance, and when he would have time off. Faraday was able to go home to see his mother and family in Weymouth Street on most evenings, but knew that he could not join Abbott on the coming Wednesday at the City Philosophical Society because 'I shall be occupied until late in the afternoon by Sr H Davy & must therefore decline seeing you at that time'. Nonetheless he hopes and expects to see his friend every Sunday as far as possible.

There is a perceptible change in tone from the earlier set of letters to those Faraday wrote to Abbott over the next six months, a growing self-confidence as he spent his days beside Davy in the laboratory, and a stronger philosophising manner in which he uses the letters to outline his developing views. One letter, which he describes as 'patch work', he claimed to have begun with no connected thought in his head, ending it with an analysis of man, as if 'man' were a chemical compound: 'compound', indeed, is the keyword:

> What a singular compound is man – what strange and contradictory ingredients enter into his composition – and how completely each one predominates for a time according as it is favoured by the tone of the mind and senses and other existing circumstances.[53]

Faraday lists man's 'contradictory ingredients' as 'grave circumspect & cautious' and 'silly headstrong & careless'; 'conscious of his dignity' and 'beneath the level of the beasts'; 'free frivolous & open his tongue', then 'ashamed of his former behaviour'. There is a maturity in this reflection which already marks out the self-educated young man. Faraday's life had changed radically in the past few weeks. At twenty-two years of age he had been reborn as a natural philosopher newly apprenticed to the greatest teacher of the subject in the land.

Faraday's rooms high up at the back of 21 Albemarle Street overlooked Jacques Hotel in Bond Street, a noisy place of parties and dinners, music and dancing. The night before he philosophised to Abbott about the ingredients of man he was distracted from the beginning of his letter by loud music from a 'grand party dinner' at the hotel. An orchestra had been hired to play that evening, 'bassoons violins clarinets trumpets serpents and all other accessories to good music', and with every new piece they played, Faraday could not 'for the life of me help running . . . to the window to hear them'.[54] His natural jollity and good humour, his love of good companionship that had led him to play the flute and know 'a hundred songs by heart',[55] to enjoy fireworks in Ranelagh Gardens and any number of river and country outings, led him also to share with his friend his excitement at the changes in his life, which had flowed directly from his determination to follow science.

Once he had been shown the door into the Royal Institution, everything that happened subsequently to Faraday came as a result of his own efforts, determination and self-possession. The letters to Abbott amply demonstrate the calibre of the intellect that Riebau had taken on as an apprentice, and that Sir Humphry Davy had now engaged. Within three months of starting as Davy's assistant, Faraday had become by observation as much an expert on lectures and lecturing techniques as anybody in London. There are four long letters to Abbott which examine in detail the finer and the coarser points of the art of lecturing, and consider too a lecturer's needs, his equipment, illustrations, the design of the lecture theatre, its ventilation, seating, sight-lines, and entrance and exit arrangements. The most extraordinary thing about this is that Faraday, who had done no public lecturing himself, and who had not experienced any university lecturing, with its syllabuses, regular classes and so on, should so rapidly find the key to clarity in an art that was so widely abused. His notes, since they were first published in 1870,[56] have for more than a hundred years been widely and influentially used as benchmarks to guide aspiring lecturers. The only other person in Faraday's ken who had come to lecturing afresh was Sir Humphry Davy himself in his professional journey from Penzance and Bristol to London. Between them they comprised the new wave of lecturing techniques, and re-invented the art.

Sir Humphry Davy threw Faraday in at the deep end. A month after he had begun at the Royal Institution, Faraday was working with Davy on the same nitrogen trichloride that had blown Dulong's finger off, and sent glass into Davy's eye. Faraday coolly told Abbott, 'I have been engaged this afternoon in assisting Sr H in his experiments on it during which we had two or three unexpected explosions.'[57]

We know practically all there is to know about how to make nitrogen trichloride from Faraday's letters to Abbott. The new explosive had great military potential, and, from the post-Cold War perspective of two hundred years later, it is revealing how unconcerned Davy, a man of the establishment and deeply anti-French, was about the security of information about the explosive.

Davy may not have given his assistant much warning about what might happen when the greasy, butter-like compound, which smelt curiously of almonds, was put into a basin of water, and then phosphorus was added to it. They concocted the compound itself the same day by making up solutions of ammonium nitrate and ammonium chloride, and then, using a scrupulously clean air jar, inverting over them some 'fresh made pure clean' chlorine gas. There is a note of triumph in the expression of that recipe – Davy was inordinately proud of chlorine. There must be no trace of oil, grease or any other impurities anywhere in the equipment, and it was Faraday's job to see that everything was spotless. By now Davy was fully confident of his assistant's care and dexterity in handling fragile laboratory equipment, his attention to detail and his physical bravery. A month after taking Faraday on Davy was prepared to trust his young assistant to work side by side at the bench with him on murderous substances.

Davy and Faraday began by keeping the ammonium solutions as cold as possible by surrounding the basins with ice, but soon they relaxed that operation as they found it slowed the process down. When the chlorine came into contact with the solution, the liquid began to rise dramatically up the jar, and drops of yellow oil rose and then gently dropped down into the liquid to lie as an oily layer at the bottom. They found slightly different rates of absorption between the nitrate and the chloride, but the compound that lurked at the bottom of the retort was more or less the same in both versions of the experiment.

Having formed itself, this compound then began to give off nitrogen very actively. The liquid seethed with a sharp, stinging smell, 'bringing forth tears in abundance it excites also a very disagreeable sensation in the nostrils and lungs'. When separated from the liquid the compound solidified in a buttery way, and lay pregnant with potential on its dish. This was where the excitement began again. Davy and Faraday put a tiny piece of it into some water and dropped some phosphorus into the basin. Suddenly, bang! – the whole thing exploded, shattering the basin and throwing glass, earthenware, water and the remains of the evil compound up into the air and everywhere. The two men were shocked, but slowly raised their heads above the bench as the clink of precipitated glass fragments died away. They tried once more to tame the beast by reversing the process and adding the compound to the phosphoric solution. This made a sudden flame, but there was no explosion. While they were doing the experiment, Davy blithely reminded his assistant how he had nearly blinded himself the past autumn by trying to heat it up.

Another of Faraday's jobs that afternoon was to collect the compound together from the various retorts and basins. This he did very gingerly, knowing its explosive power in combination. Davy was not discouraged by the dangers – they seemed to empower him – and this gave confidence to his assistant. Together they set to work again on new ways of attacking the chloride of nitrogen. They tried mixing hydrochloric acid with it in a glass tube, and this caused a rush of gas out of the liquid, filling the tube with bubbles 'which expanded as they ascended in a beautifull manner to fourteen or fifteen times their original bulk and the tube quickly became full of this gas'. The gas was piped to a trough of water, and its smell and colour immediately revealed it to be chlorine, with a tiny admixture of oxygen. The resulting precipitate was ammonium chlorate. They tried the trick again, this time with nitric acid, and nitrogen alone came off. Then they tried a third time, with a solution of potash. For a fourth time, Davy told Faraday to do it with ammonia, and this immediately produced thick acrid smoke, ammonium chloride, which filled the laboratory, making them both choke violently. Once the smoke had cleared they took some more glass bowls and tubes and tried again with ammonia. The smaller tubes constrained the reaction, but in an instant the whole lot exploded. That brought the experiments to an end, and it was Faraday who had to clear up the mess.

The next day they tried again, this time with yet more violent results. There were four big explosions in the laboratory that day,[58] audible throughout the building. Perhaps they caused some alarm, and staff ran downstairs to see what had happened; or perhaps the Royal Institution, being used to the Professor's stinks and bangs, took little notice. So the Professor and his new boy carried on, undaunted, ducking down behind the bench when they felt the need. They wore glass masks, which were some protection, but the day's work came to an abrupt end when Faraday had his hand nearly blown apart. The tube he was looking at rather too closely exploded in front of his face, blew violently out of his hand, shattered his mask and took part of his fingernail with it.

Working side by side, the two men were the vanguard, the thin line between the known and the unknown. In his first Elements lecture, Davy stressed the importance of instruments, and the progress that had been made in chemical discovery simply through the development of new, better and yet more ingenious pieces of equipment. 'Nothing,' he wrote, 'tends so much to the advancement of knowledge as the application of a new instrument.'[59] Davy was a gadgets man, perfectly at home with glass tubes, bottles and retorts, ground glass stoppers and brass taps and mounts, jointing them together like infinitely variable skeletal remains, with gutta percha, caoutchouc, string or wax or a combination of some of these, though safety was never taken much notice of.

We know nothing of the talk that went on between Davy and his assistant in the laboratory. Davy, who had recently enlarged and published his *Elements of Chemical Philosophy* lectures, cannot possibly have been silent about them to his companion as they worked together. In a later remark, Faraday described Davy as 'a mine inexhaustible of knowledge & improvement',[60] and it is likely that that knowledge and improvement will have emerged, by demonstration and example, from the mine from their first day together. Davy will have shown Faraday the importance and efficacy of accurate and accurately-made instruments. Engravings in the back of the *Elements* volume suggest that the equipment was neat and precise, but the reality at Davy's chaotic bench, where instruments might have to be devised on the spot at speed, was rather different. Davy, quick in movement, might carry on several unconnected experiments at the same time, and 'was perfectly reckless of his apparatus, breaking and destroying a part in order to meet some want of the moment . . . With Davy, rapidity was power.'[61]

Faraday, who was himself already an expert maker of electrical equipment, was more careful and circumspect, perhaps shocked by Davy's bullish approach. But he had much to tell Davy about his own experiences with batteries, electrolysis, the making of crystals and so on, and with two such articulate and involved men on common ground the talk cannot have been idle.

The importance of chemistry, its role as a civilising force in world affairs, was a topic that Davy had written about extensively. Chemistry in the early nineteenth century had been shown by Davy to be the key to industrial and economic progress in peace and war. The manufacture of porcelain and glass, dyeing and tanning, advances in medicine and agriculture, improvements in the composition and manufacture of gunpowder, were all dependent on the growth of chemical knowledge, and that, in its turn, depended on the progress that Sir Humphry Davy was personally making in his laboratory in the Royal Institution basement. In his correspondence with Abbott Faraday revealed that his own private experiments were careful and ordered, and followed more or less a course of self-improvement in science. What may once have seemed to Faraday, through Tatum's lectures and his conversations with friends, to be an involved and complex subject, dissolved through talk with Davy into a perspective of reasoned, reassuring and repeatable processes. Davy saw the simplicity of the subject, the inter-connectedness of chemical laws, and he put this across clearly in his writings:

> It is indeed a double source of interest in this science, that whilst it is connected with the grand operations of nature, it is likewise subservient to the common processes as well as the most refined arts of life . . . Complexity almost always belongs to the early epochs of any science; and the grandest results are usually obtained by the most simple means.[62]

In putting the discipline to which he had dedicated his life and health into its place, Davy brought comfort and reassurance to Faraday, quite as much as he imparted knowledge. Working and talking with Davy, Faraday found a structure for his knowledge, and a purpose for acquiring and categorising it. He now had somebody with whom to share his instinctive appreciation of the visual beauty of chemicals – the sheer,

relentless black of carbon, the yellow of sulphur, purple of potassium –
and their changes in colour, nature, texture, state, even taste if they were
bold enough, that took place in reactions in the laboratory. The harmony,
novelty and magic of the chemical names that tripped upon the tongue
– silicium, aluminium, zirconium, ittrium, glucium, manganese, zinc,
tin, iron, lead, antimony, bismuth, tellurium, cobalt, copper, nickel, pal-
ladium, uranium, osmium, tungsten, titanium, columbium, cerium, iridium, rhodium, mercury, silver, gold, platina (now 'platinum') – all these
wonderful names had run in their turn from Davy's own pen,[63] and
through the smoke and fume of experiment many must have found their
moment in conversation.

Humphry Davy and Michael Faraday are connected for all time as
teacher and pupil, master and assistant, milord and valet, tyrant and
subject. From a perspective of two hundred years, however, they stand
at equal but separate stature. Michael Faraday's upbringing, with its twin
constraints of impending poverty and strict religion, had a third ingredient of tight urban boundaries. Unlike Davy, who roamed the Cornish
moors as a youth and declaimed poetry into the winds, Faraday did not
see a moor, or any wild space, or much green, until he travelled abroad
with his master. Davy wrote poetry, and had friends among poets, and
his interconnected lifelong series of personal quests for discovery began
through his poetic writing as he divined the nature of the earth and his
place in it. The core of his achievement is in the isolating, naming and
proving of unique entities – nitrous oxide, chlorine, potassium, iodine,
the Davy Lamp – each a link in a chain. By the time he died in 1829 he
was separated from the culture to which he had contributed so much by
illness, distance and attitude. His final years, spent apart from his wife
and wandering in Europe, found him speaking largely to himself in a
series of visionary writings about travel, the rise and fall of civilisations,
interplanetary voyaging and fishing. Davy was a man of the early Romantic movement – prodigious, interrogative, eye-catching and original are
words that illuminate him. Nobody can securely be named as Davy's
teacher.

In the late summer of 1813 Sir Humphry and Lady Davy laid plans for
a tour, lasting perhaps two or three years, to France, Switzerland, Germany, Italy, and thence into Greece and Turkey. The first object was to
enable Davy to collect the medal awarded him by the Emperor Napoleon

and the Institut de France for his electrochemistry. This itself had been the cause of controversy, of accusations of treating with the enemy. Davy wrote to Thomas Poole:

> Some people say I ought not accept this prize; and there have been foolish paragraphs in the papers to that effect; but if two countries or governments are at war, the men of science are not. That would indeed be a civil war of the worst description: we should rather, through the instrumentality of men of science, soften the asperities of national hostility.[64]

Along the route Davy planned to meet, talk and experiment with the continental scientists with whom he had corresponded. Though Britain was at war with France, Davy, a scientist renowned in France and now honoured by Napoleon, obtained a passport for himself and his party. This comprised his wife, her lady's maid, his Flemish valet La Fontaine, a footman, and Michael Faraday as Davy's assistant. Sir Humphry had not had personal staff before, this was an introduction of Jane's: a man in his position must have a valet. A few days before departure, however, the valet's wife refused to let her husband go to Boney's France for so long, and Faraday was asked to do his job, with the promise that Davy would hire a replacement in Paris. Attending to Sir Humphry's personal needs was not quite what Faraday had bargained for, but he could hardly refuse and risk being left behind.

'I'll see you tomorrow about 1 o'clock,' Faraday wrote briefly to Benjamin Abbott early in October, perhaps to give him the news,[65] and on 13 October 1813 the party of five set off.

CHAPTER 4

'The Glorious Opportunity'

At eleven o'clock on that crisp autumn morning the coach rolled off from the Davys' house in Grosvenor Street. Sir Humphry and Lady Davy and the lady's maid travelled inside the shining black carriage; Michael Faraday and the footman were outside, on the roof, with the driver. Those three had to stand all the force of the weather, but they also got the fresh air and the view, and for Faraday this was central to his enjoyment of the journey and his record of it.

In one of the fullest and most exciting travel documents of the period, Faraday wrote a long account of his tour with the Davys.[1] The peculiarity of the Journal is not only its detail or its length – nearly four hundred pages of Faraday's fluent hand, whippy, spiky letterforms, sloping elegantly to the right – but its purpose and arrangement. The volume contains descriptions of two extended tours made by Faraday, the first to Europe from October 1813 until April 1815, the second to south Wales in 1819. The accounts blend into one another: on page 46 the continental diary breaks off in mid-sentence and, after a blank sheet or two, dives straight into 150 pages on the Welsh trip. Then the continental journey takes over again, with a description of the Parisian water supply, and leads us for a six-month dance through France, over the Alps, down to Genoa, Turin, Florence, Siena and Rome, where it cuts off again in mid-sentence, this time finally. A diary of the subsequent months of the journey, to Naples, back to Rome, into Switzerland and Germany, and back to Italy again before returning home is now lost, but long extracts were published in Henry Bence Jones's biography of Faraday in 1870.[2]

The document that we have must be a second version, written up from initial notes, at home in some of the long evenings before Faraday married in 1821.[3] A pencil note inside the front cover gives his reasons for writing the diary:

This journal is not intended to mislead or to inform or to convey even an imperfect idea of what it speaks. The sole use is to recall to my mind at some future time the things I see now and the most effectual way to that will be I conceive to write down be they good or bad or however imperfect my present impressions.

The keeping of the diary was thus Faraday's attempt to grapple with the chronic memory loss which dogged him from his youth in bouts and flashes, an inability to recall anything from common events to complex thoughts, and which would lead him to deep melancholia and threaten at times to destroy his career. This also drove his compulsion, encouraged by Isaac Watts's advice, to take detailed notes, and to write them up – from John Tatum's and Humphry Davy's lectures, and from his own laboratory experiments. The deliberate and full process of laboratory notes that Faraday practised and introduced as a standard for all scientists thereafter derived not so much from a desire to record, as from his deep-seated and desperate fear of forgetting.

Everything Faraday writes of the days on the move comes from the elevated perspective of the top of the carriage, is bathed in the light of day, and swings with the rhythm of the coach. He was apprehensive when they set off – quite naturally, for as he wrote in his opening paragraphs, he had never before 'within my recollection' been further than twelve miles from London. 'But curiosity has frequently incurred dangers as great as these and therefore why should I wonder at it in the present instance.'[4] 'This morning formed a new epoch in my life,' he mused, as he awaited the fresh curving landscapes and the insights to come.

The party trotted off along Park Lane to Hyde Park Corner, through Kensington and west towards Hammersmith and Kew. Their destination that evening was Amesbury, north of Salisbury, eighty-five miles away along what is now the A30. At the comfortable pace of ten miles per hour, with a change of horses at Basingstoke, they should have made it before nightfall. The next morning was cooler, probably cloudy. They skirted the edge of Salisbury Plain, seeing Stonehenge across the fields, but made all speed for Exeter, where they 'arrived rather late and put up for the night', Faraday wrote. 'I have before me at this time the Cathedral but it is too dark to see it distinctly.'[5]

If the first two days' journey was a novelty for Faraday, the third was a revelation: 'Reached Plymouth this afternoon. I was more taken by the scenery today than by anything else I have ever seen. It came upon me unexpectedly and caused a kind of revolution in my ideas respecting the nature of the earth's surface.'[6]

The first sight of Dartmoor and the journey round its southern edge had been the jolt that, by his own admission, first took Faraday out of the limited horizons of London, into the beginnings of a new world view. No amount of reading of Ali Baba or of the *Encyclopaedia Britannica* had prepared him for it: 'The mountainous nature of the country continually put forward new forms and objects and the landscape changed before the eye more rapidly than the organ could observe it. This gave me some ideas of the pleasures of travelling and have [*sic*] raised my expectations to future enjoyments to a very high point.'[7] Appetite whetted, Faraday and the party retired to bed at the Commercial Inn in Plymouth: 'Travelling I take it is fatiguing work but perhaps a little practice will enable one to bear it better.'

It was in Plymouth that Faraday's Journal, and his journey, really began. What survives of the manuscript is a narrative of eighteen months' adventure by an extraordinarily receptive young man who has been lifted by accident, perseverance and a succession of events from the humdrum life of a bookbinder's apprentice to stand beside the greatest man of science of the day. There was pain with the pleasure, for although Sir Humphry Davy was instructive and sympathetic to his assistant, and had undoubtedly answered his questions about the geology of Devonshire, he was changeable, and could be vain, high-handed, and overly deferential to his difficult wife. For her part, Lady Davy was snappy and irritable, particularly to the servants, and especially to Faraday. Until the promised replacement for the absent valet came in Paris, Faraday had some extra duties to perform. There was Sir Humphry's shaving to attend to, the laying out of his clothes in the mornings, the ascertaining of proper standards in the hotels and inns they stayed at, the marshalling of the hotel staff and other servants, and the disposal of the contents of his master's nightly piss-pots, a chemistry lesson in itself.

They had hoped to leave Plymouth the morning after their arrival on a cartel, a ship licensed to ply between countries at war, carrying messages, essential mail, and prisoners for exchange. But the wind was too high, had been for several days, and had generated an 'enormous swell of waters which comes rolling in from the Atlantic ocean'.[8] This was Faraday's first sight of the sea. Its strength surprised and entranced him, and over the next few days he observed it with the eye of a natural scientist. The ship's captain, however, was observing it with a sailor's eye, and the following day, Sunday, 17 October, he warned the party that having dismantled and loaded the carriage and stowed the luggage, they should come on board to prepare to leave at a moment's notice. This may have been the first time that Faraday had failed to attend a meeting at the Sandemanian chapel on the Sabbath, and as the continental journey unrolls it becomes clear that he is not as fully committed to the Sandemanianism of his parents as we might expect. He is at best semi-detached, and allows himself to come close to the pleasures of worldly temptation. His first cultural shock came, however, before leaving Plymouth, when he and the party found themselves suddenly and unexpectedly caught in one of the practices of Jewish law that he had read about in Leviticus.

Davy needed to change some money into francs, but as it was the ninth day of the Jewish Feast of the Tabernacles the money-changers in Plymouth refused to do business until after sunset. So the captain devised a charade. He put his watch forward, closed the shutters, lit some candles and assured the money-changers that, yes, the sun had now set, and they really did need to change their money and set sail for France on the tide. 'He would have prevailed,' wrote Faraday, spotting the transparent collusion between the captain and the money-changers. But just as a money-changer was 'about to take the bag out of his pocket, his wife came and to his sorrow told him the hour. And as *she* knew that *he* then knew it, he patiently and we impatiently waited until the sun was beneath the horizon.'[9]

While this went on, the captain sailed the ship out of the harbour on the evening tide, and lay waiting in the Sound. With time ticking away, Sir Humphry and his party changed their money, pocketed their francs, jumped into a little boat at the quay, sailed with all speed to catch the cartel and clambered breathlessly aboard.

There was a good swell running that night. The Davys had a cabin, but Faraday stayed on deck, pacing up and down, sitting wrapped in a blanket, leaning on the rail, drinking it all in. His excitement at the new experience of the wind in his face on a night sea voyage rises up out of his Journal. What he writes has a youthful, prosaic directness about it which engages and endears. His impressions are still very present nearly two hundred years later, and we breathe the sea-salt with him. Early in the voyage he is entranced by the phosphorescence shining in the water as the ship's bow cuts through the waves; he has 'a fine opportunity of observing the luminous appearance of the sea and was amused by it for a long time. The prow . . . seemed to turn up a vast number of luminous bodies about the size of peas.'[10]

As day came on and the light increased, Faraday captured the roll of the sea, the rise and fall of the ship, the distance of the far horizon, and the cold green darkness of the wave troughs. A French privateer passed by, a speck in the distance, but although the captain did his best to point it out to him, Faraday could not spot it. There was nothing to be seen 'except sky and immense waves striding one after the other at a considerable distance. These as they came to us lifted up our small vessel and gave us when on their summits a very extended horizon, but we soon sank down into the valleys between them and had nothing in view but the wall of waters around us.'[11]

They made landfall at Morlaix on the Brittany coast too late in the evening to disembark, so had to anchor and spend 'another night tossed about on the waters. The evening was very fine but cold. I found the deck however a better place than the cabin.'[12]

When he first saw France Faraday had pangs of 'regret for home', intermingled with fear and apprehension. At eleven o'clock in the morning they sailed past the guard ship, their flag of truce flying,[13] and came to anchor in the harbour. There they had to wait, writing letters home and amusing themselves with the cabin boy's banter, until an official was ready to come aboard to give permission to land. The sudden arrival of an enemy ship in a small French port was a significant event, and the local officials needed time to prepare themselves, agree procedure and puff themselves up. This was a big day in Morlaix. They may not have known that the ship's party included the great natural philosopher Sir Humphry Davy and his entourage, landing with a passport approved by Napoleon himself. The functionaries gathered themselves together, and 'late in the afternoon the mighty man of office came attended by several understrappers and a barge full of Frenchmen apparently beggars and porters'.

Everybody was questioned and thoroughly searched. Faraday had his hat removed by an official, and it was patted and prodded and inspected, and laid carefully on the deck. Then he was frisked, and his pockets and clothes inspected. He had to take off his shoes so that the officials could ensure there were no secret messages stuffed into them. He was found to be clean – they all were – and they were allowed to pass. But the letters they had written as they waited in the harbour were confiscated, and they were firmly told that they were not permitted to write home about their arrival and reception in France. If they were caught doing so, they risked arrest as spies.

The order was given to unload the party's carriage and luggage, and

immediately the crew of Frenchmen pounced on them and conveyed them in every direction and by the most awkward and irregular means into the barge alongside, and this with such an appearance of hurry and bustle, such an air of business and importance and yet so ineffectually that sometimes nine or ten men would be round a thing of a hundred pounds weight, each most importantly employed, and yet the thing would remain immovable until the crew were urged by their officer or pushed by the cabin boy.[14]

Released of its cargo and passengers, the cartel sailed for home, and 'with no pleasurable feeling', Faraday watched it go. By now the loaded barge was stuck in the mud as the tide flowed out. So they waited some more, and as the evening drew on Faraday watched the same phosphorescence that he had seen out at sea becoming visible in the ebb tide, rising and falling in brightness, disappearing and reappearing. When the waters rose again they felt the barge creaking and shifting heavily, and beginning to make a quiet way upriver between high wooded banks in the moonlight. They landed at the town quay, took essential luggage with them, and were led on foot through filthy streets to the only hotel in Morlaix. They thought that this could not possibly be the place, as a horse wandered idly through the front door. But, yes, this was it – 'one of the dirtiest pig-sties I ever saw . . . I sat down without consideration in a very hungry plight for supper. It was clean and with my appetite its quality was no object, and being also considerably fatigued I had no difficulty in going to sleep, though singularly accommodated.'[15]

After breakfast in the unspeakable hotel, they went down quickly to the Customs House where their belongings had been taken. They waited 'patiently or otherwise for some time looking on our things but not daring to touch them. At last business commenced.'[16]

The local soldiery marched up and formed a ragged line on the edge of the quay. Then thirty or forty inhabitants of Morlaix tumbled chattering out of the town and down the steps to help unload the belongings of this exotic party that had just blown in – enemy English, civilian, finely dressed and seemingly immune from touch of the law. Banging, bumping and crashing, the crowd leapt into the barge, 'seized some one thing, some another and conveyed them to the landing place above . . . destitute of all method and regularity. It seemed as if a parcel of thieves was scampering away with what was not their own.'[17]

The townsfolk had the greatest difficulty with the carriage. There were no cranes on the quay so they had to heave its bits up, chassis and cabin swaying dangerously amidst the muddle of willing hands. With the carriage waiting in pieces, all the travellers' possessions were taken into the Customs House and laid out, with a soldier posted at every door. First the carriage was searched, 'all the corners and crannies for what they could find and thumped over every part of [it] to discover hollow and secret places'.[18] Then, 'disappointed in their hopes of booty from the carriage', they came inside and started on the luggage. 'They seemed determined to make up for their loss here. Package after package was opened, roll after roll unfolded, each pair of stockings unwrapped and each article of apparel shaken.'[19]

Again they found nothing suspicious, but confiscated two or three dozen new cotton stockings for good measure. Davy, who had restrained himself for long enough, now lost patience. The stockings were theirs; they were marked with their names; they needed them for the journey.

Perhaps threats followed, and if they had no effect, a bribe did the trick. 'At last the business ended with everything in the possession of the rightful owners, and a gift to the officers for their *polite* attentions.'[20]

So the workforce got on with the business of reassembling the carriage. They had none of the proper tools, just brute force and glimmering common sense: ''tis true they made the job appear a mighty one, but they got through it, and after having exclaimed "levez, levez" for an hour or two everything was in a moveable state and horses being tied to, we proceeded in order to the Hotel'.[21]

If they had hoped to be on their way directly, they were disappointed. Just one more formality, messieurs, mesdames. The Governor of the town had to check with Paris, 'to learn whether the government continues in the same mind as now, that they were in when they sent Sir H Davy his passport to England. If it does not we of course are prisoners.'[22]

It took another day for the good news to get back from Paris to Morlaix, and for the party to be cleared for onward travel. In the meantime Faraday had time to walk about.

I cannot refrain from calling this place the dirtiest and filthiest imaginable. The streets are paved from house to house with small sharp stones, no particular part being appropriated to foot passengers. The kennels are full of filth and generally close to the house. The places [squares] and corners are occupied by idle loiterers who clothed in dirt stand doing nothing.[23]

Horses, pigs (the strangest kind of pig, more like greyhounds, Faraday thought), poultry, human beings 'or whatever has connection with the [hotel] or the stables and pigsties beyond' passed indiscriminately through. This was the same everywhere in the town. Idlers, beggars and nondescripts hung about the fires in the hotel's kitchens, chatting and getting in the way. There was an extraordinary mixture of luxury and squalor: 'on the left of the passage is a dining room ornamented with gilded chairs, tables and frames, but with broken windows and stone floors . . . [and] if pigs do not go upstairs at least animals as dirty do'.[24]

The next morning the party got their permission to proceed. The postillion – 'mostly a young, always a lively man', Faraday generalised of the profession of hired local coachmen – gave a laugh and showed off his jackboots as he walked stiffly from the fireside to the horses to prepare for the journey. Faraday's interest in high technical detail brings him to describe fully the appearance, purpose, weight (fourteen to twenty pounds a pair) and construction of the jackboot, the iron and leather leg armour that protected the postillion, who rode the near-side lead horse, from breaking his legs in an accident. The party climbed aboard the carriage to their allotted places, the postillion checked the trappings, clambered up to his saddle, fixed his jackboots into position and tucked in his coat. With a glance back at the driver, he cracked his whip, 'a most tremendous weapon to dogs, pigs and little children. With a handle of about 30 inches, it has a thong of 6 or 8 feet in length, and it is constantly in a state of violent vibratory motion over the heads of the horses, giving rise to a rapid succession of stunning sounds.'[25]

There was Faraday, ever-ready with his observing eye, out in the air on top of the coach, and off they went with a lurch towards Paris. They had hoped to cover the ground like the wind, the whip-thong crackling over the heads of the horses. But the roads were potholed and rutted, and they were shaken about desperately. They may not have considered just how big France is. The distance between Morlaix and Paris is about the same as that between Land's End and Dover, a major expedition by the standards of the day. One dark evening outside Rennes a horse stumbled and broke its traces. While they were waiting in the cold for the postillion to calm the animals and refix the harness, Faraday saw a glow-worm shining on the road. He had never seen one before, and its light entranced him. He picked it up, poked at it, watched how its light came from two luminous spots which brightened and faded, brightened and faded and then failed altogether. 'On examining it afterwards . . . I found it to be a small black worm not three fourths of an inch in length and having no parts particularly distinguished as those which had been luminous.'[26]

They lumbered late into Rennes and put up at the cold and desolate post house, which Faraday describes in the tones of a gothic novelist, reminiscent of Mrs Radcliffe's *The Mysteries of Udolpho*: 'from being built of stone, from containing long galleries, winding stone stairs, narrow passages, deserted rooms &c [it] strongly reminded me of the interior of a romantic castle, and a black man as cook, attendant &c wonderfully assisted the fancy'.[27]

They carried on through Laval, Alençon and Dreux, picking up bread and wine in villages on the way, putting up at post houses and huddling in front of miserable fires. Faraday noticed that travellers were provided with firewood in the bedrooms, but the wood was always green, and needed bellows to keep it alight – and of course, there were never any bellows to be had. Late on the seventh day after leaving Morlaix, the party approached Paris. Thirty or forty miles out, the roads began to improve, practical signs of the effects of Napoleon's public works strategy. The roads were straight, and for four or five miles would stretch ahead in a line, and then, with a slight bend would stretch on again. 'The eye,' Faraday writes, 'is enabled to perceive at once all it will see for the next hour [and] the expectation slackens and a monotonous effect is produced.'[28]

They had their last change of horses in the square in front of the Palace of Versailles, and then off they went for Paris, rolling up outside the Hôtel d'Autriche, 'where I cannot imagine we shall stop. It is deficient in common accommodation, and yet withal it bears a very respectable character.'[29]

As quickly as they reasonably could, the party moved on to the Hôtel des Princes, a highly fashionable and well-appointed hotel at the northern end of the rue de Richelieu. The Hôtel des Princes was one of the most sumptuous in Paris, brightly lit, panelled and furnished throughout with marble-topped furniture which, perhaps after conversation with Davy, Faraday identified:

One beautiful slab is valued at 800 livres. It is formed of various minerals arranged mosaically and contains between four and five hundred specimens, among which are Porphyry, Serpentine, Marble, Sulphate of Baryta, Carcareous Spar, Fluor Spar, Lapis Lazuli, Jasper, Agate &c &c &c. The appearance of the whole being very beautiful. There are also in these apartments three fine large slabs of black encrina marble, in one of which was the head of an animal.[30]

The expectations Faraday had had when he set off for France were that he would act as Sir Humphry's valet until they reached Paris, where a replacement would be hired. He would attend Sir Humphry at his scientific work 'as his assistant in experiments and in writing',[31] at meetings with men of science, and would continue to learn from him as he had at the Royal Institution in London. But from the evidence of the diaries he was left much to his own devices in Paris, and during the thirty-one days they remained there on only six does he note that he was attending Sir Humphry on scientific duties. He must have been working with him as a secretary or accompanying him on other days, but he was fairly well lost, ignored and depressed on his first full day in Paris, Friday, 29 October.

> I am here in the most unlucky and irritating circumstances possible . . . I know nothing of the language or of a single being here, added to which the people are enemies & they are vain . . . I must exert myself to attain their language so as to join in their world.[32]

His spirits perked up the next day when he accompanied Davy to meet Davy's old friend Thomas Underwood. Described by John Davy as 'an artist of some talent, with a fondness for science',[33] Underwood had been a proprietor of the Royal Institution in its early days, and indeed had recommended in 1800 that Davy be appointed as Lecturer. He and Davy had travelled in England together, making a geological tour to Cornwall in 1801.[34] But Underwood was a republican, and had made too many approving noises in England about the French Revolution. He went to France in 1802, but after the Peace of Amiens had ended the following year, was arrested by the French. Napoleon, however, tolerated him, and licensed him to stay as a 'détenu' in Paris, where he patrolled the fringes of the Emperor's court, and appears to have been on good terms with the Empress Josephine.

As a foreigner, Underwood had a pass to enter the Louvre at will, and he took Davy and Faraday to see the treasures that Napoleon's armies had amassed during their victorious years in Europe. This was a special concession, given so that foreign visitors could enjoy and take back good reports of the riches of the imperial museums, and of how well the looted treasures were being cared for. Works of art and antiquities had been removed as spoils of war from the Vatican, from Italian Papal and city states, and from the Netherlands, Flanders and other subject nations, to be displayed in the Louvre.[35] Since the first haul had arrived in 1797 French people and foreigners had flocked to see them at the Musée Napoleon, the shiny new revolutionary name for the former palace.

[61]

I saw the Galerie Napoleon today but I scarcely know what to say of it. It is both the Glory and the disgrace of France ... [W]hen memory brings to mind the manner in which the works came here and views them only as the gains of violence and rapine she blushes for the people that even now glory in an act that made them a nation of thieves.[36]

Sir Humphry Davy had a rather different response to seeing the treasures. He remarked with a sniff, 'What an extraordinary collection of fine frames,'[37] and stalked out, unable to stomach the injustice of the cull of works of art from vanquished nations. Faraday, however, showed no such political instinct, and took his opportunity to see as much as he could of 'the works of the old and most eminent masters'. He noted the ancient Greek statues, including the Apollo, Laocoön, Venus de Medici, Hercules and the Dying Gladiator, and the paintings 'in a gallery of enormous length ... some thousands of pieces'. Walking out of the Louvre, Faraday passed the multi-coloured Arc de Triomphe du Carrousel, raised eight years earlier in honour of Napoleon in 'the rarest and most valuable marbles', and crowned with the four bronze horses sequestered from St Mark's, Venice. He carried on through the Tuileries and turned north across the rue de Rivoli to the place Vendôme. Taking a candle, he climbed to the top of the column erected to Napoleon, and looked out wide over Paris.

For the next eleven days, Faraday seems to have explored the centre of the city very thoroughly, walking about on his own.[38] He was dismissive of the Seine, 'a very poor dirty river, not at all what I expected to find it. It has of course no tide, and is therefore almost unfit for navigation, at least such as is required by a large city. Scarcely anything moves on it but charcoal barges and washing houses.'[39]

The grandeur of imperial Paris also struck him – the statues, fountains and gardens of the Tuileries – 'It is the Parisian lounge and is much frequented' – and the programme of 'sticking up N's in every spot central and lateral where they can. This is a principle scrupulously attended to in every public work. The Museum and the Gallery &c abound with N's and silently recall the Emperor to mind at every step and turn.'[40]

But as a natural-born analyst, Faraday is engaged most of all by observing how the city works as an organism – the generous public water supply, the way wood is brought in for fuel from the north by barge, the washerwomen working in their dozens in the fountains and from barges on the river, and above all the Parisian road systems. Encircling the city at different distances from the centre, he noted, were 'two circles of boulevards ... two great circumscribing roads', the inner and outer tree-lined rings shaded in the summer and autumn, with 'shops, stalls, coffee houses and various places of public amusement' presenting 'a light, airy, pleasant and inviting variety'. How different this all was from London, where there were no gushing fountains, no broad encircling boulevards, no wide roads at all to speak of except the new Portland Place, and no embankments on the river. Paris, however, was built for the fierce heat of summer and for public show; it is a summer and autumn city, at its best when the people dress up and spill out onto the walks and *pavés*. But beyond the imperial façade, 'the streets of Paris are in general narrow. At the same time there are many of great length and width and noble appearance, but the number is not so great as might be expected in a city so much vaunted.'[41]

Faraday had to leap for his life, and risk being soaked in the flooded central drain, to avoid the cabriolets which 'men drive furiously and make streets already dangerous from the absence of foot paths still more so'. He became footsore from the street surface of stones 'very small and sharp to the foot', but despite that, over those few days he walked for miles.

There was an undercurrent of excitement in Paris, a kind of thrill or *frisson* at the naughtiness of it all; how different it was from the home life of the devout Faraday family. Michael Faraday was not yet a Sandemanian, not having made a Confession of Faith, but nevertheless he found the French hard to take. Living with Sir Humphry and Lady Davy, socialites both, both with a more flexible outlook on the proprieties of life, he had to maintain what he could of his moral defence and religious observance with no help from his employer: 'Travelling ... I find is almost inconsistent with religion (I mean modern travelling) and I am yet so old-fashioned as to remember strongly (I hope perfectly) my youthful education.'[42]

The casual attitude in Paris to the Sabbath, 'a day of pleasure instead of work', bemused him. Shops were open as usual, and 'accordingly you will find the streets as gay on such a morning as this as on any other morning, and without a good memory or an almanack it would be difficult to tell the Sabbath from other days, for no visible distinctions exist'.[43] They shut their shops earlier on Sundays, Faraday noted, 'but why do they shut them up? To go to the theatre.'

Faraday's account of autumn and early winter 1813 in Paris is unique not only because he was himself so perceptive, fluent and lengthy in his diary, but also because there were no British visitors half as articulate as he in Paris at this time. A flood of Britons had come to the city in autumn 1802 during the short-lived Peace of Amiens, and the flood would briefly become a torrent after April 1814 when Napoleon was removed to Elba, and then permanently after June 1815, when Paris was an occupied city once again. Among the new influx would be two Scotsmen, Walter Scott, whose *Paul's Letters to his Kinsfolk* (1816) gave a vivid picture of occupied Paris, and the painter Andrew Robertson, whose journal of autumn 1815 in Paris boils over with enthusiasm at his first experience of an extraordinary foreign culture. Like Faraday, he was taken aback by the Parisians' lax attitude to the Sabbath: 'it is quite orthodox to go from the theatre to the church and vice versa'.[44] But Michael Faraday alone drew an Englishman's picture of a tense Paris in the months before Napoleon's first downfall.

A week or so after arrival, Faraday had to apply for a passport, and present himself at the Prefecture of Police, 'an enormous building containing an infinity of offices' opposite Nôtre Dame. Nobody would tell him which of the infinity was the one for him, until he had paid for the information. Then a door was pointed out to him, and behind it twenty clerks were sitting behind twenty desks and twenty enormous ledgers, each with a long queue of people in front of him waiting to be dealt with. What little French Faraday might have picked up in the past few days deserted him now, and, tongue-tied, he became the centre of attention. A handy American noticed his discomfort, and helped him explain himself, but was bemused when he saw a Frenchman calmly making out a passport for an enemy Englishman. Faraday got a squint at the ledger, and seeing Sir Humphry Davy's name written down ahead of his, was told that he and Sir Humphry were the only two free Englishmen in Paris at that time.

'A round chin, a brown beard, a large mouth, a great nose &c &c' was how the passport clerk unflatteringly described Faraday.[45] He does not wear a beard in any subsequent portrait, so we might conclude that he grew his beard either as a youthful extravagance, or because with his valet's duties for Sir Humphry, he did not have time to shave himself. Besides all the optimistic exhortations written on the passport asking Parisian authorities to respect and aid the travellers as required, the paragraph which pleased Faraday most was the one which gave him free entry to museums, libraries and other public property on any day of the week.

The first duty for Sir Humphry that Faraday records was to accompany him on 11 November to the Imperial Library, now the Bibliothèque Nationale, a hundred yards down the rue de Richelieu from their hotel. 'Any person of a decent appearance may go in,' Faraday writes, and books could be read at the tables provided. 'By a proper application to the principal Librarian', books could also be borrowed for a few days. This was a novelty to both Davy and Faraday, and it may be that one purpose of Davy's visit, if not also to consult particular books, was to study the library's organisation and see if he could begin to advocate such a system at home: 'It contains an immense number of books in all languages and on all subjects arranged in several long galleries separated into divisions.'[46]

In the library galleries Faraday saw the bronze cast of Louis Garnier's *Le Parnasse Française* (1718–21; now at Versailles), a three-foot-high sculpture of Mount Parnassus surmounted by Apollo, and peopled with figures of the great French writers of the seventeenth century. There were rooms of rare manuscripts, antiquities and, where two galleries met, a wooden model of the pyramids of Egypt. But what particularly caught his eye were two globes, about fifteen feet in diameter, 'the largest I believe that have ever been made', set at either end of the library, and projecting through two floors.

So, with much sightseeing and walking the streets, the bright young *boulevardier* passed his time in Paris. Over the next few days he tried, but failed, to get into a sugar factory to see how the French manufactured sugar from beet, and tried, but failed the first time, to visit the museum at the Jardin des Plantes – 'but I got a fine walk in the Garden, and found amusement for some hours'. He had 'an easy walk' around the Palais Royal, now 'a collection of public exhibitions, coffee houses, shops &c.', and in the evening, with another Englishman 'who had been in

France 12 years' (this was most probably Thomas Underwood again), went to a coffee house 'said to belong to the handsomest lady in Paris. She is always in the room and is one of the principal attractions.'[47]

There is more than a trace of exasperation in Faraday's account, a reflection perhaps of his Sandemanian desire for plainness, at the excesses of decoration and sumptuousness that he found at the Palais Royal:

> Pillars of marble rise from the floor to the ceiling; glasses and piers line the walls of the room and garlands of flowers run from one to the other. Luxury here has risen to its height and scarcely any thing more refined or more useless can be conceived.[48]

He walked through the markets, and noted their organisation into separate sections for poultry, flour, vegetables, meat and corn: 'They are in general small and roofed over.'

On 18 November, the day after he had failed to get into the museum of the Jardin des Plantes on his own, Faraday returned there with Sir Humphry to meet Nicolas Louis Vauquelin, Professor of Chemistry at the University of Paris, highly respected as the discoverer of chromium. This discovery, in 1798, brought Vauquelin plaudits from the revolutionary French government, and secured him the post of official assayer of precious metals for Paris when Napoleon became First Consul in 1799. The year before Davy and Faraday's visit, Vauquelin had isolated glucinium, a white metal obtained from the semi-precious gem beryl, later to be named beryllium. His area of study was among these special metals and their compounds, whose common property was an entrancing chromatic quality, something which gave added delight to Davy and Faraday when they discussed his work with him and saw his specimens.

Many years later, Davy wrote some notes about the scientists he had met in Paris.[49] He had been quite taken aback by Vauquelin's domestic *ménage*. On his first visit (on 31 October; this may have been without Faraday) he had been ushered into Vauquelin's bedchamber, which doubled as a drawing room, where he also met the scientist's two elderly housekeepers, sisters of an even more eminent chemistry professor, Antoine Fourcroy. One of the sisters was sitting up in the bed, peeling truffles for the kitchen, and Vauquelin insisted on Davy being given some for breakfast.

'Nothing could be more extraordinary than the simplicity of his conversation,' Davy wrote.[50] By 'simplicity', he means 'lewdness': '[Vauquelin] had not the slightest tact, and, even in the presence of young ladies, talked of subjects which, since the paradisical times, never have been the objects of common conversation.' By now, as Davy put it, Vauquelin was 'in the decline of life', and reminded Davy of pre-Lavoisian chemistry, 'of the French chemists of another age; belonging rather to the pharmaceutical laboratory than to the philosophical one'.

But if he was writing Vauquelin off, Davy was premature. The housekeeper's truffle-paring may have been part of a chemical rather than a culinary exercise, for in 1813, the year of Davy's visit, Vauquelin had isolated asparagine, an amino acid found in asparagus.

Fifteen years later, in June 1828, when Davy himself was nearing death, a spry Professor Vauquelin wrote to Faraday asking for some letters of recommendation for a young man intending to visit British cloth-bleaching factories.[51] This letter carries clues that may shed some mild light on Davy's growing attitude to Faraday during the continental tour of 1813. Vauquelin writes of Faraday's 'great reputation . . . justly acquired amongst chemists', but begins, 'although I have not yet been in direct contact with you . . .'. Vauquelin had forgotten that he and the younger Faraday had met long before, suggesting that Davy kept Faraday in the background, at best his amanuensis, at worst his invisible valet.

Nevertheless, Faraday had fond memories of his day in Vauquelin's laboratory. He saw potassium chloride being manufactured by passing chlorine, held in earthenware vessels of '11 or 12 gallons capacity', through a solution of potash in a six- or seven-gallon jar over a low heat. The chloride collected at the bottom of the solution, a different method, Faraday noted, to the one practised in England, where the chlorine was passed through several different portions of the potash solution. Talking with a laboratory workman, Faraday heard talk of Pierre Louis Dulong, the discoverer of the explosive nitrogen trichloride, who also worked with Vauquelin. Faraday, who had damaged his hand while experimenting with the explosive, could show his scars and relate how he, like Dulong, had been blooded for science.

CHAPTER 5

Substance X

Sir Humphry Davy's arrival in Paris had been eagerly awaited. For weeks before he came French scientists had been discussing the visit, and making plans for the ceremony at the Institut de France on 2 November 1813 when he was to be awarded the Napoleonic gold medal. Ampère had been especially eager to meet the man he considered 'the greatest chemist that had ever appeared',[1] and for his part Ampère was the first person Davy had wanted to meet. Davy was majestically received at the Institut de France, and, seated to the President's right, was told during the *éloge* by the Secretary Georges Cuvier that the meeting was 'honoured by the presence of Le Chevalier Davy'.[2] He attended receptions and dinners in his honour: at the anniversary dinner of the Philomatic Society both he and Underwood were guests of honour. Toasts were drunk, but as a deference to the two Englishmen all declined to drink Napoleon's health.[3] Despite being a guest in a foreign country, Davy did not curb his opinions of people he met. John Ayrton Paris, his first biographer, reported that it had been observed that 'during his residence . . . his likes and dislikes to particular persons were violent, and that they were, apparently, not directed by any principle, but were the effect of a sudden impulse'.[4] Though Davy expressed dislikes privately, they did not appear in the character sketches of French scientists that he wrote some years later, and which were first published by his brother John: the sketches, of Guyton de

Morveau, Vauquelin, Cuvier, Humboldt, Gay-Lussac, Berthollet, La Place and Chaptal, are invariably spirited and appreciative.[5]

On 23 November a deputation of three distinguished French scientists called at the Hôtel des Princes to see Sir Humphry, and set him a problem which not only gave renewed purpose and direction to his months in Paris, but delayed his departure for Italy and held him up in January 1814 in the south of France. André-Marie Ampère, Nicolas Clément and Charles Bernard Desormes were shown into Davy's drawing room. One of them opened a box and took out a bottle of blackish flakes which had a shiny quality, deep violet in the light, lustrous, not unlike the lights that Davy had seen in Vauquelin's chromium, though less iridescent. They called it 'Substance X'. There was not much of a smell to it, and one of the scientists said it was quite brittle in larger lumps. The visitors looked enquiringly at Davy – Faraday was hovering behind trying to see but also trying to be invisible – and Davy looked at the flakes. Then one of the French scientists broke the silence, telling Davy that about two years earlier a gunpowder manufacturer, Bernard Courtois, had produced some crystals when making saltpetre at his works. He had had no idea what the stuff was, but when it was heated it gave off a sharp-smelling, poisonous, lurid violet smoke. The extraordinary thing was that it did not liquefy; it just disappeared on heating in a violet cloud.

There was a great deal of money in gunpowder manufacture in France at that time: there was a war on. Many thousands of barrels had been shipped out to supply the French armies in Spain, Portugal, Russia, Italy and the Austro-Hungarian Empire. Yet more was stockpiled in strategic dumps around France, much of it intended to damage English armies and interests. Gunpowder-making was a very sensitive industry, and the discovery of this strange by-product had to be handled carefully. The nature of the material had stumped even the flamboyant young French chemist Joseph Louis Gay-Lussac. He was a brave and daring figure, popular and famous for undertaking dangerous balloon ascents to gather samples of air for analysis and to take measurements of the strength of terrestrial magnetism. With Alexander von Humboldt he had formulated the law that oxygen and hydrogen combine precisely at the ratio of one to two by volume to make water, and that all gaseous reactions are in such simple proportions. These were revelations of the fundamental driving forces of life, and it was a matter of intense pride for Napoleonic

France that a Frenchman was leading the way in analysing them. But even Gay-Lussac could not give a clear answer to what 'Substance X' was. He had found that it produced an acid very like hydrochloric acid, and both he and Nicolas Clément had ventured that it was indeed the same acid. And yet . . .

After two years without reaching any serious conclusion, Ampère seems to have decided that the only thing to do was to ask Sir Humphry Davy. There were clear risks; the dangers of asking a citizen of an enemy country to identify a by-product of gunpowder were obvious. But who else was there to ask? And so the deputation made its way to the Hôtel des Princes.

Sir Humphry asked his visitors how the material was obtained, but they could not or would not tell him. Faraday records: 'The process by which it is obtained is not as yet publicly known. It is said to be obtained from a very common substance and in considerable quantities.'

Davy took out his travelling box of chemical equipment, and heated a few of the flakes. True to form they vaporised in a dramatic and quite beautiful but poisonous violet smoke. The men choked; someone ran to the window and flung it open. When the smoke had cleared, they took some more of the substance and heated it in a sealed jar. It did not need much heat to start to smoke, and very soon, as it cooled again, it condensed into purple crystals around the neck of the jar. They then dissolved some in alcohol, and formed a deep brown liquid which precipitated silver nitrate. Sir Humphry tipped a bit of this onto a sheet of paper and put it in the sun to dry, where it very quickly tarnished to a dirty black.

Then Sir Humphry tried some other tricks. He leant over his tubes and jars like a magician. He rubbed some of the mystery substance with zinc filings and found that a liquid formed. When it was put into a tube with potassium and heated it flared violently, and the men all backed off. It reacted even more violently when heated with phosphorus, and in combination with mercury a heavy metallic liquid formed which on heating became first orange, then black, then red. Faraday was taking notes of all this, as was his practice, and it is because of these notes, later transcribed into his Journal, that we know so much about this critical scientific meeting. In making the chemical combinations that Faraday described – and in a rented hotel room too – Davy was skimming the edges of extreme physical danger, not only from poisoning by the gas but from the effects of being showered by burning phosphorus or potassium or heated mercury. He was also risking expulsion from the hotel.

Over the next few days Davy made more experiments on the mysterious purple flakes. The visitors probably left him to it, but Faraday was present, as his notes, written out in the Journal under 1 December, make clear. There was much controversy in Paris over whether Davy should have been given a sample to work on alone – Thénard and Gay-Lussac were 'extremely angry' with Ampère for giving some to Davy, because Gay-Lussac was intending to publish an analysis of 'Substance X'.[6]

Davy repeated some of the experiments he had earlier tried in the presence of his visitors: bangs, whooshes, smoke and great stinks issued from the hotel room as he tried combining 'X' with iron, zinc, tin, potassium, ammonia. It was all done in tiny quantities, but the results were prodigious: 'When solution of ammonia is poured on to the new substance and left in contact with it for a short time,' Faraday recorded, 'a black powder is formed which when separated, dried and heated, detonates with great force.'[7]

In carrying out all these tests, Davy was rapidly eliminating possibilities for the flaky substance, and approaching a definition. He was racing, in the short time he could spare, to find a solution to the puzzle, and above all to find it before Gay-Lussac or any other Frenchman did. Despite Gay-Lussac's anger over the freedom Davy had been given to work on 'Substance X', Davy had a great respect for his rival. He described him as 'quick, lively, ingenious, and profound, with great activity of mind, and great facility of manipulation. I should place him at the head of the living chemists of France.'[8]

This was undoubtedly a private battle of wits. Nicolas Clément moved into the fray when he gave a paper at the Institut showing that the substance could be produced by passing sulphuric acid through seaweed ash. But Gay-Lussac was the true rival, not least because Davy had unfinished business with him: three years earlier Gay-Lussac had allegedly suppressed the French publication of a paper on alkalis by Davy.[9] Perhaps to size up the opposition, Davy and Faraday went to hear Gay-Lussac lecture on vapour to his students at the national school of chemistry in the École Polytechnique. 'My knowledge of French,' Faraday wrote later, 'is so little I could hardly make out the lecture, and without the experiments I should have been entirely at a loss.'

After the lecture they were shown the enormous voltaic battery at the

École, comprising six hundred pairs of plates, each seven or eight inches square, which at its best could produce six hundred volts. With some grim chagrin, Faraday noted that the battery had been paid for by the French government, while Davy had had to appeal to the patriotism of the Royal Institution Managers to raise money to buy one for England. He did not ask the government – there was not a hope of government money for scientific equipment in England until Charles Babbage drummed money out of the Exchequer for his Difference Engine in 1823.

Ten days after first being introduced to 'X', Davy went to the Jardin des Plantes, where Michel Eugène Chevreul had a laboratory, and the two scientists discussed and worked on the flaky substance together. Faraday was with them, taking notes. By 11 December Davy had concluded that it was an element standing alone, and he coined the name 'iodine', from the Greek for 'violet-like'. On that day he did some final, conclusive tests, trying to pass a current through the material using Chevreul's voltaic pile. He confirmed that it was an element, individual and apart, an analogue of chlorine, and thought it might come to be used to manufacture pigments, and in gunpowder. That was a fine triumph over French science, although as Faraday put it, with a trace of still lingering caution, 'as yet it must be considered as a simple body'.[10]

With characteristic speed, Davy wrote a paper on iodine, with Faraday's help as secretary in transcribing his atrocious handwriting and crossings out, which he rushed to the Royal Society in London to be read to his peers.[11]

While Davy was concluding his tests on iodine, Faraday was already expecting to leave Paris – he had written to his mother on 9 December saying as much.[12] Sir Humphry had received his medal from the Institut, he had met fellow scientists, and he had clinched the iodine question. Nevertheless they stayed on for another three weeks, perhaps so that Davy could discuss iodine further and discover economic natural sources for it, less inherently dangerous than saltpetre. The Monday after Davy had reached his conclusions on iodine, Faraday records that he had at last seen the museum at the Jardin des Plantes; if he was accompanying Davy that day it suggests that Davy's obsession with finding a source for iodine might have led him to pick over the exhibits in the museum and to discuss them with Cuvier, the Professor of Anatomy at the Jardin des Plantes. It is quite within Davy's impulsive nature that he should change plans at a moment's notice, and keep his entourage in uncertainty over what was to happen next. Davy had had many conversations with Cuvier. He had found the Frenchman eloquent in conversation, with 'a great variety of information on scientific as well as popular subjects ... the most distinguished man of *talents* I have known; but I doubt if he is entitled to the appellation of a man of genius'.[13]

From Davy this was a great compliment. Davy too was loquacious, a formidable conversationalist, and, like Cuvier, he came by the end of his life to extend his thought and philosophy to the widest realms of human society and happiness. Davy, however, merely thought and wrote about social progress; Cuvier, as a politician and courtier as well as natural scientist most famous for his interpretations of fossil remains, actually tried to put it into practice. He became a minister after the restoration of the monarchy under Louis XVIII, and stood up to Charles X when he put an end to the freedom of the press in July 1830. Under King Louis-Philippe Cuvier became Minister of the Interior.

The day after Faraday had seen some fossils at the museum in the Jardin des Plantes, those 'astonishing organic remains' of mammoths and other mammals that Cuvier had discovered at Montmartre, he walked across the city up the hill to Montmartre to try to find where they had come from, and with luck perhaps to dig up some more. But try as he might, with hand signals, a smattering of French and perhaps some exasperated English, he could not make the plaster-burners in the quarry understand what it was he wanted to see. It could not have been easy to make an early-nineteenth-century French workman understand by hand signals what a fossil was. As a result, Faraday did not get to the cliff to poke about, but he did take a good look at the geology of the place and, remembering Davy's teaching, noted that 'The rock is limestone and selenite and is burned for plaster on the spot ... This stone is very imperfectly crystallized and looks more like calcarious sandstone. It is nearly all soluble in acids.'[14]

If the day had been clear, he might have been rewarded by an incomparable view of Paris. There in the middle distance, then beyond woods and ramparts, lay the city – a small carpet of white, cream, grey, and threads of dark red. The towers of Nôtre Dame stood out crisply, then as now, beside the florid Tour St Jacques, and the roofs of the Louvre draw a line which divides Paris in two along the river. The Seine, low-lying and kept in its place by embankments, is and was then barely visible from Montmartre. Floating upon the city like tethered hot-air balloons are the gleaming domes of the Institut, Les Invalides and the Pantheon, the only building to break the skyline at Montparnasse. But Faraday noted nothing about the view; what instead caught his eye was the clunking telegraph mounted on a tower nearby, which passed its unending semaphore messages to Paris from Boulogne and Lille. By means of the telegraph, Napoleon's officials could communicate with each other rapidly. According to Andrew Robertson, who also saw the telegraph at work, it took six minutes for a message to reach Lille from Paris, and for an answer to be received.[15] Faraday describes the telegraph relay, and adds a little drawing for good measure. He points out that 'They are very different to the English telegraphs, being more perfect and simple.'[16]

There, standing on a Paris hillside, was a young citizen of an enemy country, who had already aroused the curiosity of the plaster-burners, sketching the equipment that kept Napoleon's intelligence flowing around the country. How extraordinary that he was not arrested as a spy.

Wandering in these last few days more widely about Paris, Faraday watched a man touting for custom at a 'Try your Strength' machine on the Pont des Arts. He also tumbled to the answer to a problem that had been pestering him for some time – what was the occupation of 'certain men who carry on their backs something like a high tower finely ornamented and painted and surmounted in general with a flag or vane', which had a flexible pipe attached to it? The answer was that 'these men are marchands des everything that is fit to drink',[17] water- or lemonade-carriers.

Sir Humphry had not yet made it clear to the party when they were to leave Paris. It had been on and off for days, but there must have been some indication that departure was imminent because on 18 December Faraday went to the Prefecture of Police to get a passport for interior travel in France, and on Christmas Eve he was writing: 'we expect shortly to leave this city, and we have no great reason to regret it. It may perhaps be owing partly to the season and partly to ignorance of the language that I have enjoyed the place so little. The weather has been very bad, very cold, much snow, rain &c have continually kept the streets in a foul plight.'[18]

But there was one final fine Parisian extravaganza before they departed:

Napoleon and the Empress Marie-Louise were to visit the Senate in full state on 19 December. The weather was cold and wet, but Faraday stuck it out on the terrace of the Tuileries, and eventually the long procession of trumpeters, guards and officers of the court wound into sight. At the end of the procession Faraday caught a glimpse of Napoleon in an opulent carriage surmounted by fourteen footmen, 'sitting in one corner of his carriage covered and almost hidden from sight by an immense robe of ermine, and his face overshadowed by a tremendous plume of feathers that descended from a velvet hat. The distance was too great to distinguish the features well, but he seemed of a dark countenance and somewhat corpulent.' The Emperor was received by his citizens in complete silence: 'no acclamations were heard where I stood and no comments'.[19]

There were, however, joyful acclamations from some members of Sir Humphry Davy's party in the morning of 29 December, for, as Faraday writes, 'this morning we left Paris'.[20]

CHAPTER 6

A Point of Light

They were all elated. It was freezing cold, bad enough for Sir Humphry and Lady Davy sitting inside the carriage, but deadly for those outside in the air. They were heading for Nemours, forty miles south of Paris, to spend the night, but it was evening before they reached the Forest of Fontainebleau. There had been no heat in the sun all day, and by evening the trees were still covered in hoar frost. This moved Faraday to lilting, Coleridgean prose.

> . . . we did not regret the severity of the weather, for I do not think I ever saw a more beautiful scene than that presented to us on the road. A thick mist which had fallen during the night and which had scarcely cleared away had by being frozen dressed every visible object in a garment of wonderful airiness & delicacy. Every small twig and every blade of herbage was encrusted by a splendid coat of hoar frost, the crystals of which in most cases extended above half an inch. This circumstance . . . produced an endless variety of shapes and forms. Openings in the foreground placed far-removed objects in view which in their airiness, and softened by distance, appeared as clouds fixed by the hands of an enchanter: then rocks, hills, valleys, streams and roads, then a milestone, a cottage or human beings came into the moving landscape and rendered it ever new and delightful.[1]

Sir Humphry was also moved to such pictorial levels of passionate exclamation as they galloped through the forest. The experience drew the romantic poet out of him, forty lines of passion. This is a sample:

> The trees display no green, no forms of life;
> And yet a magic foliage clothes them round, –
> The purest crystals of pellucid ice,
> All purple in the sunset . . .[2]

This poem captures an essential difference in outlook between Faraday and Davy. In worldly affairs Faraday was naïve, ignorant, and wilfully avoided considering political issues. His understanding of the very dangerous situation in France was practically non-existent. Blundering about a Parisian quarry, patently the uninformed Englishman, openly sketching Napoleon's telegraph equipment, he was being careless in the extreme. He felt an unfortunate, but at the time perfectly commonplace, kind of juvenile superiority over the French and the Italians, and this emerges regularly in his account of the continental journey.

Davy, however, though feeling superior to most people around him, had political antennae. He saw the importance of racing to an understanding of what iodine was before Gay-Lussac got to it; knowledge was power. He saw, too, the importance of putting on a theatrical show of chemical effects for the French scientists, and making them nervous. And he saw the importance of not appearing impressed by the treasures in the Louvre. So, at the end of his versification, Davy gives the lines a twist, and turns them into poetry. He draws a picture of a golden eagle on the gorge at Fontainebleau:

> . . . the bird of prey, –
> Emblem of rapine and lawless power:
> Such is the fitful change of human things:
> An empire rises, like a cloud in heaven,
> Red in the morning sun . . .
> . . . soon its tints
> Are darken'd, and it brings the thunder-storm, –
> Lightning and hail, and desolation comes;
> But in destroying it dissolves, and falls
> Never to rise!

Davy could handle allegory; indeed his whole imaginative life was wreathed in it, his visionary writings were driven by it, and his later writings suggest that towards the end of his life he was taken over by it. Faraday, on the other hand, saw the natural world as part of the revealed truth, the real thing, and his life's work came to be dedicated to understanding the purposes behind nature – God's purposes, in his view – and to explaining them in their most direct terms to humanity.

Riding through the Forest of Fontainebleau as the winter's day, and the year 1813, drew to their close, Davy and Faraday were separated by more than the roof of the carriage. Davy was inside, looking out of the window to the right or left. Faraday, however, sitting up with the driver and the luggage, could see from an aerial perspective the entire 360 degrees around him, and the zenith of the skies. The man of allegory was enclosed from the world; the budding scientist of revealed truth was out within the elements.

It took them five days to reach Lyons. Faraday writes of travelling hastily, faring meagrely and arriving 'fatigued and at a late hour' at one of their stops on the way.[3] It was a difficult and uncomfortable trip, to say the least. But even after the ecstatic experiences of Fontainebleau there were more natural joys for them to witness. They set off before dawn, without knowing where they would sleep that night. 'These dark hours however have their pleasures, and those are not slight which are furnished at such hours by the memory or the imagination,' wrote Faraday. As the sun went down in the Burgundian hills they saw crepuscular rays, or 'Zodiacal light', as Faraday described it. 'It appeared as an emanation of light in enormous rays from the sun into the expanse. There were about seven rays diverging upwards and sideways and ascending many degrees into the heavens. They continued for nearly half an hour . . .'.[4]

The horses splashed through the waters at the edge of the Loire as they galloped down to Lyons in the starlight. In the gorges of the Auvergne they walked 'for some miles through these wild valleys and passes', to rest the horses and for Sir Humphry to investigate the extinct volcanoes.[5] This was one of the main purposes of this part of the journey – Napoleon himself wanted Davy to study volcanoes.[6] 'We seem tied to no spot, confined by no circumstances, at all hours, at all seasons and in all places,' Faraday wrote, using words which have a distinct echo, remarkable in a young non-conformist, of a significant passage in the Anglican Holy Communion service.

We move with freedom. Our world appears extending and our existence enlarged. We seem to fly over the globe rather like satellites to it, than parts of it, and mentally take possession of every spot we go over . . . We have lived hard this last day of the year.[7]

But a few days into January 1814 they began to feel the welcome of the warm south. The weather gradually lost its icy grip, and their spirits rose at these first hints of a Mediterranean climate. Sir Humphry reached for his pencil:

> The air is soft as in the month of June
> In northern climes; a balmy zephyr blows,
> And nothing speaks of winter's harshest month
> Save that the trees are leafless . . .[8]

Looking about the Rhône near Lyons, he saw the landscape with the eye of an eighteenth-century connoisseur:

> . . . and all the tints
> Which human art bestows upon the scene
> Are chaste as if the master-hand of Claude
> Had traced upon the canvass their design.

They first saw the Alps from outside Lyons. Mont Blanc 'was readily distinguished', Faraday writes, giving the facts as he saw them:

It appeared as an enormous isolated [?] mass of white rocks. At sunset as the light decreased, their summits took a hundred varying hues. The tone of colouring changed rapidly as the luminary sank down, became more grave, at last appeared of a dull red as if ignited, and then disappeared in the obscurity, until fancy and the moon again faintly made them visible.[9]

Sir Humphry, however, put his first view of Mont Blanc in his own poetic way:

With joy I view thee, bathed in purple light,
Whilst all around is dark; with joy I see
Thee rising from thy sea of pitchy clouds
Into the middle heaven . . .[10]

They were heading for Montpellier, where Davy knew there would be a good supply of seashore plants and sea creatures that might be rich sources of iodine. When they reached the town, eleven days after leaving Paris, Faraday climbed to the Place Peyrou, the highest point. From there he had 'a clear unsullied view of the beautiful and extensive landscape. From this spot I could see around me the Alps, the Pyrenees, the Mediterranean and the town as well as the country in the near neighbourhood.'[11]

They remained a month in Montpellier. Sir Humphry disappeared into the hinterland and to the sea's edge to look for sources of iodine, and presumably he took Faraday with him, though the Journal is not clear about this. They must have gone together on a four-mile walk to Mont Ferrier, an extinct volcano, which had blown a huge ball of basalt for two miles when it erupted in deep geological time, and this had become a small mountain in its own right. By now the volcano had become a settlement, and gave evidence to suggest that the earth had been formed through the heat of volcanic activity. Faraday and Davy were both attracted by the olive and pine trees: 'the pines are short but airy', Faraday noted. Davy, however, went much further, and the day after their visit to Mont Ferrier composed thirty-one lines of verse to 'The Mediterranean Pine':

Thy hues are green as is the vernal tint
As those fair meads where Isis flows along
Her silver floods . . .

From this poetic description Davy moves into the ancient past, describing places and events in world history on which the pine has cast its shade – the teaching of Socrates and Plato, Greek democracy, Roman virtue, the teachings of Christ and the wanderings of the Jews.

There is a powerful energy crossing the gap between Faraday's approach to what he is seeing, and Davy's. The natural distance between enthusiasm and experience, pupil and teacher is palpable. Writing as they do in such different ways about the same landscapes, the same views, the same daily experiences, even the same kind of tree, suggests that during the conversations that must have taken place on Faraday and Davy's walks – even if they were broken by the effort of the walk, or stilted by the gap in status, age and social position – there was also a growing fault-line in attitude, laying down early markers of the distance and distaste that later grew between them. At the moment, however, the distance was small, and for Faraday, if not for Davy, the ideas that flew from one to the other were like electric sparks passing between two separated wires.

While Sir Humphry picked over the Mediterranean flora, Faraday made his own wanderings about Montpellier. The weather had taken a turn for the worse, but even so Faraday was very much happier in Montpellier than he had been in Paris: 'The shops are pretty, and many well-furnished and kept. The markets seem busy places, the coffee houses well frequented. The inhabitants are respectable and I have found them very good natured and obliging. The weather alone is what we did not expect it to be.'[12]

He had time on his hands once again, and he writes of pacing the aqueduct at the Place Peyrou to discover its length, 792 of his paces.[13] Here is another example of Faraday's enthusiastic concern for facts, dimension, physical reality and record emerging yet again, as it did in the notes he took of Tatum's and Davy's lectures, and in his accounts of the continental journey so far. But as Faraday was rambling about pacing the antiquities and Sir Humphry was gathering plants, Montpellier was gearing up for war. There was a straggling resident army, a fort above the town, and some hot-headed inhabitants. Their enthusiasm to resist the oncoming armies of the Duke of Wellington was consuming and patriotic. Nevertheless, Michael Faraday, an innocent abroad, did not seem to sense the dangers. On the Esplanade he noticed the pillar surmounted by Napoleon's eagle and the gilded letter N, but dismissed it as 'ostensibly placed as an embellishment, but really intended to produce a political effect'.[14] He even took the extraordinary risk of walking around the fort, which was full of soldiers, while the cannon were firing – 'I do not know what for, nor could our host tell me.'

'The stroll around the ramparts was pleasant,' he writes disarmingly, 'but I imagine that at times whilst enjoying myself I was transgressing, for the sentinels regarded me sharply, and more particularly at least I thought so as I stood looking at one corner, where from some cause or other the fortifications were injured.'[15] But nobody challenged him, and he had a wonderful view. After his rash behaviour when confronted by Napoleon's semaphores at Montmartre, it was just as well he did not take out his notebook and sketch at Montpellier.

Great world events were passing under Faraday's very nose in that place, but he did not seem to fathom their importance. His entry for Tuesday, 1 February is restricted to: 'This morning the town was all in uproar and running to see the passing of a large train of artillery which is going up towards Lyons. They seem in great haste.'[16]

And four days later, having amused himself by standing at the edge of the parade ground and watching the clumsy square-bashing:

Drilling is now the occupation of the town, and the Peyrou looks like a Parade. During the morning it is covered by clusters of clumsy recruits who are endeavouring to hold their arms right, turn their toes out, keep their hands in, hold their hands up &c according to the direction of certain corporals who are at present all authority and importance.[17]

Then, as if it were merely a passing show, 'The Pope passed through this place a few days ago in [*sic*] his way to Italy. He has just been set at liberty . . . Almost every person in the town was there but myself.'[18]

Faraday's indifference to Pope Pius VII's return to Rome may reflect Sandemanian attitudes, but nonetheless Sandemanians were encouraged to keep abreast of current affairs. What did catch Faraday's attention in these few weeks in Montpellier, however, was the French manner of weighing goods in the market, and of sawing large logs of wood, a technique he recorded in a sketch. Neither method had he seen in England. He trawled around the booksellers, he watched peddlers performing in the market, and he went to the theatre. Although he did not understand the dialogue, he 'unexpectedly found out the meaning by that universal language of gesture, for it was most exuberantly employed'.[19]

While Faraday ignored the climactic events, their significance was clear to Sir Humphry. He wove the grand sight of a British fleet in the Gulf of Lyons, which Faraday too must have seen, into his poem 'The Canigou', in praise of the peak in the French Pyrenees.

> . . . On the wave
> Triumphant ride the fleets of Ocean's Queen.
> My heart throbs quicker, and a healthful glow
> Fills all my bosom. Albion, thee I hail! –
> Mother of heroes! mighty in thy strength!
> Deliverer! from thee the fire proceeds
> Withering the tyrant; not a fire alone
> Of war destructive, but a living light
> Of honour, glory, and security, –
> A light of science, liberty, and peace![20]

Though he had been admitted to France as a guest of Napoleon, perhaps also as a political pawn, a sign to all warring parties that science was above politics and warfare, Davy had no doubt at all where his loyalties lay. Science, to him, was a real part of the war effort, part of Britain's fire, the living light sent out to wither the tyrant, as he expressed it. His role, as exemplified by his analysis of iodine, was to be the leading edge of the fire, and being jealous of French achievements, he aimed to humiliate French science before he returned to England.

Leaving Montpellier before sunrise on Monday, 7 January, they arrived in Nîmes at noon. They spent the rest of the day, and the next, picking about the Roman remains, the Pont du Gard, the Amphitheatre, the Maison Carré and the Grand Fountain. Faraday goes into much detail about these – some of the information reads as if it has been lifted out of a guidebook – but he seems to be more greatly taken by the geological activity around the Grand Fountain than by the antiquities themselves: 'Rocks of enormous magnitude and height are so thrown together by nature as to form a broken kind of crescent.'[21] He is prosaic about the remains, descriptive, matter-of-fact:

This place was by the various and overwhelming accidents of time nearly buried and forgotten. The canal was filled up with earth and the springs stopped or diverted. It was not more than a century ago that the encumbring rubbish was cleared away and the broken or destroyed parts rebuilt, but this has been done in a manner approaching to the ancient style and thus an adequate idea may be formed of what it originally was.

From Nîmes they went to Avignon, across the Rhône on the rope-ferry, their carriage perched precariously across the beam. Then to Vaucluse to see the famous fountain and the home of Petrarch. The place inevitably drew out the poet in Davy, and warmed his fellow-feeling with Petrarch:

> A scene of pastoral beauty glads my eye,
> Well suited to a pastoral poet's song.
> . . .
> I wonder not the poet loved thy wave, –
> Thy cavern'd rocks, – thy giant precipice;
> For such a scene was suited well to break
> The tyrant-spell of love . . . [22]

Davy, the romantic scientist, is hopelessly revisionist when it comes to writing poetry. Although he performed his science with the aplomb of a man of the Romantic era, his poetry drives him back to the first half of the eighteenth century, the golden age of Thomson, Pope and Akenside. From Faraday's perspective, however, we have a more detached reading of Petrarch's vale:

> At some little distance from the head, and after having passed two or three beautiful cascades, the stream divides into branches forming three rivers of considerable size. The water is extremely clear and pure, and of a beautiful green colour. The bed of the river is carpeted with a thousand water plants, and an eternal verdure seems to reign in the environs of Petrarch's haunts.[23]

Faraday is wholly susceptible to natural beauty, and writes in a style that can evoke the high colour, sparkle, light and jewels in a landscape. It is a language that Goethe, Humboldt and Coleridge knew best.

There are signs in the Journal that Sir Humphry explained things regularly to Faraday as they went along, discussed the geology of the country, talked about scientific phenomena as the occasion demanded.

Much of the geological information that Faraday records must have come from Davy there and then; because there are only a few recorded instances of direct instruction we should not suppose that that was all there was. In the foothills of the Alpes Maritimes Sir Humphry expatiated on the nature of the wind coming down the valley at Vaucluse, on the melt-water running off Mont Ventoux, and together he and Faraday seem to have discussed the dramatic crepuscular rays that they saw on the road to Aix-en-Provence.

They were now travelling along some of the most beautiful coastal roads in Europe, and after forty-seven days on the road from Paris, the ecstatic responses that burst out of Faraday in the Forest of Fontainebleau had been temporarily blunted: 'Left Aix this morning. Nothing particular the whole day, for pretty scenery has now become common, though not less interesting.'[24]

It was not the grand sweep of landscape that captivated him now, but detail and opportunities to exercise, so he ran around after the small green lizards, 'too nimble to be caught', that he found basking in the sun on banks of lettuces. He was amused at being told by an innkeeper that the Pope had spent the night at his inn six days earlier; to induce them to stay they were given the Pope's bed to sleep in. Faraday was surely the only Sandemanian ever to have been offered the Pope's bed, an event for which his religious training gave no particular guidance.

They travelled on through Fréjus, 'the delightful town of Nice', and on towards the Italian border. Faraday's sense of wonder returned to him in a flood.

I never saw such fine scenery as on this part of our road. It was magnificence and immensity itself. The rocks often rose perpendicularly on the side of the road for many hundred feet, and sometimes overhung it in the most terrific manner. In one place the way had by blasting and hewing been actually cut out of the side of a leaning rock, and with the roaring river at the bottom and the opposite precipices was an inconceivably romantic situation. The whole here limestone.[25]

They had now turned north up the valley of the Roya. The freezing weather had caused enormous icicles to form where water poured out of the rocks, and many of these had broken off and scattered onto the road, 'threaten[ing] destruction to the passing traveller'. They had to move them aside to make a way through, but, Faraday wrote, 'the fragments were often too heavy for me to lift'.[26] On Saturday, 19 February, they rose at dawn and girded themselves to make the final climb over the Col de Tende into Italy. Faraday put on an extra waistcoat and two pairs of stockings under the thick leather overalls and shoes which were his travelling garments. Instead of putting it away when he dressed that morning, he kept his nightcap on. He was ready to go.

There was a deep snowfield all around them as they set off. The men they had hired to help them over the mountain were beginning to gather. There would be about sixty-five of them altogether, mountain men from the villages whose job it was to dismantle the carriage and rope it to sledges, and manhandle the lot up to the peak and back down the other side. They whistled and talked, totally familiar with and unimpressed by the dramatic mountainscape, and scaring the travellers with their warnings about avalanches and precipices. Sir Humphry and Faraday kept their nerve by taking readings on their barometer to gauge their height, and discussing the geology. Davy pointed out the micaceous schist, and told Faraday that where there was micaceous schist there was also granite. There were two sedan chairs, one each for Lady Davy and her maid, who both went on ahead. Travellers coming the other way passed them, and the men with the sledges set off at a run, shouting and cheering as they went. The party was soon scattered into groups, Davy and Faraday taking up the rear. They followed the mule tracks, and Faraday stopped to sketch how the mules' footsteps enlarged and softened as the sun on the snow warmed them. Far ahead in the distance they could see the sedan chairs crawling along a ridge, 'and a bird soaring below it – the men pointed out to me as an eagle'.[27]

By late afternoon they had reached the summit, six thousand feet above sea level.

The view from this elevation was very peculiar, and if immensity bestows grandeur was very grand. The sea in the distance stretching out apparently to infinity. The enormous snow-clad mountains, the clouds below the level of the eye and the immense white valley before us were objects which struck the eye more by their singularity than their beauty, and would after two or three repetitions raise feelings of regret rather than of pleasure.[28]

The sledge with the carriage paused at the top, while the foot-passengers and some of the mules went ahead. They had been warned about hollows in the snow, practically invisible on the surface, but nevertheless Faraday slipped many times and found himself up to his chest in snow. One animal and its load were nearly lost – it missed its footing and tumbled over, rolling several yards down the mountain, and had to be dug out and righted by all hands. Looking back, they saw the carriage on its sledge setting off, gathering speed rapidly, with the men running alongside skidding down the mountain, practically out of control. As night fell, they heard the dong, dong of a village bell, and carried on through the snow until they crossed into Italy and reached Limone Piemonte, where they spent the night.

Continuing northwards for two days, they reached Turin during Carnivale. The following day was Shrove Tuesday, and Faraday 'strolled' – his word – into the whirling streets in search of a party. Faraday's stroll in a new town had become a ritual for him, and in Turin he went to the edge of the city and among some trees by the River Po he listened to the bands and watched the dancers spin around the musicians in rings. Between the bands and the circles of 'ever-moving and never-tired dancers' were 'singers, leapers, boxers, chestnut merchants, apple stalls, beggars', everyday Italian life, enchanted by the excitement and celebration. Faraday then strolled back into town, where he saw the Corso, the even more extraordinary custom of the well-to-do of Turin who despatched their 'carriages, curricles, saddle horses &c' to be driven empty for several hours up and down for show, as the crowd looked on.

There were . . . an immense number of persons who stood on each side of the street looking and gazing with great apparent satisfaction, and who if they had been conscious of the comparison I was then making between the scene before me and the one I had just left would have looked down on me with contempt and derision, no doubt equal at least to that which at the same time occupied my mind.[29]

The continental journey was, for Faraday, beginning by now to develop a pattern of its own. Long, weary travelling from town to town was enlivened by *ad hoc* instruction from Davy, and landscapes and antiquities that he had read or been told about and perhaps never dreamt he would one day see. His Journal record is detailed and engaging, and although scientific subjects are regular themes, they do not dominate. He writes as if he is taking notes (which he probably was), quite as much as making an account for his own future reflection, enjoyment and remembrance.

Davy and Faraday were among the very last of the Grand Tourists, those wealthy Englishmen and their companions who in the decades leading up to the war with France had travelled in their thousands through France and Germany to Italy in search of antiquities and classical learning. Davy's mission was science, while for Faraday there was an ambivalence about the true aims of the journey. He had scientific duties to perform for Sir Humphry, certainly, but for himself the dividend would not be science but a widening knowledge that it brought him of the depth, richness and pattern of European culture. This came to underpin Faraday's outlook all his life, and as the decades passed we can see how crucial these eighteen months in Europe were for him, and how they influenced the pattern and direction of his career and achievement.

The character that the Journal most directly evokes is of a receptive young man, talkative, animated, urgent, eager to know, determined to understand, one who happily disregards the discomforts in exchange for the riches that travel will reveal. He is curious about religious practices on the continent, but there is little clear evidence of his own religious beliefs. On his travels this reluctant Sandemanian comes across as a *bon viveur* who enjoys good food and wine, attending the theatre, dressing up and taking part with enthusiasm in masked balls. He has read his guide books, and is precise in recording details of distance and dimension, as if he too were writing a guide. As a tourist, slogging round the towns he visits on foot, he is energetic and assiduous, keen to find the high point for the panoramic view, eager to visit museums, galleries and gardens, and to watch local celebrations and processions. He does not waste his time. Whether in the marketplace, the inn or the museum, Faraday is curious, and works very hard to feel and to express the textures of the continent, and the customs of the people around him.

All these qualities, which the continental Journal articulated, emerge in their time in Faraday's later life. The Journal is the seedbed where we can see the shoots of his coming character beginning to poke through. The fact that he wrote it up a second time, perhaps nearly ten years later, also tells us something worth noting: without making too much of it, Faraday is preserving the young, ebullient Mike for posterity before he is sucked down into adulthood, marriage, responsibility, social conformity, religious non-conformity, decisions, and the perpetual need to earn a living.

In many of the towns he visited, Faraday sought out the bookshops, printers and bookbinders, looking back through them at his earlier, now abandoned, life. He wrote to Riebau: 'My old profession of books has oftentimes occurred to my mind and been productive of much pleasure.'[30] He bought books at 'every large town we came to', but soon found he had accumulated too many, and had to deny himself, though he may have lost some of those he had bought somewhere en route.[31] He tried to buy a French grammar in France, an Italian–English dictionary in Italy, and later in the journey an English–German dictionary, but try as he might, languages always had a tendency to elude him. He went to the theatre on two or three occasions, but never really understood the dialogue, unable to keep up with its relentless speed.

A recurrent and characteristic theme in the Journal is Faraday's fascination for detail. There was the phosphorescence in the harbour mud at Morlaix; the analysis of a postillion's equipment; the glow-worm on the road to Rennes; the telegraph at Montmartre; notices of the various methods of weighing goods in the marketplace, with comparisons between the English, French and Italian practices. Together, these and many other observations add up to an extended series of insights into continental life of a depth which would have graced any great travel writer of the nineteenth century – Richard Ford or Sir Richard Burton come to mind – and could have provided material for a painter on his travels. If Michael Faraday had achieved nothing else in his lifetime, this Journal would by now have had due recognition, and we would know him well as an incisive travel writer who sparkled once and vanished like a shooting star.

There is another beam along which we can take a fresh perspective on Faraday's youthful life and character. This shines out from his letters home, to his mother, sisters, and principally to Benjamin Abbott. Each letter is heavily and opaquely overwritten, but they have an immediacy which time and revision might have blunted in the Journal. The first surviving letter, to Faraday's mother, is dated 9 December 1813, six weeks after the party had arrived in Paris.[32] The war frustrated the free flow of correspondence between France and England, and this letter was carried home by 'a person who is now here, but who expects soon to part for England'. It is a short letter, a mere wave, with no news, just the apologetic 'I could say much more, but nothing of importance.'

Margaret Faraday gets a longer letter four months later, from Rome, and it is from this that we can begin to take a new view of the journey. From the start there is a studied deference to Sir Humphry, which reflects the style of the pair's day-to-day relationship: 'by a high favour Sir H. Davy will put [this letter] with his own, and it will be conveyed by a particular person'. There are tiny hints of unhappiness such as a loving son might try to suggest to his mother, but not so much as to worry her. The journey had been 'as pleasant and agreeable (a few things excepted, in reality nothing) as it was possible to be'. Faraday runs quickly over events in Paris, how Sir Humphry's 'high name' in the city gave them easy access to everything they wanted to see, and how their passports were granted 'with the utmost readiness'. He sweeps his mother down through France in a line or two, gives her a hint of the dangers of travel in a remark about their stormy passage between Genoa and Lerici, writes nothing about Florence, and tips her out at Rome, 'in the midst of things curious and interesting'. But with this and the letter written a fortnight later to Benjamin Abbott, we begin to get additional information that adds depth to the Journal account.

They had been held up by bad weather in Genoa, while trying to take a boat across the bay to Lerici. Taking advantage of the delay Sir Humphry called on Professor Viviani, who had some electric fish in captivity, and tried to discover if the fishes' electric charge was strong enough to decompose water; he found it was not, but nevertheless they gave some good shocks.[33] The short voyage to Lerici was rough and dangerous, but it had the effect of silencing Lady Davy, who seems not to have stopped talking since they left England. Faraday was beginning to get fed up with her and her imperious ways, treating him like the servant he did not consider himself to be. In a later recollection Abbott wrote an account of what Faraday must have told him when he came home:

When in a boat in the Gulf of Genoa a sudden storm of wind . . . placed them for some time in some danger, and she (Lady D) was so alarmed that she became almost faint and in consequence ceased from talking. This, he told me, was so great a relief to him that he quite enjoyed the quiet and did not at all regret the cause that produced it, though the situation was for some time critical.[34]

Passing through Italy, they drove into Lucca a day ahead of the English army that had landed at Livorno, and received a surprising and rapturous welcome. The entire town, waiting outside the gates, cheered and ululated as they trotted past. The crowd did not care that the carriage carried no guns to drive the French out; all that mattered was that the passengers were English, and grandees too apparently, smiling and waving as they passed along the line of people. To Abbott Faraday wrote:

> . . . since we have left the French dominions we have been received with testimonies of pleasure & gratitude as strong as it was possible for the tongue to express. At Lucca we found the whole population without the gates waiting for the English . . . The town was decorated in the most brilliant manner by colours, drapery and embroidery flying from every window, & in the evening general illuminations took place done as expressive of their joy at the deliverance from the French government, & the English were hailed everywhere as their Saviours.[35]

They arrived in Florence flushed and delighted. It was a glorious morning, enhanced by the good fortune of finding the best hotel, 'a Palace both outside and inside', as Faraday described it,[36] and that is probably just what it was. For the next two days he took himself off on his strolls about town. He discovered the River Arno, admired the bridges, particularly Ponte Santa Trinità, with its 'air so light and free one can scarcely imagine it to be of stone'.[37] He walked to the Duomo, the Baptistery, considered climbing Giotto's campanile for 'the finest possible view of Florence & the environs', and then on to the Piazza Signoria. The bronzes in these public areas caught his eye particularly – the Baptistery doors, 'bronze and most beautifully cast'; in the square 'the bronze is a fine figure of Perseus with the head of Medusa'.

The great object of the visit to Florence was to go with Sir Humphry to see the scientific instruments formerly in use at Accademia del Cimento, once the working place of Galileo, and by now in the Museo di Storia Naturale. Faraday told Abbott all about it: 'here is a fine Museum of Natural History containing an immense quantity of things curious & instructive and some wax works in anatomy & botany of the most delicate kind. The collection of apparatus is numerous and rendered invaluable by the instruments of Galileo & the Duke of Tuscany.'[38]

He goes on to describe the telescope with which Galileo discovered the moons of Jupiter in 1610, the 'vast quantity' of electrical machines and apparatus, the magnets – one of which could support a weight of 150 pounds[39] – and particularly the great lens that Grand Duke Ferdinand III had commissioned. There were minerals, shells, insects, and stuffed birds and their eggs. The last room 'contains some singular specimens of carving and modelling representing the horrors of death in the Plague and in a sepulchre. There were some Egyptian mummies in the room, one of them opened.'[40]

For two days Sir Humphry and Faraday worked on iodine in the museum's laboratory, and also began to prepare for a dramatic experiment to show that diamond is pure carbon, a chemically identical substance. They set the Duke's lenses, the larger one fourteen or fifteen inches in diameter, out in the garden. It was a sunny morning, and they tested their strength and efficacy by putting a piece of wood at the focus. Instantly the wood burst into flame. These were also the days of the Feast of the Annunciation, celebrated in Florence with great excitement. Faraday recorded the atmosphere in his Journal: 'The country people flocked into the town in their best attire, the women ornamented with enormously large ear-rings and an abundance of gold and silver lace about the head.'[41] People were shouting, cannon firing, and fairground booths had been set up in the streets between the cathedral and the Annunziata. Faraday went into the cathedral 'at about 11 o'clock' and heard the Te Deum to the sound of trumpets and cannonfire: 'The sound of the trumpet in so large an inclosed space produced a striking effect on the mind – the music beautiful.'

On Sunday morning, the Feast of the Annunciation, Sir Humphry set a diamond on a perforated dish mounted on a platinum rod inside a thick glass globe. This was filled with a stream of hydrogen, ignited to heat the diamond. They had moved the equipment out of the garden, and now they were upstairs in the museum, by a south-facing window. On a wooden framework to one side was an air pump whose iron arm and oiled joints glistened in the sunshine as Faraday gently wound them up and down. Adjacent was a bubbling retort with potassium chlorate being heated to produce oxygen. Pipes joined the pump to the globe and the globe to the retort. As the hydrogen was drawn out of the globe by the pump, the oxygen, with a huff and a sneeze, was drawn in. Thus, the diamond was bathed in an atmosphere of oxygen, as pure as Davy and Faraday could make it.[42]

They all kept an anxious eye on the sun, for the sky must be clear and the sun as high and as hot as possible to give the required heat to the lens. With the noise of the Annunciation crowds sussurating across the garden, and the bangs of the cannon going off at the cathedral, Sir Humphry adjusted the lenses. The large one, nearest to the window, took the sunlight first and focused it onto the smaller one, set about three and a half feet away. This focused the light yet again, into an intense, dazzling, severe point which passed sharply through the wall of the glass globe and fell like a pinprick onto the diamond. This too sparkled, glorying in the experiment, but nothing else seemed to be happening. For about three-quarters of an hour they let the heat point play on the diamond, adjusting the apparatus from time to time to let the wall of the globe cool and to compensate for the relentless motion of the sun. Then, 'on a sudden Sir H Davy observed the diamond to burn visibly, and when removed from the focus it was found to be in a state of active and rapid combustion. The diamond glowed brilliantly with a scarlet light inclining to purple, and when placed in the dark continued to burn for about four minutes.'[43]

They must have cheered and danced, having achieved what many thought impossible, the creation of about seven hundred degrees centigrade of heat at a tiny point of light, and the sudden, incandescent, unearthly consumption into a pile of black dust of the hardest substance known to man. Cheers echoed in the distance from the celebrations of the Feast of the Annunciation, where the crowds were celebrating another creation at a tiny point, one which would generate more light and heat than any diamond.

Over the next few days they repeated the experiment. It failed once because the sun was not strong enough, but as they progressed they found they could light up and damp down the burning diamond at will. They tried the procedure in different atmospheres – with carbonic acid and nitrous oxide – but the prize of the experiment was the proof that diamond is pure carbon, one and the same as graphite, pure and black. The experiments went on so long, day by day across a week, that Faraday was too late on one of the days to get into the Uffizi to see the paintings. But it was an intense, magnificent and spectacular week, comparable in excitement to anything in the long months of laboratory work in London and Paris that Sir Humphry had shared with Faraday. It was a definitive instance of the star scientist creating spectacular effects to pluck one more certain fact from the bosom of nature.

The party left Florence early on Sunday, 3 April, a week after the first success with the burning glass. 'In no place since I left England have I been so comfortable and happy,' Faraday wrote.[44] They had been welcomed to Italy as conquerors, and left Florence with a conquest of their own. 'Englishmen are here respected almost to adoration,' Faraday wrote to his mother from Rome, 'and I proudly own myself as belonging to that nation which holds so high a place in the scale of European Powers.'

CHAPTER 7

Mr Dance's Kindness Claims my Gratitude

On the way to Rome Sir Humphry became more buoyant than he seems to have been on other parts of the journey, and he spoke with excitement about the geological features of the landscape. The double success of the iodine discovery and the burning of diamonds must have loosened his tongue, for the geological information that Faraday writes down in the Journal is fuller and more detailed than any earlier notes. They were also, now, well away from the French.

They spent the first night in Siena, where Faraday visited the cathedral, a building 'of great magnitude and covered externally with black and white marble'.[1] Some of the designs in the mosaic floor were uncovered for him, and he also looked at illuminated missals in the Libreria Piccolomini. South of Siena, where they spent a second night, they passed through a volcanic ridge of the Apennines and stopped to climb one of the peaks.

> The summit was lava & pumice of various kinds, below under the lava basalt occurred, split irregularly in a perpendicular direction. There were many cavities in the basalt, some of them contained very minute cubical crystals of a black colour and opaque. In others were larger semi-transparent white and prismatical crystals. These Sir H Davy thought to have been formed by the cooling of a substance rendered fluid by heat.[2]

They travelled on to Lago di Bolsena, the largest volcanic lake in Italy, past 'mountains singularly ridged and rifted on their south and western sides, as if cut into their present form by enormous torrents'.[3]

As they made their way down into the Tiber valley, they looked out anxiously and with growing excitement for their first glimpse of Rome. Then, coming round a turn of a hill, there was the dome of St Peter's and, surrounding it, gradually the eloquent panorama of Rome revealed itself. They clattered down into the city, through the Porta del Popolo, and took the Via del Babuino to their hotel in the Piazza di Spagna.

Faraday got away as soon as he could for his first stroll. He crossed the Ponte Sant' Angelo and visited St Peter's, 'of which more anon if I am able'.[4] This was Easter week, and the cathedral was being prepared for the celebrations. He went back to St Peter's the next day, Thursday, 7 April, to see the spectacle.

Towards the evening the illumination of the churches for which preparations had been making for two days took place and St Peter's presented a magnificent sight. A large cross was suspended over the middle of the aisle, nearly under the centre of the dome, and illuminated in a brilliant and perfect manner on all sides. The effect it produced on the mind on entering the church was singular and powerful. In the chapel of our saviour was an illumination consisting of above two thousand wax candles of great size, and everything was arranged for the reception of the pious or curious. The various religious societies in the city came in procession by turns with lighted tapers and chaunting to give homage, and the whole city appeared engaged in the service of religion. On the Saturday after at about 10 o'clock a general firing of all the pistols, guns &c &c in the town commenced, and continued for nearly two hours, the people taking this method of expressing their joy for the resurrection.[5]

Overwhelmed as he was by the religious spectacle, Faraday's interest was taken more by the antiquities than by the buildings which he had described earlier as 'modern work'.[6] There is genuine amazement in his voice at the size, extent and magnificence of ancient Rome. Though he may have had ample opportunity in Riebau's shop to read pre-war histories, such as Gibbon's *Decline and Fall of the Roman Empire*, the perspective of Faraday's generation as it reached adulthood was one of rebuilding, reconstruction, analysis and discovery. Michael Faraday was one of the first Englishmen to enter Rome after Napoleon's abdication, and he saw the city with the eyes of a young citizen of a newly triumphant nation. Travelling through France, he had been a licensed visitor to an enemy country; in Italy he was a welcomed and admired representative of a liberating power. This gave him an altered perspective, and as a young man of modest manner and enquiring outlook, he handled the change in viewpoint with courtesy and tact. There was also a new moral ingredient: Faraday's generation looked at the ruins of ancient Rome in the light of their experience of the new Europe, which had itself suffered ruin during thirty years of war.

Faraday tended to set off on his sightseeing walks at about eight or nine o'clock in the morning, and to stay out until four in the afternoon. On one morning he started by climbing the Antonine Column 'to trace out from it the route I wished to go'.[7] He walked to the Piazza di Pietra, to the Church of the Gesù, and up the hill to the Capitol, where he saw the bronze equestrian statue of Marcus Aurelius: 'the air and energy of the horse is wonderful: it is considered as the most perfect work of its kind'.[8] Then he slowly picked his way across the Forum, and walked on to the Colosseum, to the Campo Vaccino and the Palace of the Caesars to San Giovanni in Laterano, 'a magnificent piece of architecture, and within abounds in riches paintings and statues'. He was now near the easternmost part of the city walls, approaching Porta Maggiore, 'formerly part of the aqueduct of Tiberius Claudius, but being the part under which passed the public road it was formed in a more magnificent and imposing manner than the other arches'. Turning for home, Faraday noted the ruins of the Temple of Minerva Medica, and walked up Via Merulana to Santa Maria Maggiore. He was 'astonished' by the baths of Trajan,[9] some of the finest of the baths which

> inclosed temples, perystiles, games, the schools of philosophers, libraries, theatres, alleys, arbours &c, indeed everything that the arts could contribute to their magnificence, their convenience or their luxury . . . There were at Rome twelve public baths or therma, and 860 were counted which were private. In the reign of Nero their number was almost infinite.

That was about enough for one day, and 'turning off took my road home hungry, thirsty and fatigued'. But at eight o'clock the next morning he was off again, this time in the other direction, towards the Pantheon, south to the Teatro di Marcello and, via the Arch of Janus Quadrifons and the Cloaca Maxima, to the Circus Maximus, the baths of Caracalla and the start of the Appian Way. The Journal breaks off in mid-sentence just as Faraday writes 'I rambled along . . .';[10] and so he probably did for the rest of that day. These are entirely manageable expeditions for a man of his age, and it was early April, not high summer, but nevertheless the assiduity, energy and single-minded determination to get about on his 'rambles' reflects the importance to Faraday of seeing as much of Rome as he possibly could.

The letter to Abbott that Faraday began in Rome on 1 May he continued in Geneva nearly three months later. There he reflected on what he had seen in Italy, and with the benefit of distance wrote:

> . . . the things [in Rome] would affect anyone, and that mind must be dull indeed that is not urged to think & think again on these astonishing remains of the Romans when they appear in sight at every corner . . . The two things here most striking are the Coliseum and St Peter's, and one is not more worthy of the ancients than the other is of the moderns. The Coliseum is a mighty ruin & indeed so is Rome & so are the Romans, & it is almost impossible to conceive how the hardy warlike race which conquered the globe has degenerated into modern, effeminate, idle Italians. St Peter's appears to have been erected on the plan of some fairy tale, for every luxury, every ornament and every embellishment & species of embellishment have been employed in its erection. Its size is mighty, it is mountain-ous, its architecture elegant, its materials costly. They consist of Marbles of every hue & every kind of mosaics, statues, casts, bronzes, Jewels, Gold & silver not spread [?] sparingly but shiny & glittering in every part.[11]

There is a break in the record of Faraday's weeks in Rome, because the first draft of the Journal is lost, and something must have distracted him when he was writing it up years later, for he never returned to finish it. His first biographer Bence Jones, however, who was working from the original draft, picks up the story fifteen days later on 5 May. There was not much science done in Rome by Sir Humphry and Faraday, by all accounts. After a long early-morning walk on 15 April from the Piazza di Spagna to the Colosseum, the Forum and the Campo Vaccino and back again, Faraday had breakfast and went with Sir Humphry to the Accademia dei Lincei in the Palazzo Corsini to experiment with charcoal. This was probably to continue ideas Davy had developed during the burning of the diamonds, but 'in two experiments the globes burst and the results were lost'.[12] Just before they left Rome they went together to the home of Domenico Morichini, where they repeated his experiment which aimed to show that violet light, when isolated in the spectrum, had the property of magnetising a needle. From the Journal account, Faraday was convinced by what he saw, but Davy remained sceptical.

At about two o'clock in the morning of Saturday, 7 May they left Rome for Naples, driving past the Colosseum, 'beautiful in the extreme' in the moonlight.[13] They had set out so early to avoid robbers, and at dawn met the party of gendarmes detailed to escort them through dangerous country. The Journal record now goes silent for a week, until we find Sir Humphry, Faraday and a boy servant at the foot of Mount Vesuvius preparing to climb. They paused halfway up to enjoy 'the extensive view of both sea and earth',[14] and continued over 'rough and hilly' ground broken by lava streams, impeded by layers of ash, 'a very bad foundation for the feet, continually receding as the foot advances; nevertheless, by the aid of strong sticks and two or three restings, we attained the top by about half past two o'clock'.

There was a huge column of smoke, a foul and dangerous stink of sulphur, and flames licking out of the ground ahead of them. 'When silence was made,' Faraday writes, 'the roaring of the flames came fearfully over the ear.' Above the noise, Sir Humphry pointed out the yellowish iron chloride encrusting the lip of the crater. They scraped some away to take home, but had to run for their lives as the wind changed and brought the whole poisonous, suffocating cloud down upon them. From a place of safety Sir Humphry resumed his lecture, and explained that the steam which they could also see was water that in other circumstances would have run off down the mountainside as streams.

Their servant boy pulled some eggs from his bag, cracked them and fried them on a stone. Then he set out some bread, wine and glasses, and the travellers sat down together in this poisoned landscape to eat a hearty lunch. The ground shimmered in the heat; red, white and yellow salts danced in the wavering atmosphere around them. On this extraordinary mountain Faraday witnessed the action of a gigantic chemical retort, much as an ant, wandering across the Royal Institution laboratory bench, might observe a melting pot with Sir Humphry and his assistant in attendance.

They went back to their hotel that evening, but returned to the mountain late the next afternoon, to see the spectacle of a grumbling volcano at night. As they reached the summit, it became dark very quickly, and

the flames . . . issued forth in whirlwinds, and rose many yards above the mouth of the volcano. The flames were of a light red colour, and at one time, when I had the most favourable view of the mouth, appeared to issue from an orifice about three yards, or rather more, over.[15]

The party was rather more organised on this second trip up Vesuvius. They had brought a good dinner with them, which they spread out in the sulphurous light.

Cloths were now laid on the smoking lava, and bread, chickens, turkey, cheese, wine, water and eggs roasted on the mountain brought forth, and a species of dinner taken at this place . . . Old England was toasted, and 'God save the King' and 'Rule Britannia' sung; and then two very entertaining Russian songs by a gentleman, a native of that country, the music of which was peculiar and very touching.[16]

As they picked their way back down the mountain, some of the locals who had attached themselves to the party skittered on ahead, sending lumps of lava and ash flying, shouting and yelling in the darkness as they bumped into one another and ran uncontrollably downhill. But Faraday could not leave so quickly. He paused and turned and looked back. There he was rewarded with the exquisite sight of the flaming mountain, and 'the long black cloud, barely visible by the starlight, appeared as a road in the heavens'.

There is no record in Faraday's Journal or letters of how the party spent the rest of their days in Naples, but we do know that they were entertained in the highest society, the Queen of Naples presenting Davy with a pot of ancient pigment for analysis.[17] The year was drawing on, and they wanted to escape the heat of Italy to summer in Switzerland. They headed quickly back to Rome, where on 24 May Davy may have witnessed Pope Pius VII entering Rome in triumph through the Porto del Popolo. Sir Humphry suggested he was present at the triumph when he wrote years later, in the voice of The Stranger in Dialogue III of *Consolations in Travel*, that he was 'with almost the whole population of Rome' as the Pope was welcomed back to his city.[18] But was this just Davy's imagination at play? And was Faraday there too? This was a moment of great historical importance, and it is a curious coincidence that the missing pages of the Journal should straddle a day on which we might, perhaps vainly, hope for a clear reflection from Faraday of his attitude towards the Pope, Roman Catholicism and the cataclysmic events around him.

Heading further north, for Geneva, they next appear on 3 June at Terni, fifty miles from Rome. Faraday writes seductively about the two-hundred-foot-high waterfall at Terni, which, viewed from its lip,

> calls the attention with an immense roaring. The rocks are perpendicular and the water falls nearly free in a stream of the purest white. The force with which it descends causes a considerable quantity to be dispersed in the air in mists and fine rain; and this produced the beautiful phenomena of a rainbow in the utmost perfection.[19]

They walked up to Lake Velino through air scented with 'woodbine, geraniums, myrtles, thyme, mint, peppermint etc', and took a boat and rowed about on the lake, which was 'surrounded by mountains of fine form and situation, and the views are delicious'. All the time the geology of the country was in their minds, and Sir Humphry gave his customary discourse: 'the base of this part [of the lake] is travertine or calcareous matter deposited by water, which appeared in strata and as stalactites; in many places agates appeared in the limestone'. At the bottom of the falls 'the masses of travertine were enormous, forming ledges over the present streams and appearing in various singular forms'.

Passing through Milan on 17 June Faraday met one of the giants of eighteenth-century science, Alessandro Volta, 'a hale elderly man bearing the red ribbon, and very free in conversation'.[20] The red ribbon was the Légion d'Honneur, given to Volta by Napoleon. Davy's account of Volta is at odds with Faraday's. Davy remembered him as being

> at that time advanced in years, – I think nearly seventy, and in bad health. His conversation was not brilliant; his views rather limited, but marking great ingenuity. His manners were perfectly simple. He had not the air of a courtier, or even of a man who had seen the world. Indeed, I can say generally of the Italian savants, that, though none of them had much dignity or grace of manner, yet they were all free from affectation.[21]

Although we have a graphic description of the party crossing the Alps on their first arrival in Italy, there is no note of their second crossing. This was the much longer journey over the Simplon Pass, clear of snow by now, to Geneva, where they were to spend the summer.[22] For three months they lived in a villa on the banks of Lake Geneva, the guest of Charles de la Rive, Professor of Chemistry at Geneva, and there Sir Humphry spent the days fishing, writing and enjoying 'the charm of the best society (chiefly English)': 'Our time has been employed lately in fishing and shooting and many a Quail has been killed in the plains of Génève and many a trout and grayling have been pulled out of the Rhône.'[23]

Faraday performed the valet's job of loading Sir Humphry's gun, but when not out hunting they became scientist and assistant, working together on iodine and the prism: '[Davy] has lately been making experiments on the prismatic spectrum at Mr Pictet's. These are not yet perfected but from the use of very delicate air thermometers it appears that the rays producing most heat are certainly out of the spectrum and beyond the red rays.'[24]

During this stay de la Rive noticed the special genius of the young man who accompanied Sir Humphry. Lady Davy expected Faraday to eat with the servants, and sent him down to do so; but de la Rive refused to allow him to go, said he would also eat with the servants if Faraday did, and brought him back upstairs to share his conversation.[25]

For his own pleasure, Faraday wrote extensive notes, of which only the part about his experiments on glow-worms to determine the nature of their light survives.[26] His letters home give the clearest account of his feelings and activities in Geneva during the summer. To his mother he reflected on the celebrations in London following the fall of Napoleon: 'Things run irregularly in the great world; and London is now I suppose full of feasting and joy and honoured by the presence of the greatest personages in Europe.'[27]

To Robert Abbott he describes the patriotic feelings he holds as an Englishman abroad at a time of victory:

I valued my country highly before I left it, but I have been taught by strangers how to value it properly, and its worth has been pointed out to me in a foreign land ... Englishmen are considered every where as a band of brothers, actuated by one heart, and one mind and treading steadily & undeviating in the path of honour, courage & glory ... [T]he English are respected, received & caressed every where for the character of their country; may she ever deserve that character ... [28]

He praises Sir Humphry, whose 'constant presence ... is a mine inexhaustible of knowledge, & improvement', and reflects on the 'many sources of information [that] have been opened to me, and many new views [that] have arose of men, manners, & things, both moral & philosophical'.

It should by now have become quite clear to both Benjamin and Robert Abbott that the Michael Faraday who would return to London would not be the same ebullient but innocent young man who left it. There are even hints in recent letters that Faraday was optimistic about learning French or Italian – he was certainly complimentary about both languages, and although he never in the event fully mastered any foreign tongue, out there, among French and Italians, he was gaining in confidence and beginning to understand the customs of the countries he was passing through, and to appreciate their differences:

I who am an Englishman, & who have been bred up with English habits, of course prefer English civilization to the civilization of

France; but everyday's experience teaches me that others do not think so, yet though I have no right to suppose I excell all those who differ from me, I still am allowed the liberty of forming my own opinion.

By this time Faraday knew something of Sir Humphry's plans, and he told Robert Abbott what he had heard: 'I expect [our future route] will lay in Germany for a short time, for from hence we shall pass (in 5 or 6 weeks) on the North of the Alps to Venice, and from Venice we shall go to Rome, & there spend the winter.'

As the summer went by, domestic tensions grew in the Davy entourage. Faraday touches on this in a letter to Benjamin Abbott, written only a week or so before they left for Venice, when he refers to his situation, 'which is not at all times pleasant and what I expected'.[29] There are some more clues about the distress that Lady Davy's high-handed behaviour was causing Faraday. His unhappiness poured out in a later letter to Benjamin Abbott,[30] and it is clear that the hate (as he described it) that she had felt for him from the beginning of the journey, and her 'evil disposition' were now beginning seriously to undermine him. There is no hint of Lady Davy in the Journal. Faraday just did not allow her in; but she may never have allowed him to forget that he was her husband's valet, and that personal service to Sir Humphry, not scientific frolics, came first.

Though a strong-minded and determined man of science, as a husband Sir Humphry was in thrall to his rich and well-connected wife, and needed her social contacts to get about socially himself, even though her money was now, legally, his. He was not required to defend his valet; still less to give him any kind of elevation within the party. Lady Davy had been born to riches and position; Sir Humphry, by contrast, had come from a modest country family, and his wife may have reminded him of that from time to time, very clearly. Reflecting on the Davys years later, Maria Edgeworth remarked that Jane 'had fallen in love with celebrity';[31] now perhaps, in the reality of an interminable journey cramped together in a carriage, her love affair with celebrity was unravelling. Under the circumstances, Lady Davy's attacks on Faraday reveal the strength of his character, his determination not to be destroyed by this difficult and demanding woman, and his ambition to better himself and to take all the opportunities life offered. It is not surprising that he went off on long walks by himself, and there is a note of despair later in the letter when he admits to Abbott that 'I am certain if I could have foreseen the things that have passed I should never have left London . . . I have several times been more than half decided to return hastily home.'

All this gives a fresh perspective on the delight that Faraday feels when receiving letters from home and in writing to his friends. He takes great pains to tell the Abbotts and his mother and brother where to write to and how to address letters to him:

> Dear Ben . . . inform my friends that I wish whatever letters they will send me may be directed to me alone or to me at Sir Humphry Davy or chez Monsieur le Chevalier Davy. I have already given this notice in a letter to my brother but for security . . . I give it again to you . . . [32]

He wants to hear news of home, of George Riebau, of Mrs Greenwell,[33] the housekeeper at the Royal Institution, who had been unwell lately and no doubt had kept a motherly eye on him from the time he began to live in Albemarle Street. He asks after John Newman, the Royal Institution instrument-maker, who had clearly been pleased by the young man's fascination with the scientific instruments he made; and he even asks tenderly after de la Roche, the bad-tempered bookbinder: 'I should like to have my name mentioned to him with thanks on my side; but he is perhaps in France, and if I see Paris again I shall search for him.'[34]

Although writing from a thousand miles away, Faraday sends comfort to Benjamin Abbott in his own troubles. Abbott was working in a counting house, and was having the same kind of difficulties that Faraday himself faced when he tried to change from the trade of bookbinding to a life in science.

> I have always perceived . . . that those things which at first appeared as misfortunes or evils ultimately were actual benefits and productive of much good in the future progress of things. Sometimes I compared them to storms and tempests which cause a temporary derangement to produce a permanent good. Sometimes they

appeared to me like roads stony, uneven, hilly and uncomfortable it is true, but the only roads to a good beyond them; and sometimes I said they were clouds which intervened between me and the sun of prosperity, but which I found were refreshing reserving to me that tone and vigour of mind which prosperity alone would enervate & ultimately destroy.[35]

Faraday's advice and succour may have a ring of the sermon, but it is also mature and ruminative. It reveals the solidity of Faraday's friendship, his loyalty and concern at a time when he may on the surface be enjoying himself in exotic locations, but when he too is suffering bitter persecution which he is powerless to control, and can only try to avoid. He adds wryly: 'I have experienced too that pleasures are not the same when attained as when sought after, and from these things I have concluded that we generally err in our opinions of happiness and misery.' But whenever he had cause to reflect on his present lot, Faraday knew he had fallen squarely on his feet, despite the difficulties that Lady Davy put in his way:

> ... the glorious opportunity I enjoy of improving in the knowledge of Chemistry and the Sciences continually determines me to finish this voyage with Sir Humphry Davy, but if I wish to enjoy those advantages I have to sacrifice much, and though those sacrifices are such as an humble man would not feel, yet I cannot quietly make them.[36]

The party must have set off eastwards very soon after Faraday had finished his letter to Benjamin Abbott. Their destination was Munich, and they travelled, as he told his mother, by way of 'Lausanne, Vevay, Berne, Zurich, Schaffhausen, and the Falls of the Rhine in Switzerland, and many other towns in Germany'.[37] Faraday was more forthcoming to Benjamin Abbott, describing the 'immense body of water' at Schaffhausen, 'the largest waterfall in Europe ... tremendous and magnificent'.[38] The extraordinary variety of costumes in Switzerland also caught his eye. Each town, each canton, had dozens of varieties, the details in each standing for a particular attitude or allegiance: 'to the passing traveller the change of place is shewn first by the change of the women's dress'.

They stayed only three days in Munich, and turning south travelled across the Tyrol back towards Italy, through a landscape which, in Sir Humphry's words, was

> as fine as I have ever seen. Deep glens – in two of them two blue rivers, rolling and foaming over rocks of syenite and micaceous schist. The depth of the glens, much greater than in Switzerland; narrow, and pine and larch below; then cultivated patches, and then pine and birch, and larch again; and, above all, very high mountains, dark and frowning, but having snow in their gullies and bosoms, and on their tops. The sky harmonised with the grandeur and solemnity of the scene; it was clouded, but something like a soft October day in England.[39]

The route to Innsbruck, where they were on 6 October, and Vicenza (13 October) took them through the Brenner Pass, where they saw wild strawberries growing at six thousand feet. The surviving entries in Faraday's Journal pick up again in Vicenza. It was the time of the grape harvest, and they passed country people carrying grapes in baskets, and treading them and collecting their juice by the roadside. It was a fertile, good-hearted scene which Faraday describes with gusto. The postillion marked the season by fashioning a whip handle out of vine, 'five or six of the year's branches being twisted together and tied at the top and bottom with packthread . . . the poor horses are thus honourably and everlastingly flogged by whips of the vine'.[40]

Despite the time of year, and the plenty, the party was pestered by beggars, who were as inventive in their techniques as they were pathetic. As the carriage approached children would kneel down in the road ahead and kiss the ground, then jump up and run alongside the carriage crying 'Carità, caro Dio &c &c'; others would do five or six acrobatic tumbles until the carriage reached them. Faraday wrote in his Journal:

> Begging has increased wonderfully since we left Germany, indeed it is almost the birthright of modern Italy . . . [T]he poor people of the country universally lay aside their work and run by the carriage

begging. A shepherd will leave his flock at half a mile distant to beg at the road as the carriage passes . . . It must produce a humiliating and depressing effect on the mind of the people in general, and appears as a curse spread over the country.

Passing on through Padua, they reached Venice, which Faraday had long wished to see and knew only from his reading and from an engraving of the Rialto and the Grand Canal which hung over the parlour fireplace at home.[41] 'On approaching it by water . . . the houses appear actually to rise out of the waves, for not a bit of ground is to be seen . . . We entered the city up a canal and went to the hotel, even to the very door, in our boat.'[42]

Faraday went on his customary strolls around Venice, on foot and by boat, poking about the bookshops, observing the townscape and the method of construction of the city. He found out about the 'very peculiar and complicated and curious' government system, and the fact that 'a horse is not to be found in Venice'. The party left after two days,[43] sufficient for Faraday to see 'the place in a general manner', his 'curiosity perfectly satisfied'. Evidently Venice disappointed him, for as he wrote to George Riebau, the city, as a historic centre of the printing trade, appeared to him 'bare and little worthy of its character'.[44]

They now set off to return to Rome, making a stop at the village of Pietra Mala, near Florence, to collect samples of an inflammable gas that emanated from the soil and caused tongues of flame to dart into the sky. They took the samples to Florence to analyse 'in the now almost deserted laboratory of the Florentine Academy',[45] and found them to be 'light hydrocarburet pure', or methane.

Faraday's priorities were now clearly forming. The ease with which his curiosity about Venice was 'perfectly satisfied', and the depth of his fascination in the scientific discoveries he had witnessed on his journey, makes an eloquent comparison. His particular attitude to science was voiced by Benjamin Abbott in one of the few surviving letters sent to Faraday on the continental tour. Benjamin is greatly missing his old friend in science, and reflects on the physical risks that Faraday was always prepared to take to advance his knowledge. Other London acquaintances, he writes, 'are not so fond of Science as to stand at a furnace till their Eyes are scorched, or risk a convulsion of their Muscles from the unexpected touch of a Voltaic battery . . . for such a one I must wait till *you* return'.[46]

Abbott tells Faraday news of London, of the courses of lectures just starting at the Surrey Institution, on Chemistry, Extemporary Eloquence, 'Passions and Affections of the Mind & their Influence on Language and the Polite Arts', and Music. He intends to go to all of them, he says, and talks about the practices of the various lecturers as if Faraday knew them all, which he probably did. Replying to an anxiety that Faraday must have shown about the state of the Royal Institution's finances, Abbott says: 'the members this summer submitted to a great sacrifice & all the debts are paid off so that . . . a dissolution . . . cannot take place within a period of time much longer than it is even probable that you will be absent'.

Now that the summer was over and they were back in Rome, Faraday's duties for Sir Humphry increased. 'My time is extremely occupied,' he writes to Abbott, 'so that I can scarcely look in my Italian books, & I have been three days in manufacturing this letter.'[47] Davy was analysing the pigments used in the ancient frescoes discovered in Herculaneum, and with the help of the sculptor Antonio Canova, who was the Pope's surveyor of works of art, had been given permission to take samples. This, with more work on iodine and hyperchlorides, fully occupied him and Faraday.

As Christmas approached, Rome prepared itself for the celebrations. Faraday wrote to his elder sister Elizabeth: 'You will have sincerity amongst you and we hypocrisy. This is a season in which modern Rome shows forth her spirit. Her churches (in number innumerable) are filled with the crowd who in the same hour fill the streets with licentiousness and riot.'[48]

The Carnival, which ran in parallel with the Christmas festivities, was about to begin. For a week the Pope traditionally relinquished control over the Romans. The streets were given over to men in fools' costumes battling with sugar-plums, to puppet shows, processions and clowns mocking religious orders. All these are remarked upon by Faraday, who took eager part in celebrations with Humphry Davy and other foreign visitors to Rome, German, English and French together: 'It was cheerful and we kept Christmas day, Christmas week and Twelfth day with a Ball, feastings and other games suited to the season and the place.'[49]

In the time he had free, Faraday revisited many of the sites he had seen earlier in the year. In writing about them to Elizabeth he mentions one 'Mr D', and says how 'often I have wished Mr D could see what I saw, that he could wander with me over the mighty wilderness of ruins the Coliseum presents . . . D would be delighted with them and his art and skill would enable him to bring faithful ideas of them home.'[50]

The vocabulary that Faraday uses to describe the Roman ruins in his letters and Journal is throughout precise and informed. It may have come from guidebook instruction, but it may also have come from recollections of conversations with 'Mr D' and others who shared and fostered Faraday's interest in antiquity. This 'Mr D' is, I would suggest, one and the same as the Mr Dance who first gave Faraday a ticket to hear Sir Humphry lecture, and who I have argued is George Dance, the eminent architect of the Roman Revival in London.

George Dance had also asked after Faraday at this time through Riebau, so the respect and interest was evidently mutual. Faraday replied to Riebau acknowledging the good wishes of 'Mr Dance, Mr Cosway and Mrs Udney . . . Mr Dance's kindness claims my gratitude, and I trust that my thanks, the only mark I can give, will be accepted.'[51] The significance here is that while walking amongst the ruins of Rome Faraday calls to mind a highly influential teacher, architect and proselytiser of the antique, and the context of his remembrance of him directs us to the conclusion that it was Dance who had fired his lifelong interest in the classics and the antique.

The tone of Faraday's letter to Riebau may echo the manner in which he held and addressed Sir Humphry. As his acknowledgement of Dance's, Cosway's and Mrs Udney's attention shows,[52] Faraday was acutely aware of his position in relation to those whom he considered to be his superiors. He opens to Riebau:

> It is with very peculiar but very pleasing and indeed flattering senti-
> ments that I commence a letter intended for you, for I esteem it a
> high honour that you should not only allow but even wish me to
> write to you.

He signs himself 'Faraday', presumably because that is how he was known in the shop. This is to the man who looked after him as a young apprentice, knew him very well, and probably took the place of his father in his affections. The two men had a great mutual respect for one another, which suggests that the humility Faraday shows in his letter is not false, but an expected courtesy which happened also to be his natural style. It held throughout his life, and evolved equally out of a Sandemanian ethic in which all men and women were to be honoured and of considered value. This instinctive attitude to others exaggerated the gap between Faraday and the Davys, whose own tendency was to emphasise their superiority and the social and financial gulf between themselves and those below them.

In Rome for the second time, Faraday haunted the printsellers and bookshops.[53] He bought six small gouache Italian views, including Vesuvius, Baiae and Pozzuo, and perhaps other pictures as well.[54] He complained to Riebau that there seemed to be no new books available in Italy, that what there were came from France, and that the Italians 'seem latterly to have resigned printing and to have become satisfied with the libraries their forefathers left them'. He also found it practically impossible to buy a Bible, 'either Protestant or Catholic . . . In all shops in Rome where I ask for a small pocket bible the man seemed afraid to answer me, and some Priest in the shop looked at me in a very inquisitive way.'[55]

The reason for this was that in early-nineteenth-century Rome the common translation of the Bible was seen by the Vatican as subversive, because it exposed the Latin mysteries of the Roman Catholic liturgy to the vulgar tongue. Thus it was effectively suppressed. This, at the very least, put Roman Catholicism and Sandemanianism at the furthest ends of the Christian spectrum from each other. For the Sandemanians clarity of the Bible text was fundamental to their teaching – and we might ask why it was that Faraday was looking for a Bible in Rome. Did he not bring one with him? Did he feel that he had let his religion slip after so many months far from home with the Davys? He had after all already reflected that travelling and religion did not go well together.

It was easier to have a good time in the Carnival than to buy books. Rome was alive with gaudy and noisy crowds celebrating the extended period of Epiphany. The most talked-about event among Romans and visitors alike was the Corso, the riderless horserace which was run each year in the Piazza del Popolo. Having heard about the race in England, Faraday was determined to see it, and got himself a good seat on scaffolding under the obelisk by the start. He could see the entire length of the course, and watched the preliminary parade of carriages, the rush for safety when the first warning gun went off, the troop of horse guards cantering around the course, and then the arrival of the racers.

The five competing horses were paraded by their owners and handlers in a dazzle of family colours, and bucked and tossed as the noise of the crowd enraged them. They were harnessed with rope and wore tin-plate armour with dangling spiked lead balls which struck their flanks cruelly as they moved. One horse 'got over the starting rope and dragged the men with him, and the master cried out that he could hold the horse no longer. The trumpet sounded and the rope dropped, and the animals were instantly at full speed.'[56]

They were infuriated by the pain from the spikes which hammered against their flanks and by the baying of the crowd. The plates of tin flew off their backs; the crowd howled as the terrified animals hurtled round the track. They only stopped when a cloth was stretched across the course, but Faraday heard one story of an English horse, unused to the race, which refused to stop, burst out of the square and ran out of town.

After the Corso the Masquerade began. 'All Rome glittered with Princes, Princesses, Dukes, Lords, Spaniards, Italians, Turks, Fools &c, all of which were in profusion. I went this morning to a masquerade ball between 2 and 5 o'clock and found it excellent.'[57]

Faraday threw his decorum to one side when he dressed in a 'domino', a priest's cloak and hood with a half-mask, and merged with the crowds on their way to a ball in a theatre lit with 'a vast number of chandeliers', with illuminated boxes, waltzing in the pit, and cotillion and country dances on the stage. The revellers spilt out into the square, where 'confetti', little lumps of white plaster, were thrown about out of windows and passing carriages. 'I found the English were much more eager at this sport than the Romans. I know an English window from which eight crowns' worth of confetti were thrown this afternoon.'[58]

Though dressed for the Masquerade, Faraday was in fact on his way to the Accademia dei Lincei, where he was to meet Sir Humphry to help him with some scientific work. He fell in behind another procession wearing dominoes, and walked with it for some time expecting the fun to start at any moment, when it suddenly became clear that this was not another masked procession, but a funeral.[59]

When Faraday last wrote to Benjamin Abbott at the end of November,[60] he had been, as he confessed in the next letter, 'in a ruffled state of mind'.[61] He and the Davys had been cooped up together on their continental tour for more than a year, and, worse, Faraday was still working as Sir Humphry's valet despite the clear assurances before they left that he would soon be relieved of domestic duties. He had a growing feeling that despite all the 'glorious opportunities' he was having, he had been invited along under false pretences. Davy had made it perfectly clear at the outset that Faraday's duties as a valet were strictly temporary: 'I felt unwilling to proceed on this plan, but considering the advantages I should lose & the short time I should be thus embarrassed I agreed.'[62]

Sir Humphry had kept his word at first and had tried to find somebody else to be his valet; he had tried all the way down France and into Italy: 'At Paris he could not get one … At Lyons he could not get one, at Montpellier he could not get one, nor at Genoa, nor at Florence, nor at Rome, nor in all Italy & I believe at last he did not wish to get one and we are just the same now as we were when we left England.'[63]

As the journey wore on Sir Humphry lost interest in finding a new valet, becoming too content with the *status quo*: 'A thousand reasons which I have now forgot caused the permanent addition of a servant to our family to be deferred from time to time, and we are at present the same number as at first.'[64] Faraday allowed that it was 'the name more than the thing which hurts', but nevertheless tensions of anger and frustration built up in him, and these burst out in Rome. He loathed Lady Davy. When he wrote to Abbott his reflections 'ran from my pen as they were formed at that moment when the little passions of anger and resentment had hooded my eyes'.

Lady Davy had a volcanic temper. She was domineering, arrogant, 'proud to an excessive degree and delight[ed] in making her inferiors feel her power'. She sought gratification continually, wishing 'to roll in the full tide of pleasures such as she is capable of enjoying', but when Sir Humphry was not looking made every effort to ensure that the rest of her 'family', as Faraday described the party with a quaint seventeenth-century turn, were deprived of enjoyments. Her life revolved around etiquette, protocol and hierarchy, and she was the despot. Sir Humphry was no match for her, and dithered when he had to take a decision affecting the family, finding it impossible to 'keep neuter, and from different reasons he can scarcely choose his side'. Lady Davy put Faraday down, keeping him in his place whenever she could, and despised his special relationship with her husband. This was an understanding that she could never share. Faraday's intelligence propelled him out of the condition of valet, and so she could never be the centre of attention when science was the subject. We might also infer that Lady Davy was jealous of Faraday: he deflected her husband's attention, he talked the language of science rather than of service, and he was an attractive but unavailable man on the fringe of her unsatisfactory marriage.

Faraday gradually began to develop protections against Lady Davy: 'I learned to despise her taunts & resist her power, and this kind of determined conduct, added to a little polishing which the friction of the world had naturally produced in your friend, made her restrain her spleen from its full course to a more moderate degree.'

Having learned to deflect her anger, Faraday began to be able to laugh at her whims, and when the storms renewed themselves, he fought back. 'At each [quarrel] I gained ground & she lost it, for the frequency made me care nothing about them & weakened her authority & after each she behaved in a milder manner.'[65] After the quarrels there were coolnesses 'between us all for two or three days'.[66] These tense, extended silences may have created the perfect opportunities for Faraday to get away on long walks on his own.

There were times when he wanted to dump them all and come back to England on his own. Indeed, one particular thought of this kind led him as near as he ever came to quitting science completely: 'At all event when I return home I fancy I shall return to my old profession of Bookseller, for Books still continue to please me more than anything else.'[67]

But Faraday bounced back, and in the next sentence began with enthusiasm to relay to Abbott some new excitements. Sir Humphry was continuing his analysis of ancient Greek and Roman pigments from the Herculaneum samples, and from a piece of blue glass from Hadrian's Villa, given to him in Milan. Faraday goes on to transcribe the central findings in the paper on ancient pigments that Davy was composing for the Royal Society and which Faraday himself had helped to write out.[68] And far from dumping the Davys and going off home on his own, telling of Sir Humphry's new discoveries had sufficiently shaken him out of his despondency for him to make the next proclamation:

Now for news!!! We shall part in a few weeks for Naples and from thence proceed immediately for Sicily ... application is made for passports to travel in the Turkish Empire & to reside at Constantinople ... to be amongst the Greek Islands in March and at Athens early in the spring.[69]

Three weeks later the plans had been amended, but writing to his mother, Faraday did say that 'I can tell you to a moral certainty that we are to see Constantinople.'[70]

In the meantime, Sir Humphry and Faraday worked together on chlorine and iodine, and on the explosive gas chlorine dioxide, a 'new compound of oxygen and chlorine which Sir Humphry discovered a few days ago'.[71] They were able to contain Lady Davy's constant demands by engaging an extra servant for her alone, 'to do everything she can want, & now I am somewhat comfortable; indeed at this moment I am perfectly at liberty, for Sir H has gone to Naples to search for a house or lodgings to which we may follow him, & I have nothing to do but see Rome, write my journal and learn Italian'.[72]

They were, however, never to see Constantinople, the Greek islands or Athens, and although Faraday did not yet know it, their great excursion was coming to its end. They did visit Naples again, and climbed Vesuvius, where they felt the mountain shake more dramatically than it had at their last visit, throwing lava into the air 'in lumps of various size from ½ lb to 25 lbs or more'.[73] But this was as far south as they were to get. After Napoleon's escape from Elba war threatened again, and the news from France, just as much as further news of quarantines being imposed on the road to Constantinople,[74] impelled Sir Humphry to curtail the journey and come home. As Faraday characteristically put it: 'I heard for news that Bonaparte was again at liberty. Being no politician I did not trouble myself much about it, though I suppose it will have a strong influence on the affairs of Europe.'[75]

By the time they reached Mantua, 'everybody,' Faraday wrote, 'is preparing for war.'[76] The soldiers and border guards were now pernickety and bureaucratic about the party's passports, and examined and re-examined them. Avoiding France, they crossed the Tyrol, travelled north through Austria, Germany and Holland, and embarked for Deal at Ostend. 'You may be sure we shall not creep from Deal to London,' Faraday wrote to his mother from Brussels, 'and I am sure I will not creep to 18 Weymouth Street, and then . . .'.[77]

They returned to London on 23 April 1815, St George's Day.

CHAPTER 8

We have Subdued this Monster

Britain was on the verge of profound change when Faraday returned from the continent. Over the subsequent eight weeks the armies of Napoleon, Wellington and Blücher, with their winding columns of baggage carts and camp followers, snaked mile by mile across the landscape of northern Europe, to converge on 17 and 18 June at a crossroads near the nondescript village of Waterloo.

The day after he and his party came home, Sir Humphry Davy attended a meeting at the Royal Institution, and was elected a member of the controlling group of Managers.[1] At Weymouth Street Faraday embraced his mother, brother and sister, and danced on the doorstep; 'My Michael!' his mother cried. A few days later, ruddy-faced, sunburnt and cheerful, Faraday turned up at Benjamin Abbott's front door. He was dressed in his travelling gear, the clothes, bought on the continent, that had protected him on the roof of the carriage for thousands of miles. As Abbott later recalled:

The trousers ... were open from the knee to the ankle on the outside, and provided with a row of loops and eyelet holes to keep them closed. His coat shewed evident signs of having been much exposed to rain, dust and sunshine, and his whole appearance shewed the effects of a long journey made in variable weather.[2]

Faraday lost no time in going back to the Royal Institution. He needed to be seen again in Albemarle Street, for he had given up his job eighteen months before and was looking for work.[3] He attended lectures and offered his help in the laboratory as soon as he could. If, in a dark moment in Rome, he had been serious about going back to bookbinding, by now, re-entering the Royal Institution, all such negative thoughts had evaporated. Events moved rapidly. On 8 May Sir Humphry was elected Vice-President of the Royal Institution,[4] and a week later, at William Brande's request and with Sir Humphry's full support, Michael Faraday got his old job back with an enhancement of responsibility – 'Assistant in the Laboratory and Mineralogical Collection and Superintendent of the Apparatus' – and also accommodation and thirty shillings a week. This was a small pay-cut from before, and reflected the uncertain finances of the Institution, which depended totally on the income it generated from subscribers.[5]

News of Wellington's victory at Waterloo reached London within twenty-four hours. The rejoicing infected everybody and everything, even down to the tone of Faraday's next letter to Abbott. He wrote of a titanic struggle between himself and William Harris – the Librarian of the Royal Institution – and his niece, who resisted the Managers' attempt to winkle Miss Harris out of his old rooms. But Michael Faraday was back, sharpening an extended metaphor to prove it:

> The Enemy having been completely beaten in the contests that took place, notwithstanding the reinforcements which he endeavoured to bring into action, his party was obliged to quit the spot contested for & retire; and I last night found all hindrances removed and the place ready for my reception . . . [6]

Back in the thick of life in London, Faraday threw himself once again into the activities of the City Philosophical Society. Having dealt with the subject of throwing the enemy out of his rooms, he bounces further along in the letter, saying: 'Tomorrow bye the bye is Lecture night in the City. If it is a good lecture come and take me there – I should like to know more exactly how that Society stands at present & intend to join it as soon as can be.'

Science teaching in London was widely available in the years immediately following Waterloo. The City Philosophical Society may have been for members only, but John Tatum's fortnightly lectures at Dorset Street were open to all comers. Lectures at the Royal Institution were open by subscription, and to the determined man or woman tickets were possible to come by. There were lectures in the London Institution at Blackfriars and the Surrey Institution at Southwark, and a profession of itinerant science teachers had grown up whose performances could be attended on payment of a small fee on most nights during the season.[7] A decade and more earlier at the Royal Institution the genius and personality of Sir Humphry Davy had been the catalyst for this explosion of opportunities for learning about science. As a result of his lecture series a small publishing industry had developed to fuel the enthusiasm for knowledge. Aimed at Sir Humphry's audiences, and at those who missed the flurry of educational activity at the Royal Institution, were the series of books by Mrs Jane Marcet, of which *Conversations in Chemistry* (1806) had fired Faraday, and became one of the best-known.[8]

Teaching at the Royal Institution was challenged by this competition. With Sir Humphry Davy no longer on the teaching roll, the responsibility fell to William Brande to maintain the momentum that Davy had so energetically initiated. The Royal Institution and the many other teaching institutions had to compete for their financial security and for the services of teachers who were both learned and could draw a good crowd. As the best-equipped and at this time the only 'official' laboratory in England, the Royal Institution also made money from fees generated from government research contracts, as they would now be called, and from requests from individual industrialists, entrepreneurs and lawyers who wanted scientific analysis of one kind or another. The Institution had competition in science matters from military and trade interests, such as at the Military Academy at Woolwich and the East India Company Academy at Addiscombe, Surrey, but with demilitarisation in Britain accelerating after 1815, the advantage was turning towards Albemarle Street.

Nevertheless, by 1815 the Royal Institution was in deep financial trouble. It had come near to bankruptcy in 1814, being baled out only by an emergency subscription from some of the membership. Davy must have been aware of the Institution's plight when he gave up his professorship in 1813, but being driven by his old creative demon, and indeed by the impulses of his wife, he lacked the selflessness at the time that might have encouraged him to stay and help to save the sinking ship. When they were on the continent the finances of the Institution must have been a topic of conversation between Davy and Faraday, as Faraday wrote anxiously to Abbott from Rome asking him to make sure his books were not sold at auction, were the worst to happen.[9]

William Brande succeeded Davy as Professor of Chemistry at a critical time, and although it is partly to his credit as a lecturer that the Royal Institution did not go under, it did only limp along financially: the coal bill for 1816 could not be paid until 1818,[10] and in that year part of the Institution's capital had to be spent to pay off debts. Brande was a steady, reliable fellow, who had risen to the professorship by hard work, through running teaching programmes at the New Medico-Chemical School in Windmill Street and at the Royal Institution, and by being in the right place at the right time; he also had a large family, and a pressing need to earn money to support it. Brande had been apprenticed in London to his brother, an apothecary, following one of the standard routes into a life in medicine and drug dispensing, and as a result of his work on gallstones had been made a Fellow of the Royal Society in 1809, aged only twenty-one. He had none of Davy's charisma as a lecturer, and coming between the explosive influence of Davy at the Royal Institution, and Faraday's subsequent illuminating tenure, he has been eclipsed. Nevertheless, Brande had his ambitions, and in 1816 became the founding editor of the Institution's *Quarterly Journal of Science and Arts*. This journal spread the Royal Institution's name and influence afield, and provided a review of scientific activity wherever it took place. The 'Advertisement' to the first issue made its intentions clear, pronouncing that 'the Royal Institution appears a proper point whence a work like the present should emanate'.[11] As a practising chemist, Brande carried out pioneering work at the Institution on coal gas, and, gracefully acknowledging Faraday's 'accuracy and skills as an operator', wrote the *Manual of Chemistry* (1819) which, drawn chiefly from his lecture notes, set out for a new generation of students the principles of chemistry.[12]

Faraday slipped as naturally into the role of assisting Brande in 1815 as he had into that of working at Humphry Davy's right hand. He was now well practised as a lecturer's assistant, and had become so smooth and efficient at hovering behind the speaker that Brande was described at the time as 'lecturing on velvet'.[13] After a lifetime's instruction in humility and service from the Sandemanian church, and as Davy's valet for nearly two years, Faraday had become a natural manservant, with a speciality in the needs of a science lecturer. Over the preceding few years he had moved to the frontiers of science under instruction from John Tatum and from Davy, and it is characteristic of him that although Brande was only three years older than he, Faraday saw him as a role model and recognised and learned from Brande's greater depth of experience and knowledge. Among the first entries in the Common Place Book that Faraday kept from 1816 are accounts of Brande's lectures on geology and on the burning of mercury in chlorine:[14] 'This is the first time I believe that the actual inflammation of mercury in chlorine has been noticed, at least Mr Brande and myself were both ignorant of it until this morning. MF.'[15]

Although Brande was now Faraday's immediate superior at the Royal Institution, Humphry Davy, as Vice-President, remained an active presence. Even when absent from London he impinged upon Faraday, giving him instructions by letter to do this or that – to send his 'little light single barrelled gun which I begged you to keep in your room' to him at Lord Somerville's, in Melrose.[16] In the same letter he asked Faraday to collect some ripe berries from mountain ash trees in Kensington Gardens, and to repeat the experiment that the Irish chemist Michael Donovan had carried out. Donovan claimed to have produced sorbic acid from the berries; Davy was convinced, correctly, that it was malic acid. 'Pray make an investigation of this subject. I think you are a better chemist than Mr Donovan.'

Davy's most fruitful demand on Faraday, however, came when he rushed back from his 1815 tour of Scotland and the north of England to carry out some urgent experiments on the properties of gases and flame. He had been implored by Revd Dr Robert Gray, the Chairman of the Society for Preventing Accidents in Coal-Mines, to use 'his extensive stores of chemical knowledge'[17] to try to find ways of combating the terrible loss of life caused by explosions in coalmines. Coal was the fuel that had driven the Industrial Revolution, and which Britain depended upon to drive its steam engines and to maintain its economic and industrial power. As demand for coal increased, so colliery owners and managers were digging deeper and deeper, putting their miners at increasing risk as they dug out the coal in ever-greater quantities.

The enemy of the miner was fire-damp, the naturally occurring, highly inflammable gas methane, that would explode violently with little warning. The deeper the pit, the more at risk were the miners. Fire-damp was exploded by the candles that miners carried for light, and there were no effective protections against it. A small bird in a cage was all they had – the bird would rapidly faint and soon expire when the oxygen diminished, giving the miners a very short time to escape before the gas suffocated them or exploded. But the bird test was hopeless, and having known Humphry Davy, Gray appealed to him as the person most likely to overcome the problem through rational scientific analysis.

Davy set to work at once. Claiming a natural right to the Chemical Assistant's time, he called on Faraday's help even though mid-October had become one of the busiest periods of the year at the Royal Institution. The annual cycle of lectures to medical students, following the Apothecaries Act (1815), was now beginning, and Brande needed Faraday to ensure that the lectures continued to run smoothly. Sir Humphry Davy, however, whose own research peak each year had always been the autumn, was not a man to be brooked, and as a result, as Faraday himself told a Royal Institution audience in 1829, 'I was witness in our laboratory to the gradual and beautiful development of the train of thought and experiments which produced [the Safety Lamp].'[18]

Faraday's exact role in the development is not clear, but in the preface to his account of the experiment, Davy gives credit to three people in particular. He first mentions the Revd John Hodgson, the Vicar of Jarrow, and John Buddle, the 'viewer', or overseer of the Wallsend colliery. These two men had had direct experience of pit disasters and their aftermath, and gave Davy the technical and practical information he needed to begin his experiments. The third name is Faraday: 'I am myself indebted to Mr Michael Faraday for much able assistance in the prosecution of my experiments.'[19]

Working side by side – for that is the only inference we can reasonably draw from the combination of Davy's ungarlanded acknowledgement and Faraday's modest reminiscence – Davy and Faraday together discovered the parameters of the proportions of methane to air at which it would and would not explode. 'The great object,' as Davy wrote in his account of the experiments, 'one rather to be ardently desired than confidently expected, was to find a light, which, at the same time that it enables the miner to work with security in explosive atmospheres, should likewise consume the fire-damp.'[20]

Davy did not want simply to combat the fire-damp, but to make use of it as fuel to light the miners' lamps. That would be a dramatic victory indeed, akin to a knight in armour vanquishing a fire-breathing dragon, and using its flames to boil a kettle to make a cup of tea for the maiden in distress.

Davy and Faraday first sought to discover what brightness of light they could raise from burning fire-damp safely, and began a 'minute chemical examination' of the gas. They had already had some experience of methane when they collected samples from Pietra Mala in Tuscany, so they were well aware of its properties. They mixed it with increasing volumes of air, and found that it exploded 'with most energy' when the portions were seven or eight of air to one of methane. Much less air and the explosion was feeble or non-existent; much more and it just gave a brighter flame to a burning taper. Then, trying carbon dioxide, 'carbonic acid or fixed air' as it was then called, they found that in proportion of one part carbon dioxide and seven parts methane, there was no explosion. Testing the gas in foot-long glass tubes a quarter of an inch in diameter, Davy and Faraday found that the flame took more than a second to travel along the tube. In a narrower tube it took longer, and metal tubes were better still because the cooling effect of the tube effectively doused the flame.

They were now approaching the great technical breakthrough. Davy's powers of scientific reasoning were immense, but so were Faraday's; and during these reasoning processes Faraday was at Davy's right hand. So when Davy writes, 'in reasoning upon these various phenomena it occurred to me . . .', what he may more truthfully have meant was that it 'occurred to us'. The discovery turned on the fact that Davy had observed that methane needed 'considerable heat' to inflame, but that when burning it produced a cool flame. The introduction of carbon dioxide, given off after the oxygen in the air had been burnt, cooled the methane, as did the metal tubing, making inflammation and explosion impossible.

Here was the theoretical solution they were seeking. Their next job was to perfect a piece of equipment that would create the conditions they required. There was nobody in Davy's immediate vicinity in the laboratory more nimble-fingered than Michael Faraday, and we can comfortably take it that when Davy called for metal tubing of one-seventh and then one-eighth of an inch in diameter, it was Faraday who procured it for him. And when he talks of his 'several attempts to construct safety lamps', and of 'complicated combinations', the fabrication of these safety lamp prototypes, of which there were five, was done in part at least by Faraday. The ideal specification, Davy eventually found, was a series of concentric wire gauze cylinders set around the burning wick 'composed of wires from one-fortieth to one-sixtieth of an inch in diameter, and containing twenty-eight wires or 784 apertures to the inch'.[21] This spread the heat evenly across the gauze surface when methane caught fire, cooling it as it did so, and the lamp was safe under all circumstances in explosive coal-gas atmospheres.

We shall never know what Faraday contributed in terms of ideas, but he was no intellectual passenger in any debate, and if his contribution to the development of the safety lamp had been restricted to making prototypes, forming wire tubing or writing up notes,[22] Humphry Davy would have been unlikely to have acknowledged 'much able assistance' from Faraday. It is arguable that with the knowledge he had gleaned from Tatum and Davy, Faraday was at the very least a catalyst in Davy's explorations.

From then on, Faraday's contribution, whatever it was, was written out of the history of the safety lamp, which is known simply as the Davy Lamp. Sir Humphry took all the plaudits – the publication of the paper;[23] the triumphal reception in the Newcastle coalfields; the dinner in his honour at the Queen's Hotel, Newcastle; the three cheers; the set of plate presented to him by Lord Lambton. 'We have subdued this monster,' John Buddle proclaimed.[24] Returning his thanks at the celebration dinner Davy said: '. . . it was in pursuing those methods of analogy and experiment, by which mystery had become science, that I was, fortunately, led to the invention of the safety lamp'.[25]

'I', indeed. Faraday made no claims for himself when writing about the Davy Lamp a year or so later. In lecture notes written in 1817 he referred to the lamp as 'the result of pure experimental deduction. It originated in no accident, nor was it forwarded by any, but was the consequence of a regular scientific investigation.'[26]

When in 1829 Faraday acknowledged his own witness of the 'gradual and beautiful train of thought' and reflected on the rival solutions to the problem, he added generously: 'the honour is Sir H. Davy's, and I do not think that this beautiful gem in the rich crown of fame which belongs to him will ever again be sullied by the unworthy breath of suspicion'.[27]

CHAPTER 9

The Chief of All the Band

Beyond the Royal Institution and his immediate family Faraday had a social life based around the City Philosophical Society. After two years on the continent his welcome back to Tatum's rooms at 53 Dorset Street will have been warm and generous, and very soon he was formally elected a member. Already having the special glamour of being Sir Humphry Davy's assistant, Faraday's accomplishment of the Grand Tour, a rare enough feat by now, will have brought him yet added lustre and fame among his friends.

One of the City Philosophical Society members wrote a long poem which reveals something of the appearance of the Society's meeting room, the pattern of its meetings, and the characters of Tatum and some of the members. Faraday transcribed the poem, a narrative in mock-heroic verse, into his Common Place Book, covering twenty-one pages. A direct parody of John Dryden's satire on the court of King Charles II, *Absalom and Achitophel* (1681), the poem tells the story of what appears to have been a very serious dispute within the Society, the allusions to members indicating the patterns of their allegiances.[1]

The poem, 'Quarterly Night, October 2nd 1816',[2] describes the evening, one of the four quarter days of each year, on which the Society's administrative business took place. On this particular occasion a Muse happens to turn up to hear a lecture. She pauses outside the building, hearing rowdiness, a 'war of tongues' going on inside, sees gas jets illuminating the words 'Theatre of Science' on the door posts, and, having paid her shilling entrance fee, goes upstairs. The meeting room is pink-washed, with a pair of green folding doors, a ceiling decorated with clouds, a soaring eagle and a balloon 'that seems to pierce the skies', carrying a man and woman in its basket.[3] The poet names the pair as 'venal Sadler' and 'coarse Miss Thompson', that is the balloonist Windham William Sadler, who made a historic flight from the courtyard of Burlington House to Coggeshall, Essex, on 29 July 1814, accompanied by 'Miss Thompson', an actress 'renowned in the dramatic corps', and 'an inmate [*sic*] of Mr Sadler's family'.[4]

The poem describes the room as lit by gas, and in the strong light its dusty, cobwebbed condition is plain to see. 'Slight gilded frames' giving the names of lecturers line the walls, and amongst the tables and chairs there are two globes, one presumably terrestrial and the other astronomical. High around the sides of the room, which was clearly designed for meetings or performances of one kind or another, runs a gallery.

> But Ah! The luckless Muse! No lecture grave
> Or learned discussion is she doom'd to have
> The night to plodding business was devoted
> Which th'secretary's cloudy brow denoted
> The laws were read and members names called o'er
> Committee acts for thirteen weeks before.

In the narrative of the poem, which describes a fierce argument about reforming the Society, the names of the members are vaguely hidden – 'Tête-hum with mind alarm'd and twinkling eyes' is clearly John Tatum; another, 'Nick-all', is probably Robert Nicol, who became a solicitor;[5] another, 'Maghard', is a near anagram for (Edward) Magrath. This follows the model of *Absalom and Achitophel*, in which Dryden substitutes the names of David, Absalom and the city of Sion for Charles II, James Duke of Monmouth and London respectively, among many others. The clearest and most extended character-drawing in the City Philosophical Society poem, however, is this one:

But hark! a voice arises near the chair!
Its liquid sounds glide smoothly through the air
The list'ning muse with rapture bends to view
The place of speaking and the speaker too.
Neat was the youth in dress and person plain
His eye read thus *Philosopher in grain*
Of understanding clear reflection deep
Expert to apprehend and strong to keep
His watchful mind no subject can elude
Nor specious arts of sophists e'er delude
His powers unshackled range from pole to pole
His mind from error free from guilt his soul
Warmth in his heart good humour in his face
A friend to mirth a foe to vile grimace
A temper candid manners unassuming
Always correct yet always unpresuming
Such was the youth the chief of all the band
His name well known – – – – right hand.
With manly ease towards the chair he bends
With Watts' Logic at his finger ends.

When Silvanus Thompson published this extract in 1898 he substituted the line of dashes, present in Faraday's script, with the words 'Sir Humphry's'.[6] Thompson may have been correct; equally the poet might have been referring to Tatum. It is self-evident, however, that these lines describe Michael Faraday, and their high regard reveals the extent of his popularity and honour in the Society – he is a respected peace-maker, having become a kind of gilded Victor Ludorum among the membership. Clearly the poem was written by a devoted admirer – Benjamin Abbott may be an initial suspect on account of his fondness for Faraday, but from what little we know of Abbott's literary skill this is unlikely. What is surprising is the fact that of all the characters in the poem this one alone does not get a nickname – we have to be satisfied with the mysterious observation 'His name well known . . .', and the obscuring line of dashes.

If we rule out Benjamin Abbott as author we may be left with Faraday himself as one credible alternative. Faraday certainly had the talent to write the verse – his wide reading and fondness of books, his extended diaries, notebooks and travel notes are ample witness to that, and some poems by him survive; but was he quite so vain? The most likely and remarkable candidate, however, seems to be the parodist William Hone, already notorious as a subversive author and radical, and under government surveillance. Hone was a member of the City Philosophical Society, and known to both Abbott and Faraday.[7] As a bookseller and publisher he had been in hot water with the authorities, bravely satirising the Prince of Wales and the government of William Pitt and, in partnership with the illustrator George Cruikshank, publishing broadsides and pamphlets during the unrest surrounding the passing of the Corn Laws (1815) and the Seditious Meetings Act (1817). Hone's published satires and parodies had teeth, and with their witty allusions, driving rhythms and wide circulation, unsettled the establishment.[8] He was finally pinned down towards the end of 1817 when he published three parodies of Christian texts, the Catechism, the Litany and the Athanasian Creed, turning their forms into three vicious but very funny attacks on the government. Hone was arrested on charges of blasphemy, and sent by the Attorney-General for three separate trials on successive days in December 1817. He defended himself, and by outwitting the prosecution and showing the charges to be foolish, was acquitted on all counts. He became a public hero overnight, and a focus of outrage against a repressive government. The anger and disharmony apparent in 'Quarterly Night' might reasonably be said to reflect Hone's political temper, though that does not of itself necessarily suggest authorship.

In his addresses to the City Philosophical Society, Hone, as Abbott recalled, 'entirely submitted' to the rules of the Society, and 'never touched upon either [religion or politics]'.[9] Under the terms of the Seditious Meetings Act meetings of societies such as the City Philosophical were banned, unless granted a licence by magistrates. The Act deemed that any place in which people paid to enter or join in a debate 'shall be deemed a disorderly House or Place', and this applied to the City Philosophical Society as much as to any other.[10] Tatum applied to the Quarter Sessions of the City of London on 14 April 1817, but the licence was refused because the magistrates required the names of members to be registered, and to be 'in possession of the list of questions submitted to their discussion'.[11] For more than two weeks, until the magistrates licensed the Society on 2 May, after the matter was raised in the House of Commons by Sir Matthew Ridley MP, the City Philosophical Society was an illegal organisation.[12]

The tenor of 'Quarterly Night' suggests that the City Philosophical Society certainly could be described as a 'disorderly House or Place'. But out of the rumpus emerged the quiet, motivated Michael Faraday. The ambition of the youth is conspicuous; the particular combination of talents as described in the poem, allowing for some exaggeration for effect, was a potent force – a liquid voice, neat but plain in dress, reflective, guilt- (and error-) free, warm-hearted, good-humoured, temperate, and so on. Formed in the fire of the City Philosophical Society, Faraday's character as a lecturer and researcher began to take its own particular shape.

The Common Place Book, which Faraday himself bound,[13] had a purpose for him beyond that of carrying his day-to-day notes and remembrances, as his 'Philosophical Miscellany' had done. The blank pages of the book were sold with a printed preface which outlined 'the principles recommended and practised by John Locke', and some instructions about how best to use it:

To men of reading and reflection, the advantages of a Common Place Book, in which thoughts, remarks, and quotations may be arranged and digested in such a manner as to be referred to with ease and dispatch, are sufficiently obvious. The Divine, the Poet, the Philosopher . . . will all participate in its benefits; there is indeed no man, whatever may be his station in Life, who has not often lamented that he has allowed ideas to pass away which he could have wished to have retained, and in vain solicited his memory for passages which he might easily have treasured up in such a repository.

These words reflected Faraday's own particular needs. The sudden memory losses continued to afflict him, and so, following Locke's example, and having already formed the habit of keeping a daily journal on his continental journey, he set himself up with a Common Place Book. In this he was also following Isaac Watts's advice in *The Improvement of the Mind*:

Rule 9. Once a day, especially in the early years of life and study, call yourselves to an account of what new ideas, what new proposition or truth you have gained ... and what advances you have made in any part of knowledge ... It is a wise proverb among the learned, borrowed from the lips and practice of a celebrated printer: '*nulla dies sine linea*'.[14]

Watts specifically referred to Locke when he itemised 'five eminent means ... whereby the mind is improved in knowledge of things', the first being 'Observation: includes all that Mr Locke means by sensation and reflection.'[15]

On some early pages of the Common Place Book Faraday has written notes to explain a complicated pen-and-ink diagram of numbered boxes with objects inside them.[16] This Faraday had devised to follow a popular system of object association devised by Gregor von Feinaigle in his book *The New Art of Memory* (1812), intended to aid failing memory.[17] Faraday was taking every step he knew to improve his memory, which was becoming a grievous difficulty for him. He was very well aware that if anything could put paid to a career in science, it was memory loss. He may have taken some comfort from Isaac Watts, who understood the problem perfectly well, and said so:

It is often found that a fine genius has but a feeble memory for where genius is bright, and the imagination vivid, the power of memory may be too much neglected and lose its improvement. An active fancy readily wanders over a multitude of objects, and is continually entertaining itself with new flying images; it runs through a number of new scenes or pages with pleasure, but without due attention, and seldom suffering itself to dwell long enough upon any one of them, to make a deep impression thereof upon the mind, and commit it to lasting remembrance. *This is one plain and obvious reason why there are some persons of very bright parts and active spirits who have but short and narrow powers of remembrance; for having riches of their own, they are not solicitous to borrow.*[18]

Faraday must have identified with Watts's passage, and may already have discussed his memory problem with Sir Humphry, as it were son to father, because in July 1816 Davy introduced him to Abia Colburn, the father of Zerah Colburn, from Cabot, Vermont. The boy had been brought across from America to demonstrate his extraordinary memory for numbers and the lightning speed of his mental calculations to those in society who might pay to see him perform. Davy became one of his patrons, a member of the committee of management which organised Zerah's introduction as a novelty entertainment.[19] He told Faraday: 'Mr Colburn, the father of the American boy who has such extraordinary powers of calculation will explain to you the method his son uses in confidence.'[20]

Zerah Colburn performed his feats in front of audiences in London, Birmingham and Liverpool, and on to Ireland, Scotland and France. Although Davy had his own reasons for introducing Faraday to the Colburns – 'I wish to ascertain if [Colburn's method] can be practically used' – he may have felt that there would be some added value for Faraday personally in trying to learn Zerah's technique. Faraday threw questions at the boy to test his powers, and was evidently bowled over by his mental ability:

His memory of figures, perhaps of words and ideas also, is extra-ordinary. He can retain three or four lines each containing six or seven figures in his mind at once and he can blend those figures together without confusion, adding, subtracting, noting the sum or remainder and substituting these numbers for those he commenced with.[21]

But quite apart from the fact that Faraday had no real talent for mathematics, memory feats such as those that Zerah Colburn showed him were something he could attempt but feared he might never emulate. Watts came again to the rescue with clues about how to proceed:

The best way to learn any science, is to begin with a regular system, or a short and plain scheme of that science, well drawn up into a narrow compass, omitting the deeper or more abstruse parts of it, and that also under the conduct and instruction of some skilful teacher.[22]

Faraday must have read those sentences from Watts with delight, for science, with its essential and unavoidable systems, was the ideal course of study for somebody with a poor memory. Watts goes on:

> After we have first learnt and gone through any of those arts and sciences which are to be explained in diagrams ... we may best preserve them in the memory by having those schemes ... in large sheets of paper hanging always before the eyes in closets, parlours, hall, chambers, entries, staircases etc. Thus the learned images will be perpetually imprest on the brain.[23]

Isaac Watts, who we know today as the author of many popular hymns including 'When I Survey the Wondrous Cross' and 'O God our Help in Ages Past', was a non-conformist minister, whose work underpinned not only the teaching of dissenting congregations, but was also read by members of the established church and by all types of people seeking self-improvement.[24] His English was lucid and expressive, and he urged clarity of life and expression on his readers.

Faraday first practised his talents as a lecturer at the City Philosophical Society on 17 January 1816, with an address on Chemistry, which in his notes he defined as 'a knowledge of the powers and properties of matter and of the effects produced by those powers'.[25] Introduced by John Tatum, he stood up, his wavy brown hair shining in the gaslight. He looked around the room, glanced down at his notes, and began a lecture that opened the most influential career in teaching of the nineteenth century.

> With much diffidence I present myself before you this evening as a lecturer on the difficult, and refined Science of Chemistry, a Science which requires a mind more than mediocre to follow its progress; but I trust that my efforts to fulfil my duty as a member of this Society, will be received favourably, though I may fail in them.

After this opening, Faraday progressed to discuss the extension of matter, solidity, the divisibility of matter, gravitation and electricity, which he dwelt upon for twenty pages of written text. He must have been very well received by the audience, because it was on the strength of this lecture, and the seventeen others that followed it between early 1816 and May 1819, that his reputation as the most brilliant member of that gathering of ambitious and talented young men was based. Whoever it was that wrote 'Quarterly Night', the members of the City Philosophical Society were probably unanimous in their sentiment:

> Such was the youth, the chief of all the band,
> His name well known . . .

Writing many years later, in a tribute to Faraday after his death, Benjamin Abbott recalled: 'Here too [at the City Philosophical Society] were made our first attempts at lecturing, which certainly in his case gave promise of what he afterwards became in this department of scientific teaching.'[26]

Faraday's Common Place Book was where he not only wrote notes on lectures, experiments and natural occurrences that had caught his eye, but jotted down pieces of writing that appealed to him. From the *Spectator* he found the following paragraph by Joseph Addison:

> *Hope* quickens all the still parts of life, and keeps the mind awake
> in her most remiss and indolent hours. It has habitual serenity and
> good humour. It is a kind of vital heart in the soul, that cheers
> and gladdens her when she does not attend to it. It makes pain easy
> and labour pleasant.[27]

In Faraday's choice of texts one senses a need to select those which are optimistic, hopeful, positive, as if he is using his Common Place Book as a source of inspiration to which he could return when his spirits needed to be shored up. There is, however, only one extract from a sacred text in the book,[28] so if he ever did collect his favourite religious writings together, they were kept elsewhere and have not survived. There are further passages about Language, Friendship, and Wonder, which he quotes Dr Johnson defining as:

> a pause of reason, a sudden cessation of the mental progress, which
> lasts only while the understanding is fixed upon some single idea,
> and is at an end when it recovers force enough to divide the object

into its parts, or mark the intermediate gradations from the first agent to the last consequence.[29]

There are jokes and puns in the Common Place Book, and, over a thirty-year period of use, many pages of anagrams, suggesting that they were part of Faraday family entertainment. These are some of them:

Horatio Nelson — Honor est a Nilo
O Poison Pit — Opposition
Telegraph — Great help
No more stars — Astronomers[30]

Keen to improve his lecturing manner, Faraday attended Thursday-evening classes in 1818 on Oratory given at the Royal Institution by Benjamin Smart. The notes he took from Smart were extensive and detailed, running to nearly 150 pages, and reflect his determination to get his style right, and to acquire the tools he needed to succeed. From an early age Faraday's determination to succeed in science was followed, step by step, by an equally firm desire to teach what he knew in the clearest possible way. If by this stage in his life he had had any expectation that he might one day become a preacher, he must also have known that skill in lecturing techniques would spill over from the pulpit, and give him clarity and insight when he came to preach the word of God.

Smart's lectures covered topics such as Mechanical, Significant, Impassioned and Dramatic Reading, giving advice on intonation, pauses, timing, and the positioning of the speaker's feet, arms, hands and eyes.[31] He will also have taken the edge off Faraday's accent, and may also have coached him out of his soft 'r'. Here, once again, Faraday was in the landscape that Isaac Watts had walked before him:

There is something more sprightly, more delightful and entertaining in the living discourse of a wise, learned and well-qualified teacher, than there is in the silent and sedentary practice of reading. The very turn of the voice, the good pronunciation, and the polite and alluring manner ... will engage the attention, keep the soul fixed, and convey ... the ideas of things in a more lively and forcible way.[32]

This chimes well with Faraday's own remarks about lecturing in a letter to Benjamin Abbott, written five years earlier, before he travelled on the continent, and indicates that he had taken Watts's advice long before he had heard Smart lecture or had embarked on lecturing himself:

A Lecturer should appear easy and collected, undaunted and unconcerned his thoughts about him and his mind clear and free for the contemplation and description of his subject. His action should not be hasty and violent but slow easy and natural consisting principally in changes of the posture of the body in order to avoid the air of stiffness or sameness that would otherwise be unavoidable.[33]

Lecturing and studying with Tatum took the members of the City Philosophical Society to the edges of scientific knowledge of the day. Faraday's notes in his Common Place Book show that the topics for discussion included not only the widest discussion of chemistry, with experiments and demonstrations, but also the nature of electricity, the uses of apparatus, and the theoretical actions of one body on another at a distance. Faraday wrote down some questions he had in mind to raise at Dorset Street: 'Bodies do not act where they are not: Query, is not the reverse of this true? Do not all bodies act where they are not, and do any of them act where they are?'[34] Of electricity, still a profound mystery as to its origins, power and potential, Faraday was unable to come up with a definition. In the notes for his Chemistry Lectures of 1816–19 he wrote: 'Electricity – instances of it – no definition can be given of it – proof that its first principles are unknown.'[35]

The notes headed 'Questions for Dorset Street' move from subject to subject to such an extent that we might suggest that there was another undercurrent powering Faraday and his friends at the City Philosophical Society. This was their mutual desire for self-improvement, an urge that touched many aspects of their lives. In Faraday's case the greatest step he had taken in this direction came when he embarked for the continent with Sir Humphry Davy. But in each other's company, and with the guidance of the energetic and intelligent John Tatum, the members of the City Philosophical Society set themselves subjects for discussion, lecture and study. Faraday's 'Questions for Dorset Street' continue:

Query – the nature of courage, is it a quality or a habit?

Query – the nature of pleasure and pain, positive, comparative, and habitive? Observations of the inertia of the mind. On the improvability of mental capacity.[36]

The members gave lectures to each other on non-scientific philosophical subjects, Faraday choosing 'Observations on the Inertia of the Mind' on 1 July 1818,[37] followed a month later by 'On Argument'.[38] 'Man is an improving animal,' he told the members in his lecture on the inertia of the mind:

> . . . he is continually varying; and it is one of the noblest prerogatives of his nature that in the highest of earthly distinctions he has the power of raising and exalting himself continually . . . The goal before us is perfection, always in sight but too far distant to be reached.

The study of man as an improving animal might have been the mission of the City Philosophical Society. Of its members and aspirants whose futures can be traced, many improved themselves and led distinguished lives.[39] Benjamin Abbott, then a clerk in the City, became a teacher by 1822, and later was admitted to the Society of Friends, the Quakers. Alfred Ainger became an architect;[40] Timothy Claxton a mechanical engineer, and wrote on the subject;[41] Robert Cocking a landscape painter and pioneer aeronaut – he gave a lecture to the Society in August 1814, which he later repeated to the Society of Arts, on his parachute and its capabilities.[42] Cocking took part in many parachute experiments, his final jump, which Faraday witnessed, proving fatal when his parachute failed over Lee, Kent.[43] Other members included William Hone and Thomas Huxtable, and Thomas Morson,[44] William Goodwin and Thomas Pettigrew, who went into medicine, Pettigrew becoming a distinguished surgeon and antiquary.[45] Of two of Faraday's closest friends, Edward Magrath became the Secretary of the Athenaeum Club, and Richard Phillips a lecturer in chemistry at the London Hospital and at Sandhurst.[46] Charles Woodward became an FRS, and Cornelius Varley a painter and inventor who patented optical drawing instruments.[47] One extraordinary thing about the disparate young men who came together within John Tatum's embrace is that out of the twenty-five whom Frank James has identified as being members in 1815, six improved themselves to the extent that nearly a century later their achievements were worthy of public record in the *Dictionary of National Biography*, and a further seven or eight became professional men with successful and notable lives. Evidently they needed no persuasion to get on; but nevertheless it is a remarkable tribute to the character and teachings of John Tatum that so many of his young men should have done so well.

It may have been common practice among members of the Society to take notes on things they had read or heard or picked up from conversations overheard in |the street. With Faraday the practice of writing things down was established early. 'General practical observations', he writes in 'Questions for Dorset Street':

Whilst passing through manufactories, and engaged in the observance of the various operations in civilized life, we are constantly hearing observations made by those who find employment in those places, and are accustomed to a minute observation of what passes before them, which are new or frequently discordant with received opinions. These are generally the result of facts, and though some are founded in error, some on prejudice, yet many are true and of high importance to the practical man. Such as come my way I shall set down here, without waiting for the principle on which they depend; and though three-fourths of them ultimately prove to be erroneous, yet if but one new fact is gathered in a multitude, it will be sufficient to justify this mode of occupying time.[48]

Although Faraday announced this determination, most of the notes in the Common Place Book come from published sources, rather than from the lips of factory workers and others. One anecdote illustrates chemistry as a corrective of pride: Faraday tells how a German nobleman commissioned a chemist to analyse his blood and compare it with that of a common working man, to see if it was of an intrinsically better quality. The blood from both sources was found to be identical in composition.[49] Beside the jottings from Dr Johnson and the *Spectator* are extracts from poems, such as sixty-six lines from *Lalla Rookh* (published 1817) by Thomas Moore.[50] These are written between geological notes made on Faraday's July 1817 visit to Devon, and the January 1818 Oratory lecture

Michael and Sarah Faraday. A pair of silhouettes cut in 1821, the year of their marriage.

Sarah Barnard. A pencil drawing, c.1820, of Faraday's fiancée. It appears to have been drawn using an optical aid, and may be either by Faraday himself or by Cornelius Varley, a Sandemanian associate of the Faradays and the Barnards who had invented and manufactured 'Varley's Patent Graphic Telescope'.

Michael Faraday in his late thirties. Engraving by Samuel Cousins after a portrait by H.W. Pickersgill, 1829.

Faraday aged forty. Pencil drawing by William Brockendon, 1831. Drawings such as this and another by George Richmond made Faraday look much younger than he was at the time.

Faraday in his early fifties.

Faraday with John Frederic Daniell in the early 1840s.

Faraday with William Brande, Humphry Davy's successor as Professor of Chemistry at the Royal Institution, late 1850s.

Faraday lecturing at the Royal Institution in 1855.
Among the audience are Prince Albert and the Prince of Wales, later Edward VII.

Michael and Sarah Faraday in
the mid-to-late 1840s.

FARADAY GIVING HIS CARD TO FATHER THAMES;

And we hope the Dirty Fellow will consult the learned Professor.

A cartoon published in *Punch* in 1855, at the height of the public controversy over the filthy state of London's River Thames.

A SCIENTIFIC CENTENARY.

Faraday (returned). "WELL, MISS SCIENCE, I HEARTILY CONGRATULATE YOU; YOU HAVE MADE MARVELLOUS PROGRESS SINCE MY TIME!"

Punch cartoon published in 1891, the centenary of Faraday's birth.

Margery Ann Reid, one of Faraday's favourite nieces, and the author of fond childhood recollections of her uncle. Pencil drawing, mid-1830s, by George Barnard, Faraday's brother-in-law.

Edward Magrath, a lifelong friend of Faraday who became Secretary of the Athenaeum Club.

Sir Humphry Davy. Portrait by Sir Thomas Lawrence, 1821.

Faraday's friend Richard Phillips, a practising chemist and editor of *Annals of Philosophy*.

The artist John Martin.

J.M.W. Turner by John Linnell, 1838.

Mary Somerville.
Marble bust by Sir Francis Chantrey, 1840.

Ada, Countess of Lovelace.

C.F. Schoenbein – friend, fellow chemist,
correspondent and confidant of Faraday's
latter years – in 1858.

Harriet Moore, 1854.

notes, which suggests that he read *Lalla Rookh* as soon as it reached the bookshops.

Faraday's reading at this point in his life is full and varied, if the Common Place Book is any guide. There are quotations from La Place:

> The true march of philosophy consists in rising by the path of Induction and calculation from phenomena to laws and from laws to forces.[51]

A few pages later there is a note to remind Faraday that he has spotted a line about the conduction of electricity from Ossian's *Fingal*,[52] 'the lightning flies on wings of fire'; and he has transcribed in full the alphabetical rhyme beginning

> An Austrian army awfully arrayed
> Boldly by battery besieged Belgrade,
> Cossack commanders cannonading come . . . [53]

This, first published anonymously in the *Trifler* of 1817, has entered the repertoire of English anonymous verse,[54] and in picking it up so early, almost certainly from the original edition of the *Trifler*, Faraday once again reveals the instinctive love of words and word-play that comes out also in his love of anagrams, in his diaries and in the writing and performing of his compelling lectures. He probably knew by heart most of the poems he transcribed: to the end of his days he could, and would, recite Thomas Gray's 'Elegy',[55] he knew chunks of Shakespeare and Byron, and in a conversation in 1820 or 1821 with William Wollaston, he decorated his contribution with a quick-fire quote from Samuel Butler; he recalled that story in a lecture when he was in his sixties.[56]

When Faraday did visit factories as a young man – and indeed while he was an apprentice Riebau encouraged him to spend some of his spare time looking at industrial sites – he made notes not so much of what he overheard, as of what he saw and was engaged by as a scientist. He writes of a visit with Edward Magrath to a ribbon-dresser's workshop, and describes the entire process that the ribbon goes through from the loom to the shop.[57] A few years later he went to the factory of the American émigré inventor Jacob Perkins, where he saw the new process of softening steel to make it suitable for engraving, and then of hardening it again so that the plate would print many times without wearing out.[58] This was part of Perkins's practical research into making plates suitable for printing banknotes. There are further long descriptions of industrial processes in the continental Journal and in Faraday's account of his visit to Wales in 1819. Technical description was his stock-in-trade, and in the Common Place Book and the journals we see it beginning to develop into a finely-tuned talent.

The ban on discussing religion or politics in the City Philosophical Society, a measure taken to avoid trouble from the authorities, was obeyed by most members, but one or two found subtle ways around it.[59] Faraday himself might just have been infringing it when he introduced his lecture 'On the Inertia of the Mind' by claiming that

> whatever I may say has no reference to a future state or to the means which are to be adopted in this world in anticipation of it. Next I have no intention of substituting any thing for religion; but I wish to take that part of human nature which is independent of it. Morality, Philosophy, Commerce, the various institutions and habits of society are independent of religion and may exist either with or without it.[60]

Another member, Williams, was less light-footed. Abbott recalled how Williams, 'rather older than most of us, and I think a Dissenting Minister', sometimes attempted to evade the rules by beginning a lecture:

> Now I will tell you a story – 'Once upon a time there lived in a distant country a man named Job' (or Moses as the case may be), and this, though not altogether approved of, was never actually condemned.[61]

The furious debates and factions within the Society wove in and out of the different interest groups within it. Pettigrew ran anatomical classes,[62] Faraday and Magrath organised a language group.[63] One member complained of the personal invective and dissent that 'disturbed the regularity of the meetings'.[64] Timothy Claxton failed to be elected to the Society because he did not have 'friends enough at court', nor could he fit in with 'the very scientific style of language and the gentleman-like appearance of their members'.[65] During the dispute which drives 'Quarterly Night', Tatum appeals for calm:

> Tête-hum with mind alarm'd and twinkling eyes
> Stood up to say 'Peace and goodwill I prize
> Indeed my friends it cuts me to the heart
> To see you from good order thus depart
> I always do from quarrels turn my face
> Because they're unbecoming to this place.'[66]

The member who noticeably resisted the temptation to discuss politics or religion was William Hone.

The breadth of activity that Tatum encouraged within the City Philosophical Society clearly attracted attention, and contributed to the magistrates' suspicion in the wake of the Seditious Meetings Act. But Faraday used his experience and opportunities at the Society to improve his language and teaching skills, and, instinctively as the son of Sandemanians, to dress smartly. This may well have further alienated Claxton, but it began to form the public image of the Michael Faraday we know. Faraday's route to success was greatly aided by the fact that he assumed the manners and apparel of a gentleman.

The City Philosophical Society did not survive for long after its treatment by the magistrates. Members began to drift away, most notably to the Society of Arts (now the Royal Society of Arts), which had managed to avoid coming under the terms of the Act. Robert Nicol and Richard Phillips joined the Society of Arts in January 1818, and Faraday followed them in December 1819.[67]

CHAPTER 10

A Man of Nature's Own Forming

With Sir Humphry Davy increasingly absent from the Royal Institution, Faraday settled down to work for William Brande. He was given the 'Miscellanea' pages in the *Quarterly Journal of Science* to compile and edit, and having an eye for what was topical, acquitted himself well. There are pieces on the return of the young trainee-architect C.R. Cockerell from his seven-year-long tour of Greece and Asia Minor, where he studied archaeology; others on cleaning chimneys; and, drawing on his own recent experience, another on the combustion of diamond.[1] Brande had sufficient faith in his assistant that when he left London for the summer in August 1816 he put the production of the new journal entirely in Faraday's hands.[2] He also gave Faraday the opportunity to publish under his own name, initially as 'Mr Faraday' or 'MF', and in early issues of the *Quarterly Journal* we find Faraday's first by-lines, on articles analysing Tuscan caustic limes, and an account of a species of tea plant from South America.[3]

Perhaps because they were more of an age than were Faraday and Davy, Brande was open and specific about the help that Faraday gave him on experiments that were later collected together in Brande's *Manual of Chemistry*. There is no equivocation or opacity in the acknowledgement in Brande's Preface:

Much of the work has been written in the Laboratory, where the results of experiments have been immediately transferred to its pages; and where I have uniformly received the active and able assistance of Mr M. Faraday, whose accuracy and skill as an operator have proved an essential service in all my proceedings.[4]

Faraday too got away on holiday, and in June 1817 travelled to Devon to visit Thomas Huxtable. This may however have been to recuperate after he was hurt in what appears to have been a serious laboratory accident. Writing to Abbott on 9 June Faraday tells how busy he is:

I now begin to get sight of a period to this busy time and hope by the beginning of next Month to have cleared away the mass of cleanings & preparings & arrangings &c that now impede my way. Our lectures are nearly over & our Evening Meetings will soon cease for the season and then I really mean to relax.[5]

The next surviving letter, written to his mother nearly three weeks later, is from Barnstaple:

... I have much pleasure in telling you that ... I am improved in every way. My strength is greatly increased, all my scars have disappeared; I am growing quite merry, and am in every way far superior to what I was.[6]

Faraday made sure he had a good time despite his injuries:

I have seen a great deal of country life since I left town, and am highly pleased with it, though I should by no means be contented to live away from town. I have been at sheep-shearing, merry-making, junketings &c., and was never more merry; and I must say of the country people (of Devonshire at least) that they are the most hospitable I could imagine. I have seen all your processes of thrashing, winnowing, cheese and butter making, and think I could even now give *you* some instructions; but all I have to say to you on these subjects shall be said verbally.

Never one to miss an opportunity to increase his knowledge of the natural world, Faraday made some pages of notes of the geology on the road home from Devon. A striking characteristic emerges here, one which was embryonic in the continental Journal, but which comes with a new clarity in the descriptions of the Devon landscape. Travelling as he was in high summer, Faraday sees the landscape in terms of colour, form and scale modified by distance. In short, he sees it with the eyes of a painter:

Soil bright red – the effect of distance in modifying the colour is very curious and striking. The surface of the soil which when at hand appears of a dull but strong red colour takes the appearance of carmine as it recedes from the eye, and has a very fine tone of colour thrown over it – the effect was so strong as to make me doubt that the spot I had seen in the distance was the same I had come up to.[7]

This response is a prelude to what became for Faraday a lifetime's involvement with art and artists. His unique talent was to be able to combine a life in creative and interpretive science with an understanding of and empathy for the practices and processes of art. As a youth he had mastered perspective through Masquerier's instruction, George Dance's attention, and his own perseverance; in later life he worked closely on the science and art of lithography with the artist and entrepreneur Charles Hullmandel, and on photography with Henry Fox Talbot and others. By many routes, including through his future brother-in-law, the painter George Barnard, he met and became a friendly adviser in the 1830s and 1840s to some of the most important artists of his generation.[8]

There comes an apotheosis of Faraday's feeling response to the appearances of the natural world in his journal of the tour he made in Wales in July and August 1819. He travelled with Edward Magrath to visit the iron and steel works at Dowlais, near Merthyr Tydfil, at the invitation of the owner Josiah Guest, and on to John Henry Vivian's copper works at Swansea. Having spent some days inspecting the industrial processes, Faraday and Magrath travelled north to Caernarvon and Anglesey through the Cambrian Mountains. They saw Rhayader, the Devil's Bridge near Hafod, Machynlleth and Dolgellau, passing through some of the most sublime landscapes in Britain, and seeing sights that had attracted artists since the mid-eighteenth century. Faraday's Welsh Journal, written up like its continental counterpart at a later date, shows his extensive and instinctive responses to the people, the landscape and the human activity within it.[9] His empathy as a man of feeling and understanding comes across clearly, more maturely now than in the continental Journal. He was particularly interested in the people he met as human beings with tales to tell and experiences to share. Through Faraday's pen we meet in Bristol a seventy-five-year-old man who had been born in Jamaica, served in the Royal Navy, and lived for thirty years on a naval pension of £5 per year. He had worked as an ostler for the past twelve years, but had lost his job because he was too old.

> He said he had the satisfaction to see that ... he had not been surpassed by any man [his employer] had had since; though they had changed no less than 7 times; and the poor fellow pointed out with wonderful facility the reasons why the new men could not do, and why he could.[10]

The Welsh Journal also contains some singular passages in which Faraday shows that so in tune with nature is he, he seems to melt into the landscape like a sylph. Hearing some children singing in a schoolroom he writes:

> I never heard sounds that charmed me as these did. Never did music give me such pleasure before. I regretted the moment when they ceased to vibrate and left us to sink down into common life again. But all pleasures are fleeting and this was amongst the most so that I ever possessed.[11]

Admiring Cader Idris, Faraday wrote as might the eighteenth-century divine, artist and traveller the Revd William Gilpin when describing one of his Picturesque tours:

> The scenery became more and more enchanting as we proceeded, equalling all the cultivated beauties of Hafod and surpassing them

in the introduction of peasants huts of this finest form and state for a picture.[12]

As a souvenir of the tour Faraday commissioned a group of eight or ten oil paintings of waterfalls and other landscapes he had visited from the artist Penry Williams, and asked for them to be sent on to him.[13] His emotional responses to the experience of being in this wild part of Wales reach their highest pitch when he describes how he is guided to the waterfall of Melincourt by

a little damsel ... who could not speak a word of English. We however talked together all the way to the fall though neither knew what the other said ... I was delighted with her burst of pleasure and on hurrying round a corner she first showed me the waterfall and then she ran along more and more rapidly that she might bring me under the stream before I could recover from the impressions it had first made on me ... While I was admiring the scene my little Welch damsel was busy running about, even under the stream, gathering strawberries. When she saw me at leisure she gave me a whole handful and would not take one for herself; they were excellent. I wanted to look down the river and she, perceiving my intention, waded to a stone she was too little to jump to and then pointed out where I might, with safety, put my foot. On returning to the fall I gave her a shilling that I might enjoy her pleasure; she curtsied, and I perceived her delight ... Sterne may rise above Peter Pastoral and Stoics above Sterne in the refined progress of human feeling and human reason, but he who feels and enjoys the impulses of nature however generated is a man of nature's own forming and has all the dignity and perfection of his race, though he may not have adopted the refinement of the art. I never felt more honourable in my own eyes than I did this evening while enjoying the display this artless girl made of her feelings.[14]

This is heartfelt writing, typifying the depth of response that Faraday could summon to the natural and human world. It represents a refinement of that power in him that would also find expression in scientific analysis, experiment and intuition, and in the strength of his feeling for music and art.

In 1819, Faraday was twenty-eight years old, but being short and curly-haired looked young for his age. A group of tidy wives whom Faraday and Magrath had met on the ferry near Swansea in 1819 whispered to each other when they saw the not-so-young men that they must be runaway schoolboys.[15] Some of Faraday's letters to Benjamin Abbott reflect his fondness for young women, and it may be that by now he had already become good friends with Sarah Barnard, the fifth of nine children of Edward Barnard, a distinguished silversmith, and his wife Mary. A pencil profile of Sarah survives from around this period. It was drawn, almost certainly by Michael Faraday himself, using an optical telescope of the type patented by Cornelius Varley. Sarah was evidently a plain girl with firm, even heavy, features, who, with round shoulders and a slight stoop, seems not to have been taught to stand properly. But she had an eye for style: her hair was close-cropped and curled in the fashionable manner, and the dress she wore for the portrait has a high Empire-line cut, edged with lace.

The Barnards, like the Faradays, were devout Sandemanians, and worshipped at the London chapel in Paul's Alley. That, undoubtedly, is where Michael and Sarah met, as perhaps ten years earlier had Michael's elder sister Elizabeth met and married the Sandemanian saddler Adam Gray. Faraday's brother Robert was also to marry a Sandemanian, Margaret Leighton, and his youngest sister Margaret married one of Sarah Barnard's brothers, the artist John Barnard.[16] The Sandemanian community in London was as tightly knit as any small exclusive group can be, and intermarriage among the co-religionists was expected, even required.

Faraday involved himself in some Sandemanian activities, although he was not perhaps wholehearted. In 1817 he was instrumental in organising a singing school connected to his chapel, but writing to Abbott in July that year he was frank in his disappointment that a prior commitment to a singing rehearsal would prevent him from having a good evening out with his friends.[17]

Quite possibly Faraday had been rebuffed once or twice by young women he had been attracted to. There is a long poem in the Common Place Book which rails at the curse of unrequited or unwanted love:

> What is the pest and plague of human life?
> And what the curse that often brings a wife?
> 'tis Love.
> What is the power that ruins man's firmest mind?
> What that deceives its host when alas too kind?

and thirty-five lines more, ending:

> Love, then thou 'ast nothing here to do.
> Depart, depart to *yonder* crew.[18]

Michael Faraday courted Sarah Barnard with determination. Still suffering perhaps from the rush of blood that produced the evocation of the Welsh girl at Melincourt, he wrote poems for Sarah, and sent one at least to her. The one that survives has none of the passion of his prose:

> You ask'd me last night for the lines which I penn'd
> When, exulting in ignorance, tempted by pride,
> I dared torpid hearts and cold breasts to commend,
> And affection's kind power and soft joys to deride.[19]

Faraday's amorous attentions may have become too much for the nineteen-year-old Sarah, who recalled in later life that his 'passions were so ardent, that she for a time doubted her ability to return it with adequate strength'.[20] His attentions were too much at least for Sarah's parents: they sent her off to Ramsgate for a few weeks when Faraday wrote this to her:

Again and again I attempt to say what I feel, but I cannot. Let me, however, claim not to be the selfish being that wishes to bend your affections for his own sake only. In whatever way I can best minister to your happiness either by assiduity or absence, it shall be done. Do not injure me by withdrawing your friendship, or punish me for aiming to be more than a friend by making me less; and if you cannot grant me more, leave me what I possess, but hear me.[21]

Sarah's father's response to this was to say that 'Love makes philosophers into fools.'[22]

Bravely, Faraday went down to Ramsgate in pursuit of Sarah. He was nothing if not determined to get the girl who had taken his heart. He began badly, by being uncharacteristically critical and disagreeable in Sarah's company. That got him nowhere, so he took her on a walk to a windmill. He encouraged the miller to show them the machinery, as if the motion of great wooden cogs, wheels and pulleys would turn a young lady's mind to love. That did not work either, so he tried a third approach. He took Sarah to Dover, where they climbed up to Shakespeare's Cliff and looked across at the 'brilliant sparkling ocean, stirred with life by a fresh and refreshing wind, and illuminated by a sun which made the waters themselves seem inflamed. On its surface floated boats, packets, vessels, beating the white waves, and making their way against the feigned opposition of the waters.'[23]

That was better; now he would make progress. On their last evening together Michael and Sarah took a curricle and drove to Manston, two miles inland from Ramsgate: 'I could not have imagined a ride so pleasant . . . Not a moment's alloy of this evening's happiness occurred: everything was delightful to the last instant of my stay with my companion, because she was so.'

By his urgent embassy to Ramsgate, Faraday seems to have turned the corner with Sarah. He was besotted, and his expression of his feelings for her was as eloquent and fluent as we might expect from one who also responded with such poetry to children singing, to a waterfall in summer, to a simple country girl giving him strawberries, to chemical and electrical activity in a laboratory: '. . . every moment offers me fresh proof of the power you have over me. I could not at one time have thought it possible that I, that any man, could have been under the dominion of feelings so undivided and so intense; now I think that no other man can have felt or feel as I do.'[24]

No letters from Sarah to Faraday survive, and we know of those from Faraday only from Bence Jones's edited transcriptions.[25] It is clear that Faraday's wooing of Sarah was not easy; he was firm from the beginning, but due perhaps to her youth, inexperience or a determination to test his mettle she remained, or appeared, unsure. She suffered from family meddling in her affairs;[26] he had to contend with bouts of dumb frustration brought on by trying to balance his professional and private life:

I want to say a thousand kind and, believe me, heartfelt things to you, but I am not a master of words fit for the purpose; and still, as I ponder and think on you, chlorides, trials, oil, Davy, steel, Miscellanea, mercury and fifty other professional fancies swim before and drive me further and further into the quandary of stupidity.[27]

Faraday's 'professional fancies' were not fancies at all, but the strong realities of his life at the Royal Institution: the busy laboratory in the basement; the time-consuming preparation of equipment and materials for lectures; the keeping up with new developments in science; the corresponding with the most senior and influential figures in the world of science and industry; the compiling of his Miscellanea pages for the *Quarterly Journal of Science*; and as if there was not enough to do, the fielding of demanding letters from the ever-present even when absent Sir Humphry Davy.[28]

Michael Faraday, in his late twenties, was a model amanuensis melded into a watchful, intuitive and adaptable scientist. The combination of a youthful attitude, natural modesty, total loyalty and relatively mature years made him a prize employee. He was gradually given more responsibilities at the Institution, notably the care, maintenance and display of the valuable mineral collection, and new, larger private apartments on the second floor of 21 Albemarle Street.[29]

Davy, who was abroad on scientific missions for just over two years, from May 1818 to June 1820, made much use of Faraday at a distance. He had travelled first to Flanders to look at the miners' lamps in use in the coalmines there, and to encourage mine owners to use his lamp: 'They have promised me to follow the model very strictly,' he told Faraday.[30] Among his other assignments Davy went back to Naples to see how science could be put to the service of archaeology and literature, by discovering methods of using chlorine to unroll without fragmentation the papyri discovered at Herculaneum. Faraday had been instructed to forward the English newspapers to Sir Humphry, and from time to time demanding little notes would come asking him to forward an enclosed packet of letters, or send some fishing flies and line, some snipe shot of a particular size, or a set of thermometers.[31]

Sir Humphry found it impossible to let go, impossible also to remember that Faraday had other duties. But behind the peremptory demands, expressed as they are in a late-eighteenth-century manner which we can so easily misinterpret today, there is a real affection for Faraday, and an admiration for his qualities as a scientist. Davy knew that in Faraday he had a staunch, highly-geared young man, a one-off. He shares chemistry news with Faraday: 'I have seen Count Stadion's expts from which it is certain that there is a Chloric acid containing less oxygene [*sic*] than the acid in the Hyperoxymuriate of Potassa . . .',[32] and: 'Dr Morichini has found abundance of Iodine in the ashes of the sea weeds of the Mediterranean working on a large scale . . .',[33] and: 'As soon as I saw Thenard's first paper I said to Dr Morichini "All this [word unintelligible] of *hyperoxygenised acids* will turn out to be the simple but curious fact of the oxygenation of water. I am glad to have been right." '[34]

That is all shop talk, which Davy knew of course that Faraday would respond to. Davy did not have this relationship with anybody else; indeed William Brande, who as the new Professor of Chemistry one might suppose should be in line for some chemical chat, hardly communicated with Davy at all: 'Be so good as to give my best remembrances to Mr Brande . . . I have received only one short note from [him] since I have been abroad & I have written to him three times.'[35]

So we can feel the genuine warmth flowing out of closing remarks such as these to Faraday:

> Mr Hatchett's letter contained praises of you which were very gratifying to me & pray believe me there is no one more interested in your success & welfare than your sincere well wisher & friend H. Davy.[36]

Meanwhile, back in the laboratory, Faraday was becoming involved in a wide variety of chemical analyses for industrial and commercial interests of one kind and another. For the Royal Institution's printer William Savage he analysed specimens of paper to establish their different chemical make-up and particular qualities. This involved weighing, burning, boiling, dissolving and filtering, employing a veritable *batterie de cuisine* to bring the results needed to write up his detailed report.[37] He corresponded with Josiah Wedgwood in the course of analysing samples of clay from different parts of the country – Cornwall, Flintshire, Devonshire and Purbeck;[38] and with Simon Cock, Secretary of the African Trading

Company, over a brewing patent dispute which ultimately went to the Court of Chancery.[39]

These were highly responsible matters to be handled by the Assistant in the Laboratory, but in the course of his work Faraday also became a highly skilled forensic scientist, justifying the faith Davy already had in him, and spreading his reputation. In these same few months the *Literary Gazette* had made a particular mention of Faraday's paper 'On the Sounds produced by Flame in Tubes', lately published in the *Quarterly Journal of Science*,[40] and in response Faraday wrote to the editor to 'return my thanks for your very flattering and polite attention'.[41]

This was Faraday's first recorded contact with the journalist William Jerdan, the editor and later the proprietor of the *Literary Gazette*, the magazine which became one of the most influential popularisers of artistic, literary and scientific activity around Britain during the first half of the nineteenth century. The *Literary Gazette* shared many of the aspirations that Faraday himself was to pursue at the Royal Institution in the 1830s, and years later Jerdan included Faraday in a list of 'kind and liberal associates who had helped so much to pitchfork the "Gazette" into a high and influential rank as an organ of science, arts and literature'.[42] Further echoing Faraday's own instinctive attitudes as a teacher, Jerdan's magazine aimed to encourage, or as Jerdan himself put it, ' "to praise heartily" and "censure mildly" '.[43] Already Faraday was fully aware of the power that the intelligent press could wield in promoting ideas and personalities, and that to get on in his own career he would benefit from having Jerdan on his side.

In the latter years of the 1810s Faraday's talents drew him further into forensic and court work, which was variously enthralling and time-wasting. 'Now I am so tired,' he wrote to Benjamin Abbott in February 1818, 'with a long attendance at Guildhall yesterday & today, being sub-poenaed with Sir H Davy, Mr Brande, Phillips, Aikin & others to give chemical information on a trial which however did not come on that I scarcely know what to say.'[44]

He had a more productive experience as a forensic scientist when he was called by the Imperial Insurance Company as an expert witness in a case brought by Severn and King, a firm of sugar refiners in Whitechapel. The insurance company had refused to pay out to the plaintiffs, after a fire in November 1819 which destroyed their factory, because they had been using whale oil in a new refining process without telling their insurers. The question on which the case turned was – did the whale oil increase or decrease the risk of fire when in contact with sugar? Faraday carried out some detailed experiments on 'train oil', as whale blubber oil was called, heating it as far as 600°F, drawing off and analysing the vapour collected, burning the oil and analysing the products. He found that the new process was much more dangerous than the one the insurers had underwritten, because 'oil after distillation was rendered more volatile and inflammable than before'. In slow motion, step-by-step, Faraday described to the court the events of an explosion.[45] His side lost the case despite the fact that his evidence was detailed and clear, because the plaintiff's lawyers proved that their client had not intended to defraud the insurers.

From September 1820 Faraday began to make detailed notes of his daily laboratory work, and from these we have a picture of the variety and depth of experimental researches that he carried out. The notes, which open with an analysis of artificial camphor, are the beginning of forty-two years of minute record, contained in two quarto and eight folio manuscript volumes, which Faraday bequeathed to the Royal Institution.[46] Note-taking came to be for Faraday as natural a part of the experimentation process as the use of clean equipment. Until these records began, however, we have to rely on letters, published articles and third-party accounts to trace Faraday's scientific and social activity. Writing to Benjamin Abbott in April 1819 he tells how the business of the Royal Institution presses 'hard upon me at this time and during the whole of the Lectures'. He sketches out a typical week of occupied evenings: Monday – 'a scientific meeting of Members here and every other Monday a dinner to both of which my company is requested'; Tuesday – 'I have a pupil who comes at 6 o'clock and stops till 9 engaged in private lessons'; Wednesday – the City Philosophical Society; Thursday – 'my only evening for accidental engagements'; Friday – the pupil again for three hours; Saturday – 'my little private business'.[47] On Sundays he was at the Sandemanian chapel for most of the day.

Among the 'business of the Institution' around this time was his forensic analytical work, and whatever other commissioned work came along. A project that ran for nearly five years from 1818 engaged Faraday with the cutler James Stodart, who had a shop in the Strand selling surgeons' instruments, razors and other cutlery made from an Indian steel known as 'wootz'. Stodart, a member of the Royal Institution, had made some of the first experiments on wootz when samples came to England from Bombay in the mid-1790s. He promoted wootz, 'preferred by Mr S. to the best steel in Europe after years of comparative trial',[48] and had discussed its properties with Humphry Davy.[49]

The idea of experimenting on iron and steel, a hot, heavy, noisy and time-consuming business even on a laboratory scale, had never appealed to Davy, who was happier with test tubes and retorts. Stodart's conversations with him fell on stony ground, but to Faraday they created an immediate link with his childhood. We do not know how much time Faraday had spent with his father in the smithy, but the family had lived over the shop for years, and the sounds, sights, smells and conversations were close at hand. As a much older man Faraday ruminated about his memories of his father and blacksmithery when he saw some nail-makers at work in Switzerland in 1841: 'Cloutnail-making goes on here rather considerably, and is a very neat and pretty operation to observe. I love a smith's shop and anything relating to smithery. My father was a smith.'[50]

The opportunity that Stodart presented had added value for Faraday – the chance to carry out important research which would have repercussions for trade, industry and science; the chance also to pursue a project that would be entirely his own, away from the interference of Sir Humphry; and further the opportunity to return to the smithy, to experience again the great heat of the furnace, the clanging of the hammer on the anvil, the smell of hot iron. It was perhaps for some of these reasons that Faraday settled naturally into the research with Stodart.

Their aim was to find ways of replicating and improving on wootz by alloying iron with a variety of other metals, including rhodium, silver, platinum and nickel.[51] In a long letter to Charles de la Rive, Faraday describes the progress of the researches. De la Rive was editor of the *Bibliothèque Universelle*, and Faraday had hopes that he might publish reports of the work with Stodart.[52] One particular problem was to find crucibles strong enough to withstand the intense heats required to fuse the metals in the furnace:

You cannot imagine how much we have been plagued to get crucible[s] that will bear the heat we require and use in our experiments

– Hessian [i.e. German, from Hesse], Cornish, Pipe-clay crucible[s] all fuse in a few minutes if put into the furnace singly, and our only resource is to lute two or three, one within another, together so that the whole may not fuse before our alloy has had time to form in the centre.[53]

The heat they had to produce was so intense that silver evaporated and formed a 'fine dew' inside the furnace on cooling. They were unable to melt titanium samples, which melt at 1675°C, but they might have reached temperatures of around 900°C. Nevertheless, Faraday began to think they were getting nowhere, adding to de la Rive:

Pray pity us after 2 year's experiments we have got no farther, but I am sure if you knew the labour of the experiments you would applaud us for our perseverance at least. We are still encouraged to go on, and think that the experience we have gained will shorten our future labours.

The work with Stodart took Faraday out of the Royal Institution to discuss the problem with iron founders elsewhere in London, and it was this that had taken him to Guest's iron foundries in Wales in the summer of 1819. There is no discussion of the iron-making process in Faraday's journal of the tour, which attends instead to the geography, layout and social arrangements of the works, and the welfare of the employees. Although he wrote that he intended to discuss iron-making later in the journal, he did not in the event do so, though there are other contemporary notes about iron- and steel-making matters in the Common Place Book.

Iron was becoming increasingly important as a building material as larger and stronger buildings were being constructed all over the country to house printing presses, looms and other heavy industrial machinery, and Faraday was as interested in its failure as its success. One particular failure which he noted in the Common Place Book concerned the report of the cracking of the cast-iron columns around the Opera House in Covent Garden after only a few months' use. The columns were heard to explode like a gunshot, and 'were seen immediately after in a state of violent vibration and producing a ringing sound'.[54]

The chemistry of iron took Faraday into another of his profound interests, the improving of means of image reproduction, which drew him to experimenting with lithography[55] and photography, as well as steel-engraving in the light of Jacob Perkins's process of softening and hardening steel plate for engraving and printing.[56]

The delight Faraday found in working at the Royal Institution was the constant variety of the tasks that confronted him. With Brande greatly taken up with teaching, Faraday was free to organise his time and make his own priorities, fielding the projects as they came in. Alongside the extended programme of research on iron with Stodart, and the work on the inflammability of whale oil for the Severn and King court case, he was investigating the activity of gases flowing at low pressure; improvements to lightning conductors; gunpowder analysis for the East India Company; the compounds of chlorine and carbon; and the drying of beef, veal, cod, pork and chicken for the Admiralty. Despite the pressure of work, which he had little control over, he still expressed guilt at his delay in answering some enquiries. Writing about lightning conduction to William Flexman, a surgeon he had met in Devon in 1817, Faraday wrings his hands:

> . . . I am continually saying to myself that I have not yet time to do this or that thing, and yet, when the performance has been delayed until an hour rendered inconvenient from its lateness, when it must be done, I have suspected that an undue admission of small but dangerous delays has been the cause of the whole evil. I have not written to you before, because at each time when I thought of it I had something else in hand; and yet I must confess that many convenient opportunities for the purpose have passed away since I received yours. I hope you will not deny me pardon. My honest confession ought to mediate for me in some degree; and though a promise not to do so again will not remove the error already committed, it may perhaps tend to diminish the punishment not yet inflicted.[57]

Faraday's extreme remorse is painful to read. It is certainly genuine, rooted in the religious teaching and practices that he felt that he had transgressed. We can feel the weight of the Sandemanian Elder sitting at his shoulder, wagging a reproachful finger at him, for not having carried out quickly enough a promised experiment with the lightning conductor. What he did for Flexman was to climb up to the Royal Institution roof – perhaps he sent somebody up to do that – tie a specially adapted wire with brush-wire rolled around the top to a chimneypot, run it down through the chimney, 'taking care that it touched nothing on the way', to the lecture room in the basement, wait for a thunderstorm, and charge up a Leyden battery with the sparks collected. 'Now I think,' he added to Flexman, 'you could easily make an apparatus of this kind, and it would be a constant source of interesting matter.' It was this extreme attention to detail, driven by a horror of wasting time or dilly-dallying, and of not making best use of every moment given to him, that was at the root of some of Michael Faraday's special qualities. He wanted to get things right, and he wanted to please. In another this might have been irksome, but Faraday had another gift that lightened the Sandemanian burden – an ironic sense of humour. He concluded to Flexman: 'only take care you do not kill yourself, or knock down the house'.

In September 1819 the *Literary Gazette* published a brief paragraph reporting the experiments of a German, Professor Meinicke, who had produced light by electricity. Meinicke, the item reported, had suggested that 'it will in future be possible, by means of a single electric machine . . . to light up a whole city'.[58] Faraday might have seen this paragraph – we know he read the *Literary Gazette*. He was particularly interested in the ways towns might be lit at night, and the year before had sent de la Rive some information about gas lighting for small-scale users, describing how by linking together eighteen or twenty gas lamps in a circuit of pipes 'two or three shopkeepers may join together and have [the apparatus] amongst them with very little cost'.[59]

There is no evidence that he ever thought at this stage that electricity could light cities, certainly not when, about the middle of October 1820, Sir Humphry Davy came bouncing into the laboratory to tell him of the recent discovery by the Danish scientist Hans Christian Øersted of an interaction between electricity and magnetism. Øersted had published his findings in Latin in Copenhagen, and they were now republished in English in *Annals of Philosophy*.[60]

The article had a startling effect on Davy, who had just been elected to the senior post in science in Britain, the Presidency of the Royal

Society, and on fellow scientists in London. With Faraday at his right hand Davy set about straight away repeating Øersted's experiments, the published text open like a cookery book on the bench in front of them. They took some wires, a battery, a magnetic needle and some iron filings to measure the strength and location of the magnetic forces that they already knew acted around a live wire. Looking at the effect of the needle flicking when the current was passed through the wire, they could see no reason why the phenomenon should not be explained as ordinary magnetic attraction and repulsion.

Another scientist who was puzzled by Øersted's discovery was William Wollaston, who had made a fortune out of his patent process for purifying platinum and making it malleable. Davy disapproved of the way Wollaston had become rich by patenting a discovery; he himself had consistently refused to patent his safety lamp, preferring to pass the benefits directly on to his fellow men without payment. Nevertheless, Wollaston and Davy were good friends and regular fishing companions, who laughed together a good deal, dined and drank together; in affection for his friend Davy drew a pen portrait of Wollaston in his book *Salmonia* (1830) as Physicus, a man of science who took up fishing late in life.[61]

Wollaston and Davy discussed electrical theory with much determination in the first three or four months of 1821.[62] In their conversations, some of which took place in the Royal Institution laboratory in Faraday's presence over equipment that Wollaston had devised, Wollaston suggested that perhaps the electricity flowed in a helical fashion down the wire, making the wire magnetic as it went and thus affecting the compass – what Wollaston called 'vertiginous electricity'. But still neither he nor Davy could give a convincing reason why the compass needle moved as it did. Øersted had given his explanation – that current in a wire forms a magnetic field that circles round it; and Ampère had shown the attraction of two wires carrying current in the same direction, and the repulsion if one flowed the other way. But nobody could show what tied all this together. These men had been brought up to see Newton's laws of gravity and motion as inviolable: bodies attract one another, and the earth is vast and massy enough to draw all objects to itself with the force of gravity. The motions between a little electric wire and a compass needle, however, are different altogether, an insult indeed to the grandeur of Newton's laws. How could the one visibly attract the other?

Some of Wollaston and Davy's conversations certainly took place in the Royal Institution, but it is a large building, and their talk could not all have been within Faraday's earshot. This became a crucial point, threatening to destroy Faraday's career before it had fully begun, because almost exactly a year after these first inklings of this strange ability of electricity to create motion came to the forefront of scientific discussion, he did some experimenting and thinking of his own, and came to radical new conclusions. But for the time being he had little time for all that. He was working extensively on chlorine and chlorides of carbon from October 1820, preparing himself for the Severn and King trial in December, continuing also the long-drawn-out iron alloy work with Stodart; and, further and deeper, he was in love with Sarah Barnard, walking out with her, and sighing over the 'chlorides, trials, oil, Davy, steel, Miscellanea, mercury, and fifty other professional fancies'.[63]

Michael Faraday and Sarah Barnard married at St Augustine's church, Watling Street, at the south-west corner of St Paul's Cathedral, on 12 June 1821.[64] The law did not allow them to marry in the non-conformist Sandemanian chapel. Faraday for one took the marriage in his stride, refusing to get too excited over the event. A few days earlier he had written to Sarah's sister, Mary Reid:

There will be no bustle, no noise, no hurry occasioned even in one day's proceeding. In externals, that day will pass like all others, for it is in the heart that we expect and look for pleasure.[65]

If that day did 'pass like all others' it was nevertheless the prelude to a lifetime's attachment and loyalty for them both. In a letter written a year later Faraday told Sarah:

The theme [love] was a cheerful and delightful one before we were married, but it is doubly so now. I can now speak, not of my heart only, but of both our hearts. I now speak, not only with [?] any doubt of the state of your thoughts, but with the fullest conviction that they answer to my own. All that I can now say warm and animated to you, I know that you would say to me again. The excess of pleasure which I feel in knowing you mine is doubled by the consciousness that you feel equal joy in knowing me yours. Oh, my dear Sarah, poets may strive to describe and artists to delineate the happiness which is felt by two hearts truly and mutually loving each other; but it is beyond their efforts, and beyond the thoughts and conceptions of anyone who has not felt it. I have felt it and do feel it, but neither I nor any other man can describe it; nor is it necessary. We are happy and our God has blessed us with a thousand causes why we should be so.[66]

During their first summer as husband and wife, Michael and Sarah Faraday settled into the Royal Institution. The Managers gave them an extra room, vacated especially by William Brande,[67] and now they occupied rooms 18, 19 and 20 on the second floor.[68] While Sarah kept house upstairs, Michael organised the basement laboratory to his satisfaction. Under two adjoining chimney breasts were two furnaces, one of brick, another, standing on a table, of iron. There were a plethora of benches in the middle of the room, and a sand bath under the skylight by the lecture-room archway. Above the benches, supported on iron arms, was an enormous set of bellows, like a big black bat, resting upside down. There was nothing on the floor, just bare oak boards, worn, stained and pitted by spills, and laid on stone flags that themselves lay on the bare earth. All these details are shown in the engraving made of the laboratory by William Tite, published as the frontispiece to William Brande's *Manual of Chemistry* (1819), and reflect the changes made since John Davy wrote his description of how the laboratory was arranged during Humphry Davy's tenure. Faraday's tidy eye had also organised the shelves and corners, making the room legible once more as a space, with everything to hand. There was always a smell of something in the air: whatever had been cooking – chlorine, iron, naphtha, sulphates – hung about for days until the next smell was strong enough to drown the previous inhabitant out.

But the most interesting, most evocative equipment for Faraday now was the electrical apparatus, which was kept in an adjacent room. Standing alone in the half-light he could run his hands over it, turn his fingers round the wires, and press the wax, india rubber and gutta percha used for insulation. There were columns of silver and copper discs which would give an electrical charge when soaked in salty water, heavy zinc troughs packed with rows of metal plates shimmering below the turbid surface. Nearby were coils of silk-bound wire, a silvered jar with a plunger, a crate of more silvered jars connected together by wires. Some light reflected from these peculiar objects, but overall it was grey, black, ponderous impedimenta, phenomenal, outlandish.

CHAPTER 11

There they go! There they go!

The scientific world in Britain and Europe was already rushing to some collective conclusions about what it was that electricity and magnetism do with each other when, in the summer of 1821, Richard Phillips, by now the editor of *Annals of Philosophy*, asked Faraday to write a paper summing up the research to date, where the scientific world was in the fashionable subject of electricity and magnetism – an overview.[1] Faraday had read Øersted's new observations; Ampère had published on electrical subjects in 1820 and 1821, as had de la Rive, Berzelius and Claude Berthollet. At home, Humphry Davy had written lucidly on 'The Magnetic Phenomena Produced by Electricity',[2] acknowledging Faraday's assistance, while Brande's article 'On the Connexion of Electric and Magnetic Phaenomena' appeared in the *Quarterly Journal of Science* in 1821.[3] William Wollaston, a highly respected figure in London science, had spoken widely about his views, but had not committed himself to print. Even John Tatum added ideas of his own in the *Philosophical Magazine*.[4] Swirling around the subject of electricity and magnetism was a host of senior scientific sharks. In its time, the subject was as hot, crowded and significant as was the discovery of photography in the late 1830s and the development of the hydrogen bomb in the 1950s.

To aid his writing Faraday ran through the various published experiments in the laboratory, and read and put into chronological order the published articles he had assembled. No doubt he also remembered conversations between Davy and Wollaston, and reflected on them. Faraday's paper duly appeared in two initial parts, anonymously at his own request, in September and October 1821, and the editor was very pleased with it: 'I need hardly say that it has my entire approval, being exactly the thing I wanted.'[5] But nevertheless the paper did not go far enough for Faraday himself; something else was nagging at him. Another session at the laboratory bench with the wires and batteries was needed.

At the beginning of his working day on 3 September 1821 he lit the lamps and fetched a stool. He cleared a space on the bench, and pulled closer to him the heavy plate-battery and other things he wanted. To one terminal of the battery he attached a length of wire which in turn he attached to an egg-like object, bound in silk and gutta percha, speckled with bits of dark red sealing wax, with two bare wires sticking up like the antennae of a butterfly. This was a tight coil of wire, that he had wound to provide resistance to the flow, each turn being insulated from the next to avoid sparks and flashes of sudden electrical discharge. Once this connection was made, and another between the far end of the battery and the coil, every inch of wire, around the coil and back to the battery, would be alive with electrical movement and power, unseen and silent, but as real as the sap rising through a blade of grass in spring.

Faraday moved a compass needle towards a straight length of wire which he had hitched up between a pair of insulating glass rods. Watching the needle, he made the second connection. Flick!, the needle moved. He leaned over and swapped the wires on the battery terminals. This changed the direction of the current, and flick!, the needle turned the other way. Faraday knew as he was connecting the wires that this would happen. Other brilliant men in laboratories in London, Copenhagen, Paris and Vienna had done the same thing a dozen times, but now he was seeing it all afresh, with new eyes. He realised that if the magnet was fixed – a bar rather than a needle on a swivel – the motion would be transferred to the wire; the wire would move. The task he now had to face was to devise a tricky piece of apparatus that would harness the vigour that nudged the wire, and embrace it and dance with it. This is where the artist in Michael Faraday came to the fore, the ability to visualise a way in which an unseen force may be translated into a manifest continuous physical action; to enable the particular characteristics of the problem to reveal the solution.

At some point during that day Sarah's fourteen-year-old brother George Barnard came down into the laboratory.[6] Faraday did not generally like company in his laboratory, but children were different. They had open minds, lightness of intellect, innocence, grace, qualities which Michael Faraday himself had never lost. Perhaps, knowing George was upstairs, he had called him down, suspecting that there might be something special for him to see.

Faraday assembled some bits and pieces: a cork, some wire, a glass jar, a silver cup. He pricked the end of the wire into the cork, put some water in a jar with mercury lying at the bottom, and floated the cork on the water, allowing the end of the wire to make contact through the cork with the mercury. He then put the top of the wire into an inverted silver cup with a globule of mercury held under its rim. Connected at each end to a battery, this made a circuit which would allow the wire to flex without breaking the flow of electricity. He brought a magnet up to the live, vertical wire – there!, it moved. He did it from the other side, and the wire moved again. The motion was entirely dependent on the wire carrying current, and the magnet moving up to it: no electricity, no jerk on the wire when the magnet moved towards it. He made some adjustments to the ramshackle apparatus by fixing a magnet in a glass tube and arranging it so that the wire on its cork in the mercury could revolve around it when the current flowed. Then he joined the circuit, and, flick-flick-flick, the wire spun round the magnet. 'There they go! there they go! we have succeeded at last!'[7]

Faraday grinned in delight, rubbed his hands and danced around the table, cheering with George. What he had invented, and what the fourteen-year-old boy had witnessed, was the first electric motor – free motion, derived from electric power and a magnetic field alone. From the notes he made that day in his laboratory diary we can understand exactly what it was that he and George had seen:

The effort of the wire is always to pass off at a right angle from the pole, indeed to go in a circle around it . . . From the motion above a single magnet pole in the centre of one of the circles should make the wire continually turn round . . . The battery arranged with the

wire as before. In this way got the revolution of the wire round the
pole of the magnet ... Very satisfactory, but make more sensible
apparatus.[8]

Disconnecting his wires and wiping his hands on a rag, Faraday said
to George: 'Let's go to the theatre: where shall we go?'

'Let's go to Astley's,' said George, 'to see the horses.'[9]

And so they did.

As he watched the circus horses run round and round the ring and
perform their tricks, Faraday must have reflected on his own little circus
act, flea-sized by comparison, in the Royal Institution basement. Very
rapidly he came to a decision. He had gained enough self-assurance
amongst the bantering young scientists in the City Philosophical Society,
and on the roads of Europe with Sir Humphry, to know that he too had
a view, and it was worth expression through his light and rapid pen: he
would not limit his contribution to reporting on other men's research
to date. Over the following eight days, Faraday wrote his long and detailed
article – it runs to sixteen pages of printed text – and submitted it under
the title 'On some new Electro-Magnetical Motions, and on the Theory
of Magnetism' to the *Quarterly Journal of Science*, with the by-line 'M.
Faraday, Chemical Assistant in the Royal Institution'.[10]

Faraday knew that what he had discovered was important, and discussed it with friends – perhaps including some of his old City Philosophical Society colleagues. He tried to call on Wollaston to talk to him, but
he was out of town.[11] Faraday had no suspicion of the fuss his discovery
was to cause, only of its value. Less than a week after completing the
paper he told de la Rive that he had written up an experiment that might
be of interest to him and Ampère: '[It] will appear in a week or two and
... will as it contains experiment be immediately applied by M Ampère
in support of his theory much more decidedly than it is by myself. I
intend to enclose a copy of it to you . . .'.[12] Then he went into the country
until the end of the month.[13]

Within days of publication on 1 October,[14] Faraday was being crucified
by the scientific world. Hour by hour the prediction Davy had made in
1812, that Faraday would know soon enough that scientific men had no
moral superiority over anybody else, was coming painfully true. Despite
having the high prestige of being the newly-elected President of the Royal

Society, and despite the companionship they had shared in Europe, Davy did nothing to ease Faraday's torment. Early in October, only a month after his experiment, Faraday opened his heart to James Stodart:

I hear every day more and more those sounds which though only whispers to me are I suspect spoken aloud amongst scientific men and which as they in part affect my honour and honesty I am anxious to do away with or at least to prove erroneous in those parts which are dishonourable to me. You know perfectly well what distress the very unexpected reception of my paper on Magnetism in public has caused me and you will not therefore be surprised at my anxiety to get out of it though I give trouble to you and others of my friends in doing so.[15]

Faraday spelled out the charges that had been levelled against him:

I understand I am charged 1. with not acknowledging the information I received in assisting Sir H. Davy in his experiments on this subject; 2. with concealing the theory and views of Dr Wollaston; 3. with taking the subject whilst Dr Wollaston was at work on it; and 4. with dishonourably taking Dr Wollaston's thoughts and pursuing them without acknowledging the results I have brought out.

These are all such specific, clear and serious allegations that they show how rapidly news ran about within the little world of science, how short the lines of communication were, and how furious the grandees were when a servant ran off with the silver. Faraday's critics, as well as those who brought the bad news to him, were the members and Managers of the Royal Institution, Fellows of the Royal Society and a number of wired-up gossips and literati. He could quite easily have subsumed his discoveries within his survey articles, and even claimed credit for them there, but he had decided to give them a frame of their own, and move them into the sun. Although the *Quarterly Journal* would have been circulated to the Royal Institution membership – about four hundred people – only a comparatively restricted number could possibly have read Faraday's paper in the few days it took for the chattering to begin.

Still fewer would have been able to understand it and would have the capacity to distinguish Faraday's ideas from those of Wollaston and Davy. The proposal that Wollaston had been contemplating was that the live wire revolves about its own axis, that is, spins like a top, when subjected to magnetic influence, while Faraday had demonstrated that the force made the electrified wire revolve as a whole round the magnet, like the earth round the sun.

In writing to James Stodart so soon after the painful publication of his article, Faraday begged to be 'liberated from the dishonour unjustly attached to me in these charges. I am anxious to apologise to Dr Wollaston in any way that I can for not having mentioned his theory & experiments, if I may be permitted.'[16]

It was specifically the imputation of dishonour that hurt Faraday; if he were dishonoured he could not be considered a gentleman, and he would also have to answer for it in the Sandemanian chapel. Nevertheless, he was not so humiliated that he could not send a copy of his paper, and a tiny version of the rotation apparatus, set in a glass tube one and a half inches long, to the German scientist Ludwig Wilhelm Gilbert in Leipzig,[17] and another to J.N.P. Hachette, the French mathematician and physicist.[18] At the end of October Faraday settled down to write a grovelling letter of apology to Wollaston, explaining the circumstances, offering to present him with the same minuscule apparatus that he had sent to Gilbert, and asking to have

> the favour of a few minutes conversation with you on this subject simply for these reasons: that I can clear myself satisfactorily – that I owe obligations to you – that I respect you – that I am anxious to escape from unfounded impressions against me – and if I have done any wrong that I may apologise for it.[19]

Wollaston replied coolly, but with some grace – 'You seem to me to labour under some misapprehension of the strength of my feelings upon the subject to which you allude'[20] – and invited Faraday to come over to discuss the matter. According to Faraday's recollection of nearly two years later, he and Wollaston then met 'two or three times' and went over the experiments together.[21]

Who could have been so jealous of Michael Faraday to cause such trouble for him so rapidly? The field of suspects is a very narrow one. Wollaston may have complained to friends, but he was a mild-mannered, generous man who had already found success and riches in science. He must have known that Faraday had tried to contact him, and he should have been able to see the fundamental difference between his proposal and Faraday's. William Brande was a friend and colleague of Faraday's; they had worked very closely together at the Royal Institution for six years. Further, Brande and Faraday went on to become lifelong friends, and there is no trace of early bad blood. It is unlikely that Brande sniped at him, but on the other hand Christian forgiveness can go a long way. Then there are the Managers, servants and regular habitués of the Institution; some of these may have listened to the gossip and passed it on, but they would have had to be quick.

There were, however, two people at least who may have felt they had cause to make Faraday's life a misery at this time, to trip him up during his rise to prominence. One was Henry Warburton, a political radical and Fellow of the Royal Society, who became the MP for Bridport at the 1826 election. Warburton had been a member of the Royal Institution since 1808 and was a close friend of Wollaston's. His resentment at Faraday's publication of his electrical discoveries was so profound that eighteen months later he brought the issue up again when Faraday stood for election to a Fellowship of the Royal Society. In a letter written then to Faraday, Warburton regretted that he had not made 'remarks in public on that part of your conduct to which I objected'.[22] Objectionable conduct was how Faraday's publication of his electro-magnetic discoveries was being perceived by some older members of the scientific establishment; in going into print the young man had upstaged the highly respected Wollaston and Davy.

The second suspect is Sir Humphry Davy himself, who reopened the wounds over the rotations affair in March 1823 when he attempted to put his perception of Wollaston's achievement on record in a paper to the Royal Society. At the beginning of his paper Davy referred, with perhaps a trace of sarcasm, to Faraday's publication of his 'ingenious experiments on electro-magnetic rotation'. Davy's main implication, however, was that Fellows of the Royal Society knew that Wollaston had played a major part in the discovery, but had not been properly acknowledged:

I cannot with propriety conclude, without mentioning a circum-
stance in the history of the progress of electro-magnetism, which
though well known to many Fellows of this Society, has, I believe,
never been made public, namely, that we owe to the sagacity of Dr
Wollaston, the first idea of the possibility of the rotations of the
electro-magnetic wire round its axis, by the approach of a magnet;
and I witnessed, early in 1821, an unsuccessful attempt which he made
to produce the effect in the laboratory of the Royal Institution.[23]

When this was reported more widely in the *Annals of Philosophy* an
editorial gloss took the matter further, revealing that 'had not an experiment on the subject, made by Dr W, in the laboratory of the Royal
Institution, and witnessed by Sir Humphry, failed, merely through an
accident which happened to the apparatus, he would have been the
discoverer of that phenomenon'.[24]

Davy, however, knowing that a wire rotating round its own axis was
quite different to one rotating round a magnet, denied that he had ever
claimed that the apparatus had failed, or that Faraday's discovery and
Wollaston's conjecture could ever have been one and the same. Amid
claim and counter-claim, the affair rumbled on, spoiling the sweet edge
of success that Faraday had thought he had at last tasted in science.[25]

Richard Phillips showed himself to be a true friend, and a good journalist, by maintaining a staunch support of Faraday, and giving him a further
platform in *Annals of Philosophy* to conclude his 'Historical Sketch of
Electro-Magnetism'.[26] Phillips himself added some final paragraphs which
outlined once again Faraday's new discoveries and concluded: 'we earnestly recommend [Faraday] to continue his researches on a subject which
he has so ably illustrated and enriched by his discoveries that are in the
highest degree curious and important'.

While Faraday had his growing body of supporters in London, his
strongest intellectual support and encouragement came from abroad.
Already he was corresponding with J.N.P. Hachette, Charles de la Rive,
Gay-Lussac and Ampère about electrical and other matters. These men
were all leading European scientists, of the generation of Davy and older,
and through them Faraday was defining his constituency of science as
the world, rather than the narrow limits of London. He sent copies of
his papers to these scientists, who shared them with others, and received

theirs in exchange. What Faraday was seeking was discussion and comment across the continent, and status as a scientist. He was deeply discouraged by the accusations of dishonour in the electro-magnetism affair, reflecting to Stodart: 'I am but a young man and without name and it probably does not matter much to science what becomes of me.'[27] But nevertheless the misunderstanding and dishonour cut him to the quick, driving him to rehearse the whole affair in public, from his own point of view, in a 'Historical Statement' published in the *Quarterly Journal of Science* in 1823.[28]

To London science, Michael Faraday was still a servant, a status which Sir Humphry Davy strove to maintain for him. Throughout the summer of 1821 Faraday had continued to be bombarded by demands from Davy. These were not written to Faraday the scientist, but to Faraday the valet – please look for my game certificate and send it to me in Ireland; please ask my housekeeper to get a bed ready for my brother; tell my servants to put a carpet down in my bedroom and have the bed aired.[29] Clearly Davy had a big problem with Faraday – despite himself, he seems never to have been really able to believe that the bright young man whom he had taken abroad with him had broken out of the servant class. This was despite the fact that at much the same time Faraday was receiving letters from foreign scientists such as the one in which Hachette sent him 'a thousands thanks for the copy of your beautiful work on chlorides'.[30]

Before priorities at the Royal Institution obliged him to put his work on electricity and magnetism aside for the coming decade, Faraday moved his ideas forward over Christmas 1821 by dangling a length of wire from the laboratory ceiling, electrifying it and making it rotate under the influence of the earth's magnetism alone. Wollaston visited him in the laboratory over these weeks, and together they discussed electrical matters, putting the controversies of the autumn behind them. As a Christmas surprise Faraday showed Sarah the electro-magnetic effects, but the most impressionable witness of this new step forward was George Barnard, and once again the boy saw Faraday's extreme excitement when the experiment succeeded: 'All at once he exclaimed, "Do you see, do you see, George?" as the wire began to revolve ... I shall never forget the enthusiasm expressed in his face and the sparkling in his eyes.'[31]

There is no letter from Faraday to Benjamin Abbott throughout the electro-magnetic affair, and no hint of Abbott's opinion of the controversy. Faraday no longer confided in his old friend by letter, and since he had returned from the continent the letters had become scarcer and less about science than about trying, usually unsuccessfully, to fix a date for them to meet. But they did manage to see each other from time to time – Abbott later recalled visiting the Royal Institution where he saw the progress being made on the safety lamp, the liquefaction of gases, electricity, steel alloys and optical glass, which suggests that he came many times, and over a long period, well into the 1820s.[32] When they began finally to drift apart, it was because of Faraday's 'increased and continually increasing absorption in the work of the Laboratory and on mine a severe illness which entirely changed my path in life'.[33] Then they both married, and Abbott and his wife moved away from London.

CHAPTER 12

Use the Right Word, my Dear

A month after he was married, Faraday presented himself to his Sandemanian brethren at St Paul's chapel and made his confession of faith.
Sarah had made her own confession two years earlier, and, with no
discussion about it at home in Albemarle Street, Michael followed her.
Sarah will certainly have been present when her husband stood up in
front of the congregation on Sunday, 15 July 1821, and was very surprised,
for she later asked him why he had not told her he was about to take
such a big step. 'That is between me and my God,' he replied, perhaps
with a smile, but certainly without any further explanation.[1]

Faraday seems to have been leaving it rather late, at approaching thirty,
to become fully admitted into the Sandemanian fold, and we might
reasonably ask why. There had been some signs that he had struggled
with keeping a balance between science and religion – his refusal in 1812
to insist on the historical accuracy of the biblical flood, as Sandemanians
should, may reflect deeper doubts.[2] His many youthful contacts, across
a seven-year apprenticeship, with the bunch of Swedenborgians and radicals around Riebau's shop, or the lively people at Tatum's, may equally
have given him pause about the religious practices of his parents. So
might his eighteen months on the continent with the Davys, a thousand
miles from the nearest Sandemanian chapel, and peppered with distractions. But now he had married the daughter of a Sandemanian who had

recently been elected an Elder,[3] and a desire indicated if not by Sarah, then certainly by her father, may have been that Michael Faraday should make his confession of faith and become a full member of the church.

In front of him in the simple chapel, with its long lines of pews, was the bench of Elders of the church, a raised platform about twelve feet long with a door at the centre leading from the vestry, surmounted by a sounding board.[4] Below that was another long bench where more senior church members sat. So, collectively, the congregation was faced with two rows of senior churchmen who could watch them closely as they worshipped. The confession of faith that all Sandemanians had to make to become full members of the church set out in stern language the 'abominable and filthy' state that humankind finds itself in, redeemed only by the love of God through Jesus. (The words that Sarah's grandfather had used in his own confession of faith in 1760 are set out in Appendix Two, and over the intervening sixty-one years the form is unlikely to have changed.)

Having confessed, Faraday was ready to face questions from the Elders and from any member of the congregation who wished to examine his motives and faith, to test his resolve. According to the rules of the church, candidates were expected to 'appear to understand and believe the truth, and express a readiness to do whatever Christ has commanded'. When the questioning had ended, and after a moment of silence, the presiding Elder admitted Michael Faraday to the Sandemanian church. Then the entire congregation poured out of the pews to gather in the aisles and greet him with a kiss and embrace, 'to testify hearty welcome into the fellowship, and love for the sake of the truth professed'.[5]

Faraday found complete fulfilment with the Sandemanians, though there would be profound crises which upset him deeply and shook his faith. He attended Wednesday-evening and Sunday services regularly, rose to become a Deacon in the church in 1832, and an Elder in 1840. Sandemanianism became the cornerstone of his life, the mark against which he measured his conduct, attitudes and relationships. Though he moved inexorably to the centre of world science, successful and acclaimed, he remained, as a Sandemanian, one of the flock, submissive to the collective and coercive will of the Elders and to the word of God. Sandemanianism ran through and within him like the veins in marble, ineradicable and absolute. Such firm spiritual purpose, perhaps more than any other aspect of his character and circumstances, is what distinguishes Faraday from all other scientists called to explore the workings of nature. He saw what he did as reading 'the book of nature . . . written by the finger of God',[6] and it was such a profound sense of a mission directed that relates him as much to Emanuel Swedenborg, Pierre Teilhard de Chardin and Albert Schweitzer as to Newton and Davy.

Faraday and Sarah were, as far as we can tell, happy, intimate and supportive of each other in their extended apartment at the top of the Royal Institution. They had no children of their own, but they did have a wider family life which entertained and gratified them. Enjoyment of a family wedding, or 'rambling about' happily in the country together, are two of the rare insights into the Faradays' home life that emerge from surviving correspondence.[7] During the mid-1820s two of Sarah's nieces, Constance Reid and Jane Barnard, came to live with them, and they were all there together as a family for many years. As a devout Sandemanian, indeed as any young wife of her class and period, Sarah considered it her duty to tend to Michael, to help him entertain visitors, and to provide him with all the domestic support and comforts that he needed; indeed, on marriage, that 'power you have over me' that Faraday succumbed to when he and Sarah were courting had evolved quietly into benign domestic management.[8] Sarah was always there for her husband, not as an intellectual support but to make his home. At the end of his life Faraday told her that she had been 'a pillow to my mind',[9] a compliment that suggests that although there may have been plenty of sing-songs and word games, there was not much serious discussion of chlorides in the flat upstairs.

Looking at the pattern of contemporary Sandemanians' family lives, the Michael Faradays were exceptional in not having children.[10] Michael's sisters Elizabeth and Margaret had nine and ten children respectively; his brother Robert had four. Sarah's siblings, Mary, Elizabeth and Edward, had six, nine and twelve children. Sandemanians bred furiously, creating clans which worshipped and worked together – Chater, Deacon, Leighton, Vincent and Whitelaw are some of the names that crop up regularly in the Sandemanian lists,[11] as do Faraday and Barnard. We may well ask why it was that neither Michael Faraday nor Humphry Davy, who like Faraday loved children and, also like Faraday, was something of a child himself, had children of their own. One factor they had in common was that both of them spent most of their reproductive lives handling highly poisonous chemicals, some of which, such as mercury, are now known to cause madness and impotence.

Michael and Sarah Faraday were warmly remembered by their niece Margery Reid, daughter of Sarah's eldest sister Mary. As a seven-year-old child in about 1823 she remembered how her Uncle Michael would give her lessons in elocution, repeating to her techniques he was then learning from Benjamin Smart.

> [He taught me] to read with good emphasis, and I well remember how unweariedly he would go over and over one sentence, and make me repeat it with the upward and downward inflections, till he was satisfied; and then perhaps would follow a good romp, which pleased the little girl much better than elocution.[12]

The persistence, patience and concern for the proper education of children that is revealed here is a trait in Faraday that is rooted in the teachings of John Locke, Isaac Watts and Sandemanianism, and in Faraday's memories of his own unsatisfactory schooling. It is reflected further, as the pattern of his life develops, in his vocation as a teacher of students at the Royal Institution and the Military Academy at Wool-wich, and especially in the series of Christmas lectures he set up for children at the Royal Institution in 1826.

Margery Reid seems to have stayed in her uncle and aunt's apartment for an extended period from 1826, and had warm memories of her childhood:

> When my aunt was going out . . . she would occasionally take me down to the laboratory, and leave me under my uncle's eye, whilst he was busy preparing his lectures. I had of course to sit as still as a mouse, with my needlework; but he would often stop and give me a kind word or a nod, or sometimes throw a bit of potassium into water to amuse me.
>
> In all my childish troubles, he was my never-failing comforter, and seldom too busy, if I stole into his room, to spare me a few minutes; and when perhaps I was naughty or rebellious, how gently and kindly he would win me round, telling me what he used to feel

himself when he was young, advising me to submit to the reproof
I was fighting against . . .

My uncle read aloud delightfully. Sometimes he gave us one of
Shakespeare's plays or Scott's novels. But of all things I liked to hear
him read 'Childe Harold'; and shall never forget the way he read
the description of the storm on Lake Leman. He took great pleasure
in Byron, and Coleridge's 'Hymn to Mont Blanc' delighted him.
When anything touched his feelings as he read – and it happened
not unfrequently – he would show it not only in his voice, but by
tears in his eyes also.[13]

These are important insights into the depths of Faraday's emotions
and the way he chose to reveal them with his wife, sisters-in-law and
nephews and nieces gathered around him. Direct, incisive and business-
like in the laboratory, he could weep at great literature in his home. We
might add to the poetry that moved him the sixty-six lines from Thomas
Moore's *Lalla Rookh* that he transcribed in his Common Place Book in
1817 or 1818.[14] They come from near the end of the long, painterly poem,
set in the deserts, oases and palaces of Persia, and driven by battles,
treachery, love, death and honour, with all the high colour and agonies
of ripe romantic poetry. The passage Faraday copied out tells of the
reconciling of a lovers' quarrel:

> . . . And hearts so lately mingled, seem,
> Like broken clouds, – or like the stream
> That smiling left the mountain's brow,
> As though its waters ne'er could sever
> Yet ere it reached the plain below
> Breaks into floods, that part forever
> Whose life, as free from thought as sin
> Slept like a lake till Love threw in
> His talisman, and woke the tide,
> And spread its trembling circles wide.

When things went right in the laboratory, extreme outbursts of joy
were as natural for Faraday as they were when he was reading romantic
poetry or praising God with his Sandemanian brethren. His rapturous

moments, such as the one when he first discovered electro-magnetic rotations, were the counterpart of the days of drudgery that he complained of in his correspondence,[15] and those in the early years of the 1820s when he had both to do the job of lecture assistant for Brande and keep up scientific research in his own right. He was not alone amongst his circle in this exuberant trait: Humphry Davy danced too, most ecstatically when he realised in 1807 that he had isolated potassium. But Faraday also had a temper which showed itself in his hatred of Lady Davy, and in mood swings, 'quick transitions of expression' which he had to learn how to control.[16] He told his good friend and protégé, the scientist John Tyndall: 'You can hardly imagine how often I have been heated in private when opposed, as I have thought, unjustly and superciliously, and yet have striven and succeeded I hope in keeping down replies of the like kind: and I have I know never lost by it.'[17]

A year after Faraday's death, Tyndall put this temper into perspective:

Underneath his sweetness and gentleness was the heat of a volcano. He was a man of excitable and fiery nature; but through high self-discipline he had converted the fire into a central glow and motive power of life, instead of permitting it to waste itself in useless passion . . . Faraday was *not* slow to anger, but he completely ruled his own spirit, and thus, though he took no cities, he captivated all hearts.[18]

Clarity of thought and explication was Faraday's greatest asset. He was determined that the children who came under his influence should also be perfectly clear about the importance of decisiveness in life, of clarity of thought, of the scourge of woolly-headedness. Margery recalled: 'Once I told him of a professor, previously of high repute, who had been found abstracting some manuscript from a library. He instantly said: "What do you mean by abstracting? You should say stealing; use the right word, my dear."'[19]

A passion for clarity allowed Faraday, despite his patchy memory, to make intuitive leaps of understanding. These carried him to the heart of the theory and practice of electro-magnetic rotation – the electric motor – and, exactly ten years later, to the theory and practical demonstration of electro-magnetic induction – the electric transformer. Through those two steps, the second made as a kind of *jeu d'esprit* when he had time to think seriously about electricity again after interference from many other scientific and administrative matters, the world began to move forward from the era of the horse, cart and candle, to the motor car, refrigerator and electric light. It is really (with hindsight) only a very short jump from electro-magnetic rotation to induction, but notwithstanding the fact that many scientists across Europe spent the 1820s looking for it, the world had to wait for Michael Faraday's desk to clear before the link could be demonstrated and humanity move on.

These were transitional years for Faraday, and if he felt put upon and given a junior's work to do, he might well have reflected momentarily on Matthew 13.57, 'A prophet is not without honour, save in his own country.' In at least two other countries, Italy and France, this prophet was greatly honoured. In July 1823 the Accademia Economico-Agraria in Florence elected Faraday to its body of Academic Correspondents,[20] and two months later the Institut de France in Paris gave him a similar honour. Ampère, one of his chief supporters, wrote to him the day after the election:

I at last had the pleasure yesterday that I had hoped to experience earlier, of seeing you nominated by the Académie des Sciences in Paris to the number of its Correspondents. I know few philosophers who have more right to this and this justice done to your numerous and important discoveries is at the same time a very happy event for me since I then become the colleague of one of the men who has shown me the feelings of a friend and to whom I prided myself on being able to give this name.[21]

As an analytical scientist, Faraday was juggling a continuing series of briefs, large and small, some deriving from the big wheels of government, the Admiralty and industry, others coming directly from public enquiries that interested him. For the astronomer George Fisher, a member of Captain William Parry's expedition to search for a north-west passage, Faraday spent two days in February 1824 analysing atmospheric air brought in glass flasks from the Arctic, finding that Arctic air contained 2 per cent less oxygen than London air.[22] His practicality was his strongest suit, and the root of his value to the Royal Institution. Faraday was not the type to disappear airily on long fishing trips like Davy, but would settle down with application to the task in hand.

For the Holyhead Roads Committee, a parliamentary body appointed to improve communication between London and Dublin via Holyhead, Faraday wrote a 3500-word report in May 1822 on the analysis of sea water and its effect on the boilers of steamships. He recommended copper over iron for the boilers, and gave additional advice about the best kind of coal to use at sea. Even when dealing with such technical matters Faraday's written style is light and readable, full of good sense and simple additional practical advice, such as his suggestion that iron pipes carrying thermometers be run through steamships' coal bunkers so that checks could be made to ensure that the heaps of coal would not overheat and catch fire.[23]

The steel alloy trials with Stodart were continuing, leading to two further papers on their discoveries published in 1822, jointly written with Stodart.[24] These were of great interest to the French and German scientists with whom Faraday corresponded, de la Rive and Hachette in particular, and to manufacturers and industrialists in Britain and Europe who were eager to know of means to improve the quality and availability of steel. One Sheffield steel manufacturer, Charles Pickslay, invested in new work-shops to carry on the improved practice that Faraday and Stodart had developed, and offered Faraday some fenders made of improved steel if he would tell him where the new alloys could be obtained 'on the best terms & the price'.[25] Faraday had continued contact with Pickslay, whose company sent him a pair of razors in gratitude for his work, along with a specimen of steel 'alloyed with Silver, Iridium and Rhodium, which they consider the best they have produced ... the report of the Forgers is that the steel works better under the hammer, than any they have before used, and likewise hardens in a much superior manner'.[26]

A few weeks after completing his reports to the Holyhead Roads Committee, Faraday was invited to go to Swansea with Richard Phillips to advise on one of the worst cases of industrial pollution that had yet affected urban and farming areas around an industrial plant. Correspondence was appearing in the Welsh press about the fallout of 'copper smoke', a deadly mix of sulphuric and sulphurous acids, sulphur, copper and arsenic from copper-smelting and brass-making furnaces around Swansea. John Henry Vivian, whose works Faraday had visited in 1819, faced legal action, opprobrium and ruin. One published letter claimed that:

> The substances falling in the surrounding country have not only greatly injured, but almost totally destroyed vegetables and animal life in that vicinity. Thousands of acres are rendered useless entirely from the arsenic falling in showers upon the surfaces of the land, and indeed numberless instances have occurred of the teeth dropping from the mouths of cattle that have grazed in the neighbourhood of these furnaces and upon examination of such teeth they have been found to be coated with a strong coating of copper.[27]

This was an urgent local issue, with lives, livelihoods and the economic future of Swansea at stake. The Vivians had been indicted at the Crown Court in Cardiff, and the huge copper works, with its eighty-four furnaces which worked day and night, were threatened with closure. As the most respected and energetic analytical chemist of his day, Faraday was the best possible choice as adviser, while Phillips, lately elected a Fellow of the Royal Society, was an able chemist and mineralogist whose editorship of *Annals of Philosophy* had brought him some professional celebrity. Young, articulate and coming from London, as special consultants in applied science these two men were the best possible team.

They were expected in late July 1822, and before Faraday left home he packed Sarah and his mother and mother-in-law off to stay in Ramsgate together. Writing to Sarah before his departure, Faraday told her touchingly of a windfall he had received from a satisfied client, Mr Lawrence, who

> insisted on my accepting two ten-pound bank-notes for the information he professed to have obtained from me at various times. Is not this handsome? The money, as you know, could not have been at any time more acceptable; and I cannot see any reason, my dear love, why you and I should not regard it as another proof, among many, that our trust should without a moment's reserve be freely reposed on Him who provideth all things for his people.[28]

We do not know what information Faraday had given to Mr Lawrence that had proved so helpful, but the gift is indicative that the employment agreement, however vague, that Faraday had with the Royal Institution allowed him to do private work and keep the fees for himself. Lawrence's gift emboldened him, and continuing to Sarah he wrote of the coming mission to Swansea: 'I fancy we are going to a large mansion and into high company, so I must take more clothes. Having the £20, I am becoming bold.'

There was a social side to the serious business of chemical analysis which Faraday had certainly anticipated, but with which he did not feel entirely comfortable. He wrote to Sarah from Swansea:

as dinner was to take place at 6 o'clock, and there were great persons to be at it, I was obliged to haste in my dressing, so as not to detain them. After dinner the tedious fashion of remaining at table could not be broken by me alone; so at half past nine, and not before, we went into the drawing-room to tea; here I was detained half an hour, and then stole away to converse a little with you.[29]

On his first Sunday morning in Wales Faraday and Phillips walked out to Mumbles Point, and had lunch in a 'small, neat, homely house' in Oystermouth on the way back. Later that day, Faraday, now on his own, had tea 'in a little cottage', indicating how accepted it was in far-flung rural areas for travellers to knock on any likely door and ask to be fed. He wanted to avoid having dinner with the Vivians, and came home late, hearing 'sacred music in the drawing-room' as he tiptoed down the hall to his room. 'They have all been to church to-day, and are what are called regular people,'[30] he added to Sarah.

In addition to gathering chemical evidence, Faraday and Phillips were attracted by the reward of £1000 offered by a fund set up in Swansea by Vivian and others to find ways of disposing safely and effectively of the poisonous by-products of smelting plants. They suggested that the smoke be passed through pits and showers to wash out the pollution, and long flues and higher chimney stacks be built to carry the poisons away – although the effect of that would have been to spread the problem wider. In the event, Vivian having pointlessly considered moving his plant to a less-populated area, the matter was settled out of court and damages were paid to landowners. The £1000 was not awarded.[31]

When their work in Swansea had come to an end, Faraday and Phillips

returned to London, Faraday travelling on to the south coast to meet
Sarah in Kent. It may have been during the weeks he spent there that
he gathered together some miscellaneous notes he had kept on odd pieces
of paper and transcribed them into a notebook. This he gave the title
'Chemical Notes, Hints, Suggestions and Objects of Pursuit', underlined
with a bold flourish.[32] In the manner that had served him well in the
past, he drew up an index for the notes, which cover many of the subjects
he had investigated or intended to pursue further – nitrogen, sulphur,
phosphorus, electricity, heat, light and so on. There are entries on
lithography, on the use of charcoal as a high-temperature pyrometer,
and a suggestion that working on iodide of nitrogen might be fruitful.
The notes are alive with ideas and prospects, demonstrating how
Faraday's thought processes and priorities were flashing here and there
about the natural world, settling momentarily and then moving on.
They help also to suggest how he was able to keep abreast of his own
work and that of his contemporaries, and, in microcosm, they illustrate
the restlessness of his mind, his mission to explain, and his ability to
reveal connections and parallels between disparate natural phenomena.
The 'Chemical Notes', which he dated 1822, and may have continued
into subsequent years, differ from his Laboratory Diaries in that they
are not running records of processes, moment by moment, but notes
made when the heat was off, suggesting that they were brought together
when he was away from the pressures of London. Nevertheless, Faraday
cannot resist a teacherly word at the beginning of the notebook, advising
all scientific men to follow his example. One wonders, for they have the
appearance of private notes, who he thought might read this opening
paragraph:

I already owe much to these notes and think such a collection worth
the making by every scientific man. I am sure none would think
the trouble lost after a year's experience. MF 1822.

A few days after the Faradays came home, Michael wrote to Ampère
in reply to a long letter the Frenchman had sent in July,[33] and which had
lain unanswered on his desk. Ampère's letter had enlarged on electrical
and magnetic effects and phenomena, and had shown his heartfelt admiration for Faraday's achievements. In his reply, written by coincidence a

year to the day after his first discovery of electro-magnetic rotations, Faraday spoke ruminatively to the man who, in the place of the now estranged Sir Humphry Davy, had become his mentor by correspondence. Thinking perhaps of the small boats he had seen and travelled in on the Kent coast, Faraday wrote:

> On reading your papers and letters I have no difficulty in following the reasoning but still at last I seem to want something more on which to steady the conclusions. I fancy the habit I got into of attending too closely to experiment has somewhat fettered my powers of reasoning and chains me down and I cannot help now and then comparing myself to a timid ignorant navigator who though he might boldly and safely steer across a bay or an ocean by the aid of a compass which in its actions and principles is infallible, is afraid to leave sight of the shore because he understands not the power of the instrument that is to guide him.[34]

This is the sort of letter that only a rare kind of scientist could write to another of his own intellectual and spiritual level, one who is at once great and humble. Faraday's letter recognises the limits of experiment, of laboratory work and conjuring with test tubes, and suggests that there is another way forward, where reason is freed from the results of experiment, however intuitive the methods might have been. We are in the realms here not of science but of art and faith, and the imagery that Faraday uses – 'timid ignorant navigator . . . afraid to leave sight of the shore' – recognises one of the central metaphors of the Gospels and the Acts of the Apostles, where the Christian church is compared to a ship sailing across the sea of faith.[35] Even 'steady the conclusions' is redolent of a little boat bobbing uncertainly on the swell. When Faraday writes to Ampère of the navigator's fear of leaving sight of shore 'because he understands not the power of the instrument that is to guide him', he has God, as well as the magnetic compass, in mind.

From the beginnings of their correspondence, Ampère, who was himself devout, showed the greatest respect for Faraday and his discoveries. Behind the florid early-nineteenth-century French prose, which does not translate well, we can sense the depth of his admiration.

I would be only too happy if you would please accept the homage of my gratitude and of my sincere admiration for your beautiful discoveries in the two sciences to which I would like most to devote myself if my daily work permitted me to indulge exclusively in them, physics and chemistry.[36]

Faraday found strength in Ampère's attention, and told him how much 'such commendations of yours' encouraged him.[37] Ampère, unlike some scientists in London, saw the point of Faraday, telling him: 'Your discoveries which have enriched physics with new facts are the principal cause for my additions to my work of two years ago on electro-dynamic phenomena.'[38] Ampère empathised with Faraday to the extent that the younger man began to worry that his colleagues, spotting the letters arriving from the great French scientist for their Laboratory Assistant, might become jealous of the correspondence. This was a trigger that made Faraday pour out some of his unexpressed emotions about the way he was being treated:

Though comparatively young in science I have still had occasion to experience something of the influence of those around me and I am compelled to say I have not found that kindness, candour and liberality at home which I have now on several occasions uniformly experienced from the Parisian men of science . . . Considering the very subordinate situation I hold here and the little encouragement which circumstances hold out to me I have more than once been tempted to resign scientific pursuits altogether, but then the remembrance of such letters and expressions as yours cheers me again and I struggle on in hopes of getting results at one time or another that shall by their novelty or interest raise me into a more liberal and active sphere.[39]

Ampère is here taking the high place in Faraday's circle that Benjamin Abbott had once held. Ten years earlier Abbott had been the man to whom Faraday would open his heart – in those days Davy was a hero to Faraday, and he told Abbott so. But now the intellectual level of the exchanges had reached a height to which Abbott could not adequately respond, and so when Faraday needed a sympathetic ear that would understand the hinterland of the argument, he turned to Ampère. The implied criticism of Davy, veiled but true, will not have been lost on Ampère.

Where Faraday experienced mean-mindedness and exclusion from his compatriots, he found a welcome for his ideas and an appreciation of his value from scientists on the continent. Davy and others in London were imprisoned by their hatred of the French, and this coloured Davy's dealings with French scientists; Faraday, as his innocence in Montmartre and on the ramparts of Montpellier had demonstrated, took little heed of conflict or politics, treated people at face value, and would add lustre to his discoveries through sharing ideas with scientists regardless of nationality.

CHAPTER 13

Fellow of the Royal Society

The Royal Institution chemical laboratory was an active, noisy and smelly place in the early 1820s. When not performing research that had been contracted one way or another, Faraday was carrying out what can best be described as his 'own' work. This was chemical and physical research directed by choice, inspiration and passing advice from Sir Humphry Davy, most particularly a new experimental track, the liquefaction and freezing of chlorine. Faraday was also fulfilling another of his responsibilities, that of hovering behind William Brande in the lecture theatre, assisting with demonstration equipment and illustrations. In the best thespian tradition, it happened on one occasion in 1823 that Brande became ill and Faraday had to step in at the last minute. The lecture he gave was 'so brilliant . . . the experiments following his words with such surprising facility and with such success, that the applause was universal, and from that moment every student [in the audience] was convinced that Faraday was born to rise to great dignity and importance'.[1] Such spontaneous public acclaim was but one sign that the time had come for the Royal Society, the premier gathering of scientists in Britain, to recognise Michael Faraday by electing him to a Fellowship.

Explosions echoed regularly around the Royal Institution when Faraday was at work in the basement, one particular series of bangs following Davy's suggestion that Faraday 'work with hydrate of chlorine [i.e. frozen chlorine] under pressure and see what happens by heat etc.'[2] Perhaps that was a casual passing remark from Sir Humphry as he picked up his fishing tackle and went off to the country, but Faraday took it seriously and heated sulphuric acid and potassium chlorate in a glass tube which 'soon burst with a violent explosion'.[3] Further exploring the liquefaction of gases, he heated some crystals of ammonium nitrate in a tube, and this too exploded, severely burning his eyes. The pressure Faraday was dealing with in the tube was between twenty and thirty atmospheres, so the explosion was prodigious. A few days later there was another big bang which shattered another tube, spraying glass and fiery acids everywhere, and cut Faraday about the eyes again. Writing to de la Rive on 24 March 1823 Faraday told him ruefully, 'I fortunately escaped with slight injury only in both cases, and am now nearly well.'[4] But to Thomas Huxtable he was not so dismissive, and drew a more complete picture of the dangers of the laboratory:

I met with another explosion on Saturday evening, which has again laid up my eyes. It was from one of my tubes, and was so powerful as to drive the pieces of glass like pistol-shot through a window. However I am getting better, and expect to see as well as ever in a few days. My eyes were filled with glass at first.[5]

What was Faraday doing in the laboratory on a Saturday evening when he should have been upstairs in his apartment with his wife, preparing himself for a Sunday with his brethren? His devotion to duty, to the Royal Institution, to science, was formidable, and came as second nature to him. Loyalty to one's employer was a strong Sandemanian precept, and at the expense of his family life Faraday stuck to his duties with spirit. But it will have been Sarah, hearing the explosion, and rushing down to find her husband's face streaming with blood, who picked the pieces of glass out of his eyes.

When the bangs had subsided in the laboratory, the firing started in earnest at the Royal Society, in a concerted effort, led by Warburton and Davy, to keep Michael Faraday out. The bad blood over the rotations affair came up again, through the remarks by Davy in his paper on electro-magnetism, as a reason to doubt Faraday's integrity and originality of thought. To twist the knife in the wound Davy, once the patron whom

Faraday respected, appears also to have sown doubts about whether the liquefaction of chlorine was Faraday's own idea or had come from a course of action suggested to him by Davy. Clearly there was no sympathy for the injuries Faraday had suffered to get to the truth about chlorine, and mud was stirred up once again when Faraday read a paper to the Royal Society in March 1823 and came to publish his results.[6]

Thirteen years later Faraday wrote to Phillips to put the affair into perspective.[7] When Davy had suggested that Faraday try to heat the crystals in a closed tube, he, Davy, did not tell Faraday what to expect: 'I did not at that time know what to anticipate, for Sir H. Davy *had not told me his expectations*, and I had not reasoned so deeply as he appears to have done. Perhaps he left me unacquainted with them to try my ability.'

Assuming Faraday is remembering the details correctly, there are two possible conclusions here: either Davy did not know what would happen, and so could not claim to have had his ideas stolen by Faraday; or he knew very well, and was letting him find out for himself, as any good teacher would, while failing to warn him that he might be killed by an explosion in the process. There is no real evidence to suggest that Davy deliberately led his old pupil into a potentially lethal trap, but we may suspect that he was sufficiently irked that Faraday had reached a successful conclusion from his initial suggestion to mutter about it to his friends at the Royal Society, thus fuelling the opposition to Faraday's candidature. Faraday put his position to Phillips in a sentence:

How I should have proceeded with the chlorine crystals without the suggestion I cannot now say; but with the hint of heating the crystals in a closed tube ended for the time Sir H. Davy's instructions to me, *and I puzzled it out for myself*, in the manner Dr. Paris describes,[8] that the oil I had obtained was condensed chlorine.

This controversy, highly irritating to Faraday, came at the worst possible time, and was just one more stick for the entrenched establishment of the Royal Society to use against him. At its root was Davy's profound jealousy that his young assistant-cum-valet had risen so far and achieved heights that might have been his had he not given up laboratory work in 1813. The personal affection that Davy had developed for Faraday in the latter part of the 1810s had, by now, irrevocably curdled. The frozen chlorine affair went on for years: rumour piled on rumour until, one evening in 1827, when John Millington gave the wrong information in a lecture on gas-powered engines at the Royal Institution, Faraday pointed out quite pungently in public that he had liquefied chlorine 'unaided by any knowledge of Sir H. Davy's views'.[9] He seems to have found it very difficult to forget the sufferings he had endured in both the electro-magnetic rotations and frozen chlorine affairs, because he set out carefully detailed chronologies of both on sheets of paper he bound into his copy of John Ayrton Paris's *Life of Sir Humphry Davy*.[10]

Two of Faraday's friends in science and industry, Richard Phillips and John Vivian, had recently been made Fellows of the Royal Society. Both were sociable, gregarious and well-connected, but neither of them had contributed a fraction to the progress of scientific understanding and research that Michael Faraday had, nor ever would. Whether Faraday prompted him to do so or not, Richard Phillips organised the nomination of Faraday for election in late April 1823, and canvassed on his behalf among the most distinguished of the Fellows. 'Dear Michael,' he wrote to his friend, 'I *spose* you *noze* as I did your *bizzness* at the R.S. Did it well I thinks – *Wollaston, Children, Babington, Herschel* . . .'.[11]

Clearly Wollaston had no animosity towards Faraday; he signed his name to the nomination form along with the other members Phillips mentions. Among them were the most distinguished scientists of the day, connected through their upbringing, education and achievements to power and influence: John Children, son of a barrister and banker, educated at Eton and Cambridge, had published on electricity, and was an official of the British Museum and a good friend of Davy's; the physician and geologist William Babington, by now an old man but still honoured for his writings on mineralogy; John F.W. Herschel, a determined young scientist of the same age as Faraday, but with family connections through his scientist father and aunt Sir William and Caroline Herschel. These people all wanted Faraday inside the club, as did the Royal Institution secretary, John Guillemard, the difficult but dynamic engineer Charles Babbage, the up-and-coming geologists William D. Conybeare and Henry de la Beche, other scientists and physicians including James South, Davies Gilbert and Alexander Crichton, Royal Institution Managers Daniel Moore, J.F. Daniell and Charles Hatchett,

Royal Institution Visitors Peter Mark Roget and R.H. Solly, and Faraday's friend and partner in steel, James Stodart.[12] Many of these were also Davy's friends, and in refusing to support Faraday Sir Humphry was in a tiny, petulant minority. With supporters such as these to sign his nomination paper, Faraday could hardly fail to be elected eventually.

But still it was difficult. Henry Warburton was determinedly set against him, and Sir Humphry demanded that Faraday remove his nomination form from display at the Royal Society; but Faraday stood his ground, and insisted that as he did not put the form up, he was not going to take it down.[13] Davy then demanded that the proposers take the form down, and when Faraday told him that that would not happen Davy blustered that he would take it down himself. To that, Faraday replied coolly that he was sure that Sir Humphry Davy would do what he thought was for the good of the Royal Society. Such calm in the face of frustrated and angry fire was a position that Faraday found he was able to adopt in some of his most testing times, and which, at work alone in the laboratory, he could transmute into patience, endurance and expectation that a particular course of action would eventually lead to a successful outcome. Faraday was very touched by the level of support he garnered right at the beginning of the nomination process, and heard that Brande 'thought it impossible to be better'.[14]

In the event, Faraday's nomination took more than six months to be accepted. It was announced to the gathered membership eleven times, far more than membership proposals were usually put to discussion, reflecting the extent of the manoeuvrings for and against Faraday behind the scenes. He was finally elected on 8 January 1824, with a large vote in his favour, and only one against. The voting was secret, so there is no record of which of his antagonists it was that persisted right to the end in voting against Faraday's Fellowship of the Royal Society.

While the outcome of the election remained uncertain Faraday put his mind to other things. 'I am getting tired of the Laboratory,' he wrote to John Vivian, 'and mean to get a little fresh air by the sea side.'[15] He and Sarah went down to Folkestone where they walked along the cliffs and on Romney Marsh, watched the birds and shook the dust of London from their feet. But where most people might just look out to sea and dream, Faraday's insatiable curiosity led him to describe the formation of cloud over the cliffs between Dover and Folkestone. Writing in his laboratory diary – which came on holiday with them – he described how he and Sarah saw the cloud streaming inland, 'increasing in size, but all seemed to pour nearly from the same spot; the air which came from over the sea there taking on a visible form and passing to the interior as a cloud'.[16] As in all Faraday's didactic writings, a description of the effect is followed by a simple explanation of why and how it happened:

> Was not this effect produced by the cooling of the surface of these hills after the sunset by radiation into the clear space above, and from the consequent cooling of the moist air brought by the wind from the sea below its point of deposition?

Standing by the sea at Folkestone he watched gulls flying over the waves against the wind, looking for food. He noticed how they might remain stationary for up to three minutes without flapping their wings:

> This . . . I think could not be due to any previously acquired momentum because they would suddenly sweep round, going down with the wind, and then return against it, all without flapping the wings. I have also remarked hawks over land advance in a similar manner in similar circumstances, without having been able to detect any motion of the wing calculated to support them. They seemed to remain suspended in the air by an apparent balancing of the body on the wings against the wind.[17]

Faraday recalled also having seen gulls and hawks leave a resting place in a cliff and just hang on the air 'whilst they examined the ground beneath, and without a single flap of the wing'. Then comes the inevitable question, followed by the practical application: 'How do these birds fly? and why may not a man or a machine fly in the same way in the same circumstances?' The puzzle stayed with Faraday for a year at least, and thinking about it again on his next summer holiday on the Isle of Wight, he concluded:

> Perhaps the effect which may sometimes be observed in flying a kite may be connected with this subject. Sometimes a kite when badly rigged will, upon rising, not cease to ascend when the string forms

a certain angle with the current of air, but will continue to mount, taking nearly a horizontal position in the air, and that till the string is nearly vertical when the kite generally falls over and comes down.[18]

Although he had to make choices in his scientific work, Faraday felt free to range across the natural world wherever his interests took him. Geology, meteorology and aeronautics also engaged him; such sideways glides as this one into the problem of flight were characteristic, and further examples recur throughout his life. In a parallel way he sought to involve himself in the administration of the Royal Institution, and saw it his duty as his influence there rose to increase the organisation's effectiveness and bring the results of laboratory work out of the basement and into the public mind as quickly and clearly as possible.

Within weeks of his election to the Royal Society, Faraday found himself being drawn into work which might have been seen to increase his prestige in the London world of science, but which in fact, as he very soon came to realise, wasted his time and kept him away from the laboratory. A new gentleman's club was starting up in London, for 'cultivators of science, letters and art', as the prospectus offered.[19] It came together as a means of uniting the growing core of men who were neither landed gentry, aristocracy nor from the armed services, to create a unit that might give them some collective influence.[20] It had a further unwritten aim of providing a home for those intellectual gentlemen who were not scientists, but who nevertheless padded out the Royal Society Fellowship, and reduced its effectiveness as a voice for science. The prime mover was the MP and Secretary to the Admiralty John Wilson Croker, and he, together with others principally including Sir Humphry Davy, invited members of the Royal Society and the Royal Academy in the first instance to become the root from which the club drew its membership. The club, which came to be named the Athenaeum Club, needed a temporary secretary, and with an awful inevitability, Davy turned to his former valet, amanuensis and general run-about Michael Faraday to do the work. One can reasonably wonder why Davy chose Faraday when there must have been many other men in his wider circle who could have done the job as well – a knee-jerk reaction perhaps, lack of imagination, or an unquenchable desire to continue to patronise Michael Faraday FRS.

Faraday gracefully took the job on, but soon found himself writing hundreds of letters canvassing for members, dealing with the replies, organising membership lists and details, collecting subscriptions and calling meetings. This was the kind of work that he was very good at, but with other more important things to do it was no longer suited to him, and the strain began to tell. The initial expectation was that he should do the work for nothing, but sensing their lack of tact the first *ad hoc* organising committee of the club made matters worse by offering him in May 1824 the post of Secretary on a permanent basis, at a salary of £100 per year. This gave Faraday the opportunity to bow out, and in doing so he recommended his friend Edward Magrath to the club committee. Magrath was appointed, and Faraday could withdraw.

By his action in resigning from the Athenaeum secretaryship, and the clear signal that this conveyed to a wide and particularly influential circle that he was not going to be put upon, Faraday began inexorably to emerge from the burden of Davy's erratic and unreliable patronage. As his value to the Royal Institution began to rise, so Davy's gradually fell. Davy was now taken up to the practical exclusion of all else with Royal Society business, as a result giving more room for Faraday to move. In 1825 Faraday was appointed Director of the Laboratory, on Davy's recommendation, under the superintendence of Brande.[21] He began to give courses of chemistry lectures in his own right, rather than as the helpful figure hovering at the back, producing the equipment and illustrations and making things go smoothly.

Word began to spread that Faraday was now being given his head. The news reached the engineer Isambard Kingdom Brunel, who with his father Marc Isambard Brunel had been experimenting with some practical use of liquefied gases, following Faraday's discoveries in 1823. The Brunels were now working together in earnest on the beginnings of the Thames Tunnel, but nevertheless Isambard put time aside to attend Faraday's chemistry lectures, even over the few weeks in early spring 1825 when he and his father were preparing to lay the first bricks of the tunnel's entrance shaft on the Rotherhithe bank of the river.[22] At the same time that Isambard Kingdom Brunel was beginning to establish a personality and reputation of his own by moving away from the shadow of his famous father, so Michael Faraday moved away from Davy's patronage and began to step further into the light. From this beginning, these two great figures of the nineteenth century remained in step as their careers progressed;

but the difference was that there was half a generation between them: Faraday was a slow starter – in 1825 he was thirty-four and Brunel nineteen years of age.

The most influential of Faraday's first acts as Director of the Royal Institution Laboratory was to open the laboratory to meetings of the members, to which on three or four Friday evenings a year Faraday would give chemistry lectures, performing experiments to these particularly interested and committed men, and explaining what he was doing and what it meant.[23] This was an astute political move, drawing in people who may have been irritated, certainly inconvenienced, by Davy's high-handed manner, and who had been bothered by him for money for one thing and another. Davy's style of lecturing – theatrical, charismatic, centring on himself – was now a memory at the Royal Institution, and it was time for a new, cooler, Faradaian manner to emerge.

The informal Friday-evening meetings with the members broke the secrecy of the laboratory, blew away whatever mystique might have settled in the minds of the members. They rapidly evolved under Faraday's guidance into the weekly Friday Evening Discourses, perhaps the most influential, certainly the most enduring, public education series until the founding of the BBC almost a century later in 1922, and turned education into enjoyment. A month before the first Friday Discourse in February 1826, Brande formally acknowledged Faraday's eminence by relieving him of the job of assisting him at his lectures, 'in consequence of the rank Mr F holds in science, and his many important avocations'.[24]

In the year of his nomination as Fellow of the Royal Society Faraday was also elected Honorary Member of the Cambridge Philosophical Society,[25] a member of the Academic Correspondents of the Accademia Economico-Agraria, Florence,[26] foreign associate of the Institut de France,[27] and Honorary Member of the Bristol Institution.[28] Thus his reputation at home and in Europe was firm and general, and in the next two or three years further elected memberships came from the Cambrian Society, the Geological Society, the French Medical Chemistry Society, the Westminster Medical Society and the Parisian Société Philomatique. All this national and international honouring of Faraday bound him indissolubly as a central figure in world science, a link in a chain. Reflecting his own perception of himself as one among equals, and following an early-nineteenth-century practice, Faraday began at about this time to collect portrait engravings of his friends and peers, and came to bind them together into two large volumes.[29] Within these albums are 250 portraits of scientists, artists, actors, writers, royalty, men and women whom Faraday held in esteem and friendship, and who also admired him. It is a catholic and inclusive group of people, the *beau idéal* guest list for a Royal Institution *conversazione*.[30]

Faraday had his own portrait painted by H.W. Pickersgill in 1829, and this was engraved the following year for circulation to his friends and associates. In that engraving, by Samuel Cousins, we see the image of Faraday at his first level of worldly success and acceptance. At last, with his centre-parted curly hair, his generously cut velvet coat, his high collar and stock, Michael Faraday FRS can proclaim his full membership of social and intellectual Europe. Springing from a blacksmith's yard near Oxford Street, he has joined the nobs, those very same men and women who gathered weekly in front of him in the Royal Institution lecture theatre to see the secrets of nature revealed. The engraving also lights on the fineness of Faraday's features, the sense of enquiry that lies about his eyes, his wide, cupid's bow mouth, his firm, cleft chin. It is a sensuous face which engages the viewer from a position slightly above eye-level, so there is an illusion that Faraday appears taller in the print than he actually was. There are no clues in the portrait that this is a young scientist: we might as well be looking at (or he looking at us) the son of an earl, or at an assistant consul off to take up duties abroad.

Reflecting the thrill of delight at now becoming his own man, Faraday made sure he had fun with his science. There is a report that he built a velocipede at the Royal Institution, and took it up and down Hampstead Hill and onto the Heath. This machine, given the way pedal-power evolved, was probably a four-wheeler worked by levers and a crank axle.[31] But in riding it downhill with enthusiasm, Faraday will have been putting mechanical laws of momentum into personal practice, and shouting for the sheer pleasure of it.

CHAPTER 14

We Light up the House

Faraday opened the Friday Evening Discourse series on 3 February 1826 with a lecture on 'caoutchouc', the natural form of rubber.[1] He had made some initial analyses of caoutchouc sap in the laboratory in November 1824, and then, after having set a jar of the material soaking in water for a year, took it up again in November 1825 and made some experiments on it.[2] He heated it in tubes, combined it with copper oxide and sulphur, broke it down into its constituent products and folded, pressed and pulverised it. His aim was to find out the extent of the material's usefulness in the laboratory, to make flexible tubing with it for experiments, to test it as an electrical insulator, and to find out which chemicals it resisted and which destroyed it.

Caoutchouc was being imported in increasing quantities from the West Indies – hence the term 'india rubber' – and Brazil, and its flexibility and waterproof qualities suggested that it might be useful for filling joints in ships' timbers and reducing vibration in machinery. It also had exciting possibilities for the clothing industry. Charles Macintosh, a Scots chemist with many new applications to his credit – bleaching powder and the 'hot blast' process of converting iron into steel – had recently been elected a Fellow of the Royal Society, having patented his waterproof fabric in 1823. He was making a fortune, and his name, out of manufacturing coats with the material, by cementing together double thicknesses of fabric with india rubber dissolved in naphtha. Caoutchouc, with its extra-ordinary exotic name, was therefore a topical substance, the material that men and women of fashion should expect to be dressed in in rainy London, and of very much more than specialist interest.[3] It was an inspired choice for Faraday to lecture about on a wet February evening, an opportunity for him to take the audience through the sources, the chemistry, the uses and the by-products of the material from his own first-hand experimental knowledge, letting them into some of its secrets, while relying on the certain experience of some of the audience as to its success as a raincoat.

Topicality was the byword of the Friday Evening Discourses. The audience was to be entertained, entranced for an hour with a new light on the world around them, and given knowledge and understanding on subjects that touched general experience, passed to them without pain.[4] The following Friday Faraday spoke on Marc Isambard Brunel's condensing gas engine, a machine driven by carbon dioxide that owed its existence to Faraday's work on the liquefaction of gases; Brunel sent a set of drawings and specifications to illustrate the talk, and said he hoped to be present.[5] For the third Discourse, on 3 March, Faraday discussed the art of lithography, and how it was beginning to revolutionise the dissemination of imagery in books and periodical publications.

The Royal Institution Discourses, which started precisely at 9 p.m., finished promptly after one hour and were followed by tea and discussion. One of the secrets of their success was that they gave explanations for many of the technological advances, the applications of science, that were becoming everywhere visible: the railway, tarmacadam roads, gas lighting and macintoshes. An eager attender was the Chancellor of the Exchequer's daughter, Maria Herries, who kept a notebook of the lectures by Faraday that she attended in 1835 and 1836. She took to doodling on an inside cover, and there made a creditable parody of Faraday's signature, dressed up as her own.[6] 'H Merries', she writes, starting with the H and looping round to the M, in the same way that Faraday tended to adopt by allowing his pen to write 'F Maraday'. One of Faraday's Discourses in 1835 was 'The manufacture of pens from quills and steel', and Miss Herries' doodles may be silent witness to some of the visual aids and practical teaching methods that Faraday used on that evening to entertain the audience.

In May 1826 Faraday wrote a brief but telling description of a typical evening to Captain John Franklin, who was about to set off on his second voyage to the Arctic, taking, incidentally, some equipment made from Macintosh's fabric with him.[7] Remembering how much he had himself valued letters from home when he was on the continent, Faraday wrote to cheer Franklin on his way, telling him how at the last Friday Discourse he had referred to some experiments on vaporisation that Franklin was to carry out in the Arctic. The aim of the experiments was to establish if there was a temperature below which volatile materials did not evaporate. 'We have been very active in our Institution this season,' Faraday told Franklin,

> and have established conversaziones on Friday Evenings which have been numerously and well attended. We light up the house, bring forward a subject in the Lecture room illustrated by experiments, diagrams, models &c, and this serves as matter for the Evening. We then adjourn to the library where we take tea and seldom part till 11 o'clock or past. Last Friday we had a very interesting subject being an improvement by Lieut Drummond on the means of effecting geodisical operations.[8]

'We light up the house': though intended literally, this phrase perfectly expresses Faraday's attitude not only to creating a bright and warm environment so that his audience would learn in comfort and happiness, but also his whole attitude to science and the spreading of knowledge of the natural world.

The particular joy for Faraday about science was that he always found it truly exciting both in theory and in practice. He was like a little boy in the face of new discovery, as when he first got the electro-magnetic rotations to work. The letter to Franklin, which also discusses an invention by Thomas Drummond, is a wonderful example of what science did to Faraday, for here he is talking not about one of his own discoveries, but a discovery, and a practical application of it, by somebody else. Drummond was a military engineer who progressed the ordnance survey of Britain and Ireland, improving mapping techniques by his invention of a lamp that could throw light for great distances:

> . . . it was desirable that some object should be contrived that would have as it were power of penetration [of haze] in such cases lamps

& mirrors were found very ineffective but Lieut Drummond has succeeded admirably by placing a ball of lime in the focus of a parabolic reflector & raising it to an intense heat by alcohol lamp urged by oxygen gas. The light thus obtained is so dazzling that a person on to whom it is thrown at the distance of 50 or 100 feet cannot see the form of the mirror. Its intensity had risen as high as *90*, that of an Argand lamp being *1* only. It has been very successfully applied in the survey of Ireland.[9]

Faraday continued the enjoyment of science on Friday evenings long into the night. As he told Franklin, he and the audience adjourned to the Royal Institution Library where they could all talk further together, and above all discuss the objects that Faraday and friends and associates had assembled on the table. These might be intimately connected with the lecture the audience had just heard, but not necessarily so. The naturalist Walter Calverley Trevelyan had sent Faraday a specimen of resinous fungus for his opinion. Faraday gave it, and added in his reply that he should like to 'lay the specimen that I have on our Library Table at the *Conversazione* next Friday Evening if you have no objection to my doing so: it might excite a remark or interest some of the lovers of Natural History that may be present'.[10]

More closely connected to a subject in hand were examples of oriental gongs that Faraday sought for display and use for a Discourse on phonics in February 1828. He had to work hard to track some down, writing first to the East India Company Museum, then to the Duke of Somerset, the President of the Royal Institution; finally locating a pair from Java in Lady Raffles' collection in Lower Grosvenor Street.[11]

The *Literary Gazette* took a considered interest in reporting the Friday Evening Discourses from 1827 onwards, and as time went on it took to listing the objects displayed on the Library Table. On typical Fridays in 1830, for example, Faraday selected objects including a buoyancy waist-coat,[12] Raimbach's etching of Wilkie's *Parish Beadle*,[13] 'a great variety of works of literature and art',[14] 'two profiles of Sir Thomas Lawrence, the larger in bronze by Baily',[15] and 'a beautiful . . . simple dead-beat escapement for clocks invented by Mr Chancellor'.[16] The range was wide, embracing works of art and science, and was chosen to prompt conversation and discussion, whether following on from the topic of the evening's Discourse or about something completely different. The *Literary Gazette*'s correspondent at the Royal Institution was often Faraday himself, who sent abstracts of the papers and accounts of the evenings to the editor for publication.[17]

The *Literary Gazette* reported generously, as did the *Athenaeum*,[18] on the topics of the Discourses and gave a flavour of the audience's mood and receptivity. The *Gazette* wrote in May 1828 of Faraday's Discourse on 'The Nature of Musical Sound', which was 'throughout illustrated by the performance of all the experiments referred to'. It went on to mention Faraday's 'lucid and admirable way of exploring the nature of the subject. But for his own acknowledgement, we should have taken him for a skilled musician, as well as a most acute philosophical investigator of the science of phonics.'[19] Reporting Faraday's Discourse in May 1829 on Marc Isambard Brunel's block-making machine, the *Athenaeum* wrote of his 'clear, sensible, and intelligible manner usual in the lessons of that gentleman, which have ranked him as a lecturer so high in the estimation of all who have enjoyed the gratification of hearing him'.[20]

Brunel's machine, with which it was claimed 'six men could do what sixty had done before',[21] cut and formed ships' blocks, the complicated pulley devices through which every rope on every ship had to operate. Brunel's invention, and the mechanical perfecting of it by Henry Maudslay, had sped the fitting-out of ships in the five years before Trafalgar, and for such a patriotic reason alone it was of profound interest to the Friday-evening audiences. Faraday demonstrated from scale models, but the heat in the lecture theatre 'occasioned by the concourse of company' was so great that they jammed and failed to work properly.[22]

If he was occasionally let down by his demonstration equipment, Faraday's clarity of manner drew his audiences to him. It had been hard won: he had trained himself over the years by observation of other lecturers, and owed a great deal to the example of his tutor in oratory, Benjamin Smart. So concerned was he to keep his manner of lecturing light and sharp that he invited Smart to watch him perform in an early Discourse and, lest he slip into bad practices, give him a critique of his lecturing manner.[23] Faraday may well have gone back at this time to the notes he had taken from Smart's own series on oratory in 1816, among which he highlighted:

Never repeat a phrase

Never go back to amend

If at a loss for a word, not to ch-ch-ch or eh-eh-eh, but to stop and wait for it. It soon comes, and the bad habits are broken and fluency soon acquired.

Never doubt a correction given to me by another.[24]

Faraday's niece Margery Reid remembered the trouble her uncle took over getting his delivery right. She recalled how Edward Magrath

> used to come regularly to the morning lectures, for the sole purpose of noting down for him any faults of delivery or defective pronunciation that could be detected. The list was always received with thanks; although his corrections were not uniformly adopted, he was encouraged to continue his remarks with perfect freedom. In early days he always lectured with a card before him with *Slow* written upon it in distinct characters. Sometimes he would overlook it and become too rapid; in this case [laboratory assistant Charles] Anderson[25] had orders to place the card before him. Sometimes he had the word *Time* on a card brought forward when the hour was nearly expired.[26]

In the mid-1820s the Royal Institution was in another delicate financial state. William Brande had to take a cut in salary from £200 to £150 per year in 1824 as part of the recurrent economy drives.[27] By initiating the Friday Evening Discourses Faraday was taking effective practical steps to reverse the decline, through the dual benefits of the membership fees and the fact that the better the lectures, the more the word would spread, and the more people of reasonable wealth and curiosity would pay to become members of the Institution. Faraday had been quite open about the task ahead when he wrote to Franklin in 1826, but his tone was positive: 'We are making a hard struggle to restore the Institution and I have no doubt you will find it when you return in a very different state to that you left it in.'[28]

Faraday's runaway success as a lecturer and organiser made him attractive to the Royal Institution's rivals. He was invited to become the first Professor of Chemistry at the new London University in 1827, but turned it down because of his attachment to the Royal Institution. He told

Dionysius Lardner, one of the first members of the London University Council, that

> the Institution has been a source of knowledge and pleasure to me
> for the last fourteen years, and though it does not pay me in Salary
> for what I *now* strive to do for it, yet I possess the kind feelings &
> good will of its Authorities & members, all the privileges it can grant
> or I require and moreover I remember the protection it has afforded
> me during the past years of my scientific life.[29]

The appointment was to be held open for Faraday for two years, but nevertheless

> Two years may bring the Royal Institution into such a state as to
> make me still more anxious to give a third to it; it may just want
> the last & most vigorous exertions of all its friends to confirm its
> prosperity & I should be sorry not to lend my assistance with that
> of others to the work.

In reporting the financial situation to the Royal Institution's Managers, whose meetings he now attended as Director of the Laboratory, Faraday told the truth as he saw it. 'We are living on the parings of our own skin,' he informed them with brutal honesty.[30] When stories about the Institution's insecurity reached the press, it was given more flowery expression. The *Literary Gazette*, describing Faraday as 'one of the most successful chemical enquirers of the age', wrote in 1827:

> This meritorious and valuable institution has fortunately been rais-
> ing itself, during the last two or three years, from a state of such
> depression, into which untoward circumstances, and some little want
> of energy, has conspired to throw it. The lectures now in the course
> of delivery, are, and deserve to be, numerously attended; and the
> Friday Evening Meetings are at once the most rational and pleasur-
> able assemblies which are to be found in London.[31]

The Institution's many other lecture series also benefited from the following wind of the Discourses. Among them in 1828 were sets of six lectures on Music by the organist and composer Samuel Wesley; on Architecture by Alfred Ainger, one of Tatum's protégés; on Painting and the Fine Arts by Ramsay Richard Reinagle RA; on Hieroglyphics by the Marquis Spineto; on Natural History by Dr Harwood; and on Mechanics by John Millington.[32]

One of Faraday's most valuable assets was that he got on with people; he did not antagonise. He made it his business to develop good relations with the Managers, some of whom had become his friends. Daniel Moore, a lawyer closely involved with the Royal Institution, he described to John Franklin as being 'as usual astonishingly liberal'.[33] The chemical manufacturer Charles Hatchett had supported him from the beginning; the Secretary Edmund Daniell was another friend. By raising public interest and excitement at what was going on at the Royal Institution, Faraday generated confidence amongst the Managers who had financial responsibility for it.

A very rich man who had been a member since 1812 was John Fuller of Rosehill, Sussex, an heir to iron-making interests in Sussex and sugar plantations in the West Indies. Fuller had already been generous to the Royal Institution, having made the Managers a loan of £1000 in 1818,[34] but from 1828 he paid also for a gold medal, Fuller's Medal, which was given every two years in recognition of chemical discoveries.[35] The first year's recipients included Sir Humphry Davy, William Wollaston, William Brande and Faraday himself, and in publicising the striking and awarding of the medal, the Royal Institution was claiming prestige for itself and deliberately measuring itself against the Royal Society, whose Copley Medal, which Davy had described as 'the ancient olive crown of the Royal Society',[36] had been awarded annually for excellence in scientific research for over one hundred years. Faraday, indeed, would win it in 1835. The Fuller Medal, designed and struck by William Wyon RA, the leading medallist of the day, had a portrait of Francis Bacon on the reverse, while on the obverse was the inscription 'For Chemical Discoveries: Given by John Fuller, Member of the Royal Institution'. Faraday knew the value of prestige. He was anxious that Jerdan should draw attention to the new medal in the *Literary Gazette*, and asked him, 'Pray shall you take any notice of Mr Fuller's Medal?'[37] Duly, Jerdan came up with the right kind of paragraphs, reporting on the continuation of support from Fuller, 'by his familiars called Jack', and announcing the presentation of the medal at the Royal Institution to 'the principal persons who have distinguished themselves by chemical discoveries in connection with this society'.[38]

As a further tactic, Faraday actively encouraged men of reputation in science, in England and abroad, to attend lectures. He sent a pair of tickets to Walter Trevelyan in the hope that he might be able to attend a Friday evening;[39] and also to 'Prandi', most likely the Italian physicist Pietro Prandi.[40] Faraday was the ringmaster, and he wanted all the best people to roll up to his circus. When foreigners visited London he invited them to the Royal Institution. The German steel-maker Johann Conrad Fischer came to England in 1825 and 1827, and the Institution was a natural port of call for him. Fischer wrote in his diary that Faraday told him, 'I see well you are a practical man and the simple observations of such ones will do often more good to society than all our speculations.'[41] The Brazilian military engineer Felisberto Caldeira Brant came in 1828 to gather advice and equipment for a chemistry laboratory that he wanted to set up in Brazil. Faraday gave him his time, soon referred to him as 'a friend of mine', and sent him off with a letter of recommendation to take to Pierre Berthier, the professor at the School of Mining in Paris, where Faraday hoped Brant would find yet more useful knowledge.[42]

The Royal Institution had now become, more than ever before, a place of vivid interchange of people and knowledge. Faraday encouraged travellers abroad to return with objects that would be useful for the Institution's collections. He asked Benjamin Smith, who was leaving for America in March 1829, if he would bring back some examples of American minerals, asking especially for specimens of strontium from Lake Erie.[43] Adding that he had heard that Smith intended to fly kites carrying lightning conductors from his ship, he warned him about 'the Electric fluid', and gave him practical advice on how to earth the conductor. Ever on the lookout for topics for a future Evening Discourse, Faraday asked Smith to send word on the successes and failures of the kite-flying conductor so that it could be reported.

Although the subjects of the Discourses were wide-ranging, embracing the sciences, technology and the arts, there was a distinct hierarchy of priorities which Faraday, working through his Friday Evenings Committee, applied when setting the lecture programme.[44] He told the architect William Hosking that 'mere matter of opinion which can be settled only by reference to taste and not by reference to natural facts' was not suitable for the Discourses. Rather, 'New points in philosophy – or new modes of experimental illustration – or new applications to useful purposes are what is wished for. After these follow new matters in taste or literature.'[45]

The subjects chosen should all be demonstrable, and able to be clearly illustrated by example or experiment. A typical group of seven consecutive Discourses from May and June 1829 gives a flavour of the variety of interests the series covered, and of how Faraday managed to balance his audience's diet:

1 May: *On the audible properties of speech*; given by Benjamin Smart. 'He concluded a very eloquent and interesting discourse, amidst the approbation of a numerous audience.' On the Library Table were 'a curious collection of baggage-boats, paddles, war clubs, drinking cups and drums of the Javanese from Lady Raffles; Dutch torture instruments; specimens of German and English lithography.' [*Literary Gazette*, 9 May 1829]

8 May: *Brunel's Blockmaking Machine*; given by Michael Faraday 'before one of the fullest audiences we have seen in the Institution for several years'. Faraday, assisted by some men from the engineering firm Maudslay and Field who manufactured the equipment, demonstrated a model of Brunel's machinery lent by the Navy Board. On the Library Table were 'exceedingly beautiful specimens [brought from the East by Captain Waite] of Damascus blades and Persian armour; curious shields made from the hide of the rhinoceros, and very large drinking-cups and vases from the horn of the same animal; also many presents of fine crystals, of different substances, books, maps, engravings &c.' [*Literary Gazette*, 16 May 1829]

15 May: *A practical discourse upon 'Xylography', or engraving on wood*; given by [James?] Mason. 'Mr Mason illustrated his subject by a vast variety (almost to the confusing of himself) of rare and very old specimens of wood engravings, obtained from the libraries of HRH the Duke of Sussex, Earl Spencer, Mr Ottley, the East India Company, and various others.' On the Library Table 'were a few beautiful specimens of crystals and vegetable alkali, together with works of literature and art'. [*Literary Gazette*, 23 May 1829] According to the *Athenaeum* these included a selection of mediaeval illustrated manuscripts.[46]

22 May: *Nodal figures produced by the phonic variations of elastic laminae*; given by Michael Faraday. On the Library Table were 'minerals, crystallised glass, and works of literature presented to the Institution; Eastern curiosities from the Asiatic Society'. [*Literary Gazette*, 30 May 1829]

29 May: *On the fictile vases of the ancients*; given by Samuel Singer, Librarian of the Royal Institution. 'Mr Faraday purposes to direct his attention to the analysis of the black glaze of the ancient vases – a subject which has puzzled many chemists, and of which, as yet, no satisfactory account has been given – with a view to bringing the point before the Institution.' On the Library Table were 'mineralogical and geological specimens from India, presented by Captain Blake, a curious historical flag representing the emigration of the cinnamon peelers of Ceylon'. [*Literary Gazette*, 6 June 1829]

5 June: *The Ascent of Mont Blanc*, given by Edmund Clarke 'with great freedom and spirit, and accompanied with excellent illustrations, consisting of paintings, drawings, models, specimens of the instruments used in the ascent, and of the rocks and plants of the mount and its neighbourhood'. On the Library Table was an 'ancient Arabian astrolabe'. [*Literary Gazette*, 13 June 1829]

12 June: *Experimental researches ... for the purpose of improving the manufacture of glass for optical use*; given by Michael Faraday. 'Mr Faraday made his farewells at the last of the season's meetings ... calling the members' attention to the principles and practice which, within the last few years, have made the Institution so highly interesting. He also claimed their united assistance for the next year in the good cause of advancing and diffusing science and knowledge – the only objects that the Institution had in view.' On the Library Table were a coral fan in the shape of Venus and casts of sculptures of the Canterbury Pilgrims and Ivanhoe by John Henning. [*Literary Gazette*, 20 June 1829]

Faraday's peroration at the end of the 1829 season of Friday Evening Discourses defines their true purpose and the overarching purpose of the Royal Institution: 'the good cause of advancing and diffusing science and knowledge – the only objects that the Institution had in view'. The way he made it all happen, however, with a widely spread net of subjects, a varied list of speakers, and the encouragement of loans for display on the Library Table, was inspirational. People like *things*, particularly the curious, evocative and extraordinary, and in loading his Library Table with the kind of objects he did, Faraday had created a Cabinet of Curiosities which overflowed with delights. The difference between Faraday's Library Table and the Cabinets of Curiosity of the seventeenth century was that now the objects came with explanations. One visitor from Germany, Friedrich von Raumer, wrote home about 'the model of a steam-engine half a finger long, and of the power, not of many horses, nor even half horses, but of half a flea; and the little monster moved with as much rapidity and regularity as those enormous sea-dragons which force their way against the elements'.[47]

The system of loans to the Library Table fostered co-operation between individuals and societies – the East India Company, the Navy Board, Maudslay and Field, the Asiatic Society and the Duke of Sussex were among the lenders to Discourse evenings in May and June 1829 alone – and reveals the Royal Institution to have become central within the web of interchange between learned and trade organisations. The illustrations for the lectures and the discussions afterwards were seen by Faraday as fundamental to their purpose: 'I think experimental lectures owe all their value to the experiments and visual illustrations which are given in conjunction with the theoretical details and it will be my object to make these demonstrations as distinct and impressive as possible.'[48]

Though amended and improved by time, the Friday-evening practice comes straight from the suggestions that Faraday picked up from the writings of Isaac Watts, from the manner of illustrating lectures that John Tatum practised, and from the fun and companionship that Tatum and his young men had had at Dorset Street.

A member of the audience whom Faraday particularly welcomed was Jane Marcet, one of the sources of his own early inspiration. Surviving correspondence suggests that Mrs Marcet attended when she could, Faraday himself writing to her in 1846 to say: 'I do not send you a ticket because I wish you to understand that on mentioning your name You & a friend with you shall *always* pass here. I so have given an order.'[49] He held Jane Marcet in 'deep veneration', 'first as one who had conferred great personal good and pleasure on me; – and then as one able to convey the truths and principles of those boundless fields of knowledge which concern natural things to the young, untaught and enquiring mind'.[50]

It may have been his memory of this 'great personal good and pleasure' that prompted Faraday also to present the Christmas lectures for 'juveniles', boys and girls in their teen years, from Christmas 1827.[51] These became a regular event, an institution in themselves which has carried on, broadcast on television, into the twenty-first century. The Christmas lectures brought out the boy in Faraday once again, his 'wonderful juvenility of spirit' being never far from the surface: 'Hilariously boyish upon occasion he could be, and those who knew him best knew he was never more at home, that he never seemed so pleased, as when making an old boy of himself, as he was wont to say, lecturing before a juvenile audience at Christmas.'[52] The fun came to a climax in many ways, most noisily perhaps in Faraday's flinging a coal scuttle full of coal, a poker and tongs at an electro-magnet to demonstrate the powers of magnetism.[53]

Von Raumer defined precisely what it was that drew audiences back again and again to hear Faraday: it was his manner of speaking English. We must now assume that the soft 'r' of Faraday's childhood had disappeared, for no further comment is made on it as far as I can discover. It took a foreigner to make a very important point about Faraday's delivery:

He speaks with ease and freedom, but not with a gossipy, unequal tone, alternately inaudible and bawling, as some very learned professors do; he delivers himself with clearness, precision and ability. Moreover, he speaks his language in a manner which confirmed me in a secret suspicion that I had, that a number of Englishmen speak it very badly. Why is it that French in the mouth of Mlle Mars, German in that of Tieck, English in that of Faraday seems a totally different language? – because they articulate what other people swallow or chew.[54]

In a letter of the following year von Raumer described how he attended another of Faraday's lectures, and exclaimed:

Why have we [in Germany] nothing similar? Or, why do we not, at least, attempt and aim at it? Our academies . . . excite the interest of their own members rather than of the public . . . This British institution combines, in a laudable manner, external convenience, literary resources, agreeable conversation, and welcome instruction.[55]

For Faraday, teaching went all the way from the laws of nature, as expressed even by the magnetic attraction of a coal scuttle, to the musical and visual arts, where he drew musicians and artists into his embrace. Faraday's own work on the vibration of surfaces in 1831 attracted the attention of musicians such as Samuel Wesley and Charles Wheatstone, and he spoke 'On the application of new principles in the construction of musical instruments',[56] displaying – and playing – many instruments to the audience as he did so. In the visual arts he had for many years been deeply interested in the development of new ways to reproduce images. The long-standing methods of copper engraving and etching were ill-suited to the mass reproduction that steam presses could now achieve, as a copper plate soon wore out. New methods which developed in the early nineteenth century included wood engraving on boxwood blocks, pioneered by the Newcastle artist Thomas Bewick, engraving on steel plates of the kind that Faraday had seen being made by Jacob Perkins in 1820, and lithography, which was developed with Faraday's close attention by Charles Hullmandel.

Faraday and the Royal Institution were at the forefront of improving image reproduction in the 1820s and 1830s, and as a direct result of this, and of Faraday's own personal interest and experience as an amateur artist, painters and engravers attended the Institution regularly, both in the audience and as speakers. John Constable, for example, gave a historic series of lectures on landscape painting in 1836, as did Thomas Phillips RA and Benjamin Robert Haydon. As a further symptom of the widespread influence and interest of the lectures, Faraday was invited in 1838 to advise on the suitability of moving the Raphael cartoons from Hampton Court to the National Gallery, and in the same year corresponded with William Trull, a Coventry weaver, about the pigments in the Raphael tapestries that had been exhibited in Coventry and London.[57]

When a head of Voltaire, 'said to have been modelled from life', was displayed on the Library Table in 1831, 'it was considered by several of the eminent artists present rather as a cast from life'.[58] The artists were not at the lecture to consider Voltaire's head, but to hear William Ainsworth on 'The determination of the age of rocks of supposed igneous origin'. We do not know who the 'eminent artists' were, but they might have included some whom we know attended the Royal Institution such as William Brockedon, Francis Chantrey, J.D. Harding, Charles Hullmandel, John Martin, Thomas Phillips, Henry Pickersgill, Cornelius Varley and William Wyon. Of these, Cornelius Varley had a double connection with Faraday, for not only was he married to Sarah Faraday's Sandemanian cousin Elizabeth Straker, but he was also a distinguished artist with an interest in optics that went beyond the amateur and led him to the development of a succession of sophisticated drawing instruments. These, principally Varley's Patent Graphic Telescope, he produced in his factory, Mildmay Works in Stoke Newington. Varley displayed his instruments on the Library Table on a number of occasions, and in 1839 was a contributor to the early discussions of photography at the Royal Institution.

There is a revealing letter, which touches on the extent of Faraday's contacts with artists, to Charles Hatchett: 'I am very much obliged to you for the specimen you have sent me and shall get several artists to adopt it who I know are in want of such a thing. Size diluted is at present the best thing they have.'[59] What the 'thing' was is a mystery; some kind of canvas-priming solution, perhaps. The inference from the letter is that Faraday had assumed the role of managing a clearing house of technical information for artists. The painter John Martin and his wife were good friends of Michael and Sarah Faraday. Their personal affinity may have had its roots in a shared appreciation of the stark religious subject-matter of Martin's paintings and engravings. His characteristic subjects were biblical scenes such as *Belshazzar's Feast* (1820; Paul Mellon Center, New Haven), *The Seventh Plague of Egypt* (1823; Museum of Fine Arts, Boston), *The Deluge* (1827; now lost) and many drawn from Milton. From the 1830s Martin's paintings grew larger and yet more terrible in their depictions of earthly cataclysm – in *The Last Judgement* (1853; Tate, London) and *The Great Day of His Wrath* (1851–53; Tate, London) heavenly fury with the ways of humanity has reached its pictorial apogee.

But the aspect of John Martin that most fully engaged Faraday was the painter's intense practical interest in the improvement of the fabric of city life, and the dedication he showed to creating and promoting his plans. He designed means by which the River Thames might be embanked along its length in London; how a new water supply, bringing water from

Hertfordshire, would work; and how the city might be drained to improve public health and happiness. The architect Thomas Donaldson gave a Friday Evening Discourse on 'Mr Martin's plan for draining the Metropolis' in March 1833,[60] and Faraday followed Martin's progress as an engineer with respect and pleasure. He took Martin as seriously in this sphere of his work as all the most earnest art critics did in his work as a painter, and having seen his plans for the drainage of London, wrote:

> I have received and thank you most heartily for the reports. I have read them. I give you joy of the development of your most important subject and proposition, and congratulate you upon the progress which its practical application is making. I trust you will find, in this case, that your labour will be followed by that pleasure, honour and profit which is its just reward.[61]

Although Martin's contribution as an artist is prodigious, he sacrificed much of his time and art to his grand engineering schemes, none of which in the event got off the drawing board.[62]

William Brockedon was another artist whom Faraday befriended and added to his roll of lecturers at the Royal Institution. He, like Martin, was a painter of grand-scale religious dramas, such as *The Vision of Zecharia* (1821; lost) and *Moses on Mount Sinai* (1835; formerly Christ's Hospital, now lost), and with that in common we might reasonably infer that theirs was the sort of art Faraday wished to encourage, and even liked. Brockedon had trained in Devon as a watchmaker, but came to London in 1809 to study painting at the Royal Academy. He found considerable success not as a painter of biblical scenes but as a portraitist, and over the years made a large group of chalk and pencil studies of artists, writers and scientists, many of which are now in the National Portrait Gallery in London.[63] His particular interest to Faraday was his talent as a lecturer on subjects which were more allied to technical invention than art, such as wire-drawing,[64] firearm wadding[65] and the uses of india rubber.[66] But he also spoke on art at the Royal Institution, among his subjects being an account of a mezzotint process for use in lithography.[67] After his talk on colour perception in 1830 Faraday wrote to congratulate him: 'Your illustrations of colour &c is continually in my mind's eye and I am beginning to be anxious about seeing you upon it.'[68]

Unlike John Martin, William Brockedon has slipped out of public consciousness, despite the fact that he merited a five-column entry in the *Dictionary of National Biography* (1903), and that when he died in 1854 the *Illustrated London News* wrote that 'English artists are mourning the loss of an old friend.'[69] His friendship with Faraday ran as deep as any he had with artists, and evidently Faraday and his Friday Evenings Committee had great regard for Brockedon as a lecturer, the manner of his delivery and the breadth of his expertise. In public speaking, Brockedon was a man after Faraday's own heart, making himself clear to his audience and not going on for too long. The *Literary Gazette* noticed this with pleasure, reporting after his lecture on lithography: 'Mr Brockedon's subject was short but plainly and well told, and altogether that which best becomes the theatre of the Royal Institution at evening meetings of its members . . .'.[70]

Faraday knew Brockedon well enough by 1830 to know what amused him – revealing also something of the boy in Faraday – telling him that he should call round at John Ayrton Paris's house, as Paris's son 'has been amusing himself by making some models in red & black sealing wax of men & soldiers on horseback. They appear to me to be very ingenious & good. I think you would like to see them . . .'.[71]

Faraday was also deeply engaged with the work of the printmaker Charles Hullmandel. Hullmandel was a pioneer of the art of lithography, the drawing of images onto absorbent stone for reproduction, and had set up a printing shop in London to develop the technique and make it commercially viable. Subjects allied to lithography appear in the Royal Institution lecture lists in the 1820s and 1830s, indicating that the topic was as fascinating to the public as it was to Faraday and Hullmandel. Faraday himself gave a Discourse on the subject on 3 March 1826. Images light up a text, make ideas accessible, and the fact that printed matter could from the 1820s be more cheaply and splendidly illustrated by lithography was as topical and engaging then as was the spreading availability of cinema film into home video in the late twentieth century.

Faraday was instinctively aware of what the development of lithography could mean for modern life, and encouraged Hullmandel in his work. This was despite the fact that Hullmandel was notoriously difficult, being both artist and pioneer printer, and considered a tradesman at the same time. The painter James Ward RA had had rows with Hullmandel, and complained about him to Sir John Leicester, Bart, a powerful landowner and collector:

> ... being as it would appear more proud than any of his fellow mortals, [Hullmandel] thinks it proper to make it appear that the artists are under an obligation in his printing for them ... he has taken offence at the idea of being considered ... as he terms it a 'petty shopkeeper' ... I understand that all the artists are thus obliged to humbly wait at the Footstool of Mr Hullmandel and submit now and then quietly to a kick ... [72]

Faraday refused to treat Hullmandel like a 'petty shopkeeper', but honoured his art and powers of technical invention to the extent that he contributed a deeply-felt affidavit to Hullmandel's little book *On Some Improvements in Lithographic Printing* (1827):

> In reply to your request, I have no hesitation in stating, for the information of all to whom it may concern, that having been made acquainted with, and having witnessed your method, and other methods of preparing Lithographic Drawings, I know yours to be strikingly peculiar and different from the others, and from a consideration of the chemical principles of the art, should expect your process to possess that superiority which the testimony of Artists, competent to judge, assure me that it has.[73]

Hullmandel rewarded Faraday with friendship and entertainment. George Barnard remembered how he, his friend and tutor the artist J.D. Harding and Faraday attended *conversaziones* at Hullmandel's 'with actors, artists and musicians ... sometimes going up the river in [Hullmandel's] eight-oar cutter, cooking our own dinner, enjoying the singing of Garcia and his wife and daughter (afterwards Malibran) – indeed most of the best Italian singers, and the society of most of the Royal Academicians, such as Stanfield, Turner, Westall, Landseer ... '.[74]

This throws another light on Hullmandel, the hospitable, entertaining and gregarious artist-entrepreneur, quite different to Ward's image, but both aspects of character which can reasonably inhabit one man. He was the son of the German pianist and composer Nicholas Joseph Hullmandel and his aristocratic wife Mlle Cazan, who had settled in London in 1790. Charles Hullmandel was also an amateur actor and impresario: in Faraday's scrapbooks there is a poster from the 'Theatre Royal Marlborough Street' – actually Hullmandel's own house and workshop – advertising a double bill performed there on 16 February 1825. The programme included *Le Chanoire de Rheims, ou le Voyage Inutile*, the part of Le Chanoire being played by 'Mr Hullmandel, his 3rd appearance in that character'. The fact that the poster is in his scrapbook suggests that Faraday went to the play, which was preceded by another that would surely have amused him no end:

> A grand new anti-mechanical comedy, *Les Ruses de l'Amour ou Cassandre*: 'the discoveries of chemistry, steam-engines, steamboats . . . all sink into obscurity when compared with what will be offered to the public this evening.'[75]

Also in the scrapbook are a number of lithographs of mountainous landscapes (one dated 25 April 1825) which are initialled at bottom left 'GB' – presumably George Barnard – and at bottom right 'MF', evidence that Barnard and Faraday practised lithography together, perhaps under Hullmandel's guidance.[76] In an earlier treatise on his invention, *The Art of Drawing on Stone* (1824), Hullmandel wrote that lithography was 'an art entirely founded on Chemistry',[77] and it will have been this aspect of it that attracted Faraday's attention above the more mechanical reproductive arts such as engraving on metal or wood.

There were other variations on lithography, such as Brockedon's development of a mezzotint lithographic process, and all fed Faraday's interest in image reproduction. He regretted that he was unable to attend the publisher William Savage's lecture at the Society of Arts on an allied topic, 'Improvements in Block Printing in imitation of coloured drawings', and wrote to Savage to apologise, and to say how he would miss hearing 'your fine processes explained & to have given the support which the invention must merit'.[78]

Illustrations in books and on posters gave a great boost to the understanding of scientific ideas, and this was one of the constant themes of Faraday's life. He insisted on clear illustrations, both verbal and visual, in lectures, knew their crucial enlightening value, and had himself made precise pen diagrams to illustrate his lecture and laboratory notes. These, and two surviving pencil drawings of laboratory equipment, descend ultimately from the tuition Faraday had received in perspective as a boy from Masquerier and probably also George Dance. He continued his interest in art by sketching when on holiday, and by drawing elaborate pen cartouches of musical instruments, fishing gear, harvest tools, birds and so on, many of which pepper the pages of his scrapbooks. Aside from the portrait engravings that he amassed, Faraday also collected artists' prints which he stuck into his scrapbook – there is a fine proof of Rembrandt's etching *The Three Trees* (1643), a group of Dutch seventeenth-century figure engravings by Ostade and others, a proof of Claude's *Rest on the Flight to Egypt* from that artist's 'Liber Veritatis', and a miscellany of other landscape and figure prints. His small group of Welsh landscape paintings by Penry Williams has already been mentioned, as have the Italian scenes he brought home in 1815.

There was a further dimension to Faraday's interest in art: he knew the power of the image, how the stories in the Bible had been disseminated in the middle ages through woodcuts and stained-glass windows, and, in his religious life, how potently Jesus Christ used immediately comprehensible, striking and enduring imagery in his parables – the mustard seed, the camel and the eye of the needle, the mote and the beam, the lilies of the field. As a Sandemanian Faraday had sworn to attempt to live his life in emulation of Christ; as a scientist, using imagery that would rivet his audiences, he was driven to preach the truths of nature.

CHAPTER 15

Steadiness and Placidity

In the second half of the 1820s Faraday was gradually released from the influence and interference of Sir Humphry Davy. The last surviving letter from Davy, asking Faraday to forward his post during the summer, came in 1823,[1] and since then the two men had had a *rapprochement*, coming together to co-operate on a practical application of the electro-chemistry of copper and zinc, to protect the bottoms of ships. The theory, one of Davy's, was that if short iron or zinc bars were fused to the copper-lined hulls of warships, the copper would be protected through electro-chemical action from corrosion by sea water. That was a fine theory, but in practice it was found by frustrated ships' captains that barnacles and seaweed preferred the habitat of electro-chemically protected ships' bottoms, and clung to them more tenaciously than they had to plain copper sheeting or wood. The result was that the protected ships were severely fouled by growth, and disabled. Davy lost much of the government and public confidence he had gained through his invention of the safety lamp; and the nation might have lost a war at sea, had there been one in the 1820s. Davy, who was mortally ill by December 1826, gradually withdrew from Faraday's life and from science, spending extended periods in Austria, Switzerland and Italy, travelling, fishing and writing his late philosophy.

The pressures of the Royal Institution and, increasingly, of work outside it, made it essential for Michael and Sarah Faraday to get away from London for summer holidays. In 1824 and 1826 they travelled to Niton, at the southern tip of the Isle of Wight, where they went on long walks over the island, making long notes on the geology and enjoying the air and the landscape.[2] Before they left Portsmouth on the 1824 trip they called at the dockyard to look at the progress of the electrolytic protection of ships, and then crossed to Ryde. They sailed in a fierce storm which Faraday compared to one he had read about in the three-volume novel *The Entail* by John Galt, published the year before. Light reading charged Faraday's imagination; a good literary description enlivened him, gave him a thrill, sometimes even brought tears to his eyes, as Margery Reid would recall. Faraday's own powers of description were quite as vivid as any pulp fiction, and it is intriguing that while he could see natural effects with the objective eye of a scientist, he also enjoyed the rough and tumble of the popular novel. He told his sister Margaret:

Pray, have you read 'The Entail'? . . . If you have, you will remember the description in the last volume of a dry storm at sea . . . Such a storm we had in going across – every wave was white and every vessel that was out appeared to be either in the waves or in the foam. The vessel in which we were, though of good size, was so much on one side from the force of the wind that a foot or more of the deck was frequently under water for some time, and all the spars and oars swimming; then the wind was against us, so that we had to tack three or four times; and every time we tacked, such confusion, for then the vessel inclined on the other side, so that all on deck had to ship across, or they would be swimming in the water.[3]

Faraday took work with him on holiday. When he and Sarah were at Niton in 1826 he was writing *Chemical Manipulation*, a treatise on laboratory practice for students, which John Murray published in 1827. 'I am writing away here,' he told Edward Magrath, '& get on pretty well but it will be a more laborious job than I expected – I tire of writing day after day but have stuck to pretty well thus far.'[4]

This did not prevent him from writing a long letter to Sarah's brother

Edward Barnard the younger, in which he comes very close to defining his own philosophy of life:

> I have been watching the clouds on these hills for many evenings back: they gather when I do not expect them; they dissolve when, to the best of my judgement, they ought to remain; they throw down rain to my mere inconvenience, but doing good all around; and they break up and present me with delightful and refreshing views when I expect only a dull walk. However strong and certain the appearances are to me, if I venture an internal judgement, I am always wrong in something; and the only conclusion I can come to is, that the end is as beneficial as the means of its attainment are beautiful. So it is in life . . . But I think I derive a certain degree of steadiness and placidity amongst such feelings by a point of mental conviction, for which I take no credit as a piece of knowledge or philosophy, and which has often been blamed as mere apathy. Whether apathy or not, it leaves the mind ready and willing to do all that can be useful, whilst it relieves it a little from the distress dependent upon viewing things in their worst state. The point is this: in all kinds of knowledge I perceive that my views are insufficient, and my judgement imperfect. In experiments I come to conclusions which, if partly right, are sure in part to be wrong; if I correct by other experiments, I advance a step, my old error is in part diminished, but is always left with a tinge of humanity, evidenced by its imperfection . . . My views of a thing at a distance and close at hand never correspond, and the way out of a trouble which I desire is never that which really opens before me.[5]

Faraday wrote these words during the same days in which he was writing parts of *Chemical Manipulation*. 'Steadiness and placidity', as he put it, is a kind of mental detachment, an ability to separate himself from things as they are and accept the given – certainties and uncertainties together. When he writes of the 'tinge of humanity', he is describing the real gap between a solid fact, the unquestionable experimental result, and the nagging little doubts that he found besetting him when he looked carefully at the facts and figures that he had obtained. These are the same kind of doubts, though translated into personal rather than scientific terms, that he had described to Ampère in 1822.

Faraday could, however, reveal no such doubts to the wide and unknown army of students who would read *Chemical Manipulation*. The boundaries of his knowledge, his fringes of doubt, were far beyond where all but a handful of theirs would ever be. In the Introduction, he writes about how experiment has created new facts, extending enormously those 'presented to us spontaneously by nature'. Manipulation, the actual per-forming of an experiment, is the key to real knowledge:

> By accurate and ready manipulation ... an advantage is gained independent of that belonging to the knowledge of the principles of the science, and this is so considerable, that of two persons having otherwise equal talents and information, the one who manipulates best will very soon be in advance of the other; for the one may obtain satisfactory results from his experimental enquiries, while the other is left in doubt or led astray by his imperfect reasonings.[6]

Faraday could not, would not, spread any suggestion of doubt to his students, but to his brother-in-law Edward Barnard, who from clues in Faraday's reply was writing poetry and going through some kind of personal crisis, it was a different matter. Here he was writing not as a teacher of science but as a Sandemanian and a brother. Faraday first found certainty in natural facts; then looking further he felt doubt; but further still, as he very gently and enigmatically reminded Edward: 'You quote Shakespeare: the quotation may be answered a thousand times over from a book just as full of poetry, which you may find on your shelf.' That is, of course, the Bible.

In *Chemical Manipulation*, Faraday takes his readers straight into the laboratory, and describes the best size, layout and arrangement of equip-ment. Then he describes the means to achieve the first basic information about a substance – the weighing of it, the measuring and the heating. The succeeding chapters discuss subsequent activities – granulation, solution, distillation, precipitation and so on. This is not a book about elements and substances – Brande had dealt with those in his *Manual of Chemistry* – but about the *doing* of chemistry, how to use things, the practice. The titles of some short chapters give the essence of Faraday's book – 'Uses of corks', 'Uses of paper', 'Uses of copper wire'. While he had honed his interpretative and analytical skills through years of experience, manipulation – the practice of chemistry – had been with him from his youth, and we can recall how in Riebau's shop he made little experimental machines, or could strike a hammer a thousand times without resting.[7] As a child he could trust a fact; as a man he could trust his hands.

We may reasonably guess that Faraday sent a copy of the book to Jane Marcet. He had got into the habit of sending copies of papers to his 'first instructress', whom by now he must have met: 'You may imagine my delight when I came to know Mrs Marcet personally,' he told Auguste de la Rive, Charles's son, in 1858, 'how often I cast my thoughts backward delighting to connect the past and the present; – how often when sending a paper to her as a thank offering I thought of my first instructress.'[8]

Chemical Manipulation, published in April 1827, was the only book Faraday ever wrote (his publications were with this sole exception scientific papers) and he was showered with praise by his friends and colleagues. He sent a copy to Edmund Daniell, who replied immediately in words that indicate how united the Managers and staff must have been in their efforts to bring the Royal Institution back to the centre of scientific affairs and to solvency, and in particular how freely Faraday shared credit for his successes with others:

> . . . it will always be a source of gratification by recalling to my mind the part I have taken in the renovation of an establishment which whatever may be its other titles to esteem will always stand preeminent for the share it has had in the development of talent & for the encouragement it has afforded to the exertions of genius.[9]

Scientists were more direct and no less immediate in their praise. John Ayrton Paris considered *Chemical Manipulation* to be 'an invaluable treasure to every practical Chemist. I have read it with much pleasure.'[10] William Henry, the Manchester chemist, found that it 'abounds with matter of the greatest use to all who embark in operative chemistry, conveyed too in a manner which is distinct and intelligible without being tediously minute'.[11] But the best praise came from the great Georges Cuvier, who, writing as Permanent Secretary to the Institut de France, accepted the work for the Institute library.[12] Cuvier will have noticed that the epigraph Faraday chose was in French, a line from the *Dictionnaire de Trévoux*:[13] '*Ce n'est pas assez de savoir les principes, il faut savoir MANIP-ULER.*' With the whole world of English letters to provide an epigraph, Faraday's choice of French must be significant, and in choosing it he was distancing himself from the Anglocentric approach of the older generation – specifically Sir Humphry Davy – who had hated Napoleon and the French for decades, and allying himself with the new post-war world of scientific internationalism, the community of science that knew no boundaries.

A long and involved task with which Faraday was now centrally concerned was the search for recipes for clear, highly refractive optical glass, suitable for use in the wide range of optical instruments that were being invented and patented. In 1825 the Royal Society formed a committee, comprising Thomas Young, Faraday, John Herschel, James South and George Dollond, to research the properties of glass, initially at the Falcon Glass Works, Whitefriars, and, from 1827, at the newly-built furnace of the Royal Institution. This became one of Faraday's principal occupations for the next five years.

To assist him in the work Faraday employed a former soldier, Sergeant Charles Anderson, late of the Royal Artillery, of 4 Little Stanhope Street, Mayfair, ten minutes' walk from the Royal Institution.[14] Anderson was 'steadiness and placidity' personified, careful, exact, quiet and loyal, the perfect laboratory companion for Faraday, who preferred to be alone in the basement, and who, with Anderson silent beside him, practically was. Anderson's first task was to keep the glass furnace stoked and at heat, and this he did with such application that when Faraday forgot to tell him to go home one evening and let the fire die out, he remained at his post, keeping the fire hot, all night, until discovered the next morning.[15]

Humphry Davy died in Geneva in May 1829, at the age of fifty. He had been travelling in Italy, and having had a series of strokes, wrote to his brother John from Rome asking him to come quickly. Lady Davy also hurried to Rome. Humphry was a long time dying, for somehow John got him to Geneva, and read to him daily from his manuscript 'Dialogues'. 'His mind was wonderfully cheerful,' John wrote, 'and tranquil, and clear, and in a very affectionate and most amiable disposition, and the expression of his countenance corresponded.'[16] When the news of his death and burial in Geneva reached London, Faraday remained enigmatic about it – although a brief note to Masquerier in June is all we have to go on for his immediate reaction to the news.[17] Faraday's religion taught him not to make too much of death, seeing it as a mere passing, and he refused to attend non-Sandemanian funerals or memorial services.

But at the end of the year, in answer to a request from John Ayrton Paris who was writing Davy's biography, Faraday's response was affectionate and touching, but nevertheless very briefly put. He wrote of Davy's 'goodness of heart',[18] which was generous under the circumstances of his having suffered from Davy's meanness of mind, and he lent Paris the letter that Davy had sent him in 1812 inviting him to the Royal Institution to talk about a life in science.[19] Faraday had always treasured the letter – 'you may imagine how much I value it'. He did not repine or linger in the aftermath of Davy's death, but in the next few weeks took a major step that spread further the word of science and forwarded his career.

After lengthy negotiations involving duties and salary, Faraday accepted in June 1829 the offer of the post of Professor of Chemistry at the Royal Military Academy, Woolwich, in succession to the geologist John McCulloch. This position, for which he was paid £200 per year salary, entailed his giving twenty-five lectures each year, visiting the Academy weekly in term time. It did not, however, mean that he would have to leave the Royal Institution, being additional to his lecture programme there. This was a tight timetable, as evoked in a letter to Percy Drummond, the Governor of the Academy:

> It is my intention to be at Woolwich tomorrow to examine the state of things. I shall leave this house directly after my Morning Lecture ie at 10 o'clock & expect to be at the Academy at 12 or thereabouts. Will you have the goodness to leave the key for me.[20]

CHAPTER 16

Facts are Such Stubborn Things

Faraday's temperament was put under some strain in the early 1830s, his anger bursting out when goaded or criticised for the amount of time the experiments on optical glass for the Admiralty were taking. His researches had provided material for his first Bakerian Lecture at the Royal Society at the end of 1829, but now government paymasters were becoming restive for more tangible results. Faraday was asked in May 1830 by Davies Gilbert, the caretaker President of the Royal Society, how much more the experiments were going to cost, and how much longer they would take. The work had been stumbling on for six years, and already Herschel had resigned in frustration from the experimental sub-committee, leaving Faraday and Dollond to carry on alone.

George Dollond, whose role was to grind lenses and prisms from the glass made under Faraday's direction, was building up his commercial practice as a manufacturer of optical instruments on the strength of the experimental results. Only Faraday, who had originally taken on the work as a means to raise income for the Royal Institution, got little tangible out of it. He had assistance in the work at the furnace from Charles Anderson, and perhaps also from a pupil assistant, William Cookson,[1] but his anger was real. In a tone that might have been aggravated by the fact that he was recurrently ill with headaches, exhaustion and lassitude during 1830, he burst forth in a letter to Gilbert:

I ... wish you most distinctly to understand that I regret I ever allowed myself to be named as one of the Committee. I have had in consequence several years of hard work: all the time that I could spare from necessary duties (and which I wished to devote to original research) [has] been consumed in the experiments and consequently given gratuitously to the public. I should be very glad now to follow Mr Herschel's example & return to the prosecution of my own views and it is only because I do not like to desert my post at the critical time if you and others think it worth while to keep it filled that I am obliged to pursue the experiments further.[2]

Nevertheless, practical results of Faraday's efforts began gradually to emerge. The astronomical telescope that had been constructed with the seven-inch lenses made in the Royal Institution furnace was successfully tested by John Pond, the Astronomer Royal, at Greenwich in December 1830. Pond reported to the Royal Society that despite

unfavourable weather ... the result has appeared to me extremely satisfactory, and such as I hope will encourage Mr Faraday to persevere in his laudable efforts to accomplish the views of the Committee. The object glass is very achromatic, and indicates that all has been done that could be done by the artist who made the Telescope ... The nebula of Orion is shewn beautifully ...[3]

Only four weeks later, when the new-year session of Discourses began at the Royal Institution on 21 January 1831, the *Literary Gazette* reported that specimens of glass engraving and casting were on display on the Library Table, and that interest in what could now be done with optical glass was raised by Cornelius Varley, who demonstrated microscopes at the meeting.

This was a new year with a difference, for over the preceding autumn the Royal Institution lecture theatre had been renovated, presenting, as the *Literary Gazette* put it, 'a neat and comfortable appearance'.[4] It was also newly lit by gas jets, rather than oil, because Faraday had advised the Managers that gas was brighter, cheaper, cleaner and easier to use. The soot and drips from oil lamps had damaged the seats in the lecture theatre,[5] and it was fully expected that this would not be the case with gaslight. The renewal of the theatre was a major step in a series of renovations and improvements that the Managers were embarking on now that a new financial confidence was emerging at the Institution. The programme would lead at the end of the decade to the complete rebuilding of the reception rooms and the uniting of disparate eighteenth-century buildings behind one grand façade on Albemarle Street.

The reconstruction was also a very public way of moving forward from the old Davian generation which had spectacularly carried science into the public arena, into a new era of professionalism, clear presentation and sober announcement of the high status of science. Others of Davy's generation, such as Thomas Young and William Wollaston, had broadened the base and the uses of science. Young did this through polymathic abilities which led him to a theory of the undulatory nature of light, and to a translation of the hieroglyphics on the Rosetta Stone; Wollaston through his inventions of a process to purify platinum for industrial purposes and of the camera lucida. Davy, Wollaston and Young died within months of each other in 1829, and their passing enabled a changing of gear from a science driven by inspiration and opportunism to one of organisation, specialisation and synopsis.

While the Royal Institution gathered up its skirts and went from strength to strength in the early 1830s, the Royal Society laboured under a long-running sequence of bitter division and self-analysis. The central issue at the Society, after Davy's resignation from the Presidency in 1827, revolved around the question of who ran science: was it the aristocrats and gentry whose money paid for influence and prestige, or the scientists themselves whose ingenuity, commitment and genius had brought human understanding and potential to its present sophisticated position? The issue had connections running deep into the complex mechanisms by which England had operated in the late eighteenth century, and thirty years into the nineteenth century social pressures were such that these connections had to be modernised in the light of social and scientific progress. The Royal Society and the Royal Institution were not 'Royal' for nothing, and the Society in particular had benefited profoundly from patronage by the monarchy, the personal interest of George III in science being crucial to its development in both England and America.

The last two Presidents of the Royal Society, Sir Joseph Banks and Sir Humphry Davy, had been strong personalities who disliked opposition.

They were charismatic bullies whose own contributions to science, in quality and worth so far beyond that of any of their contemporaries, gave them a natural right to lead the herd. When Banks, the Sun King of science, died in 1820 there was, despite much internal manoeuvring, only one man on the horizon to succeed him, Humphry Davy, the Prince of Light shining in the reflected glory of his Safety Lamp. When Davy became mortally ill and resigned the Presidency there was confusion at the Royal Society, and there was nobody of equal stature to take his place.

As a result he was replaced by Davies Gilbert, a long-serving and influential politician and committee man. Gilbert had been born Davies Giddy, at St Erth, Cornwall, and for nearly thirty years had been MP for the Cornish constituencies of Helston and Bodmin, first as Giddy, then, from 1817 when he took his wife's more sober name, Gilbert. He was hard-working and assiduous as a Member of Parliament, and reputedly spent more time in committee than any other MP of his generation, speaking particularly for arts and science interests.[6] Through his influence in Cornwall Gilbert had encouraged Humphry Davy in his early scientific career. He had considerable wealth, which derived both from his own well-managed family estates in Cornwall and from his wife's in Sussex. His own scientific talents lay in mathematics and mechanics – he had advised Richard Trevithick on the steam engine, and Thomas Telford on the construction of the Menai Bridge – but he also had profound anti-quarian and historical interests which he expressed in papers to the Society of Antiquaries, of which he was also a Fellow. He was one of the handful of career *dilettanti* who were Fellows of both the Society of Antiquaries and the Royal Society, and became Treasurer of the Royal Society in 1820. His Presidency, when it came in 1827, was a surprise to many. William Wollaston had been a favourite to succeed Davy, but he was old and ill and no longer fully up to the job.

Gilbert hit the Royal Society as President at a time when the unrest brewing there was merely a pale echo of the social agitation in Britain as a whole. The nation was stirring over parliamentary reform, but the issue at the Royal Society was whether a scientist or a brother of the King should be the next President. In the wider picture, reform – the sweep-ing away of rotten and pocket boroughs, the under-representation in Parliament of industrial towns, issues ranging from the corrupt electoral system down to the price of bread – had to be faced by Parliament and the nation's ruling class in the wake of riots, marches, huge public meetings and machine-wrecking. Skilled committee man though he was, Gilbert's main contribution as President of the Royal Society was not to engineer a smooth modernising of the organisation, but to commission distinguished scientific men to write a series of long essays under the terms of the will of the 8th Earl of Bridgewater. The Bridgewater Treatises, essays illustrating 'The Goodness of God as Manifested in the Creation', were an attempt to keep science and established religion lashed together, with a new spin being given to them in the light of discoveries and new understandings in science. In the light also of the political and social unrest in the country, the Treatises can be seen both as an attempt to engender calm in a period of fluid change, and as well-meaning lip-service to a withering orthodoxy.

The greatest shock to the established religious and political order was that progress in geology had revealed serious conflicts between the fossil record and biblical dogma, and this meant that some very neat wording had to be devised to justify beliefs that were rapidly becoming untenable. Following Bridgewater's wishes, Gilbert invited authors such as Charles Babbage, Canon William Buckland and Revd William Whewell to attempt to hold the orthodox line while remaining more or less true to their scientific understanding. They were being given an impossible task. 'Facts are such stubborn things,' the scientist and writer Mary Somerville observed when she read Buckland's Bridgewater Treatise, *Geology and Mineralogy Considered with Reference to Natural Theology* (1836).[7] Buckland had upheld what Somerville called 'the clerical view', a line which the author himself was unable to maintain indefinitely. Faraday read some of the Treatises with interest, but consistent with his practice of remaining silent on religious matters outside his Sandemanian community, he expressed no known opinion on them.[8]

Faraday's irritation was roused in 1830 when Charles Babbage published his polemic *Reflections on the Decline of Science in England and on Some of its Causes*. The book's title alone gives warning of the sturdy point of view which Babbage set out clearly in his opening paragraphs:

> It cannot have escaped the attention of those whose acquirements enable them to judge . . . that in England, particularly with respect

to the more difficult and abstract sciences, we are much below other nations, not merely of equal rank, but below several even of inferior power. That a country, eminently distinguished for its mechanical and manufacturing ingenuity should be indifferent to the progress of inquiries which form the highest departments of that knowledge on whose more elementary truths its wealth and rank depend, is a fact which is well deserving the attention of those who shall inquire into the causes that influence the progress of nations.[9]

This is the kind of jeremiad that came to be repeated – with certain justification – countless times by inventors and scientists in Britain in the nineteenth and twentieth centuries. Babbage's lament that they do it better in France or Germany or practically anywhere else is a particularly early and eloquent example of the genre. Babbage was a genius as a mathematician and engineer, but he was no diplomat. He had been working obsessively for the past decade, with the help of his master craftsman Joseph Clement and a team of workmen, on the manufacture of a giant calculating machine, the Difference Engine, which would end the dangerous uncertainty about the rightness of abstruse and unwieldy logarithm, astronomical and marine tables. Navigation, and the life and death of a ship and its crew, ultimately depended on the accuracy of thousands of columns of numbers; and the economic and social health of the nation depended directly on the safety of shipping. By 1830, Babbage's Difference Engine was well on its way to becoming the most complicated and ambitious piece of machinery yet devised. When completed it would have had about twenty-five thousand separate moving parts cut from brass, die-cast in other metals, turned on a lathe, or hand-made in other ways. It was the apotheosis of the carriage clock, a piece of elegant and intricate machinery, of immense value to society, that stretched Hanoverian engineering to the limits of its capability. Not only that, but to make the parts required for the Difference Engine Babbage had also to devise improvements to his tools, machinery and workshop practice which had lasting benefits for the machine-tool industry and precision engineering as a whole.

But Babbage suffered from the effects of his own irascibility, his lack of diplomatic skills and his poor (or superb) sense of timing. Though it was intended as a contribution to the reform of the Royal Society, *Reflec-*

tions on the Decline of Science took matters into the open and polarised the debate. Babbage pointed a finger at the universities for teaching science in a way that took no serious account of the giant strides of the past fifty years, as if nothing had changed since Newton – he himself could have done something about it; he was a professor at Cambridge, but never lectured there. He accused the government of not supporting scientific research adequately and of undervaluing scientists; and he castigated the Royal Society, of which he had been a Fellow since 1816, for its lap-dog approach to the relations between science and government, and for not biting the hand of government enough.

Faraday's relations with Babbage during the 1820s had been uncontroversial. A letter or two had passed calmly between them, and even after the publication of *Reflections on the Decline of Science* their contacts maintained a staid professional demeanour. But to the issues Babbage raised in his book Faraday took such great exception that he encouraged the Dutch scientist Gerard Moll to write a counterblast, and published it at his own expense. Moll took an unusual view for a foreigner, criticising Babbage and other scientists for taking such an extreme position and being 'determined to see every thing in black in England and to speak highly of the Scientific institutions of foreign countries'.[10] Faraday, whose replies to Moll are lost, clearly picked up on this point and urged Moll on. Moll responded to Faraday:

> I really do not recollect what I wrote you about the present state of Science in England, but certainly I do not think it all worth printing. Still I am not ashamed of my own opinions. The English have quite enough of their natural and foreign political enemies, without waging a civil–scientific war amongst themselves. I have not the slightest doubts but that the Counts, Marquesses and Barons of the French Institute will be highly amused in seeing some of the English Philosophers so overanxious to level to the ground the venerable fabric of the Royal Society in order to have it reconstructed in the more modern form of the French Institute ... [A] neutral foreigner (if however such there be) who inquires impartially into the state of science in England and in other countries cannot help seeing with regret Englishmen scoff and rail at things which ought to have been looked upon as the pride of their country.[11]

Moll's paper, published anonymously as *On the Alleged Decline of Science in England. By a Foreigner*, took Babbage to task on the matter of English scientific pre-eminence: with scientists such as Faraday and the Herschels working in England, what could Babbage have to complain about? Babbage and Moll agreed, however, about the poor state of English universities.[12]

These were small storms by comparison with the political uprisings in England and France in the early 1830s. The restrictions imposed on the French press by Charles X in July 1830 led directly to the July Revolution that brought Louis-Philippe to power. One particular event at the École Polytechnique brought pride to French and English science, as J.N.P. Hachette described to Faraday:

There [young science students] quietly study the works of Lacroix, the Poissons, Monge etc., mathematics, physics and chemistry enriched by your discoveries are their sole pursuit. An armed detachment confronts them and invites them to march with it in defence of the violated charter. These humble, modest and unarmed young people, dressed in uniform recalling the defence of Paris in 1814, step out of the College and immediately each armed group proclaims one of the Polytechnic students its commander; each believes it is invincible, and Science and Honour go before it. Each marches with confidence, since it has the approval of all that is carried in a generous heart. Mathematical principles (Principia Mathematica) and principles of government walk hand in hand; the world's two foremost nations came together ... In France, philosophers, artists and workers feel the complete dignity of their own social position; each adds a little good to the existing good; the smallest scientific discovery is of benefit to humanity; great discoveries are heroic actions in our century. In conveying my views on the influence of the sciences, I experience a great sense of esteem for and gratitude to you and your fellow countrymen who dedicate your entire lives to scientific research.[13]

The heroic reactions of this bunch of students brought Hachette an immediate sense of pride that he wanted swiftly to convey to Faraday. The euphoria in France, however, was short-lived, as Faraday gradually came to discover from others of his correspondents. Ampère wrote in April 1831 of 'this vacuum of new scientific results, which we seem to have been experiencing in France for some time. Political passions seem to make people forget that there is always something to discover in the sciences.'[14]

Faraday's non-partisan attitude, from his influential position as Director of the Laboratory at the Royal Institution, contributed to the steadying of English science, with the result that it was barely affected, compared to the position in France, by the widespread and otherwise damaging agitation over the 1832 Reform Bill. Faraday's neat footwork in bringing Moll in to counteract Babbage's *Observations on the Decline of Science* was a considered and successful operation to maintain an even keel. With Faraday keeping a level head – his Sandemanian non-partisanship now aiding the cause – English science rolled relentlessly on in the early 1830s, the greatest light coming from the Royal Institution, the greatest noise from the rows at the Royal Society.

One faint whisper in the surviving papers that political upheaval ever impinged on Faraday personally in the early 1830s came when William Buckland sent him in December 1830 a mysterious ball of hemp, 'about a hat full tied round with a string',[15] soaked in turpentine and containing a smaller ball bound tightly with copper wire. The whole bundle, which had been found in the backyard of an Oxford bakehouse, had a loose string hanging from it that might have been intended as a sling. As the wisest man of science in Oxford, Buckland had been asked to identify the object, and he passed it on to his friend Faraday. Poking at the messy lump in his laboratory, and then bringing his professional expertise to bear on it, Faraday found shellac, gum resin and oily turpentine impregnating the hemp, and in an annotation to Buckland's letter mused that the object might have been prepared 'for bad purposes'. In the preceding months there had been an outbreak of rick-burnings in the south of England, and Faraday allowed himself the thought that the hemp ball might have been an incendiary device.

In the 1830s Faraday's social life appears to have retreated into a narrow shell bounded by his flat in the Royal Institution, the Sandemanian chapel and various boarding houses along the south coast of England, principally at Brighton, Hastings and Folkestone. He gave two excuses in one reply when invited in July 1831 by Vernon Harcourt to go to York to attend what would have been the first meeting of a new grouping of scientists determined to promote scientific research in the provinces, the British Association for the Advancement of Science. One was a knee-jerk reaction – 'I am not a Social Man never in London accepting invitations to dine out'[16] – the other a more reasonable and understandable excuse, pleading inability on account of the Woolwich lectures which 'are on until October and as they require me every week they will I fear prevent me going to a greater distance from London than 50 or 60 miles'. (Faraday's excuses declining invitations to dine are an art form in themselves; he tied himself in knots in the 1830s trying to get out of social events, being at turns too busy, too ill, never goes out on a Wednesday, poor memory and so on; but rarely are there two excuses, as here, the second of which renders the first nugatory.) How far he stuck to this reclusive régime seems to be a moot point: not going out ran against Faraday's playful nature. He made exceptions when invited by the Presidents of the Royal Institution and the Royal Society, the Dukes of Somerset and Sussex respectively, as their invitations 'I consider as commands'.[17]

Care of his mother in her last years – she died in March 1838, aged seventy-four – Faraday considered a natural duty. He paid for her keep when she was no longer able to manage lodgers, and in gratitude and respect she consulted him on everything. Margaret Faraday was the mother to a great man, and she knew it, her pride being so intense that Faraday had to tell his wife not to talk to her so much about him and his honours, because she was quite proud enough of him already, and any more would be bad for her.[18]

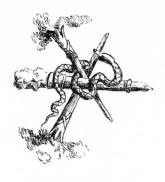

CHAPTER 17

Crispations

One particular scientific phenomenon whose detail was quite new to Faraday absorbed him from February to July 1831 to the exclusion, as far as we can tell, of all other science. This was research into vibrations formed in one body, such as a board or plank, after being struck by another, perhaps a stick or a violin bow: these vibrations and their visual expression he referred to as 'crispations'.

Faraday began by placing a variety of chemical and mineral compounds on a metal plate and vibrating it. In his laboratory diary he recorded how the different materials expressed themselves in different ways under the influence of the vibrations – with phosphate of lime, for example, he found that the finer grains settled at the centre, the coarser at the edges; red oxide of iron fell into line, 'even when rubbed with sand'; while red lead was 'very pretty; though so heavy, finest still keeps at centres and rest descend slowly to quiescent lines'.[1] There was no identifiable goal for this line of research; he seems to have proposed to follow where it led.

With Anderson's help, Faraday set up laboratory arrangements of dishes of water, funnels, an air pump to create vacuums, and complicated contraptions culminating in a deal board eighteen feet long resting on two stools. The vibrations on the long deal board produced 'quadrangular arrangements each several inches (4 or 5) in the side. They look like crossing waves but I believe they are the phenomena in question.'[2]

The crispations that Faraday obtained during the experiments were curls and undulations in the various media in the form of concentric circles, patterns of rectangles, triangles, undulating lines symmetrical about a central diagonal, and other extraordinary patterns and figures. These had first been categorised thirty years earlier by Ernst Chladni, the German pioneer in acoustics and inventor of the euphonium. Chladni had drawn up tables of patterns formed when a sand-covered metal plate was vibrated by a violin bow, but Faraday wanted to examine a wider range of causes and effects by vibrating a variety of substances in a variety of different ways.

From his laboratory notes it seems clear that there were times when Faraday was seduced away from the pure science of the effects by their sheer visual beauty. Attentive visual response is an essential requirement for all laboratory researchers, but in dozens of episodes and instances in Faraday's life his responses to the natural and artificial world, to the effects of weather and landscape, or of art and architecture, of being in Paris or Rome and points between, or his joy at just reorganising and displaying the Royal Institution's mineral collection, all these and more show the acuteness of his visual responses to have been far sharper and of a much higher degree of intensity than were those of any other scientist of his generation. This was in itself one of the principal sources of his greatness. There are many, many examples of his referring in his letters to 'this beautiful experiment', and of his correspondents responding to 'your beautiful results'.

Leading with his eyes open, it was this heightened awareness and its consequent insights that gave Faraday the edge over his contemporaries. Faraday was an artist whose mode of expression happened to take him towards the interpretation rather than the representation of the natural world, and if there had ever been a crossroads in his early life, one sign would have pointed to 'art', the other to 'science'. We may even be tempted to experiment with this idea rather more: during the months in Rome when Lady Davy was being such a scourge to him, Faraday seriously considered giving up science and making a living as a bookbinder. He did so once again when accused of plagiarism in 1821, and there are some later fainter echoes of the same despair. Had he taken this path, bookbinding would not have held him for long, and one might hazard that with the examples and guidance of George Dance, Richard Cosway and J.J. Masquerier before him, Michael Faraday might have been tempted to fall into the lap of the Royal Academy rather than of the Royal Institution.

But back in the Royal Institution basement laboratory in June 1831 Faraday explored viscosity with white of egg ('a very good thing for crispations'[3]), oil ('cold oil rarely shews crispations, hot oil readily'[4]), milk ('it has more cohesion'[5]), water, sand, hair and lycopodium, a fine powder, the spore of club-moss:

> On experimenting with white of Egg, as with the oil – it also shewed the accumulation at the centers of vibration – and as that substance shews the crispations well, it was very beautiful to trace the effect first to accumulation (lens like), then by increasing the force of vibration to see the first wrinkle appear, next quadrangular crispations and finally jets in the air upwards so as to convert the egg into froth.[6]

Clearly delighted by the effects of this experiment Faraday continued joyfully, banging on the vibrating boards and making lots of noise. Ten days later he was working with sand and water on a glass plate, exploring harmonics:

> On putting a candle exactly below this plate and holding a screen of tracing paper an inch above it, the picture given was beautiful. Each heap [of sand] gave a star . . . of light at its focus which twinkled, ie appeared and disappeared with the heap continually as it rose and fell. At the corners . . . a fainter light appeared, and then as the screen was nearer or farther lines of light in 2 or even 4 directions appeared (constant). This was exceedingly beautiful and easily rendered visible to a large Audience.[7]

Faraday always had his audience in his mind as he considered the experiments he was carrying out. While in the midst of his crispation experiments he gave a Friday Discourse 'On the peculiar arrangements assumed by particles lying upon vibrating elastic bodies' – the same paper, according to the *Literary Gazette*, that had been read at the Royal

Society a few weeks earlier.[8] The *Gazette* went on to say, using words with which Faraday may himself have briefed William Jerdan, that the repeat of the paper at the Royal Institution served

> to illustrate the difference between the Royal Society and the Royal Institution in their modes of putting forth scientific truth; and [Faraday's] conviction that everything, whether small or great, originating with the officers of the latter establishment, should be placed as soon as possible in the possession of the members at large.

With a high degree of missionary zeal, Faraday used the Royal Institution as a research centre more for the public good than as a place to serve private or commercial interest. Thus he could say, when resigning with relief from the Admiralty glass experiments in July 1831, and handing six volumes of manuscript notes over to Peter Mark Roget, the Secretary of the Royal Society, that he could not reach the ideal in the search for optically-perfect glass: 'To perfect a manufacture not being a manufacturer is what I am not bold enough to promise.'[9]

The depth and extent of Faraday's crispation experiments bordered on obsession. This line of research appears to have come from nowhere, and, when his interests moved on to other areas, to have evaporated from the core line of his scientific work. But like a chink in a rockface that allows sunlight to fall briefly onto a cavern floor, Faraday's responses to the crispations give us access to an unguarded moment in his life, and reveal a passion known only to his family and perhaps to some of his Sandemanian brethren. With crispations he was dealing with natural effects, rule and pattern that he – and anybody else – could see and repeat. This was not the invisible electricity, nor the secretive meetings and partings of molecules in a retort, but a miniature circus in which kitchen ingredients were the acrobats, a plate of glass or tin the sawdust ring, and Michael Faraday himself the ringmaster, eager to show off nature's tricks:

97. When Much lycopodium is put upon large stretched paper and struck up violently in the air, it often forms clouds in lines or masses involving.
98. Mercury on tin plate being vibrated in sunshine gave very beautiful

effects of reflection ... Perhaps a concave lens might make this a beautiful Lecture room Expt.

99. The travelling of the sun's image on each point was very beautiful and satisfactory.

100. It was pretty to see the reflection of the ceiling disappear as the vibration was induced.

101. Ink and water vibrated in sunshine looked extremely beautiful.

102. Dr Brewster* with me to-day. I shewed him some of the experiments.[10]

With crispations on his mind, Faraday noted how he saw them also in nature. Walking one rainy evening behind a brewer's dray rattling over cobbles and loaded with empty barrels, he noticed how the dray 'rumbled over the stones and the upwards jerks frequently threw the water up into heaps quite of the nature of the crispations'.[11]

Standing by the seashore at Hastings while on holiday with Sarah a fortnight or so later, Faraday realised, and expressed, something of the uses of crispations in nature, showing that they were not just pretty effects, but, like all things in the natural world, signals for something else:

Remarked a peculiar series of ridges produced by action of steady strong wind on water on sandy shore. Wherever the sand was covered by a layer of water too thin to form waves before the wind, yet flowing over the surface as where it was oozing out from above, slight ridges were formed *parallel to the direction of the wind*. These would be two, three, four or more inches long and were continually reciprocating, ie. ascending and descending in succession ... They were not high, but high enough to arrange the sand beneath, which was left lined in this way parallel to the wind's course over very extensive flats ... They are small and require careful looking for, but being once seen they are easily found again. They may serve to indicate how the wind has been during a night, etc. etc, for they are perfectly parallel to its course.[12]

---

* David Brewster (1781–1868), Scottish scientist, a pioneer of optics and editor of the newly published eighteen-volume *Edinburgh Encyclopaedia*.

This is a sharp piece of observation, not extraordinary perhaps for a man such as Faraday – rather what we have come to expect – but an instance of the beautiful connections he would make between the experimental, cloistered areas of his life and the practical application of what he had done or discovered. Revealing a way of telling the direction of the wind the previous night is the kind of 'manufacture' that Faraday was wholeheartedly engaged in, the extrapolation of laboratory discoveries into the interests of general understanding, rather than of commerce and industrial production.

The observation on Hastings beach reveals yet another instance of the wafer-thin line dividing Faraday's responses from those of such painters as J.M.W. Turner or John Martin. Turner's intriguingly titled painting of 1840 *The New Moon, or 'I've lost my boat, you shan't have your hoop'* (Tate, London), in which two children squabble on the Margate sands during an incomparable sunset, has a silent fore- and middle-ground of calmly criss-crossing waves running this way and that. There might also have been minuscule sand-ridges among them, had the painter stooped near enough to see. That Turner was as interested as Faraday in such tiny natural details as the way sand ripples under the outgoing tide is clear from a witness who spotted the painter at the edge of the Thames 'squatting on his heels ... looking down intently into the water ... apparently the object of his interest was the patterns made by the ripples at the edge of the tide'.[13] There are many more tracks on which Faraday and Turner run side by side in their natural interests – the nature of light, of electricity, the power of the wind, weather and sea being among them. On the specific case of the action of waves and the tides the two men are hand in hand in the clarity and depth of their observations. For Faraday laboratory experiment led directly to informed interpretation of the natural world; for Turner observation and experience and pages of sketchbook notes brought him to a personal understanding of the moods and tempers of the sea that could be matched only by experienced seamen.

At the same time that Faraday was completing his crispation experiments at the Royal Institution, Turner's *Life-Boat and Manby Apparatus* (Victoria and Albert Museum, London) and *Caligula's Palace and Bridge* (Tate, London) were hanging in the annual exhibition of the Royal Academy. These paintings depict two opposed moods of the sea – the former a severe storm off Great Yarmouth in which a ship is foundering; the latter a quiet tidal inlet where the sea laps into shallow pools. *Caligula's Palace* evolved from some Byronic idea of the collapse of empire, as rendered through Turner's own verse. *Life-Boat and Manby Apparatus*, by contrast, has as its central subject the deployment of a new and controversial piece of apparatus invented and promoted by Captain George Manby of Great Yarmouth. Manby was, like Faraday and Turner, an obsessive, but unlike those two men he was ruled for many years during the 1820s and thirties by a single idea: the creation of a series of stations around the coasts of Britain and France where life-saving apparatus would be permanently positioned for immediate use when ships foundered offshore. This had for years been Manby's crusade, and although he was dismissed as an arrogant and self-opinionated crank by governments in Britain and France, he was driven to do something about the repeated horror of ships' crews being lost in sight of land because there was no means of reaching them in a storm.

Michael Faraday was one of the minority of people in powerful positions who took notice of Manby and his idea, and helped him to widen public knowledge of it. Overcoming by charm, or perhaps ignoring, Manby's peppery nature, Faraday gave him a platform at a Friday Evening Discourse, on 28 May 1830, to address a Royal Institution audience on 'The means of preserving lives in cases of shipwreck'. The subject of safety at sea was close to Faraday's heart, and indeed the improvement of lighthouses became an active part of his own professional interest when he was appointed Scientific Advisor to Trinity House in 1836. In offering Manby the opportunity to speak at the Royal Institution, Faraday took pains to point out that the Friday Evenings were designed to bring forward 'what may be considered new matter'. He stressed:

> But either a new discovery or an addition to a discovery already made known or a new mode of demonstration or indeed any thing which takes from a subject the character of its being a mere repetition of what has already been made known makes it eligible for our table on these Friday Evenings.[14]

Faraday was prepared to bend the rules here, because Manby's proposals could not truthfully be called 'new matter'. He had been travelling around the country and into France on lecture tours for years proselytising for his apparatus. Faraday recognised the preacher in Manby – his were no longer new ideas, any more than the Gospels were, but their messages had to be preached again and again until they made their impact. Manby responded to Faraday's caution by promising 'experiments that would not be destitute of novelty',[15] including 'the plan lately carried into effect at [Great Yarmouth] . . . whereby lifeboats or other boats can at any time be hauled through the surf without risk, however violent the wind'. It was misleading of Manby to suggest that this idea was in any way new – a government Select Committee report had been published on the Manby Apparatus seven years earlier – but Faraday nevertheless considered the invention important enough for it to be demonstrated in London once more, and he allowed the lecture to go ahead.

Manby was duly encouraged by his reception at the Royal Institution. Early the following year he was taken by the surgeon Thomas Pettigrew to the Royal Society, and he noticed, as he told his patron, the Norfolk banker and botanist Dawson Turner, how the announcement of his name as a visitor attracted murmurs of appreciation, and how 'many came into conversation with me, having been present when I delivered the lecture to the R Institution, which they were pleased to say had afforded so much gratification to all my hearers. They hoped I would allow myself to be proposed as a F.R.S. & offered their names to the testimonial required.'[16] Manby was duly proposed as a Fellow of the Royal Society, and was elected on 12 May 1831.

During the very weeks in which Manby's application for the Fellowship was being considered, Turner's painting, with its full title *Life-Boat and Manby Apparatus going off to a Stranded Vessel making Signal (Blue Lights) of Distress* (Victoria and Albert Museum, London), was on public exhibition in the Royal Academy next door to the Royal Society in Somerset House. Just as Faraday had responded to the importance of Manby's invention, so too did Turner. The upright and highly moral scientist had bent the rules of the Royal Institution to allow Manby to speak; the painter gave the public a visual demonstration of his apparatus of the most dramatic kind. Faraday and Turner came together in their admiration and support of Manby's cause because it chimed directly with a cause that they too shared, the urgent need for the improvement and development of the safety of people at sea. It is worth adding here that the title of Turner's painting is a lecture in itself, a precise description of what is going on, together with instruction in colour coding for the correct use of flares.

Turner and Faraday had many common interests, the nature of the sea being one, the importance of teaching another. They came to know each other well enough for Faraday to give the painter advice on colour formulations and perhaps to discuss painterly renditions of storms at sea and land.[17] They had other things in common, both figurative and abstract. Both had been London lads, brought up in the last years of the eighteenth century in a lowly social class, and had had no formal schooling to speak of. Both had been 'spotted' in their youth by influential men and women and given firm encouragement at a critical moment in their early lives which enabled their genius to flourish – Faraday had this gift from George Riebau, George Dance and Humphry Davy; Turner from the pioneer educationalist Sarah Trimmer, the physician Dr Thomas Monro and perhaps others such as the classical scholar Richard Porson.[18] Both had an unquenchable interest in the effects of the sun, of weather, of light and of the way they aid or alter human perception of the world around. They were both seekers, both restless, both endlessly curious about everything they came across. Both were professionally engaged in making practical improvements to reproduction techniques, Faraday through his interest in lithography and, later, photography; Turner in his employment of legions of engravers and his exploration of the various methods of engraving in disseminating his own imagery. They had Italy in common, a profound love of classicism, and both saw themselves in the European rather than the insular British context – Faraday's correspondences with European scientists were infinitely more productive, encouraging and friendly than most of his contacts with scientists from Britain; Turner wanted his paintings to be judged against the great European masters, Claude, Rubens, Rembrandt, Ruysdael, and he regarded himself as a European artist. And if that is not enough, they also shared a sincere love of poetry and literature, particularly of Byron, Gray, Thomas Moore and Walter Scott.

Exactly how Faraday and Turner met and became acquainted is obscure, but there is one particular link that is so strong that it is possibly the one that brought them together. During the 1830s, and certainly throughout the 1840s, Turner stayed or dined regularly with the family of the physician James Carrick Moore in their various houses in Brook Street, Mayfair; Wonham House, Buckland, Surrey; and at Thames

Ditton.[19] Turner was a charming, good-hearted and long-standing friend of theirs, joining in their family parties, discussing art and travel with them, indulging in extended jokes and charades. He had a vivid nickname within the Moore family circle – they called him 'Mr Avalanche Jenkinson', which amused Turner no end, and fitted snugly with his and the Carrick Moores' vision of him as a painter of natural cataclysm, and with his own characteristic love of disguise, aliases and concealment.[20] All this can be picked up from reading the surviving letters between Turner and Mrs Carrick Moore and her eldest daughter Harriet, who became a distinguished amateur painter under Turner's influence and possibly tuition. Harriet Moore also became a close friend of Michael and Sarah Faraday, and created an important series of watercolours of the interiors of the Royal Institution laboratories and of the Faradays' apartment at 21 Albemarle Street.[21] Although there are other routes through which we know Turner and Faraday met – for example through Charles Hullmandel – the Harriet Moore connection is probably the clearest and most fruitful. It will be explored further in Chapter 23.

What Faraday pioneered in his close personal observation of the minutiae of the motions of the sea and the crispations in the sand at Hastings reached its wider expression not through publication under his name in his lifetime, but through the work of painters and poets. Matthew Arnold referred in a letter of 1849 to the 'calm, earnest look' in Faraday's expression when shown a picture of him taken from a daguerrotype.[22] It may be that Arnold's *Dover Beach* – which was written in 1851 but not published until 1867, and thus had no relevance for Faraday – can serve as a literary reflection of the kind of detached observation that Faraday achieved on Hastings beach:

> Listen! you hear the grating roar
> Of pebbles which the waves draw back, and fling,
> At their return, up the high strand,
> Begin, and cease, and then again begin,
> With tremulous cadence slow, and bring
> The eternal note of sadness in.

When Michael and Sarah Faraday came home from Hastings at the end of July 1831 Michael had scientific matters to attend to that had built up while they were away. William Tierney Clark, the Engineer to the West Middlesex Water Company, had sent him some murky-looking bottles of decayed metal and boiler sludge for analysis. Faraday's clear-cut reply informed Clark that the deposit that was damaging the boiler was copper sulphate, or blue vitriol. By way of gratuitous information, the kind of unexpected extra tuition that brings a subject to life and was to Faraday second nature, Faraday the teacher told Clark the engineer:

> You have in fact been making blue vitriol from the boiler by a process nearly the same as one expressly adopted for that purpose. Plates of copper are made hot in a Fire and then sprinkled with sulphur. Galvanic action has had nothing to do with the decay. Had any galvanic action taken place it would have been to the preservation of the Copper.[23]

This elementary chemistry lesson was duly entered verbatim into the Minutes of the West Middlesex Water Company Board Meeting for 2 August 1831.[24]

Faraday also had duties to attend to at the Woolwich Royal Military Academy. His series of chemistry lectures resumed there on 3 August, and no doubt he ran carefully over his notes and demonstration requirements in the interim. Additionally he fretted about delays in the publication of Moll's response to Babbage's *Decline of Science*. He took the job of printing the pamphlet away from one printer-publisher and gave it to his Sandemanian brother the publisher Thomas Boosey.[25] Babbage's views were so controversial and contemporary that Faraday wanted the shortest possible delay before a reply came out. This was a minor difficulty, but Faraday wrestled with it despite the fact that he now had something very big on his mind.

The six or so months of crispation experiments had amused, entertained and gratified Faraday with the pleasures of natural beauty. They had shown him the rule, regularity and predictability of wavelengths and frequency, and although they had been complex, time-consuming and delicate, requiring much ingenious setting up, they were far less intellectually demanding than many of his other experimental series, and seemed to have had no specific goal that he could, then, define. He was at this time particularly worried not only about his general state of health, which was poor, but also about his memory, whose deficiencies were reaching a new low state. 'My Memory gets worse & worse daily,' he wrote to Richard Phillips in June 1831.[26] It may be that the crispation experiments were a means of giving himself some kind of occupational therapy while not taxing his brain too greatly, before he undertook the next major step in extending human understanding of nature.

CHAPTER 18

And that one Word were Lightning...

The discoveries that Faraday made in science in the 1830s had electricity as their vibrant centre. In this decade Faraday transformed the public's perception of electricity, such as it was, from a novelty with uses limited to attempting to heal the sick or making toys revolve, to a power which would one day light cities or drive ships. During the 1830s, when Britain was shaking off a worn-out mode of government with the Reform Bills, Faraday gave a more enlightened society the rudiments of a radical enlightening science. Over the years 1831 to 1855 he recorded the core and substance of his electrical researches in a series of papers, ultimately numbering forty-five, under the general title *Experimental Researches in Electricity*.

Sometime probably in early August 1831, within weeks of his dumping the optical glass files onto the Royal Society Secretary, Faraday instructed Charles Anderson to forge in the laboratory furnace a ring of soft iron seven-eighths of an inch thick and six inches in external diameter. Having been beaten into its final shape on the anvil, the ring came out of the fire for the last time, shimmered in its furnace heat, and was plunged into the trough of water. In his own time, Faraday then took three lengths of copper wire, each about twenty-four feet long, and wound each round and round one half of the iron ring, with twine and calico insulation, testing the insulation in the water trough as he went. Then he did a second wind on the other side of the ring, this time with a total of about sixty feet of wire. This slow, repetitive task Faraday did for himself; it was calming, meditative and consumed much time in simple, sober, productive, thought-inducing manual work. As he worked, using the same kind of actions that his mother or wife would use when sewing, Faraday was freed to think about what his winding might lead on to.

He had done very little electrical work for ten years, almost to the day. Other scientists – his friends Ampère and Dominique Arago, for example – had continued with the subject and made important discoveries. Faraday, however, had been waylaid by much trivia, and ideas in electricity had lain dormant in his mind. He knew that if a wire coiled around an iron bar was electrified, the iron bar would become a magnet for as long as it had a changing flow of electricity around it. What, then, would happen if the iron bar turned on itself, and became a ring with two separate coils around it, one electrified, the other not? What effect would the thus confused magnetic field have on the state of the second coil? Faraday must have had a hunch that something extraordinary would happen, or he would not have gone to the trouble of having a ring made, with its bespoke tailoring of coils.

On Monday, 29 August 1831 Faraday attached a plate battery to one pair of wire-ends on one side of the ring: 'Will call this side of the ring A.'[1] Using his ten-year-old rotations discovery as the means to aid and abet this new experiment, he then extended the wire ends on the other coil and ran them for about three feet away down the other end of the bench to a small magnetic compass needle: 'This side call B.' Then he connected the current to ring side A.

'Immediately, a sensible effect on needle. It oscillated and settled at last in original position.' But then there was no further movement; how very disappointing . . . but how very interesting. Then he leant over and disconnected the battery from side A. 'On *Breaking* connection of A side with Battery again a disturbance of the needle.' How very extraordinary.

By creating a transient but sensible current in a wire that had no battery connections, in other words a closed loop, Faraday had induced electricity in one place from electricity in another. He had played a neat trick: a current had magnetised an iron ring – but, aha! there was another coil around the corner, and the magnetism had been deceived into making a new current in that. This was a magician's sleight of hand – the spirit

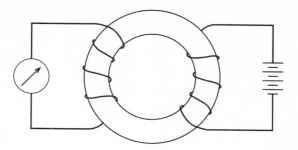

of electricity might reasonably feel aggrieved at the trickery; but there it was, it had been trapped. That was a very good day's work; Faraday had discovered and demonstrated the induction of electricity, the principle of what we now know as the electrical transformer.

He had no more time to carry on experimenting with his battery and ring, for he and Sarah had to get ready to travel back to Hastings, where they had plans to stay for a few weeks at 3 Priors Cottages, three hundred yards from the sea. As was their custom, the couple travelled outside the coach, on top behind the driver, saving money, wrapped up well in their macintoshes, and huddling together like two little mice. It poured with rain, 'but caoutchouc did good duty and we were both warm & dry. I do not think any body ever fares so well on a coach as we do. Others on the outside were wet & cold those within dry but so stewed up that I envied not their lot.'[2]

When the rain let up, Faraday was able to read as the coach swayed along over the Downs. He had a copy of a pamphlet by Richard Phillips, responding to yet another minor scientific wrangle,[3] and feeling generally buoyant despite the weather he burst out laughing from time to time. He wrote to Phillips: 'I fancy my fellow passengers thought I had got something very droll in hand; they sometimes started at my sudden bursts especially when I had the moment before been very grave & serious.'[4]

Phillips's pamphlet was not particularly funny, but what must have been enlivening Faraday's mood on that cold, wet day was his odd little discovery of last Monday. Continuing to Phillips, he remarked: 'I am busy just now again on Electro-Magnetism and I think I have got hold of a good thing but can't say; it may be a weed instead of a fish that after all my labour I may at last pull up.'

Along with their clothes and other personal belongings, the Faradays had packed the iron ring with the coils that Faraday had so painstakingly turned. He knew he was onto something big – a fish, not just a weed; that remark must have been a cautious kind of denial to Phillips. At the beginning of the journey Faraday may also have loaded the coach with some mysterious bundles wrapped in cloth, very heavy, of vaguely cylindrical shape. These were lengths of iron and copper wire, with string, calico and strips of linen for good measure. If he did not bring them with him from London, he would have acquired them from a local Sussex supplier, because in his diary, dated 12 September, when he and Sarah were still in Hastings, he writes that he has 'prepared several coils, helices etc. etc. etc.', and gives the dimensions of these things, and the lengths and kinds of wire he has used. Patently, these were made in or near his holiday cottage in Hastings, quietly wound as Michael and Sarah listened to the distant roll of the sea.

When Faraday had turned the coils – one of 310 feet of copper wire, another of 422 feet of a mixture of copper and iron wire, various spirals, helixes and coils of different sizes, all of which he had clearly marked with the letters A to L – he boxed them and got them ready to bring home. He and Sarah travelled back to London on Wednesday, 21 September, and within two days Faraday was back in his laboratory, looking at his new coils, and carefully contemplating his next move.

By the following Saturday morning, Faraday had dealt with the fall-out on his desk from the three weeks in Hastings. He set his twelve pieces of variously bound wire about him, one by one connected them in different combinations to his battery, and with the compass needle as his indicator began to perform his magic on them. Some connections gave no flicker of the needle, others made it jump and settle back again. Towards the end of the day, after creating electrical surges in one type of coil or another, Faraday took an iron bar enclosed in a wire coil and set it between the poles of a V-shaped magnet, fixed at one end, open at the other like a pair of tweezers. The pair of open ends were magnetised North and South respectively. He connected the wire ends of the coil to the galvanometer and flipped the tweezer open.

The needle flicked. He closed the tweezer again, and once more the needle flicked, this time in the opposite direction. The day had been long, and by now the light was beginning to fade. But the last entry Faraday wrote in the diary for 24 September 1831 is: 'Hence here distinct

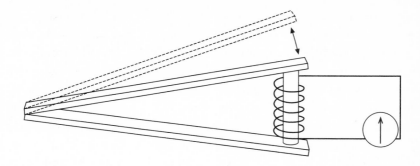

conversion of Magnetism into Electricity. Perhaps might heat a wire red hot here . . .'.[5] By the end of his second day working on his new hunches, he had discovered the principle of electro-magnetic induction.

Now he had more coils to make up, and the following Thursday he wound a total of just over four hundred feet of copper wire around a block of wood, so figuring it that it made two electrically separate insulated coils, each with thirty-four layers of wire, alternating the one with the other. This he called coil M. He put coil M to work two days later – a Saturday again – but that day in the laboratory was frustrating, with no new phenomena to report.

Other business began to intervene – a letter from the Mint had to be dealt with. There had been serious public complaints about the 'effluvia which are emitted from the Works', and could Mr Faraday please come to the Mint to inspect the Refinery

> and to investigate the causes of the complaint . . . and . . . report your opinion as to the construction of the Refinery, & whether some alteration, & contrivance, by giving height to the Chimney & improving the condensing apparatus, may be introduced, so as to destroy the noxious effects of the effluvia, & render the works perfect & free from complaint.[6]

This was the Vivian copper works problem all over again, although this time the inhabitants of Tower Hill and the surroundings were being treated to clouds of acidic gases emitted by the process of extracting silver from alloyed gold.[7] With electro-magnetic matters put to the back of his mind, Faraday took a carriage across London, inspected the works, talked to the men involved, took measurements and readings, and went home to write his report.

It was not until Monday, 17 October, more than two weeks later, that Faraday could get back to his coils in the laboratory. He had been mulling over his experiments, and where to take them next, and had found time to sit quietly to do two more pieces of coil winding. The first was a sixty-one feet four inches length (Faraday was always exact in his notes about the amounts of material used) of copper wire wound round a section of musket barrel 'in a helix passing from end to end and back again (in the same direction), so as to surround the barrel four times'.[8] This was coil N. For the second he made a hollow cylinder of paper – this must have been stiff waxed paper – and around it wound eight long lengths of copper wire backwards and forwards, up and down, carefully checking that the winds were tight, with each one nestling firmly up against the previous one. The first length was twenty-two feet, and as Faraday progressed with the winding the lengths grew longer, the final one being thirty-two feet ten inches. So there, around the paper cylinder, was 220 feet of the fine wire, making a neat little tube one and a half inches in diameter, and about six and a half inches long. This was coil O. Faraday took the eight loose ends of the wires and cleaned them and bound them together at one end of the cylinder, and did the same at the other end with the other eight loose wires.

On the Monday morning, he picked up coil O and turned it over in his hands. He took two long copper wires and connected them to the bundled ends. Then he attached these to the two terminals of his galvanometer. He found a cylindrical bar magnet, three-quarters of an inch in diameter, thin enough to fit snugly into the coil cylinder. He surely had a suspicion – or perhaps a hope – of what might happen next, for his laboratory notes clearly express the short, dramatic pause before the great moment came. These are Michael Faraday's words:

. . . then a cylindrical bar magnet ¾ inch in diameter and 8½ inches in length had one end just inserted into the end of the helix cylinder – then it was quickly thrust in the whole length and *the galvanometer* needle moved – then pulled out and again the *needle moved but* in the opposite direction. This effect was repeated every time the magnet was put in or out and therefore a wave of Electricity was so

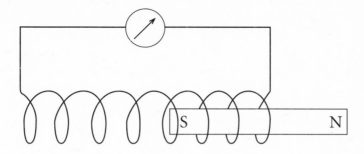

produced from *mere approximation of a magnet* and not from its formation *in situ*.[9]

That was the moment when the first electrical generator was made, and when a controlled alternating current flowed along a circuit for the first time. In Michael Faraday's shadowy laboratory, the Age of Steam was on notice to quit.

Across five more days up to 4 November, Faraday continued his elec-tro-magnetic experiments, most effectively by showing that a copper disc, spinning between the poles of a magnet, produced a constant current that could be picked up by terminals set at the edge and the centre of the disc. But in only four days in the laboratory, and about the same length of time winding coils, Faraday had already discovered the basic principles of the production of alternating current electricity.

He then settled down to write the notes up. This was, as he knew when he began the electrical work, the watershed in his life and in world science. Some inkling of this can be deduced from the way Faraday set his electrical notes in his laboratory diary. By now he was onto his second volume, in which he had already written his crispation notes. These had been numbered in paragraphs 1 to 147; in the first volume, started eleven years earlier, he had done some sporadic paragraph numbering, although this did not amount to any lengthy sequences. With his first paragraph of electrical notes, however, Faraday did not follow on from the crisp-ations by starting at 148, but began again on 29 August 1831 at number 1, 'Expts. on the production of Electricity from Magnetism, etc. etc.' Although he started the numbering system at number 1 again in August 1832, thereafter, until the end of his working life, he continued the same sequence, ultimately reaching 16,041 when he wrote his last laboratory note in the seventh volume on 6 March 1860. The experiments Faraday made before 29 August 1831 were done in the Age of Steam; those after that date were made in the new Age of Electricity, 29 August 1831 being Day One.

The importance of these discoveries was such that Faraday wanted the Royal Society to be the first to hear about them, so he wrote them up in the form of a paper to be deposited for reading by or in front of a group of the Society's Fellows. The act of depositing a paper at the Society established a date, and gave no doubt as to who the discoverer of the new facts was. Faraday submitted his paper, 'Experimental Researches in Electricity', at Somerset House on 24 November, and then went directly to the south coast to recuperate after the efforts of the past two months. This time he and Sarah went to Brighton. 'We are here to refresh,' he wrote to Richard Phillips. 'I have been working and writing a paper & that always knocks me up in health but now I feel well again and able to pursue my subject and now I will tell you what it is about.'[10] He went on to describe to Phillips the four section headings of his Royal Society paper, in which the first principles of electricity were set out publicly for the first time.[11]

By 10 December the Faradays were home again, and Michael, determined to widen scientific awareness of his electrical adventures, wrote to J.N.P. Hachette in Paris to tell him of the discoveries.[12] Hachette was greatly excited, and gave the letter to Arago, the Secretary of the Institut de France, who read it out at its 26 December meeting. What a mistake – the news got straight into the French press, the magazine *Le Lycée* publishing a report of the paper three days later, followed by a second article on 1 January 1832. Already controversy was in the air, as the second *Lycée* article maintained that French scientists had carried out Faraday's experiments first. A translation of the first *Lycée* article appeared in the London paper the *Morning Advertiser*, and this temporarily settled the controversy in Faraday's favour, but three months later it seemed as if the whole ghastly business of the electro-magnetic rotations affair of 1821 was about to be repeated. Then, Faraday, young and unknown, had been accused by Humphry Davy and others of plagiarising a theory of William Wollaston's and putting it forward as his own. This time, although there was no doubt now of Faraday's originality and greatness, his good friend William Jerdan made things worse by implying in a misleading article that the Italian scientists Leopoldo Nobili and Vincenzio Antinori had discovered electro-magnetic induction first, and that 'the researches of Mr Faraday ... were rapidly tending to the same discovery'.[13]

The truth of the matter was that, as Faraday put it, 'they are my own experiments which having gone first to Paris & then to Italy have been repeated & studied by Signori Nobili and Antinori'. At the root of the problem was the Italian journal *Antologia*, which published Nobili and Antinori's paper in an issue back-dated to November 1831, despite the fact that the Italian scientists' article, in which Faraday's priority was properly acknowledged, was itself dated January 1832.[14] This misunderstanding was the price Faraday had to pay for his openness and determination, rooted in his religious principles, to broadcast the news of his discoveries as soon as he reasonably could, for the benefit of all. Had he been driven to claim patent or what we now call 'intellectual property' rights, he might have been more circumspect. The security of a new idea or system of reasoning deposited with the Royal Society could not be assured if its own author then went and told a friend on the continent. A further dimension to the difficulty was that the events in Paris compromised Faraday's relations with the Royal Society, which never published material that had been published elsewhere in any form.

Faraday, roused to indignant anger at the apparent escape of his discovery, urged Jerdan to put the matter right:

Excuse my troubling you with this letter, but I never took more pains to be quite independent of other persons than in the present investigation; and I have never been more annoyed about any paper than the present by the variety of circumstances which have arisen seeming to imply that I had been anticipated.

What is clear from Faraday's annoyance is that electrical production was the hot scientific subject of the moment. Until he had made his discovery, and its technique was flashed across the scientific world, the only ways of producing a steady stream of electrical current were by means of a voltaic battery, by a hand-cranked static electricity machine, or through storage as static electricity in Leyden jars. Methods had been adopted of storing lightning discharge in Leyden jars, but that technique was cumbersome and dangerous, and prone to failure. A steady, reliable and prolonged voltage was now becoming an essential requirement in laboratories and manufactories, as experiments and industrial processes such as electrolysis, for example for the production of silver plate, depended upon it. It is very significant that in his experimental notes during the course of his September and October electrical work Faraday remarked with some pleasure on the quality of his battery, saying that the 'discharge of the battery between charcoal points was very powerful at the first and very good at the conclusion'.[15]

Having neatly created the foundations of the electrical industry over a few days' work in the autumn of 1831, Faraday extended the net of his ideas more widely, to explore the possibilities of electricity being generated by using that infinitely greater magnetic field, the earth itself. He got his first results on Boxing Day 1831 in the laboratory, when he made a wide loop of eight feet of copper bell-wire, attached the ends to the galvanometer, and flipped it backwards and forwards in the air. In doing so it cut through the earth's magnetic field, and induced electricity flowed in a measurable quantity. '*Beautiful*', he wrote in his laboratory diary.[16] Faraday then looked about for a way to extend the experiment onto a global scale, to see if the movement of the earth itself, spinning on its axis, could induce electricity in a wire running in a north–south direction. There seemed to be nothing to interrupt the inexorable step of his logic, except an acceptable answer to his experimental question.

Judging that the cleanest connection to the earth would be through water, Faraday decided that the Round Pond in Kensington Gardens was the best place to set up his equipment, because it had an artificial stucco bottom, was relatively free of mud, and was fed by a filtered public water supply.[17] He had first to obtain royal permission for the experiment to take place there, and applied through the King's brother, the Royal Society's new President the Duke of Sussex. By 10 January all the permissions had been cleared, and with the help of the garden staff Faraday attached each end of a coil of copper wire 480 feet long to a pair of large copper plates, and sank these to the bottom of the pond, one at the north end, the other at the south. Thus the coil, running along the pond's edge, was lying roughly north–south. Although the galvanometer needle flicked enticingly, Faraday realised that the electricity generated came through what he referred to as '*ordinary causes*', and was not the result of the earth's movement.

Faraday was his own severest critic, examining each and every result like an inquisitor. Lesser experimental scientists might have been sufficiently overwhelmed by an apparent success to have leapt to the conclusion that, yes, this electrical flow was indeed caused by the rotating earth. Not Faraday; he packed up his copper plates and wires, put the galvanometer into its box, thanked the staff for their help and retreated thoughtfully to the Royal Institution. But two days later he was out again, this time down to Waterloo Bridge in the morning when the tide was ebbing, to see if moving water had a better effect. With a roll of nearly a thousand feet of copper wire he set up the equipment in much the same manner as at the Round Pond, with two terminals being lowered into the river at the north and south ends of the bridge. Curious people gathered. Faraday noticed that there was an electrical flow and took readings. He went away to write letters at his desk, leaving his assistant Thomas Pearsall in charge of the equipment. That evening Faraday's Bakerian Lecture on Terrestrial Magneto-Electric Induction was due to be read at the Royal Society, but clearly the Waterloo Bridge experiment needed his presence, so writing to a Brighton friend Edward Hawkins that day, Faraday told him, 'I cannot be at the RS tonight,'[18] without saying why.

At half past six, when Fellows of the Royal Society were listening closely to Faraday's words being read out on his behalf, the man himself was leaning over the parapet of Waterloo Bridge in the drizzle, looking down into the murky depths. The tide was now running back upstream, 'faster than in the morning', some watermen told him.[19] There were hopeful flickers of the needle, and a certain amount of terse cross-questioning went on between Faraday and Pearsall, because the two men seemed to differ about which way the electric current had been flowing in the morning: 'Mr Pearsall who was present says they are as they were in the morning. My morning note says the reverse, but now what is the direction.'[20]

Faraday wanted to know how the sewers flowed, to see if they were affecting the readings. The watermen told him that in the evening rising tide 'the liquor in the sewers was pushed back by the tide, and that the water at the middle and sides was quite alike. In the ebb (morning) they said the middle water was the purest.'[21]

The results were inconclusive: 'I must consider further whether any source could exist in the river independent of magneto-electric induction.'[22] Despite coming back again the next day, Faraday did not get any positive results, and could not conclusively show that the earth's rotation could generate electrical current in a wire. It was a step too far for experimental science of the day, although the theory was subsequently shown to be correct. Faraday would simply not give up on devising a practical proof of a theory where he saw a glimmer of a possibility of doing so; nothing would keep this irrepressible man down. The Channel Tunnel did not come soon enough for Michael Faraday, who was now convinced that

> if a line be imagined passing from Dover to Calais through the sea, and returning through the land, beneath the water, to Dover, it traces out a circuit of conducting matter one part of which, when the water is moving up or down the channel, is cutting the magnetic curves of the earth, whilst the other is relatively at rest ... There is every reason to believe that currents do run in the general direction of the circuit described, either one way or the other, according as the passage of the waters is up or down the Channel.[23]

Crucial though the establishment of priority through a published account was, Faraday could reach his audience most effectively through his public lectures at the Royal Institution. Despite the misunderstanding over the date of Nobili and Antinori's experiments, Faraday had established his priority in induction and electro-magnetism at the Royal Society when his paper was read there in late November 1831, and on terrestrial magneto-electric induction on 12 January 1832. He chose not to discuss the experiments immediately before his home audience on a Friday Evening at the Royal Institution. Instead, at the height of his own personal excitement about his electro-magnetic discoveries that would soon reshape the world, he announced at the Royal Institution on 27 January that the following week he would himself be speaking on the reproductive powers of flatworms.

The new-year session at the Royal Institution began auspiciously, as the *Literary Gazette* reported: 'The crowded state of the library and theatre on the first night testifies that the "Friday evening meetings" have not

lost that attraction for which they have been so long and so justly celebrated.'[24] There were crowds for Faraday's Discourse on the flatworms,
and when he had finished his talk he buttonholed the members of the
Institution one by one and urged them to contribute 'as much as possible
to the intellectual pleasure of the weekly meetings',[25] meaning, presumably, that he wanted them to ask intelligent questions, get involved in
conversation in the Library afterwards, stay on for tea, contribute objects
to the Library Table display, and so on.

This appeal had the additional effect of raising excitement for Faraday's
first Discourse on electricity since making his discoveries, 'On recent
experimental investigations relative to volta-electric and magneto-electric
induction', on 17 February 1832. The week before, the audience had been
addressed by Dr William Ritchie on the voltaic pile, so when Faraday
took the floor the subject was already warm. He lifted up the iron ring
with the coils wrapped round it, with which he had first demonstrated
induction, and described how he had made it and why; he displayed
some of the other coils and magnets, and showed the flicking needle of
the galvanometer, revealing that a current flowed when a circuit was
made and broken; and he showed the experiment, which has since become
a classic – the thrusting of a magnet into a cylinder wrapped round with
a coil, and the consequent electrical flow. In the Discourse Faraday went
one by one through the processes he had adopted, and with the help of
some hapless frogs sacrificed convulsively in the interests of scientific
education, revealed the new secrets of electricity to a lay audience for
the first time.

Electricity continued to engage Faraday in the laboratory and at his
writing desk for much of the decade, but being aware of the speed at
which electrical knowledge was developing across Europe, and knowing
that he would sooner or later have his mind taken off the subject by
other research and administrative responsibilities, he sent a sealed note
in March 1832 to John Children, the Secretary of the Royal Society, to
be kept in the Society's safe. The practice of sending sealed notes with
unpublished or incomplete scientific ideas – generally hunches – to the
Royal Society was a means for scientists to put down a marker on a
particular idea as an aid in establishing priority. Faraday's embryonic
proposal, set out in his sealed note, was that magnetic action and electrical
flow are progressive, and require time. He suggested that the diffusion

of these forces travelled like waves through water, comparing them to the way light and sound travel. This is his crispation experiments translated into another, abstract, medium: he writes of a 'wave' of electricity in his laboratory diary in August 1831.[26] In linking the physical and temporal properties of light, sound, electricity and magnetism, Faraday is hammering a nail into the coffin of the old Newtonian physics, in which light was considered to be formed of corpuscles travelling through space.

The search for clear and complete answers to the question of electricity was a vocation for Faraday, who came to see electricity as the highest of God's powers manifest on earth, and the highest power known to man.[27] He was willingly being led by his work, and writing to Øersted in September 1832 he told him of the progress of his experiments, adding, 'I do not know where they may conduct me but I hope and believe they will ultimately prove of some interest.'[28]

The new impetus that Faraday's discoveries had given to the world of science, and to the wider world, demanded a new language to ease their flow out of the laboratory and into everyday speech. This need became particularly pronounced as Faraday and others continued to describe and demonstrate electricity in lectures: a phrase such as 'electrical fluid', even though it 'flowed' and had 'current', could no longer carry the burden of meaning that Faraday's discoveries were placing upon it, and was obsolete. In one of the first recorded instances of a backlash against technical jargon of the type that was to bedevil the late twentieth century, Faraday wrote to Revd William Whewell at Trinity College, Cambridge in February 1831 raising just that problem – the need for words for these new things. Whewell was an open, helpful scholar, generous with his time and ideas, the ideal confidant for Faraday. Maria Edgeworth described him to perfection: 'Fair handsome most agreeable quick conversation shining playfully with science and literature – and free from all testiness and susceptibility of some of the scientific grandees – vide Babbage par excellence.'[29]

The question that Faraday had for him would challenge Whewell's powers of free-thinking, and indeed the playfulness of his language:

I cannot help thinking it a most unfortunate thing that men who as experimentalists & philosophers are the most fitted to advance the general cause of science & knowledge should by the promulgation of their own theoretical views under the form of nomenclature notation or scale actually retard its progress – It would not be of so much consequence if it was only theory & hypothesis which they thus treated but they put facts or the current coin of science into the same limited circulation when they describe them in such a way that the initiated only can read them.[30]

Faraday well knew the passage in the Bible – Genesis 2.19–20 – in which Adam named the animals, thus putting dangers into context and fear of the unknown into perspective. To give names to the various functions, tenses, participles, conjunctions and other parts of speech of electricity was the essential next step, releasing the power of this natural force from latter-day alchemists, or whatever other silent priestly caste might arise, before they got their hands on it. With their truly public duty in the forefront of their minds, the non-conformist Christian and the deeply-established Anglican churchman forged a language for electricity that caught on rapidly and is with us today, now too deep-rooted to be superseded.

Faraday first came to Whewell with some words that he had invented but which he remained dubious about – 'exode', 'zetode', 'zetexode', and even 'eastode' and 'westode', for the terminals of a battery.[31] Whewell in his reply suggested 'anode' and 'cathode'; and these names happily remain. In creating a new terminology for the newly harnessed natural power, Faraday and Whewell were going back to the crucible of Western language, ancient Greek. 'I may mention . . . that *anodos* and *cathodos* are good genuine Greek words,' Whewell assured Faraday, 'and not compounds coined for the purpose . . . Upon the whole I think anode and cathode much the best.'[32] Nevertheless, Faraday was at first sceptical about 'anode' and 'cathode', and used 'dexiode' and 'skaiode' – from the Greek for right and left – in the first published edition of his seventh series of *Experimental Researches in Electricity* (1834), telling Whewell, 'I like Anode & Cathode better as to sound but all to whom I have shewn them have supposed at first that by *Anode* I meant *No way*.'[33]

Faraday was given some wonderfully clear instruction in Greek from Whewell, and he relished the correspondence, which was in its own way as creative as the discovery of the laws of electricity themselves. An animal is merely a beast without its name. Whewell was an essential expert witness for Faraday:

As to the objection to *anode* I do not think it is worth hesitating about. *Anodos* and *cathodos* do really mean in Greek *a way up* and *a way down*; and *anodos* does not mean, and cannot mean, according to the analogy of the Greek language *no way*. It is true that the prefix *an* put before *adjectives* beginning with a vowel, gives a negative signification, but not to substantives, except through the medium of adjectives. *Anarchos* means without government, and hence *anarchia, anarchy*, means the absence of government: but *anodos* does not and cannot mean the absence of way . . . The notion of *anodos* meaning *no way* could only suggest itself to persons unfamiliar with Greek . . .[34]

This gave Faraday the support he needed in his linguistic arguments at the Royal Institution. He wrote to Whewell:

I had some hot objections made to [your nomenclature] here and found myself very much in the condition of the man with his son and Ass who tried to please every body; but when I held up the shield of your authority it was wonderful to observe how the tone of objection melted away.[35]

With Whewell's help, the language of electricity kept pace with the steady progress of Faraday's researches. When Faraday had a problem of expression of a new idea, Whewell would generally reply by return of post with a suggestion. Thus, 'ion' and 'dielectric' came to Faraday's aid, and, much later in their correspondence, 'diamagnetic' and 'paramagnetic', and words with English roots such as 'inducteity', and a suggestion that 'machine electricity', that is static electricity, be named henceforth 'Franklinic', in honour of Benjamin Franklin's achievements in the eighteenth century.[36] That name, in the event, did not stick.

To Faraday a good name had not only to look right in print, but also to sound right; he indeed would be at the front line of its usage, the first to spin the word before the public. He tolerated the coinage of the word 'scientist' to describe his profession – this had first come into use at the meeting of the embryonic British Association for the Advancement of Science in York in 1831 – but wanted Whewell to suggest an alternative to the French word '*physicien*'. Faraday disliked 'physicist' on aural grounds: '. . . "physicist" is both to my mouth & ears so awkward that I think I shall never be able to use it. The equivalent of three separate sounds in *s* in one word is too much.'[37] In this case Whewell does not appear to have come up with an alternative, but he was aware of the importance of the task he was engaged on with Faraday:

> Such a coinage [of words] has always taken place at the great epochs of discovery; like the medals that are struck at the beginning of a new reign:– or rather like the change of currency produced by the accession of a new sovereign; for their value and influence consists in their coming into common circulation.[38]

The importance of clarity of meaning for Faraday, his understanding of the power of the right word, was a quality that had its roots and expression not only in the Bible, but further in his love of poetry. We have seen how Byron's *Childe Harold* entranced him, as did Thomas Moore's *Lalla Rookh*, and Gray's 'Elegy',[39] and he was also engaged by Laurence Sterne's wordplay.[40] His own facility as a letter writer and diarist is further expression of his literary side, as is his enjoyment of his duties as a teacher and showman. In *Childe Harold* there is a verse which Faraday must have known, and which might have touched his heart both in its relevance to his own feelings and as a poetic expression of the most powerful force in nature:

> Could I embody and unbosom now
> That which is most within me, – could I wreak
> My thoughts upon expression, and thus throw
> Soul, heart, mind, passions, feelings strong or weak,
> All that I would have sought, and all I seek,
> Bear, know, feel, and yet breathe – into *one* word,
> And that one word were lightning, I would speak;
> But as it is, I live and die unheard,
> With a most voiceless thought, sheathing it as a sword.[41]

Research into electricity filled Faraday with eagerness and delight. He searched for ways to reverse the electrical process: having induced new electricity in an empty circuit, he discovered the means by which a magnet itself could produce a visible spark. This perturbed one member of an audience in Oxford when Faraday was demonstrating the production of a spark from a magnet in 1832. A dean of the university shook his head with sorrow when the process of electro-magnetic induction was briefly explained to him: 'I am sorry for it,' he said as he walked away. '*Indeed* I am sorry for it; it is putting new arms into the hands of the incendiaries.'[42]

Faraday was in Oxford in June 1832 to attend the second meeting of the British Association for the Advancement of Science and, as part of the ceremonial university circus surrounding the meeting, to receive the honorary degree of Doctor of Civil Law. There is an irony in the fact that Faraday was being honoured by a university that only admitted students who professed to be members of the Church of England, and would not have admitted him as a student because he was a non-conformist. There was a double irony for the apolitical Faraday in that his degree, and those of three other non-conformist scientists, David Brewster, Robert Brown and John Dalton, was a political gesture, a public demonstration of the university taking a further inclusive step by honouring dissenters.[43]

Now Faraday was the hunter after the fox, though he would not have seen it quite like that. Day after day in the middle years of the 1830s he was down in the basement laboratory attending to one aspect of the phenomenon of electricity or another. According to the evidence of his laboratory diary he worked in bursts of activity, speeded and slackened by the pressures of other Royal Institution activities. Although there are indications that he might write up one or two days' work under the heading of one date, thus suggesting that that day was apparently fuller than the ones preceding it, the general pattern of the entries reveals a smooth continuity of work being picked up in the morning from apparatus and materials left on the bench at night. There were late nights and early mornings, as on 18/19 September 1833, when Faraday was working on the equivalents of elements evolved in electrolysis: 'Last night at 9 o.clk. P.M. I marked the place where the gas stood in the tube *a* under water. At 10 o'clk A.M. to-day, on examining, it had risen about a third of an inch; the effect is still going on slowly.'[44]

One senses from the diaries that Faraday is itching to reveal in a Discourse what he has just found – that certainly became clear during the crispation experiments of 1831, and it comes across also in his correspondence. He is fully aware of his duties as an experimental scientist, and indeed of the privilege of his position. A few weeks after his induction discoveries he observed to George Airy, then the Director of the Cambridge Observatory:

> ... I have been convinced by long experience that if I wish to be respectable as a scientific man it must be by devoting myself to the unremitting pursuit of one or two branches only; making up by industry what is wanting in force. I will not pretend to tell you what I think I have done in Magneto-electricity it would be too long a story but I do hope it will please philosophers & will be found to be entirely New.[45]

Faraday could not evade his sense of duty, because it brought him such enjoyment and satisfaction. Nor would he, because duty and sacrifice had been rubbed into him from the Sandemanian pulpit throughout his sensible life. He had an engine at both ends, pulling from the front and pushing from the back. And now, in 1833, the cornucopia of natural knowledge was spilling over for him, as he told the astronomer John Lubbock:

> My matter ... overflows[;] the doors that open before me are immeasurable. I cannot tell to what great things they may lead and I have worked neglecting every thing else for the purpose. I do not know whether Mathematical are like Experimental labours if they are you will have an idea of my toil but at the same time of my pleasure.[46]

CHAPTER 19

Connexions

Faraday was not being entirely frank when he claimed to Lubbock that he was neglecting everything else for his electrical experiments.[1] He might have preferred that to be the case, but he was still being bothered by Admiralty work, having been obliged in November 1832 to set his induction experiments aside to analyse thirty-two samples of adulterated oatmeal sent from a convict ship anchored in the Thames.[2] The day he wrote to Lubbock he had been testing some fruit spirit for Granville Penn of the War Department, perhaps for the purpose of developing an economic supply of alcohol for the troops,[3] and three days later he sent John Gage, the Director of the Society of Antiquaries, an analysis of a sample of ferruginous sandy clay.[4] William Richard Hamilton, recently appointed Treasurer of the Royal Institution, added his own ounce of extra burden for Faraday when he sent him a lump of metal for analysis – it turned out to be 'true bronze being compounded of copper & tin'. In his reply to Hamilton Faraday revealed something of his eagerness to get back to electricity by underlining his final paragraph: 'I found that if I did not contrive to give you an account of these matters to day I should probably be unable to do so for two or three weeks.'[5] Faraday's heart, now, was in electricity, and these were distractions he did not need, but dealt with anyway.

While he was in the midst of the experiments, Faraday was invited to speak in honour of Joseph Priestley (1733–1804), at a meeting at King's College, London on 23 March 1833 to mark the centenary of Priestley's birth. Faraday feigned bemusement at why it was that he had been asked to address the meeting, rather than 'my superior, Mr Brande, who is not here to represent the Royal Institution'. Whether it was a source of mild embarrassment or not, the fact remained that it was now Faraday, and not his titular superior Brande, whose name was connected in the scientific world as well as the public eye with the prosperity of the Royal Institution;[6] and who would now come to mind as the leader of the scientific world in London, as Davy's had before him. Faraday had that January been given the new Chair of Fullerian Professor of Chemistry at the Royal Institution, a post founded through an endowment of £3333.6s.8d by John Fuller, additional to the money he was already giving for the Fuller Medal. The appointment was marked by much praise of Faraday in the press – 'we rejoice,' said the *Literary Gazette*, 'Palmam qui meruit ferat'.[7] Faraday had come to the meeting to praise Priestley's open-mindedness, and his willingness to change his views 'as he saw nature change before him'. Faraday commended in Priestley

... that freedom of mind, and ... that independence of dogma and of preconceived notions, by which men are so often bowed down and carried forward from fallacy to fallacy, their eyes not being opened to see what that fallacy is ... I am very anxious at this time to exhort you all, – as I trust you all are pursuers of science, – to attend to these things; for Dr Priestley made his great discoveries mainly in consequence of his having a mind which could be easily moved from what it had held to the reception of new thoughts and notions; and I will venture to say that all his discoveries followed from the facility with which he could leave a preconceived idea.[8]

In describing Priestley's qualities, Faraday was also outlining how he tried to lead his own scientific life. Priestley was a hero for the current generation of scientists, as Faraday made clear. In one of his last diary entries for the centenary year, Faraday noted a remark that suggests that he and his friends had been discussing in conversation the particular contributions that Priestley had made to the understanding of electricity. Attributing the idea to Richard Phillips, Faraday observed – incorrectly, for others had preceded Priestley – 'Priestley was probably the first who put forth the view that Electricity is an important agent between mind and body in the animal system.'[9] The nature of animal electricity was one of the leading electrical issues of the day, and one of the aspects of the subject that Faraday had resolved in work on 'the identity of electricities', published in 1833, in which he showed that the different kinds of electricity – voltaic, static, animal, induced – were one and the same.[10]

John Children also eulogised Priestley at this time, and suggested that Priestley would have felt great pride at the progress that had been made in electricity, 'his darling science'.[11] It was Priestley's prescience that so impressed Faraday, Children and others, for in his *History and Present State of Electricity* (1767) he had foreseen that

by pursuing this new light, the bounds of natural science may possibly be extended beyond what we can now form an idea of – new worlds may open to our view, and the discoveries of Sir Isaac Newton himself and all his contemporaries be eclipsed by the labours of a new set of philosophers in this new field of speculation.[12]

Another of Priestley's prophecies concerned the need for philosophers to 'begin to subdivide themselves, and enter into smaller combinations',[13] a practice which, by the 1830s, was becoming the norm.

The great achievement that followed from Faraday's discovery of electro-magnetic induction was his defining of the laws of electrolysis, which later became known as 'Faraday's Laws'. The nature of the chemical actions of electricity had been fruitfully explored by Humphry Davy, but it was not until a steady and reliable current could be created through induction that electrolysis could be used effectively in industry. Faraday's two laws, ranked as 'among the most accurate generalizations in science',[14] set out that 'chemical action or decomposing power is exactly proportional to the quantity of electricity that passes', and 'electrochemical equivalents coincide and are the same with ordinary chemical equivalents'.[15] The amount of electricity required to release one gram equivalent of any element from its solution came later to be called one 'faraday'. These discoveries laid the foundations of the electro-chemical industry, of which electroplating, with its wide applications in manufacturing from the silverplating of teaspoons to the strengthening of steel, was perhaps the first and most widely visible and influential result. It is ironic that through Faraday's scientific endeavour the alchemist's dream was at last being realised – silver and gold could now, to all appearances, be made out of base metal.

When writing about a painter or a sculptor, we usually find ourselves having to wait outside the studio. Only when the work is produced and exhibited can we fall finally under its spell, and gradually determine its place in the artist's cycle, and in the wider cultural world, from where and when it is we stand. There is certainly much to be gained from watching the artist at work – film of Jackson Pollock making his drip paintings reveals his intensity, controlled energy and precision; film of Picasso assembling a figure of a woman out of terracotta guttering, some clay pipe and a branch torn off there and then from a bush outside the studio, is poignant testimony to his creativity and humility. Film of Caravaggio or Turner in front of their canvases might have been quite as revealing. In the end, however, the work is the thing.

With a research scientist it is the other way about. The creativity and invention comes in the process of laboratory work and demonstration, and if we are to judge a scientist's artistry fully it must be by watching him or her in the laboratory with its retorts, tubes and compounds, timing, weighing and testing; or in front of a monitor interpreting the brainwaves and scans of a willing subject. The object of the scientist's interest – electrolysis, reactivity, brainwaves or whatever it may be – goes on in nature willy-nilly; an artist's creativity, however, does not. The scientist is the creative investigator; the artist the creator.

There is of course no film of Faraday at work, but his extensive laboratory diaries and written expositions have the feel of early radio broadcasts or film soundtracks, to the extent that in reading them we can sense an artist at work, and can understand the enfolding drama of the processes. The art form that Faraday at work approaches most directly is theatre or cinema, with the laboratory itself providing the stage set. When he writes his laboratory diary he does so in numbered paragraphs, a method Ruskin came to adopt in *Modern Painters* (1843–60), and one which approximates to the film director's 'takes' as production progresses. Here is Faraday preparing part of his processes of research into electro-chemical decomposition; that is, the breaking down by an electrical current flow of, in this case, a solution of sodium sulphate in water into acid and alkali. Before he starts he places the current-carrying wires onto two separate pieces of tin foil on a glass plate, which is itself placed over, but raised above, a piece of white paper 'so that shadows may not interfere'. Then he twists two short pieces of platinum wire to bridge the gaps between the live tin foil and pieces of litmus and turmeric paper – to test for acid and alkali respectively – joined edge to edge and both dampened with the sodium sulphate solution. On charging the wires by turning the laboratory's electrostatic machine, Faraday observes the litmus paper turning red, indicating acid at the positive pole, the turmeric turning brown, announcing alkali at the negative. This is how he describes the next step:

The pieces of litmus and turmeric paper were *now* placed each upon a separate piece of glass, and connected by an insulating string four feet long, moistened in the same solution of sulphate of soda; the terminal decomposing wire points were placed on the papers as before. On working the machine, the same evolution of acid and alkali appeared as in the former instance, and with equal readiness, notwithstanding that the places of their appearance were four feet apart from each other.

Then Faraday applies the crucial test of extreme distance:

Finally a piece of string seventy feet long, was used. It was insulated in the air by suspenders of silk, so that the electricity passed through its entire length: decomposition took place exactly, as in the former cases, alkali and acid appearing at the two extremities in their proper places.

With his inventive twists of platinum wire – paperclip sculptures before paperclips were invented – the tin foil, the glass sheet, the long then longer solution-soaked string, Faraday is solving his practical problems as he goes along, thinking laterally and creatively, flying as artists might. His genius was to devise equipment which caused an invisible natural process to reveal *itself* by unwittingly triggering the one signal that the equipment was designed to give – the contrivance behind the Davy Lamp, electro-magnetic rotations and electrical induction are earlier examples of the same phenomenon. Faraday's final amendment to the apparatus, a seventy-foot length of wet string festooned from the laboratory ceiling in zigzags on silk lines, is a bizarre but brilliant way of proving beyond doubt that electro-chemical decomposition acts spontaneously.

The paragraphs quoted above come from Faraday's paper on electro-chemical decomposition, which he first read at the meeting of the British Association for the Advancement of Science in Cambridge in June 1833. One of the people in the audience was the decaying poet Samuel Taylor Coleridge, then in his early sixties. 'I was exceedingly pleased with Faraday,' he noted afterwards, 'he seemed to me to have the true temperament of Genius – that carrying on of the spring and freshness of youthful nay boyish, feelings, into the mature strength of manhood.'[16]

There is a wistfulness about this observation, that may have taken the fat, old, opium-raddled genius back to his youth in Ottery St Mary, or to his own impassioned lecture-performances at the Royal Institution in 1808. Where Faraday was blazing trails in science, Coleridge, through a fertile combination of genius and half-knowledge, muddied ponds. When he had himself been forty-two years old, as Faraday was now, Coleridge had been racked by his addiction to opium, on the verge of suicide and practically friendless, his life apparently in ruins.[17] Watching Faraday in action, what Coleridge could see was a popular, successful and rather beautiful man, who moved before his audience like a dancer, and looked at least ten years younger than his age, bright, capable, healthy and driven. This was the man that Coleridge might have been.

Four hundred miles to the north, Thomas Carlyle, a philosopher a few years younger than Faraday and no friend of Coleridge, defined how science – and art, literature, government, society and practically everything else – had changed in the new 'Age of Machinery', as he called it. In his article 'Signs of the Times', published in 1829 in the *Edinburgh Review*, Carlyle wrote of the waning of the individual in the face of introduced machinery, collectivisation and the creation of institutes: 'society, in short, is fast falling to pieces'. He made a pungent remark about contemporary science and its practice:

No Newton, by silent meditation, now discovers the system of the world from the falling of an apple; but some quite other than Newton stands in his Museum, his Scientific Institution, and behind whole batteries of retorts, digesters, and galvanic piles, imperatively 'interrogates Nature', – who, however, shows no haste to answer.[18]

There is a vivid contrast here between Coleridge's delight at experiencing Faraday in full flow, and Carlyle's funereal regret at the passing of the tick-tock system of society and the universe. Carlyle's remarks do, however, put a finger on the public's perception of Faraday and his practice of experimenting with complex equipment in private. Working in the background and sending forth pronouncements in the forms of scientific papers or discourses, Faraday was bound one day to fall victim to charges of distance and aloofness. As his fame reached its long, high plateau in the mid-1830s he was also, inevitably, challenged and attacked by other scientists – particularly those, such as William Henry and William Sturgeon, who called themselves 'electricians' – who envied his platform, disliked his aloofness and had alternative views.

Carlyle's and Coleridge's remarks straddle two seminal events in Faraday's life. Carlyle's 'Signs of the Times' was published just before the death of Humphry Davy; Coleridge's observation was made in the aftermath of Faraday's discovery of electro-magnetic induction. Carlyle's image of the scientist (Faraday, by implication) imperatively interrogating nature also characterises Faraday as what we might now call a 'Company Man', standing 'in his Museum, his Scientific Institution'. A Company Man was something that Humphry Davy decidedly had not been. Davy went his own way, researching where he would, without constraint from a management board. Faraday on the other hand remained the servant of the Royal Institution Managers for at least the first twenty years of his employment, until the time came when they all belatedly realised that he was much more famous and distinguished than any of them would ever be, and began to look on Faraday in a more respectful light and to free his wings.

In drawing a Faraday figure standing in 'his Scientific Institution', Carlyle is presenting a Faraday who has been liberated in the public mind from association with Davy. The fascinating thing about Coleridge's remarks, however, is that although they are here applied to Faraday, the words he used – 'that carrying on of the spring and freshness of youthful nay boyish, feelings, into the mature strength of manhood' – could have been used by him in praise of Humphry Davy, the friend of his youth.

Of Davy, Coleridge had years earlier observed: 'Every subject in Davy's mind has the principle of vitality. Living thoughts spring up like turf under his feet.'[19]

In the early 1830s the number of places in London where electrical experiments could be witnessed was growing, and rivalry between them was intense. The Royal Institution had its competitors, among them the Surrey Institution at Blackfriars, the London Institution at Finsbury Circus, and the National Repository, the museum of the London Mechanics' Institute, which had opened in 1828 and which moved to new premises in Leicester Square in 1832. The immediate rival of the National Repository was the National Gallery of Practical Science, opened in 1832 by Jacob Perkins to show off his inventions, in the Lowther Arcade, Adelaide Street, off the Strand. A fifth organisation, opened in 1838, was the Polytechnic Institution in Cavendish Square.[20] The differences between these rival institutions were largely personal, organisational, commercial and theological. The spirit that linked them, however, was a determination, driven by artisanal pride, to display inventions, and through dramatic display and demonstration to claim and register priority, and enjoy patent and exploitation rights. Their aim, inevitably muddied as rivalries flourished, was to give the working craftsmen, the men who devised, manufactured and worked the machinery, some kind of woolly ownership of the applications of the natural laws that their machines exploited.

Faraday's aims at the Royal Institution were different. He was impelled to reveal laws rather than to exploit them, and showed no interest in making money from the application of the facts of nature that he had uncovered. He took the role of detective in any investigation; he left it to others to take matters to court, to the marketplace.

The 1830s was a decade in which scientific discovery and, crucially, its technological application, took one of their occasional sudden leaps, re-energising intellectual activity and filtering down through society to transform the national economy and to extend everyman's perception of the world. London in the 1830s was becoming the capital city of the world, built on the foundations of trade and shipping, as Friedrich von Raumer observed:

> . . . on arriving at the [London] Docks, you are borne along through an absolute forest of ships. Compared with this, any thing of the

kind I have seen in Havre, Bordeaux or Marseilles, is like a single room cut out of this immeasurable palace ... Here one sees that London is the real capital of the world ... London alone is entitled to talk of being the World.[21]

Faraday's work on electricity was one of the central achievements of the 1830s, but other transforming innovations included the development of the railways: Brunel's Great Western Railway was under construction between 1836 and 1841, and George Stephenson masterminded the growth of the railway network from London to the north in the middle years of the decade. The railways could not have grown as they did without the new understanding of the science and production of steel. The improvement of the road system through the widespread use of 'tarmacadam' depended greatly on contemporary experimentations with hydrocarbons; improvements in spinning and weaving machinery and factory processes meant that even the poorer people could afford clothes that were easier to keep clean and, with the use of new dyes, prettier to look at. Improvements in optics meant that lenses could be made to look at bacteria with a microscope, at the horizon with a telescope, and at the stars with a larger telescope. Developments in printing and image-reproduction techniques and the wider use of steam-driven presses allowed books to be more widely available, cheaper and better illustrated, and thus learning could proceed with rapidity and organisation. It is salutary to begin to piece together the ultimate effects, in the cities, towns and villages of Britain and the world beyond, of the chemical and physical experiments that Michael Faraday quietly conducted in the basement of the Royal Institution. Archaeologists have shown that East Africa was the cradle of the human being; 21 Albemarle Street, London, where so many natural phenomena came to be understood and harnessed, may quite justifiably be seen as the cradle of human well-being.

With all these tangible improvements making life better came academic and research advances. Simpler and quicker means of travel meant that geologists, geographers and explorers could travel further, faster and bring back news from afar. Charles Lyell's three-volume *Principles of Geology* (1830–33) assessed the history and variety of the earth, and demonstrated that the small bit of the globe that the Englishman inhabited was intimately connected with other bits where the French, Germans and

Americans lived; that a limestone seam that went into the sea at Portland was the same seam that rose up again at Caen. John Herschel's *Discourse on the Study of Natural Philosophy* (1830) was also hugely influential, and laid down a structure for science and the practice of it, with a plea both direct and implied for the energetic study of natural phenomena. Faraday praised it warmly, telling the author:

> When your work on the study of Nat. Phil. came out, I read it as all other did with delight. I took it as a school book for philosophers and I feel that it has made me a better reasoner & even experimenter and has altogether heightened my character and made me if I may be permitted to say so a better philosopher.[22]

The four decades of consolidated research that began with Davy's years at the Royal Institution and Faraday's early period there culminated with the rush of invention in the 1830s and the writing of the key books that put those inventions into their contemporary context. Charles Babbage's *Reflections on the Decline of Science* and the Bridgewater Treatises lie like shoals across the flow of the river of knowledge.

The continued publication of the *Encyclopaedia Britannica*, which had had so profound an influence on the young Faraday, and the appearance of the *Edinburgh Encyclopaedia*, were further evidence of the explosion of knowledge and its accessibility in the 1830s. Another book, that was small in scale but encyclopaedic in its scope, and which aimed to reveal the links between the varied branches of science, was Mary Somerville's *On the Connexions of the Physical Sciences* (1834). Mary Somerville was a Scots mathematician who had lived in London since 1819. She was well-bred, beautiful, and by now married to her second husband, the military doctor William Somerville. For some years in the 1820s the Somervilles had been at the centre of science society, living in the fashionable Hanover Square, attending and giving soirées and dinners, and meeting and making friends with the widest cross-section of men and women of culture – Faraday, Babbage, Herschel, Turner and Samuel Rogers among them. Both were regular attenders at Royal Institution Evening Discourses, and William Somerville became a Manager of the Institution in 1825. During the late 1820s Mary Somerville worked on her *Mechanism of the Heavens* (1831), a brilliant translation of *Mécanique Céleste* by the

French mathematician Pierre Simon La Place, in which she brought the abstruse world of astronomical mathematics, and La Place's vision of the universe as a system with regular functions, to English scientific audiences.

Mechanism of the Heavens made Mary Somerville's name in the world of science, and prompted the Fellows of the Royal Society, who could not admit her to their number because she was a woman, to club together to commission a marble bust from Sir Francis Chantrey. But it was with *Connexions* that Somerville became a household name. For the first time, in a book written in easy prose, free of expressions understandable only to scientists, the lay public could read in mental comfort and understanding about the newly-hatched distinctions between the various branches of science, those, as Somerville put it, 'treating of the properties of matter and energy'.[23] As a highly gregarious and intelligent woman, Mary Somerville was able to involve scientists of all ages and temperaments in conversation and correspondence, eliciting ideas, advice and exchange. Many of them – most, perhaps – welcomed such attention and charm, and welcomed her flame to warm their reactions. A few days before he died, in 1828, William Wollaston wrote to tell her 'how much & how frequently he has enjoyed her society & conversation, and how ardently he wishes she would retain as a token of friendship the cabinet of models of crystals, made by Larkins, which he formerly lent her . . .'.[24]

David Brewster described Mary Somerville as 'certainly the most extraordinary woman in Europe – a Mathematician of the very first rank, with the gentleness of a woman, and all the simplicity of a child',[25] but it took another woman, Maria Edgeworth, to draw the clearest-eyed portrait:

She has no *set* smile or prim look – no mimps in her mouth – fair and fair hair with pinkish Scotch colour in her cheeks – eyes grey – small round intelligent smiling eyes uncommonly close together . . . She was dressed in geranium coloured Chinese crape . . . She is timid, not disqualifyingly timid, but naturally modest with a degree of self-possession through it which prevents her appearing in the least awkward and gives her all the advantages of her understanding at the same time that it adds a prepossessing charm to her manner and takes off all dread of her superior scientific learning. In talking to her we forget that La Place said she was the only woman in England who could understand and who could *correct* his works.[26]

When the American scientist Joseph Henry came to London in 1837 he was bowled over by Mary Somerville, then aged fifty-six but looking ten years younger. She was cultural royalty, and this impressed him to the extreme: 'She is much caressed by the nobility and gentry,' he wrote in his diary. 'While we were there several persons of these classes came to pay their respects.'[27] Henry went on to marvel at the contents of the Somervilles' house and what it revealed about Mary: 'The room into which we were shewn was hung around with Pictures of various masters and among the number some very beautiful landscapes in oil which we were surprised to learn were the production of this most talented individual.'

Faraday was particularly devoted to Mary Somerville. In his album of portraits of scientific colleagues and friends he kept two lithographs of her – 'they are both very precious to me', he told her years later[28] – and near the end of his own active life he wrote one of his most reflective letters to her. This is shot through with deep affection and gratitude, and, in tones almost of lost love, certainly of strong feeling of a scientific friendship interrupted, Faraday writes:

So you remember me again, and I have the delight of receiving from you a new copy of that work which has so often instructed me; & I may well say, cheered me in my simple, homely course through life in this house. It was most kind to think of me; but ah how sweet it is to believe that I have your *approval* in matters where kindness could do nothing, – where judgements alone must rule. I almost doubt myself when I have your approbation, to some degree at least, in what I may have thought or said about gravitation, the forces of nature, their conservation &c; and yet I do not feel that you are reproving such thoughts. As it is *I cannot* go back from them: on the contrary, I feel encouraged to go on by way of experiment; but am not so able as I was formerly; for when I try to hold the necessary group of thoughts in my mind at one time, with the judgement suspended on almost all of them, then my head becomes giddy & I am obliged to lay all aside for a while . . . I would ask [after] other friends with you but since the loss of memory have made many sad mistakes and have become afraid.[29]

As if respecting the special understanding between them, John Tyndall wrote on the envelope, presumably after Mary Somerville's death, 'A very precious letter from Faraday to Mrs. Somerville.'

Faraday's most helpful contribution to Somerville's work was discussion and talk with her. He looked over the proofs of *Connexions* and suggested amendments and corrections to the section on electricity and magnetism.[30] *On the Connexions of the Physical Sciences* was in print throughout the author's long life – she died in Naples in 1872 aged ninety-one – and ran to ten editions. Its immediate success as a channel of information for all was neatly summed up by a review in the *Athenaeum*, which praised it as being 'at the same time a fit companion for the philosopher in his study, and for the literary lady in her boudoir; both may read it with pleasure, both consult it with profit'.[31]

With this book the popular understanding of science became a possibility rather than a dream. Through her vibrant language Somerville brought an adult, reflective dimension to the subject that had been lacking in Jane Marcet's *Conversations in Chemistry*, and gave a further boost to the campaign for education that Faraday had been waging for so long at the Royal Institution. Had William Somerville's ill-health and a succession of personal financial crises not forced the couple to live abroad after 1838, Mary Somerville's influence on the direction of scientific understanding in Britain might have been even more profound.

But nevertheless Mary Somerville still kept a finger on the pulse of English science through long correspondence from Italy with her gradually ageing generation of scientists and their wives. Margaret Herschel touched the heart of the matter when, in January 1869, she wrote a postscript to a letter from her husband to Mary Somerville:

Such as you are makes the real chains work which links generation to generation – or rather you overlap the links for you spread your influence far into succeeding time ... There were giants in those days – & you did good battle yourself against the nothingnesses of women's lives & thoughts & works – though you were too polite ever to tell them how you were undermining their Paper Castles & meeting another standard of admiration *and love* . . . [32]

The particular influence that Mary Somerville had on culture in Britain was not only as an explainer, but also as a pollinator, spreading ideas, keeping people meeting and talking, and revealing crossing points between art and science. As well as her scientific achievements, she was an accomplished musician, a talented artist with a passion for Turner's paintings, a collector of pictures and *objets d'art*.[33] By the time Joseph Henry met them, the Somervilles had moved to the Royal Hospital, Chelsea, where William became Medical Officer. Chelsea then was far away from London fashion, an old riverside village with poor drains and no embankment, and an imposing but isolated hospital for sick and wounded soldiers. The Somervilles' move there followed their discovery that they had been swindled by a cousin to whom they had entrusted their investments. When their house in Chelsea was in its turn packed up in 1840 – it was by now clear that they could not afford to live in England – the inventory written by Mary's son of the remains of their possessions gives a random but touching insight into the breadth of the interweaving channels of interest that had engaged and entertained this dignified but ultimately traduced couple before they went into exile. Alongside the pictures, ornaments and furniture are a 'piano . . . crystal models, shells, fossils . . . loose minerals, mathematical instruments . . . drawing and music books . . . telescope in mahogany case . . . 2 targets and bows and arrows, easel'.[34] English science felt the loss of the Somervilles greatly, as Margaret Herschel's postscript above makes amply clear. Nevertheless, Mary Somerville continued to write from her modest Italian villa, publishing *Physical Geography* in 1848 and *On Molecular and Microscopic Science* in 1869, and overseeing and writing corrections for *On the Connexions of the Physical Sciences*.

Faraday's work on electricity continued throughout the 1830s, reaching points of completion as the years went by when he published more papers in his *Experimental Researches in Electricity* series. Further foundation stones that he laid included electro-analysis, coulometry, the 'identity of electricities', electrical discharge in gases, electro-statics and specific inductive capacities. By the summer of 1835 he had published ten papers on electrical subjects in *Philosophical Transactions*, the journal of the

Royal Society, and the *Philosophical Magazine*. Variants and translations of these articles appeared in French, German and Italian journals. Although his main field of operation was at the Royal Institution, he gave Bakerian Lectures at the Royal Society and demonstrated electro-magnetic phenomena when invited to do so. At a *conversazione* for Fellows of the Royal Society given at Kensington Palace by the Duke of Sussex, Faraday demonstrated electro-magnetic rotations to the four hundred assembled guests, who included Chantrey, Thomas Moore, Samuel Rogers and the French politician Talleyrand mingling with the scientists. The geologist Gideon Mantell was also present; he recalled Talleyrand as 'a rather decrepit old man who interrupted the rotations by removing a wire. Faraday explained the experiment in the most respectful manner, but very briefly.'[35]

Faraday also appeared at the National Gallery of Practical Science in Lowther Arcade, where in November 1833 he witnessed the public testing of a magneto-electric machine designed and made by Joseph Saxton, an American émigré electrician and inventor. Saxton was one of the small army of men, alongside William Henry, William Sturgeon and Andrew Crosse, who put electrical principles to practical, commercial and spectacular use. That Faraday was invited to be present at an event keenly reported in the *Literary Gazette* reflected on the authority he carried.[36] A few days later he borrowed Saxton's machine to demonstrate it to his own audience at the Royal Institution.[37]

Faraday was, however, scathing about claims made by most of the 'electricians'. Sturgeon, the founder editor in 1836 of the journal *Annals of Electricity*, attacked Faraday vehemently and regularly in the magazine, doubting his theories of electricity and criticising the aloof manner in which he pursued his discoveries. Sturgeon set great store by the public performance of elaborate electrical machines, whereas Faraday's practice was to work quietly in the laboratory – so quietly indeed that days might pass without him and Anderson exchanging a word – and to so manage his demonstrations that it was the phenomenon itself rather than the equipment which produced it that attracted notice.

Sturgeon, who taught science at the East India Company College at Addiscombe, has been eclipsed by Faraday, despite the fact that it was he and other electricians who developed the dynamo, the electro-magnet and many other such electrical machines out of the wire-and-wax test-bed models that Faraday had devised. Another pioneer who has slipped out of sight was Andrew Crosse, an inspired, reclusive and obsessive student of chemistry and mineralogy, and experimenter with electricity. Crosse lived the life of an eccentric country gentleman at Fyne Court near Taunton, Somerset, the house he had inherited from his father. He built batteries which made sparks fly about the house, and which kept a strong electrical charge going for days on end to make crystals by electrolysis; he fed the family silver and plate into his furnaces to make pure silver for his experiments; and he rigged up a system of copper wiring a mile and a quarter long around his house and ha-ha to capture electrical discharge during thunderstorms, and feed it into his sparking retorts. One of his ambitions was to create a perpetual-motion machine. The locals called him 'the thunder and lightning man' and were terrified of going to his house, from which, according to reports, strange lights shone out and loud explosions could regularly be heard. Obsessive and enthusiastic he certainly was, but Crosse was no lunatic. Dining with neighbours in 1816 he prophesied that one day, 'by means of the electrical agency, we shall be enabled to communicate our thoughts *instantaneously* with the uttermost ends of the earth'.[38] His friends were incredulous; but we have had the telephone for generations, and now we have the internet.

Reclusive though he was, Crosse was thrust onto a public platform when it was disclosed in 1837 that during some experiments in electrolysis he appeared to have produced insect life by passing a sustained electrical charge through a solution of powdered flint, potassium carbonate and dilute hydrochloric acid, in the presence of red iron oxide from Vesuvius. After twenty-six days a family of about a hundred little insects climbed out of the bubbling liquid. Crosse himself never claimed to have any opinion as to the cause of the generation of the insects, which came to be called *Acarus Crossii*, but news of the event leaked out and he was praised and vilified in equal measure by the world of science. He repeated the experiment time and again, he tried Somerset water and London water, but the same result occurred. The insects were sent around the scientific world in bottles, and examined under microscopes in private and public. Faraday was drawn into the dispute, and gently remarked that he had no opinion to offer. So mildly did he state his position that the press thought he was actually supporting Crosse, and he had to retrieve his reputation with some urgent backtracking. Few people dared to form an opinion about the insects – though the biologist Richard Owen pronounced them to be cheese-mites – and it is not clear whether they had fallen into the pot from Crosse's dusty ceiling, or crawled in at some point during the experiment. What is certain is that there was some impurity in Crosse's chaotic laboratory and domestic practice. He did not keep notebooks; he hardly ever washed up. 'All is chaos and chance,' the mathematician Ada Lovelace reported.[39]

Crosse's little creatures are, however, a symptom of the creative mystery surrounding electricity that began to play on the imagination of artists, writers and scientists alike in the 1830s, after Faraday in his experiments and public lectures had begun to tame and imprison it by showing how it could be induced, controlled, stored and explained. Crosse may have been the first man outside literature to have had the responsibility of having created life thrust upon him, but in fiction he was preceded by Dr Frankenstein. Despite the contrary evidence of the cinema screens, a reading of Mary Shelley's *Frankenstein* (1818) will reveal that the hero was a trained chemist, and created his monster not through a dramatic electrical charge on the reassembled body parts, but with chemicals and a great deal of clever stitching.

In music, Carl Weber's opera *Der Freischütz* was a massive hit when it opened in London in 1824. It put the supernatural creation of life into the context of high art, and so immediately popular was it that a young architect, Ambrose Poynter, wrote that 'the allegro movement is hummed, strummed, whistled and danced from Whitechapel to Hyde Park Corner'.[40] A reference to *Der Freischütz* also appeared in a review of the Microcosm, a large public microscope exhibition which was drawing London crowds in the late 1820s. The *Literary Gazette* reported: 'All the incantations of Der Freischutz are far surpassed by the monstrous forms in a single drop of water.'[41] For the first time in general human experience, whether through the evidence of the microscope, or in the persons of the little creatures that crawled out of Andrew Crosse's bubbling liquid, science had become yet more extraordinary than whatever it was that art and music could conjure up.

Faraday noticed early in 1835 that his eyesight was beginning to falter. For a scientist whose eyes were the first instrument of sense, this should have been extremely alarming; but in making a note of the situation he used language in which he places himself on the laboratory bench, describing the symptoms precisely, as if he were a responsive chemical compound, and suggesting a course of action:

> Within the last week have observed twice that a slight obscurity of sight of my left eye has happened. It occurred in reading the letters of a book, held about 14 inches from the eye, being obscured as by a fog over a space about half an inch in diameter. This space was a little to the right and below the axis of the eye. Looking for the effect now and at other times, I cannot perceive it. I note this down that I may hereafter trace the progress of the effect if it increases or becomes more common.[42]

There seems to have been no repetition of the condition, or none that gave Faraday cause to make a further note about it. It was all, however, a factor in his recurrent ill-health, which compounded with the intermittent lassitude he experienced in the early 1830s, and with his ever-present memory problems.

One matter outside his direct scientific work that gave Faraday acute consternation was the active lobbying of the Prime Minister, Robert Peel, by others on his behalf, that Faraday's name should be submitted to the King as the potential recipient of a civil list pension of £300 per annum in recognition of his scientific work. Faraday's friends at court, who included the astronomer James South and the Tory MP and Lord of the Admiralty Lord Ashley, contrived to put it into the Prime Minister's ear that it would be a fitting thing for the nation thus to honour Michael Faraday. He was not the sort of man who would take a knighthood; indeed he was reluctant even to use the title 'Dr' that the University of Oxford had conferred on him, infinitely preferring to remain plain 'Mr Faraday'.[43] Evidently Lord Ashley had been put up to the job by South, and may have been the author of a letter whose patronising tone was extreme, even by the eighteenth-century standards that still persisted in some parts of the establishment:

> Mr Faraday the great chemist is, like most persons of high Scientific attainments, very wise but not very wealthy – indeed his whole income obtained by *wearying & ceaseless labour* does not exceed four hundred pounds a year – he has but little time for reflection,

& none, I believe, to direct any undertakings to improve his circumstances . . . if you will be so kind as just to cast your eye over the
Memoir of his life (prepared at my request by a friend of mine)
you will see what toils, what privations, what sorrows this philosopher has seduced in prosecution of high & beautiful learning.[44]

The memoir (reprinted here in full as Appendix Three) plays up the
poverty of Faraday's youth, his self-help, his lucky breaks in being apprenticed to Riebau, attending Tatum's classes and in the chance encounter
by 'Mr Dance' of Faraday's neat notebooks, and all that followed. Rather
unconvincingly, it attempts to suggest that Faraday was practically illiterate until Edward Magrath's unremitting efforts over seven years, at two
hours a week, had taught him to read and write. The detail in the memoir
suggests that its author interviewed a wide range of people from Faraday's
past: these might have included George Riebau, who was working until
1836; Masquerier, who was by now living in Brighton and was still in
touch with Faraday; Edward Magrath, the Secretary at the Athenaeum
Club; or even one of the numerous Dances still around at the Royal
Institution. There is, however, one particular early detail in the memoir
that suggests that the research might have been suspect – the naming of
two of Faraday's fellow apprentices, neither of whom is mentioned anywhere else in surviving Faraday literature, the comedian William Oxberry
and the singer Edward Fitzwilliam. Although Oxberry is known to have
been an apprentice of Riebau, he seems to have left before Faraday
arrived. Fitzwilliam appears never to have been a Riebau apprentice.[45]

Although it overplays Faraday's early poverty, and the fact that for
many of the previous twenty-three years at the Royal Institution 'he has
toiled in the Laboratory from six in the morning till eleven or twelve at
night', the memoir is a generally accurate, if flat, picture of the Faraday
we know. It acknowledges the work he was also doing for the Admiralty
and the Woolwich Military Academy, and touches on the fact that he
has been 'long enrolled as a Member of almost all the Scientific Societies
of the world'. In a pointed aside it also remarks that it was not until 1832
that 'the University of Oxford did *itself* the honour of conferring on him
an honorary degree of Doctor of Civil Law'.

By the time Faraday first got wind of the fact that the pension request
had been made, the government had changed. At the April 1835 general

election Peel's Tories were voted out of office, to be replaced by a Whig government under Lord Melbourne. South told Faraday that he would be getting a letter from Peel telling him that had Peel stayed in office the pension would have been assured.[46] This is no surprise – Peel was an accomplished mathematician and a friend to science, and, indeed, had been spoken of as a possible candidate at the 1827 election of President of the Royal Society. No such letter seems to have arrived for Faraday from Peel, but, alerted to the whole affair, Faraday intended to make it quite clear that he could not accept a pension 'whilst I am able to live by my labours'.[47] He wrote to South that he could not discuss the reasons fully by letter, but would talk to him at the earliest opportunity. He explained all this clearly, but before posting the letter, which was written from Edward Barnard's house, 34 Paternoster Row, he talked the matter over with his father-in-law, the Sandemanian Elder.

In contemplating the prospect of becoming a pensioner of the state, Faraday was confronted by matters with which his church should be concerned. The Sandemanians kept themselves untarnished by direct contact with temporal government, and Faraday's immediate reaction suggests that it was his instinct to have nothing to do with the offer, however diplomatically he phrased his refusal. But there is a telling annotation, written by Faraday, on the letter to South: 'Mr Barnard prevented me from sending it & I sent another of which I have no copy.' The hierarchy of the Sandemanian church was such that the Elders demanded total obedience to their decisions from any and all of their congregation. This of course included Michael Faraday, FRS, DCL, and those letters after his name, and his many other worldly scientific accolades, withered to nothing in the face of the Elders' direction. So that letter was not sent, and another, now lost, took its place.

Faraday did, however, ultimately accept a pension from the new government, so it may be that the Sandemanian policy on this particular issue was not as harsh as he himself might have predicted. But had he persisted in refusing the offer, he would have been spared much embarrassment, and spared too the odium of being discussed in the press in connection with the sordid subject of money.

The Faradays escaped temporarily from the pensions issue by spending late June and July 1835 on a walking and sightseeing holiday in Germany and Switzerland. They crossed the Channel to Dieppe from Brighton, where they called on Gideon Mantell and his wife,[48] but despite the protection of their macintoshes, were soaked by a violent storm, and became 'so unhappy in our wetness as to be quite unconscious of anything else'. From the coast they travelled via Rouen to Paris, where they stayed for eight days and picked up George Barnard, who was to be their travelling companion. On the way south they met some scientist friends – Laurent-François Feuillet, the Librarian of the Institut de France in Paris, and Auguste de la Rive in Geneva are two that we know about from a letter home to Edward Magrath.[49]

Even four weeks after leaving England Faraday was still suffering 'with occupation fatigue and rheumatism', as he described it to Edward Magrath from Fribourg, but experience of the Alpine landscapes of Switzerland was restoring his spirits. By 'occupation fatigue' Faraday meant travelling and walking in the Alps: he was an energetic walker who could cover up to forty-five miles in a day, so we need not feel too sorry for him.[50]

Faraday's brother-in-law George Barnard was now twenty-eight years old, and making a name for himself as a landscape artist. He had been a pupil of James Duffield Harding, the watercolourist and lithography pioneer who was himself a habitué of the Royal Institution. Barnard's youth and his enthusiasm for the Alps was a further tonic for Faraday, and he sketched in the landscape, making studies for some of the many Alpine subjects he exhibited and published as lithographs over the next few years. Faraday will also have been inclined to take up his sketching pencil. The party travelled to Geneva, and then south-east along the Arve valley through Bonneville to Chamonix. They visited some of the finest geological and picturesque sights of Switzerland, including the glacier at Montanvert, the 'Sea of Ice', and travelled back by Martigny. They drove past the Castle of Chillon – made famous in Byron's poem – to the east end of Lake Geneva at Vevey, and went up through the mountains north-east to Fribourg.

It was a magnificent journey, and Faraday did not stint in recounting to Magrath his excitement at it. The paragraphs of Alpine description that he wrote to Magrath may reflect something of the conversation and friendly argument between the older scientist and George Barnard, the young artist. Faraday argued that poetry carried the higher expression, while Barnard, we might reasonably suppose, had it that painting was superior. The point is that although science was the first filter through which Faraday perceived the world, art and literature ran it very close, and, as he wrote to Magrath, they vied with each other to be the clearest means of expressing pleasure, delight and wonder at extreme natural beauty:

We are almost surfeited with Magnificent scenery and for myself I would rather not see it, than see it with an exhausted appetite. The weather has been most delightful & every thing in our favour so that the scenery has been in the most beautiful condition. Mont Blanc above all is wonderful and I could not but feel at it, what I have often felt before that painting is very far beneath poetry in cases of high expression; of which this is one. No artist should try to paint Mont Blanc, it is utterly out of his reach. He cannot convey an idea of it, and a formal mass or a common place model conveys more intelligence even with respect to the sublimity of the mountain than his highest efforts can do. In fact he must be able to dip his brush in light & darkness before he can paint Mont Blanc. But the moment he sees it Lord Byron's expressions come to mind and they seem to apply. The poetry and the subject dignify each other.[51]

Barnard, in the brief and tantalising account of Faraday among artists published by Bence Jones,[52] tells of Faraday and he going off on sketching trips together. The lithographs of mountain and other landscape scenes, some of which are initialled both 'GB' and 'MF', in Faraday's scrapbooks must be the result of this or other landscape adventures.

The pension issue that Faraday had left behind him when he sailed for France was waiting for him when he returned home. The request made on his behalf duly went up to the new Prime Minister, Lord Melbourne, who, seven months after the election, was ready to have a meeting to discuss the issue. He summoned Faraday, who attended him at Downing Street on 26 October for what may rank as one of the shortest Prime Ministerial audiences on record. Faraday made a transcript of the exchange:

Mr F – I am here my Lord by your desire. Am I to understand that it is on the business which I have partially discussed with Mr Young?

Lord M – You mean the pension, don't you?

Mr F – Yes, my Lord.

Lord M – Yes, you mean the pension and I mean the pension too. I hate the name of the pension. I look upon the whole system of giving pensions to literary and scientific persons as a piece of gross humbug. It was not done for any good purpose and never ought to have been done. It is a gross humbug from beginning to end. It . . .

Mr F, rising and making a bow – After all this my Lord I perceive that my business with your lordship is ended – I wish you a good morning.[53]

There was another account of the interview written by Faraday in a lost diary, which Silvanus Thompson referred to in his life of Faraday.[54] It seems that Faraday had a long talk with Thomas Young, Melbourne's secretary, on the morning of the interview, at which he put forward serious objections to accepting the pension, setting out religious grounds, his objections to savings banks and the laying up of wealth. This sermon must have puzzled Young, a worldly-wise, raffish and ingratiating official, whom Philip Ziegler has described as 'shrewd, unscrupulous and with a curious sensitivity, [with] a chameleon-like capacity for adapting himself to his surroundings and ingratiating himself with the object of his attentions'.[55] The radical reformer Francis Place remembered Young as 'a cleverish sort of fellow, with a vulgar air of frankness which may at times put people off their guard'.[56]

Faraday was clearly steamed up about the whole affair, and by unloading his religious convictions onto Young he may have been clearing his own conscience, as well as giving the private secretary some useful information to pass on to his master. Faraday would not accept a pension, he could tell Melbourne, before showing Faraday into the Prime Minister's office. Faraday's lost report of his encounter with Lord Melbourne says, according to Thompson, that the Prime Minister 'prefixed the word "humbug" with a participle which Faraday's notes describe as "theological"'. We might guess that what Melbourne actually said was not 'gross humbug' but 'damned humbug'. At this point Faraday 'with an instant flash of indignation, bowed and withdrew'.[57]

The way this essentially private matter was being handled was messy and embarrassing for Faraday. He had never asked for it to be raised in the first place, and it created a crisis of identity and purpose for him. Was he being granted the honour of a state pension as a private individual? If so, he would find it hard to accept. Or was he being singled out for honour on behalf of all the other men of science, in which case he had a strong obligation to accept. Further, was he being catapulted to the position of state pensioner as a recognition of his social rise? That was a current view, as the Duke of Somerset expressed to Charles Babbage:

> The story of Faraday is sure to make a great noise. There is something romantic and quite affecting in such a combination of Poverty and Passion for Science, and with this and his brilliant success he comes out as the Hero of Chemistry.[58]

It was extraordinary bad luck that the timing of the pension application should fall during a period of government change and great public controversy over higher political matters, thus putting Faraday into the category of a tiresome left-over of the last administration. Unusually, he numbered the twenty-five letters which passed between him and others in the affair, and kept copies of his own letters.[59] He was in something of a pet about it, hopelessly embroiled and not in control of the situation. When, a month or so after the meeting with Melbourne, a letter came to Faraday from Caroline Fox, sister of Lord Holland and a central figure in the Whig-supporting Holland House set, it seemed as if plans were being laid to arrange a second interview between Faraday and the Prime Minister, to clear up 'all the misunderstandings of the first', with the desired result of 'an increase of esteem and respect on both sides'.[60] Caroline Fox was a friend of both Faraday and Melbourne, and was trying to tempt Faraday out of Albemarle Street to a dinner at Little Holland House with James South and 'one or two persons desirous of making Mr Faraday's acquaintance'. Mary Fox, Lord Holland's daughter-in-law and the illegitimate daughter of King William IV and Mrs Jordan, had also written soothingly to Faraday – this all seems like a concerted Whig effort to steady the boat that Faraday and Melbourne had between them so spectacularly rocked – and calm appeared to be returning to the scene.[61] As if in confirmation, Melbourne wrote to Faraday before Caroline Fox's dinner could take place asking him to reconsider his decision, in a letter which came as close to an apology for and explanation of his conduct as might be expected. It is a masterpiece of circumlocution and careful phrasing:

> I am not unwilling to admit that any thing in the nature of censure upon any party ought to have been abstained from upon such an occasion; but I can assure you that my observations were intended only to guard myself against the imputation of having any political advantage in view & not in any respect to apply to the conduct of those, who had or who hereafter might avail themselves of a similar offer.[62]

Faraday replied immediately, with grace and gratitude, accepting the pension: 'I hesitate not to say I shall receive your Lordships offer both with pleasure and with pride.'[63]

That should have been the end of it, but within days the press got hold of the affair, and a lurid and partisan account appeared first in the Tory *Fraser's Magazine*, which was rapidly re-echoed in *The Times*.[64] This contained what reads like a verbatim report of Faraday's interview with Melbourne, and his preceding conversation with Thomas Young, and sent Faraday scuttling back to his first hardened position of refusal. The question was, who had supplied *Fraser's* with the detailed account of what the magazine described as 'some such dialogue as this'? Who was the leak? What was at stake was the public's perception of the new government's attitude to science and the arts. Was it to be one of generous acknowledgement of and gratitude for what creative people contributed to the life of the nation, or a hard-hearted view that the whole thing was 'gross', or even 'damned', 'humbug'. Two senior fixers put their heads together to see what might be done. These were Dr Henry Holland and Lord Holland (no relation). The former, as President of the Royal Institution, could have a word with Faraday, and was as influential in London society as was the latter. The doctor wrote to the peer observing that Faraday

> is still undergoing the same anxious uneasiness on this subject, not unnatural in a mind exceed[ingl]y sensitive & conscientious, & little

accustomed to the concourse of life out of doors. His feeling is . . . that he is not entitled to take a single step without the assent of Sir J. South, whom he considered to be acting for him throughout the whole; & to whom he thinks it right that any reference should be made.[65]

Dr Holland then tried to placate Faraday:

you take too uneasy a view of circumstances, which cannot possibly affect injuriously either your own conscience, or your high character in the world. I am persuaded you will so find, & feel, it hereafter, when these distressing embarrassments are gone by.[66]

When the affair rolled on and the *Courier* accused Faraday himself of having leaked details of his conversation with Melbourne to *Fraser's Magazine*, Faraday's fury broke, and he wrote immediately to *The Times* putting the matter straight: 'neither directly nor indirectly did I communicate to the editor of *Fraser's Magazine* . . . or further either directly or indirectly any information to or for any publication whatsoever'.[67]

This outburst caused James South to have a quiet word with Faraday, and the same day to write to him 'imploring' him not – in real terms practically forbidding him – 'to open your lips to any one whatever on the subject'.[68] What Faraday may not have known was that the machinery of court and government was already turning on the issue, and the pension, of £300 a year, was about to be granted by the King. The royal command to the Commissioners of the Treasury is dated 9 December 1835, the day after Faraday's letter was published in *The Times*.

The following year, the Royal Institution took a huge step towards confirming its image as a public institution in a public building. The success of Faraday's research and the many series of lectures by him and others had shown resoundingly that this was not a private club, but nevertheless it occupied an eighteenth-century townhouse which spoke with a voice of aristocracy and privilege. What the Institution needed was to address the street in the architectural language of strength, purpose, learning and culture. To that end the Managers raised over £1000 from the membership[69] to commission the architect Lewis Vulliamy to design and build what became a giant façade of fourteen Corinthian columns, with a cornice proclaiming the name THE ROYAL INSTITUTION OF GREAT BRITAIN at a high level, a new central entrance, new hall and a porter's lodge. The developed mid-nineteenth-century streetscape constrains the view of the façade so that it can never be seen frontally from the distance that its architecture demands, and even when it was completed, in 1838, its western aspect was hampered by buildings on Grafton Street, opposite. Its true antecedents, rooted in the Parthenon and the ancient Roman buildings that Faraday saw as a young man, are the Greek revival architecture of Berlin, Paris and St Petersburg, and, nearer home, buildings by Faraday's mentor George Dance and Vulliamy's teacher Robert Smirke. Vulliamy gave the Royal Institution a building that adequately reflected the true status and quality of the science that was being practised and disseminated inside.[70] In bringing its architectural image into step with its developed status as an educational organisation, the Institution was in effect picking up a dropped stitch. This was a very British way of doing things – no grand Imperial decree that great and glorious architecture would spawn great scientific deeds; on the contrary, the science had come first, and had earned the architecture.

The scientific turning point of an importance that justified the Royal Institution's grand façade was the discovery of photography. This revolutionary new application of scientific principles to technological practice was first announced in Britain by Michael Faraday at a Friday Evening Discourse on 25 January 1839. Henry Fox Talbot had sent Faraday some examples of his 'photogenic drawings', and these Faraday showed in the Library at 21 Albemarle Street before and after a Discourse on the polarisation of light. Faraday and Fox Talbot himself spoke about the new technique, and they must have mentioned the simultaneous discoveries in France of Louis-Jacques Daguerre, announced in Paris on 7 January, as the *Literary Gazette* reported that Fox Talbot's photogenic drawings were of 'the same character of those of Mr Daguerre'.[71]

The date that usually gets into the history books for the first announcement of photography in England is, however, six days after Faraday's Discourse, 31 January 1839, when Fox Talbot read his paper at the Royal Society.[72] The choice of title was highly significant, and gave a direction to Fox Talbot's initial ambition:

[290]

Some account of the art of photogenic drawing, or, the process by which natural objects may be made to delineate themselves without the aid of the artists' pencil.

There is a sense of rightness about this particular priority, that photography, the art which brought fine image-making into the reach of the common man, should have been first announced at the Royal Institution to its widely-ranging membership, rather than at an exclusive gathering of scientists at the Royal Society. A few days later Fox Talbot published his account of 'The Art of Photogenic Drawing' in the *Athenaeum* of 9 February, and then on 14 March John Herschel gave at the Royal Society 'A notice of some methods of photogenic drawing'.

Significant in the titles of the papers is the vocabulary they use: words like 'delineate' and 'drawing' are prominent. It is hardly to be expected otherwise, but the first challenge of photography was in its direct threat to artists. Two weeks after Herschel read his paper at the Royal Society, Faraday picked up the thread again, and spoke informally to another large audience of lay people about further applications of the discovery, as devised and amended by the painter William Havell. Havell had found a quick way of copying engravings by photographic action, and had discussed the process with Faraday, and given him examples to show in the Library.

Havell was a talented but pedestrian landscape painter who spent a considerable amount of his time on what he called 'photogeny'. In correspondence and conversations with Faraday in 1839 he outlined the method he had invented not of superseding art by photographing landscape as Fox Talbot and Daguerre were trying to do, but of augmenting it by using a photogenic method. Havell's illustration of his method was a photographic copy of his own sketch of Rembrandt's etching *Faust Raising a Spirit*, and he sent a proof to Faraday to display in the Royal Institution, asserting in a letter that 'there can be no doubt of its becoming a most interesting Art, for multiplying designs by a most simple process'.[73]

As Havell described it to Faraday, the process was not that simple, but a complicated, hit-and-miss method of covering the etching with a glass plate, stopping out the lighter areas with opaque white lead, the middle tints with semi-opaque white, and scratching the lines out of the painted areas with a knife or etching needle. The etching was then removed and a sheet of sensitised paper substituted, and the whole thing was exposed to the sun. Clearly, this was not a photograph of the engraving, but a redrawing of it, in the medium of light-sensitive paper. Havell had been present when Fox Talbot and Faraday had introduced the new invention on 25 January, and from his letter to Faraday it is evident that he had learnt enough to try it for himself. Fox Talbot's own practice of making negative images dissatisfied Havell, and as a result he and his brother Frederick experimented with the medium and turned negative lights into deep shadows in a series of portrait heads after the Italian baroque painter Guercino.

The great excitement of the process for Havell, as for Faraday, was that 'it is quite clear that artists may by considering the above methods multiply original sketches or designs, ad infinitum, they never wear out, may be altered, improved, retouched at pleasure, requiring no printing presses, any number may be exposed to the light at the same instant'.[74]

In raising the subject of photography at the Royal Institution just as the first news of it came through, Faraday was flagging up interests which, for him, had much wider implications. He came later to develop an interest in the chemistry of photography, which he discussed and perhaps experimented on with Herschel in 1839 and 1840, particularly in the matter of photographic varnishes.[75] He welcomed anyone who could contribute to photographic advances, such as Alfred Swaine Taylor, a chemist and medical scientist who improved on Fox Talbot's technique and made no secret of his method.[76] Through exhibiting Taylor's 'photogenic drawings' on the Library Table in the same few weeks as he showed those by Fox Talbot, Herschel and Havell, Faraday was enriching, widening and freeing the debate in a way that is in marked contrast to the process of publicity in France, where Daguerre had extracted a large sum of money out of the French government in exchange for making what he claimed to be his discoveries public.

Photography also touched Faraday's sense of vanity (as we shall see in Chapter 25). In the 1840s to 1860s he became one of the most photographed figures in public life; every kind of pose is there, leading us to the conclusion that the image of himself that he wanted posterity to grasp was the one in which science and art held hands – the photograph.

CHAPTER 20

The Parable of the Rainbow

A day or two before Christmas 1840 Faraday and Edward Magrath met to talk. Magrath was one of the few men outside the Sandemanian embrace with whom Faraday would speak freely and personally. There must have been something abrupt and disturbing about Faraday's behaviour that day, because the events of the meeting dwelt uncomfortably with Faraday, and he may even within hours have picked up his pen and written this to Magrath:

> Dont be troubled about me. I was very glad to have a little chat with you but I cannot stand much with any body or in any subject. I ought to apologise to you for my abrupt conclusion but we have known each other too long & too well to have any difficulties on that score.[1]

Faraday was, now, gradually sinking into a chronic depression, with physical effects such as vertigo and headaches. This had begun to afflict him in the last few weeks of 1839, and forced him for more than two years to lighten his administrative work at the Royal Institution, and practically to cease scientific research. He had lately been complaining about his poor memory,[2] but that was nothing new, and judging by a letter he wrote in early November 1839 to Abraham Follett Osler, the

Secretary of the Birmingham Philosophical Institute, he had then no inkling of how severe the new attack would be: 'All my time and attention,' he told Osler, 'is devoted in channels already determined, to the pursuit of Science.'[3]

The first symptoms, which forced him to lie down on 29 November 1839, had been vertigo. Faraday's doctor, Peter Mere Latham, was called, and he bled the patient at both temples and ordered him to cancel future engagements and invitations. In his case notes Latham wrote:

> He confessed to me that his mind has for a long time been dreadfully overworked – that, besides his own abstruse speculations about electricity he has had lectures pressed upon him, and is continually consulted about all sorts of subjects, which people fancy are quite easy to him, but which require considerable thought – I positively interdicted his lecturing for the present and advised him going away to Brighton.[4]

The President of the Royal Academy, Sir Martin Archer Shee, who had invited Faraday to a gathering, was the first to be turned down as the Faradays prepared to take Latham's orders seriously and travel down to Brighton.[5] For the next two years the withdrawal of Faraday from intellectual life is reflected in the changes in his pattern of correspondence. The long and generously detailed letters to fellow scientists and enquirers that had formerly characterised his letter-writing habits disappear in the 1840s. They are replaced by staccato paragraphs, usually brief notes, sometimes in reply to enquiries or solicitations, sometimes quick administrative remarks concerning the Discourse programme. It is significant that where there are longer letters in 1840, they are written from Brighton, where Faraday went at least three times that year, and where the social and professional pressures on him were practically nil. The Faradays did have visitors on these holidays, friends such as the Masqueriers and Gideon Mantell lived nearby, and they frequently called on each other. Faraday went to lectures, *conversaziones* and, once, the circus in Sussex with Mantell.[6] The Faradays' extended family came too: Michael's niece Jane Gray was with them, as were George and Emma Barnard, very recently married, who were honeymooning at a 'lodging about 5 minutes distance'.[7] Sometimes a professional acquaintance would turn up and be received as politely as possible, probably against Latham's orders – one such was the Swiss lawyer and archaeologist Johann Bachofen, who called in late April, as Faraday told C.F. Schoenbein: 'Your friend Mr Bachofen has been here & I hope enjoyed himself. You know that I should not make company for him for my retiring habits are likely to increase rather than diminish and it is for those I already know, amongst which you are a principal one that I wish to keep my thoughts.'[8]

Faraday was particularly cheered and buoyant in Brighton on 24 April 1840, when he wrote three long letters, to Auguste de la Rive, to Sarah's nephew Andrew Reid and to Charles Frederick Schoenbein, the Professor of Chemistry at Basle.[9] Schoenbein had become a close friend, but one Faraday had never met. They had been exchanging long letters for four years on scientific matters, and what began as a professional correspondence gradually flowered into something more personal when Schoenbein, concerned about Faraday's health, urged him to make a 'trip to the continent and into our beautiful Alpes [which] would, perhaps, do a great deal of good to you'.[10] When he began correspondences with foreign scientists Faraday's purpose was to exchange ideas and to sharpen his own; but with some, like Ampère, de la Rive father and son and Schoenbein, the sparks that flew from the sharpening minds lit deeper fires of friendship and empathy.

Faraday told Schoenbein that he was working on a reply to some attacks from the American scientist Robert Hare on his theory of induction: 'his criticisms have not yet driven me from my ground'.[11] Schoenbein continued to be anxious about Faraday's health, exhorting him

> not to overwork yourself and to manage a little your mental and physical forces, for your health and life are most precious to your friends in particular and to the scientific world at large. We cannot yet spare you and you must continue to be our leader for many years to come . . . you ought to listen a little to the entreaties of your friends and to grant to your mind and body some little rest. I am sure Mrs Faraday will be of my opinion and confident she will not cease reminding you of it.[12]

Sarah certainly did not, as she assured Andrew Reid: 'your Uncle is pretty well but not so strong as I should like to see him, he often needs relaxation'.[13]

In replying as he was to a long letter from Schoenbein, and in writing apologetically to de la Rive – he referred to himself as 'a miserable correspondent'[14] – Faraday was touching hands with two friends who would understand how his body was letting his mind down. During his illness he was barely able to handle science at home at the Royal Institution, barely able to look a retort in the face, being able to consider scientific ideas and his own contributions to them only when he was in Brighton, far away from the smells and pressures of London. Entries in his laboratory diary stop abruptly on 22 November 1839, a few days before his attack of vertigo, and then record only five days' laboratory work between 11 January and 11 February 1840. There are no further entries until 10 August, when Faraday undertook five more sporadic days' work, followed by no entries at all for the twenty months between 14 September 1840 and 1 June 1842. It was not, however, until a year after the illness began that the Managers of the Royal Institution formally acknowledged its severity and resolved to exonerate Faraday totally 'from all duties connected with the Royal Institution till his health should be completely re-established'.[15]

For relaxation at home and on holiday the Faradays organised family musical evenings,[16] and there were word games, charades, and times when Michael would read aloud from the Bible and from Byron, Shakespeare or Scott.[17] Knowing the sombre shades of Gray's 'Elegy' so well, he perhaps regaled his family with that as the sun went down. In the Common Place Book he writes out many lists of anagrams, which may suggest that making them up or copying them down from other sources was part of family fun. He also collected the texts of curious public notices, press cuttings, epitaphs and so on, which reflect his interest in words, double meanings, communication and jokes. He found two long palindromes and wrote them out in the Common Place Book:

> Evil is a name of foeman as I live
> Madam is an Eve even as I'm Adam[18]

With plenty of time on his hands, he also had fun with his own name, listing sixty-four variations and inventions around the theme of 'Faraday', beginning: Farady, Farraday, Farrady, Farridy, Farrada, Falady, Farridre, Farfield, Faradai, Thureydy, Ferreyday, Farday, Falliday, Pharary, Farryday, Farror, Fairday, Faradia, Fereday, Feridee, Fradday, Farraly and so on.[19] He seems to have added to the list when he was a much older man, and might have gone on for ever finding interest in his own name, a form of self-obsession that is mildly irritating.

Travel, however, was the thing, and Sarah made sure her husband got the rest and fresh air he needed. Brighton remained a regular holiday place, as did Margate, where they stayed in late July 1840, Deal, Walmer, Hastings, Folkestone, Eastbourne and many other resorts on the south-east coast of England, as well as Niton on the Isle of Wight.[20] They went round and round the coastline and back to London like a pair of wandering gulls. Faraday confided to Schoenbein from Brighton that his doctors 'want to persuade [me] that I am mentally fatigued and I have no objection to think so. My own notion is, I am permanently worse: we shall see.'[21] Schoenbein urged the Faradays to spend the coming summer in Switzerland, for 'inhaling for a couple of months the light and ethereal air of our mountainous regions would produce wonderful effects upon your frame and be the true panacea for your complaint'.[22]

In terms of the profound effect of a good holiday, a watershed for Faraday was the three months that he and Sarah, with George and Emma Barnard, spent in Germany and Switzerland in 1841. Schoenbein's letter must have prompted their decision to go, and he went so far as to offer to 'act as your cicerone for a week or two'. This was the first time Faraday had been abroad since 1835, and before he left he determined to write an extended travel diary as reflective as the one he kept on his 1813–15 continental tour with Sir Humphry Davy, and on his 1819 visit to Wales.

The 1841 diary is lost, but the spirit that breathes out of the extracts that Bence Jones published is light-hearted and vivacious, showing that the very act of travelling south was quite enough to drive the gloom of his illness away from Faraday's shoulders.[23] The party took a steamboat from a London wharf at half past six on a bright June morning, and twelve hours later they had crossed the North Sea and landed at Ostend. They drove down to Aix-la-Chapelle (Aachen), and on to Cologne to begin their journey down the Rhine towards the mountains.

Once again the Faradays were travelling with their artist companion, and George Barnard's enthusiasm for the landscape was as infectious as it was enthusiastic: 'George is in high glee with the tones of the scenery, and means to make much of it,' Faraday wrote on the day they arrived at their hotel at Thun, south of Berne.[24] Barnard also took care of all the arrangements, increasingly becoming the Faradays' courier: 'He settles when we start and has arranged where we shall go: – he takes all the care of money, passports, hours, routes – Hotels – calls etc.'[25] This was much the same sort of responsibility that Faraday himself had shouldered for the Davys twenty-eight years earlier. As they travelled the last few miles to Thun, Faraday described the view of the Alps, which 'grow in beauty greatly as one approaches them, and we have had the finest mixtures of these and the clouds which man can imagine, the latter at last dissolving in rain and rejoining the earth'.

Their rooms, on the first floor of a house detached from the Hotel Belle Vue, overlooked the Thunersee and the Bernese Alps. 'The river and lake are beautiful to-day, and the mountains also,' Faraday wrote on their first morning.

> George made a regular artistical examination of the town and neigh-bourhood to-day, and I went with him, imbibing the picturesque; there is certainly plenty of it; the morning was sunny and beautiful, and the afternoon was stormy, and equally beautiful; so beautiful I never saw the like. A storm came on, and the deep darkness of one part of the mountains, the bright sunshine of another part, the emerald lights of the distant forests and glades under the edge of the cloud were magnificent. Then came on lightning, and the Alp thunder rolling beautifully; and to finish all, a flash struck the church, which is a little way from us, and set it on fire, but no serious harm resulted, as it was soon put out.[26]

These were landscapes of a Turnerian kind – complete with the timely drama of a lightning flash and a flaming church – chromatically and theatrically described.

Like the greatly varied observations in the 1813–15 continental travel diary, Faraday's responses to the landscape and social detail he came upon in Switzerland have an engaged, enquiring touch about them. He was amused and amazed by the sight of the men and women who immersed themselves in the public baths at Leukerbad, fed by the waters of the Rhône at its source. The bathers wore gaily coloured and decorated caps and took refreshments from floating tables, staying in the water up to their necks 'for from two to nine hours per day for weeks together. What good it may do to their bodies I do not know, but it certainly must relax their minds. I can scarcely imagine a vigorous or strong-minded person submitting to it on any account.'[27]

Leaving Sarah and Emma at the hotel, Barnard and Faraday went off on long walks together. Barnard sketched while Faraday

> rambled about awhile. The courses of the torrents or avalanches here are marked by very striking appearances; a long line of pines swept down and broken or splintered in every possible way, but all in one direction, give sufficient information of the power. In some places the upturned pines have lain so long that they are rotten throughout. There are stones, too, large and small, which formed part of the destroying storm. Returning to George, I found him hard at work in the course of an avalanche, and I took a seat behind him for a while, using for that purpose both a pine and the stone which had overturned it. Heard a good deal of murmuring thundering noise, but whether of thunder or avalanches in the distance, or waterfalls, could not tell.

There were times when Faraday went for walks on his own, good strong walks which exercised his body and tested his strength and endurance. He was within a few weeks of his fiftieth birthday when he did an epic forty-five-mile walk in ten and a half hours from Leukerbad over the Gemmi Pass, then descending past the Jungfrau, down the valley and alongside the lake to return to their hotel. He endured heavy rain

> for two hours on the mountain-top . . . with the wind against me; and as the path was soon a stream, my great fear was that my shoes would not hold out . . . I arrived at Fruchtigen at one o'clock, having made twenty eight miles since six o'clock this morning. But I still felt my clothes damp, and knowing the difficulty of getting quick accommodation, I resolved to dine, and then start or stay as I might feel inclined; so with a little *eau de vie de Cognac*, and a very good dinner, and also the advantage of a rest of an hour and a half, I started again.[28]

Three hours forty minutes later – Faraday always gives precision timing – he was back at the hotel, 'in far better condition than I expected, and very glad to be there. After tea I felt a little stiff, and only then felt conscious of one small blister.' Reflecting on the walk he says: 'I think my strength cannot be bad or my reasoning very insufficient. I would gladly give half of this strength for as much memory, but – what have I to do with that? Be thankful.'[29]

There appears to be very little science in this travel diary; if there was more, Bence Jones chose not to quote it. As we have it now, Faraday's account of his 1841 Swiss holiday is an evocative and limpid-clear piece of English writing on a landscape theme. The wind and light of the Alps ripples through it, sharp natural colours depict it, and human figures – Faraday himself, George Barnard the sketcher, the determined bathers of Leukerbad – move through it, inhabiting, articulating and characterising the country that Faraday describes. Looking up at the Jungfrau from Interlaken, Faraday sees in the August evening

a beautiful series of tints from the base to the summit, according to the proportion of light on the different parts. At one time the summit was beautifully bathed in golden light, whilst the middle part was quite blue, and the snow of its peculiar blue-green in the refts. Some of the glaciers are very distinct to us, and with the telescope I can see the refts and corrugations of the different parts, and the edges from which avalanches have fallen.[30]

If there is a hint of science in the writing it is in Faraday's clear analysis of the coloration of the mountains, the way the light played upon them as the sun went down that evening, the use of his telescope, and his delight in being alive to witness it all.

But now other influences came into play that were not generally present when Faraday worked in the laboratory: the companionship of George Barnard and their unrecorded conversations as they walked together; the crisp wind in their faces; the overwhelming actuality of the Alps. Barnard was rapidly amassing material for his paintings: he showed oils of the Jungfrau and other Alpine subjects at the Royal Academy in the 1840s,[31] and in his many books on landscape painting technique he writes lucidly about the mountains, vividly evoking atmosphere and incident.[32] Being alone amongst mountains with an enthusiastic and companionable painter can have a serious influence on the nature of one's vocabulary and the priorities of one's observations, and it is hard to see how Faraday could have been impervious to Barnard's talk and viewpoint. The determined tone of Faraday's letter home from the Alps in 1835 (discussed in Chapter 19), in which he advocates the pre-eminence of literature over painting in conveying the grandeur of mountain scenery, may be a faint imprint of an argument he and Barnard had had then as they walked along. Six years later, however, things have changed, and, if Bence Jones has left us with a fair abridgement of the diary, Faraday is now seeing an underlying life-force, a rhythm and a feeling for the landscape as a record of the passage of time. Turner's Alpine landscapes come to mind as the filter through which Faraday finds the language to express what he means, as Turner's sunsets did for Mary Somerville in the 1830s. But equally, the painter-model behind Faraday's language in the Alps in 1841 is John Martin. Here is Faraday describing his experience of being within sight and earshot of an avalanche, words which evoke pictorial detail against a background of fear and companionship. It ends with a rare expression of the cataclysm in real time:

> We now heard an avalanche, and hastened our steps. We came into a wood – most picturesque. Pines were blown down and crossed our path, and we wondered how mules could ever pass along it. We came on to a rising ground on the top of a deep precipitous glen or chasm, and saw opposite to us the sources of the Silberhorn, the Jungfrau, and other wonderful summits which here rose before us, and sent down continually great streams of water rushing down in every form of fall, and every now and then the thundering avalanches. The sound of these avalanches is exceedingly fine and solemn. It is the sound of thunder known to be caused by a fall of terrestrial matter, and conveys the idea of irresistible force. To the sight the avalanche is at this distance not terrible but beautiful. Rarely is it seen at the commencement, but the ear tells first of something strange happening, and then looking, the eye sees a falling cloud of snow, or else what was a moment before a cataract of water changed into a tumultuous and heavily waving rush of snow, ice,

and fluid, which, as it descends through the air, looks like water thickened, but as it runs over the inclined surfaces of the heaps below, moves heavily like paste, stopping and going as the mass behind accumulates or is dispersed.[33]

During these few weeks, Faraday gloried in being within nature, enwrapped by it, participating in it and feeling its overwhelming effects on his well-being and senses. Although he uses some of the chemist's analytical language – 'looks like water thickened . . . moves heavily like paste' – Faraday has now thrown his chemistry book away as he runs helter-skelter out of the avalanche's path. His language has something of the lilt of Humphry Davy's, particularly in the way he places himself securely (or insecurely) within the tumultuous and shifting landscape. In facing the power of the avalanche with the words he uses, Faraday has taken further mature leaps away from the language of his youth when, on the rumbling Mount Vesuvius in 1814, he distanced himself, and wrote of 'the odour of muriatic acid and chlorine' and of water 'volatilised by heat'.[34] Then, he was learning; now, he is feeling.

There is one passage in the diary which brings Faraday to muse on a rainbow as a metaphor for his religious beliefs. He and George Barnard had hired a boat to take them across Lake Brienz to the Giessbach, where Barnard intended to draw:

The sun shone brightly, and the rainbows seen from various points were very beautiful. One at the bottom of a fine but furious fall was very pleasant: there it remained motionless whilst the gusts and clouds of spray swept furiously across its place and were dashed against the rock. It looked like a spirit strong in faith and steadfast in the midst of the storm of passions sweeping across it, and though it might fade and revive, still it held on to the rock as in hope and giving hope, and the very drops which in the whirlwind of their fury seemed as if they would carry it all away were made to revive it and give it greater beauty.

How often are the things we fear and esteem as troubles made to become blessings to those who are led to receive them with humility and patience.[35]

Here, in a small boat on the choppy Lake Brienz, within the fall of the spray from the Giessbach, Faraday, Barnard and their two boatmen were in considerable physical danger. Having experienced and written about 'irresistible force' in nature, Faraday writes what we might call his Parable of the Rainbow, and creates an image which binds together science, art and religion into a whole. This passage might help to lead us to an understanding of the nature of the balance that these three forces held in Michael Faraday's life and work.

His present anxieties may have been physically rooted in his ill-health, which, in turn, had causes such as long-term poisoning from the many toxins he had handled and breathed in daily for years. Alpine walks notwithstanding, Michael Faraday did not lead the healthy life. But there may have been more. In his science he was travelling so far ahead of his era's theoretical and philosophical thought that, being engrained also within an unyielding, relentless religion, he must have felt an insistent rub of conflict even as he tried to think his way out of it; and he may have ruefully reflected that he was a Sandemanian, not a Swedenborgian. On the other hand, another gloss might be that Faraday valued his Sandemanianism as an anchor or safety net, and a firm foundation from which to reach heavenward, with science in his embrace. This is all surmise, for we cannot really know; but something bothered him, something sent him walking for hours alone in the mountains, something made him find hope in the steadfast rainbow.

A fundamental change in Faraday's life which must have been significant in determining his mood and reflections was his election to an Eldership in the Sandemanian church in October 1840. This was a position to which all male Sandemanians, fully committed for life to their faith, should dutifully aspire. If Faraday's election came to him as a happy or perhaps rueful surprise, he will also have known that it was part of the natural evolution of things, and that the challenge was bound to come. One of his few longer letters of 1840 was written from Brighton to his Sandemanian friend and brother William Buchanan, an Elder of the Edinburgh church, in which he lists the happy band of brothers, nephews and nieces staying with him and Sarah in Brighton: 'Mr Barnard (who is here with Mrs Barnard, Jane, Mrs Reid & her daughter Elizabeth) ... Mr Paradise is also here ... there is such mingling & ought to be such community of feeling & spirit as to make us one body.'[36] The latter part of the letter, in which he writes about their co-religionist Mary Straker, is very revealing of Faraday the churchman, rather than Faraday the scientist:

> [She] is very ill & we cannot but fear that the nature of her illness is such as to indicate the breaking up of her constitution & the approach of that time which it will be well if we are all led to be waiting for . . . But she is very patient & comforted by the scriptures in the great & glorious hope of relief not merely from these things but from all sorrow & sighing through Jesus Christ and rejoices in her friends company. She has been a very remarkable character & example in the church, always in an humble station and with no worldly knowledge or worldly means but yet full of a helping, cheerful & what is more *faithful* affection to her brethren & a comfort & support in many troubles to those of her own family & acquaintance.

Compared with his incisive and clear writings about science, whether in correspondence or in his papers and lectures, the words Faraday the churchman uses about Mary Straker are clichés. Being used as we are to reading his reflective and illuminating turns of phrase, it is remarkable to see Faraday moving quite comfortably into the static language of fundamentalist religion. It might be one thing to write thus to a humble and ill-educated believer – Mary Straker herself, one might suggest – but it is quite another to slip into such standard phrases when writing to a man who is not only a senior Sandemanian, but also a well-respected Edinburgh advocate, an expert on the Scottish law of tithes and author of legal books.[37] The particular use of language seems to reveal that despite the fact that these two men were at the very top of their highly intellectual and literate professions, the sheer weight of orthodoxy demanded by Sandemanianism prevented even them from speaking with anything other than the prescribed vocabulary of their church. This may be compared with the writings of other churchmen on a broadly similar intellectual level as Faraday and Buchanan, such as John Donne, Isaac Watts and Sydney Smith, whose writings sparkle with imagery, insight and religious fresh-thinking, and gave the established and disestablished churches in England the roots of the deep understanding and expression that have built up since the sixteenth century.

After Faraday had been elected an Elder it is reasonable to suppose that his commitments at the London chapel increased. These will now have included reading from the Bible, leading services and preaching to the faithful congregation, as well as taking pastoral and administrative responsibilities at the chapel. If he had had any doubts about the compatibility of science and Sandemanianism, they would have surfaced painfully now, and it is possible that the root cause of his breakdown was not physical but mental: his inability after much (too much) thought to reconcile fully the science he was discovering with the religion that he knew.

Faraday's care for Mary Straker is but one example of his prayerful concern for the members of the Sandemanian community. In another instance he took extended time away from the Royal Institution in 1837 when his brother-in-law William Barnard was seriously ill.[38] As a capable leader of the flock, Faraday also assumed some responsibility for Sandemanian communities distant from London, particularly those at Newcastle, Dundee and Old Buckenham, fifteen miles south-east of Norwich. When in early October 1840 he told the scientist William Grove that he had just come back from Norfolk,[39] it is likely that the purpose of the journey had been to visit the Sandemanian community at Old Buckenham; and when he travelled to Newcastle in 1842 it was to visit, encourage and exhort his wider Sandemanian family as well as his own relations in that city.[40]

There are some surviving traces of Faraday's manner as a preacher. The archive at the Royal Institution holds five sermon cards which he wrote out to guide himself while preaching, and there are some more extensive notes of his and others' sermons taken by a member of the congregation.[41] The sermon cards reveal how he traced his theme from book to book of the Old and New Testaments, comparing, illustrating and exhorting, while the sermon notes, which are dated June 1862, but which reflect a manner that would not have changed since the 1840s, suggest that he preached with a much more archaic sentence structure than he used in his lectures, reflecting the practice of the chapel.[42] A typical passage, in its abbreviated form, runs as follows:

I have been greatly struck lately with the reading of Hosea. Who walk as it were in the shadow of his name – long reproofs. 1 ch.

6. vers. For I will no more have mercy upon the house of Israel. 7th But I will have mercy upon the house of Judah and will save them by the Lord their God, and will not save them by bow, nor by sword, nor by battle, by horses, nor by horsemen. 9, 10, 11, 12 takes all *this power* to break down and separate her from her lovers. Made to bow down and acknowledge her sins & iniquities.

Where the unknown note-taker has written 'long reproofs' we can suppose that here Faraday continued the practice in Sandemanian services of pointing out at length the severe human shortcomings of every individual present, and exhorting each and every one of them to improve their ways and live more soberly and prayerfully in Christ.

For reasons that are unclear, Faraday, despite being a distinguished Elder of the church, committed some transgression of Sandemanian rules that resulted, on 31 March 1844, in his rapidly being stripped of his Eldership and committed to a very real limbo where Sandemanian brotherly love was felt at its coolest. The speed and cruelty of the exclusion took no account of good service or worldly station. Faraday was not alone in this sudden fall from grace: eighteen of his fellow worshippers, including his brother Robert, his sister-in-law Margaret Faraday and even his father-in-law, the Elder Edward Barnard, were pushed to the fringes at about the same time. Whatever the cause of these exclusions, it must also have been partly a family thing – the holding of a particular point of view about Sandemanian ministry that could not be resolved with the whole congregation. Faraday's exclusion has been put down to the unconfirmed suggestion that he was commanded to visit the Queen one Sunday early in 1844, thus presenting him with an acute dilemma, a choice between obeying his monarch as a good citizen should, and observing the Sabbath as a Sandemanian.[43] No evidence has been found that Faraday was ever commanded to visit Queen Victoria at that time, and the fact that so many other Sandemanians were excluded more or less together suggests that the cull had ideological rather than personal or procedural roots.

There were some deep dissensions in the Sandemanian church in 1844, which suggest that the Elders were taking decisions that should properly have been put to the church as a whole. They read in Matthew 18 that if 'thy brother shall trespass against thee, go and tell him his fault between thee and him alone', but that if, after repeated telling by two or three more, he would still not hear his fault, 'tell it unto the church'. Interpretation of this passage may have been the root of the matter, though what the particular fault was is no longer known. The issue, however, deeply infected Sandemanians across Britain and in America, where churches 'have been visited by terrible things in righteousness'.[44] Those words were used in a letter written in December 1844 to the London community by a Dundee Elder, George Baxter, and confirmed some months later by an Elder from Glasgow, Robert Cree, who wrote that 'these were truely awfull times', and spoke of 'the hidden things of darkness . . . when many appeared to be given up to walk in their own ways'.[45] Faraday and his family evidently found themselves on the wrong side of the fence on this or a similar issue, and suffered for it. But the fact that they were excluded together indicates the presence of a strong family solidarity, stronger even than the extreme dictates of the faith they shared. Family solidarity was something that Faraday had experienced throughout his life; the fact that he continued to do so well into his sixth decade suggests that to him family was as important as religion, and perhaps also as science.

There is only the briefest mention of his agonies over the exclusion in Faraday's letters to his non-Sandemanian friends – a few words to Schoenbein, in which he speaks of 'certain private troubles [that] have brought me low in health & spirits'.[46] But writing to William Buchanan after the exclusion was over – he was readmitted to the church on 5 May 1844 – Faraday showed the kind of extreme self-abasement that Sandemanianism saw as a virtue and a duty:

> . . . I may well indeed be ashamed seeing how I have helped with the wicked to bring great reproach & contempt on the Church of God and deepest condemnation on myself. It is wonderful how I have been spared to be reproved & to write thus to you in what according to his mercy is a hope that can include even me.[47]

The direct result of the exclusion was that Faraday was stripped of his Eldership, an office he was not re-elected to for a further sixteen years. But no sooner had he abased himself in front of his brethren than he received an assurance that the wider world on the other hand had never, and would never, exclude him. Writing from her home in

Edgeworthstown, sixty miles north-west of Dublin, the novelist Maria Edgeworth paid Faraday a high, unasked-for compliment, in words that could only have raised his spirits:

Were I writing to anyone but yourself I would express without restraint or reserve and with the warmth with which I feel it admiration for talents and inventive genius directed to the best purposes, free from the petty envy & jealousy wh. too often cloud the lustre of genius and poison the happiness of the possessor. The brightness of your day the cheerfulness of your temper even under the trials of illhealth and the evident enjoyment you have in science and literature for their own sake together with your love for your private friends and the serenity of your domestic life prove (whatever Rousseau may have said or felt to the contrary) that 'Sois grand homme et sois malheureux' is not the inevitable doom of genius.[48]

This letter did not come entirely out of the blue. Maria Edgeworth, by now in her seventies, had some months earlier expressed an interest in meeting Faraday. They had many friends and associates in common – Sir Humphry Davy and William Wollaston had been friends of hers, and others included Mary Somerville, William Whewell and the Herschels – and her request to meet Faraday had come through another mutual friend, the archaeologist and recently elected Fellow of the Royal Society Sir John Boileau, Bart. Edgeworth's desire is part of a pattern in which interesting women – Ada Lovelace, Mary Somerville, Jane Marcet and now Edgeworth herself – put it about that they would like to get to know Michael Faraday. The invitation from Boileau reached Faraday thus:

Should you have the leisure to make a call at any time I think you would have an agreeable interview with a Lady whose fame in *her* department is almost equal to your own in the world of Science. Miss Edgeworth.

She is living at No 1 South Audley St. and is very desirous to make your acquaintance but cannot go out & laid her injunctions on me to make this *private* and *very marked* communication to you. As she is more than 70 – tho' still of vigorous mind I hope that I may stand excused of all indiscretion in obliging the commands of a Lady and an authoress.[49]

The productive scientist and the prolific authoress undoubtedly met in the following few weeks; Edgeworth's request refers also to her being 'gratified by your desire to have my father's Memoirs *as a souvenir from myself*', and ends with a remark in which she hopes 'that you will let my sister Wilson[50] have as much as you can spare of your time. No one can enjoy more or better appreciate your talents & character.' Evidently, Faraday had let himself be persuaded into giving some kind of instruction or counselling to Fanny Edgeworth, now Mrs Wilson, another interesting woman then at the ripe age of forty-six.

There is a further scrap of evidence that suggests that Maria Edgeworth's letter may have been written as a generous attempt – perhaps a misplaced kindness, but generous enough – to console Faraday during his travails with the Sandemanians. She had lately returned from spending some days with the Herschels at Collingwood, in the Kentish Weald:

It is impossible to be more comfortable or to have been more cordially received than we have been by these kind friends . . . The nice room I am in is Herschel's own study or working room with all his instruments put away in glass cases and presses in the corner and his books and all his things left![51]

Fanny Wilson and her husband were there too, as were Lord and Lady Adare – 'he no great shakes but a sincere admirer of the stars – double or single – and a tolerable measurer of their brightness'. It is hard to conceive that among all this science, these scientists and eager amateurs, their mutual friend Michael Faraday and his fragile health should not have been a topic of conversation. A further question arises, as to how far beyond the Sandemanian circle would its internal dissensions and punishments be known; would Faraday's exclusion have been known to any of his friends in science, or did he keep it to himself and his family? The evidence that he would only brush lightly on the subject to a man as close as Schoenbein suggests that he kept the matter to himself, and indeed the exclusion lasted for less than five weeks. Whether they knew the reason or not, Faraday's low spirits and his recurrent illness were common knowledge in his wider circle.

His exclusion could not have come at a worse time, when he was trying valiantly to recover from his breakdown, and we can reasonably consider that Maria Edgeworth's perfectly timed, complimentary and affectionate letter was an intentional, even orchestrated, attempt amongst his worldly friends to cheer the old philosopher up.

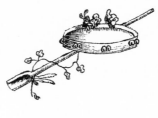

CHAPTER 21

Michael Faraday and the Bride of Science

Faraday wrote very little about his religion; or little that has survived. When he did it was usually to fellow Sandemanians, rarely touching on the subject to 'outsiders'. There is, however, one very important instance of his discussing Sandemanianism in a letter to a correspondent outside the faith. He had a flurried but revealing correspondence in October 1844 with the brilliant but highly-strung mathematician Ada, Lady Lovelace, the daughter of Lord Byron and Annabella Milbanke.[1] Ada's letters, written in ink in a bold hand, and striated with underlinings like knife wounds on the page, were so direct in their approach that one letter, which flattered him with her praise for a paper on electrical conduction, also leapt into a question that he must have found himself powerless to avoid. Before Ada Lovelace's epistolary glare, Michael Faraday was as a rabbit in front of a snake. Ada asked him:

> One reason why I desire to become more intimate with you, is my opinion of your *moral & religious* feelings.
>
> Do you agree with me, as I rather expect you do, in the impression that the *highest & most penetrating* degree of *intellect, that* species of it which is alone fitted to deal with the more *subtle & occult* agents of nature, is unattainable excepting thro' a high *spiritual & moral* development; far higher than it is usual; even to *aim* at. *I*

believe there is a connexion between the two that is not understood or suspected by mankind.

You are the only philosopher I have ever seen, who gave me the impression of feeling this in its full force.

Am I mistaken? All I can say is that if *you & I* do think alike on this point, I suspect we are very nearly a singular couple in the scientific world.

I do not know to what particular *sect* of Christians you belong, or whether to *any*; nor do I think that much matters.

I am myself a Unitarian Christian; as far as regards some of their views of Christ that is.

But in truth I cannot be said to be anything but *myself*. In *some* points I am *Swedenborgian* in feelings. Again in others I am slightly Roman Catholic; & I have also my alliance with the older *Rosecrucians*.[2]

There was no escape from that. If Faraday had felt secure in the privacy of his religion, Ada Lovelace's onslaught was quite enough to flush him out into the open and force him to explain himself.

Faraday and Ada had met, though only briefly, in the past few years, probably at the Royal Institution, where Ada was a faithful member of the Friday-night audience. In recent years, certainly since her marriage in 1835, she had become a society figure with an edge, an enchanter with a genius for mathematics, headstrong and inflammable. She had befriended Charles Babbage, and they studied mathematical problems together; but even in the 1840s some friends of Ada's parents' generation could not quite shake off their image of her as a child. The writer Joanna Baillie was astonished when she heard in 1844 that Ada had been touted as the author of *Vestiges of the National History of Creation*, a book, published anonymously, that suggested to a shocked readership that the creation of the universe was subject to natural, rather than theological laws:[3] 'This Lady whom we know so well as little Ada whose chief conversation used to be about a Persian Cat, Puff by name, is beginning to be known in the literary world.'[4]

Ada felt most sincerely that she and Faraday were kindred spirits, and at breakneck speed bombarded him with words of praise and endearment, with the added spice of conspiracy that they should get together and improve the world. Within the opening paragraphs of this first letter from Ada to Faraday – and there are many paragraphs in her letters; she sliced her thoughts like ham – she told him fervently:

> I have long been *vowed to the Temple*; – the Temple of *Truth, Nature, Science!* And every year I take vows more strict, till now I am just entering those portals & those mysteries which cut of[f] all retreat, & bind my very life & soul to *unwearied* & *undivided* science at its altars henceforward. I hope to die the *High-Priestess* of God's works as manifested on this earth, & to earn a right to bequeath to my posterity the following motto, '*Dei Naturaeque Interpres*' ... [5]
>
> All this is highly metaphysical; but there is *some literal* truth in it also, in my case. This, if we hold in future more in intercourse together, you will by degrees *yourself* perceive.
>
> For many years I have desired to be admitted to intercourse & friendship with you; & to become in *some* respects your disciple.

Clearly, Ada's zealous enthusiasms ran away with her, but Faraday took it on the chin, and answered her kindly and fully: 'The thanks which I owe you can only properly be acknowledged by an open & sincere reply and the absence of all conventional phrase.'[6] In this reply Faraday is as open with Ada as he had been as a young man with Benjamin Abbott, or latterly with Schoenbein. He compares Ada's youth – she was twenty-nine – her vivacity and determination with his own decay:

> You have all the confidence of unbaulked health & youth both in body & mind; I am a labourer of many years' standing made daily to feel my wearing out. You, with increasing acquisitions of knowledge, enlarge your views and intentions; I, though I may gain from day to day some little maturity of thought, feel the decay of powers, and am curtailing to a continual process of lessening my intentions and contracting my pursuits ... You do not know and should not know but that I have no concealment on this point from you, how often I have to go to my medical friend to speak of giddiness and reeling of the head &c, and how often he has to bid me cease from restless thoughts and mental occupation and retire to the seaside and inaction.

Ada must have hit a deeply hidden nerve to induce Faraday to reply like that. He would never normally reveal himself in such a way to someone who was practically a stranger, but with Ada Lovelace relationships were never normal. Faraday continued freely:

If I were with you I could talk for hours of your letter and its content, though it would do my head no good, for it is a most fertile source of thoughts to my mind; and whether we might differ upon this or that point or not I am sure we should not disagree.

One of the factors that may have prompted Faraday to lower his guard and open up like this was that there was no woman at home with whom he could talk on such an elevated plane. He was highly susceptible to women, and they were attracted to him. He was handsome throughout his life, and held a public position with a charisma and style which captivated women, and which certainly captivated Ada. As his portraits reveal, Faraday was a wide-eyed male English beauty, with well-made features, shining skin and hair, the kind of looks that Humphry Davy, Lord Byron and Rupert Brooke possessed. There were no comparable women in English science any more, Mary Somerville having gone off to Italy for good, and with Ada throwing herself at him Faraday was shaken to attention. To all appearances, Ada wanted to be his muse, a position that was vacant, as Sarah was not her husband's muse but his carer.

Being assiduous in covering all points, answering all questions, Faraday at last reached Ada's question about his faith. They had clearly already had at least one conversation about religion, Faraday reminding her that 'You will perhaps remember that I guessed & not very far aside your tendency in this respect.' He went on:

There is no philosophy in my religion. I am of a very small & despised sect of christians known, if known at all, as *Sandemanians* and our hope is founded on the faith that is in Christ. But though the natural works of God can never by any possibility come in contradiction with the higher things that belong to our future existence, and must with every thing concerning Him ever glorify him still I do not think it at all necessary to tie the study of the natural

Description of a Pyroneumatic Apparatus

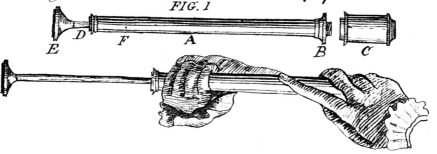

FIG. 1

The cylinder A, fig: 1, is about 9 inches long, and ½ inch in diameter: it terminates in a screw at B, on which screws the magazine C, intended to hold matches, a bougie, and some fungus. A steel rod, D, is attached to a solid piston, or plunger, not shewn in the figure, it being within the tube. This rod has a milled head, E; and at F there is a small hole in the tube to admit the air, when the piston is drawn up to the top, where a piece uni- -screws

Pen-and-ink drawing of a pneumatic apparatus by Michael Faraday in his 'Philosophical Miscellany' (1809–10).

John Tatum's lecture room at 53 Dorset Street. Pen-and-ink drawing by Michael Faraday, 1810.

A chemical balance at the Royal Institution. Pencil drawing by Michael Faraday.

Bridge and River. Wash drawing by Michael Faraday, 1820s or 1830s.

Cottage Among Mountains.
Lithograph made jointly
by Michael Faraday and
George Barnard, dated
25 April 1825.

*Rest on the Flight to
Egypt.* Engraving by
Claude Lorraine, 1670.
One of the small
group of old-master
prints collected by
Faraday and fixed in
his notebook.

The Three Trees.
Engraving by Rembrandt,
1643. Another print from
Faraday's notebook.

'Scientific Researches!' Cartoon by James Gillray, 1802.
Humphry Davy, recently appointed Lecturer at the Institution, holds the bellows.

The laboratory of the Royal Institution as it was in the late 1810s.

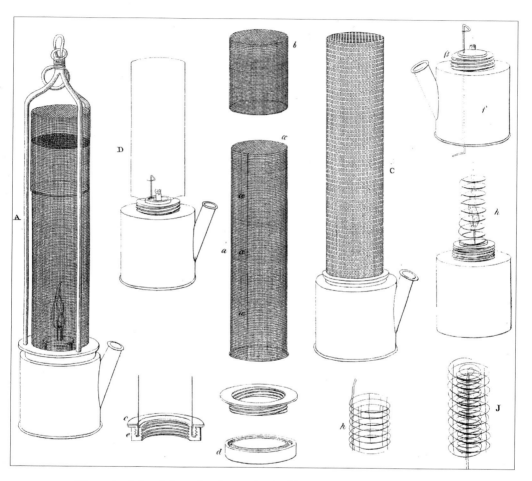

The principle of the safety lamp, devised by Davy and Faraday in 1814.

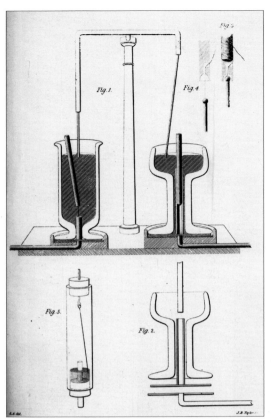

Diagram of the apparatus devised by Faraday in 1821 to demonstrate electro-magnetic rotations. The smaller version, bottom left, he made and sent to scientists on the continent for them to perform the experiment.

Faraday's induction ring: an iron ring, wound by Faraday while on holiday in Hastings in 1831, and first used that year to demonstrate the principle of electro-magnetic induction.

The electro-magnet made in 1845 at the Royal Institution. It is visible under the table in Harriet Moore's watercolour of the Magnetic Laboratory (opposite).

Faraday at work in the Chemical Laboratory. Watercolour by Harriet Moore, 1852.

Faraday's Magnetic Laboratory. Watercolour by Harriet Moore, 1850s.

Faraday's study in his Royal Institution flat (note the Turnerian storm scene in the picture on the right of the far wall: see pp.360-1). Watercolour by Harriet Moore, 1850s.

The house on the Green, Hampton Court, where Faraday lived, by courtesy of Queen Victoria, from 1858 until his death

sciences & religion together and in my intercourse with my fellow creatures that which is religious & that which is philosophical have ever been two distinct things.

And now my dear Lady I must conclude until I see you in town being *indeed* Your true and faithful Servant

M. Faraday.

Throughout Faraday's long life, only Ada Lovelace ever managed to get such a clear definition out of him of the distinct separation, as he himself expressed it at that time, of his religion and his science; but this may have been a new, even desperate form of words written out by Faraday in the light of a reasoned incompatibility between the two principal areas of his life. We must be grateful to Ada for her very direct approach, for this first letter to her reveals much. 'There is no philosophy [that is, science] in my religion' may help to explain the reason behind the use of stiff religious language in Faraday's letters – for example to Buchanan – and behind what little we know of his style as a preacher. In the tenets of Sandemanianism it was the strictly quoted words of the Bible that carried the light, and not any added illumination or exegesis of the preacher. But while Faraday says that he does not think it 'necessary' to tie the study of the natural sciences and religion together, he does not say that it would be impossible.

Faraday had settled down to write that letter less than ten days after Ada had written hers from Ashley Combe, near Porlock in Somerset. Ada's had arrived when Faraday was away in Durham, and he had since had one of his turns; but her impatience was such that, not having had a response from the great man, she dashed off another on the day Faraday happened to be composing his own reply, and the two letters crossed in the post. From Ada's point of view this was a lovers' correspondence, but an affair at this stage of the mind rather than the heart or body. She had an extremely high opinion of herself – justly – and told Faraday that he really need not reply quickly, until

sufficient time has elapsed to make a reply quite *satisfactory to yourself*. And in the *nature* of that reply, to consider *yourself* & not *me*. Do what is natural & agreeable to *you* to do; & think of *me* as a mere *instrument*. If you knew more of me, I think you would be inclined to believe (as I do) that a certain degree of scientific cooperation between us, would materially subserve the interests & objects of *both* parties. And for you to know truly my intellectual characteristics, I believe I ought to begin by becoming in a manner your pupil ... [7]

When Faraday's replies to her two letters arrived, Ada was overwhelmed by them. The second was short, saying that he would send her copies of the first two volumes of his *Experimental Researches in Electricity*: 'Give them a value by accepting them from me.'[8] In her turn, Ada empathised like a professional:

They [Faraday's letters] are in my eyes beautiful & interesting, because there is in them all that *simple sincerity*, which I have ever seemed to *feel* in you, (as if by a kind of magic); & which constitutes the feature which I repeat that I view with '*little short of reverence*'.[9]

Ada continued to write to Faraday over the following few months. Her letters were long, passionate, solipsistic, scarred, as we have seen, by underlinings. Her pen is a knife: 'My life is *one continuous sacrifice of every merely present comfort & gratification.*' Ada's passion is for herself and the freedom of her self-expression in science rather than for a lover, but her need for Faraday was acute. She shows complete understanding of his nicely drawn distinction between religion and science, and honours his godly life:

You express surprise that I should regard you as I do. It is the *singleness* of your character which is at the foundation of my feelings respecting you. I think I see in you a man who never attempts '*to serve two masters*'. I think I see in you a being who is ever willing to serve *man as under God*, but not to serve *man instead of God*, or to make man the *go-between* interposed between you & the Creator.

And, when I behold these characteristics *united* with high intellectual endowments, I cannot but look on you then as one of the *few* whom it is an honour & a privilege to know on this earth.

She ended this letter by exhorting Faraday:

Do not answer me, (that is unless you really feel you *like & can*).

And think of me as a creature who would *give all*, & ask *nothing* in return, excepting a true confidence in her own simple & fervent character. To like me & to *place faith* in me, is *all* I could ever expect.

What effect would the receipt of such letters have on a man like Michael Faraday? He kept them, indeed he endorsed them '1844', so he clearly wanted them to be anchored within his archive. He did not reply to Ada's third letter of 27 October, so another one bounded its way to him from Porlock a fortnight later. 'How much you have *said* to me by simply *not* answering my last letter!', she began, and continued by asking Faraday if there were any points he wanted to raise with Andrew Crosse, whom Ada planned to visit at Fyne Court at the end of the month. She, who had 'great influence with Mr C–', would raise whatever subjects Faraday wished to discuss with Crosse on his behalf. 'Now, let none of this *trouble* you. I would not miss a possible opportunity of being useful to *you*, or useful to Science, (*Science whose bride* I am)!'[10]

In London in the 1840s it was Michael Faraday who was the personification of science. He had held this exalted position, unasked for, for fifteen or twenty years. So in claiming to be the bride of Science, Ada was also yearning to be acknowledged as the intellectual bride of Michael Faraday. She already had strong friendships with Andrew Crosse ('hints or suggestions from me he would be apt to consider & follow') and Charles Babbage ('How I wish by the bye that *his* mind were (in *some* points) more akin to that which in *you* I so admire'), but by comparison with Faraday, Crosse and Babbage were lowly priests of science. Despite the social gulf between them, Faraday was the great object of Ada's affections, and now she was throwing everything she could at him to gain the response she craved.

Extraordinarily, Faraday must have replied to this letter by return of post, for Ada responded immediately from Porlock.[11] Faraday's letter is lost, but it clearly encouraged Ada in her affections. Her response reveals that he compared himself to a tortoise, that he referred to her 'elasticity of intellect', and that they 'must *meet*, & *talk*'. Faraday's description of himself as a tortoise – he had used the same image in a contemporary letter to Schoenbein[12] – set Ada's imagination a-jangle:

[317]

You have excited in my mind a ridiculous, but not ungraceful, allegorical picture, viz that of a quiet demure plodding *tortoise*, with a beautiful *fairy* gambolling round it in a thousand radiant & varying hues; the tortoise crying out, 'Fairy, fairy, I am not like you. *I* cannot at pleasure assume a thousand aerial shapes & expand myself over the face of the universe. Fairy, fairy have mercy on me, & remember I am *but a tortoise.*'

What says the kind gentle fairy in reply? Somewhat as follows:

'Good tortoise, then I will be to *you* of plain & sober hue. I can assume what form I like. I will be the beautiful phantom, glowing in colour & eloquence, when you so order me. But I will now be a little *quiet brown bird* at your side, & gently let *you* teach me *how* to *know* & aid you. But my *wand* is *yours* at pleasure, & into *your* hands I deliver it for your use.'

So speaks the ladye-fairy. Well! Forgive my fun & metaphor. I am as basinfull of *sportive mirth* as of science, you know . . .

You are right. We must *meet*, & *talk*. So will the Tortoise be good enough to appoint an evening for coming to this mischievous *sprite* of a *thousand forms*; (for venturing within her magic circle)? Thursday 28th, at 6 o'clock.

It is all too easy for an early-twenty-first-century reader to look at these two personalities of the mid-nineteenth century through the lens of the intervening twentieth, and to find evidence of some kind of lovers' tryst shaping up here. This may have been an inexpressible hope of Ada's, for she had admirers who may also have been lovers. But Faraday, with all his moral authority, integrity and religious commitment, was not the man to join them. On Ada's part, despite the sexual overtones in her letters, it may indeed have been enough for her to imagine herself swooning elegantly before Faraday's fine, high brow.

Another lost letter from Faraday intervened between Ada's 'tortoise and fairy' letter and her next, of 13 November. In that one he evidently set a date to meet her. 'Agreed then!', she swiftly replied.[13] 'I say Amen to every line. You must know that *the fairy* always takes to "*hard, rough, & Straightforward*" mortals.' She then unloaded on Faraday, in the new special intimacy she had granted him, news of all her illnesses:

I am subject to *two* very delightful ailments. Gastritis (alias Gastric Fever) and Asthma ... Excepting my *mother*, & you, I have not mentioned to any correspondent, that I have been ill lately ...

I know *no one so strong*, so vitalized, as myself; notwithstanding all this ... *Pain* & *suffering* have sharply & sternly schooled me, & made me *dead* to all merely *earthly* things.

Ever yours then,
The Ladye Fairy.

Ada and Faraday might have met on 28 November 1844; we have a plaintive, even inconsolable, note from Ada dated 1 December, which implies that they did, and that at some point Faraday tried to use his common origins to cool her down. Faraday himself had by 1 December left London, and Ada had tried to see him again, but

My engagements & also the rain prevented my looking in on you either yesterday or Friday [i.e. 30 and 29 November]. I do not know *when* you will return to Town, but I shall beg sometime for another hour or two from you in the evening.

We must talk *business* & *science* next time.

Pray do not fancy you are too plain & rough for me ...

I write in a hurry, & perhaps I am not over clear in expressing to you all I mean. If so we can *talk* about it.

Ever yours
A.A.L.[14]

There is one final anguished response from Faraday, in which he suddenly realises that he has gone too far with Ada for decorum:

Friday Evg Royal Institution
My Dear Lady Lovelace,

You drive me to desperation by your invitations. I dare not and must not come and yet find it almost impossible to refuse such a wish as yours. I know not how to answer you: – and do not think that my temptation is the *Gentry* for I can assure you it is for *your* kindness that I feel I make but a bad return and it is you who would draw me if anything might. Forgive me and believe me most gratefully

Yours

M. Faraday.[15]

For the next six years there was no known contact between Faraday and Ada, Lady Lovelace. But it was undoubtedly her vivacity, intellect and puppy-like affection for Faraday that bolstered his spirits, flattered him, and helped him to repair the damage in his life caused by his mental breakdown and his brief exclusion from the Sandemanians. Her wooing of him, her ambition to be his bride of science, both stirred up his emotions and appalled him, and led him to withdraw gradually into the laboratory, where he carried out his last decade of scientific research. Six years later, in June 1851, his flame for Ada was still warm. Replying to a lost request or invitation, in a letter which is an uncanny echo of a love letter he once sent to Sarah, Faraday wrote:

You see what you do – ever as you like with me. You say write & I write – and I wish I had the strength and had rest enough for a great deal more for it would give me very great pleasure to move more earnestly for those young creatures whom I rejoiced to know as your children. Their intelligence was astonishing, their manners kind & themselves in every way most interesting.[16]

In November 1852 Ada died from cervical cancer, at the age of thirty-seven.

The insurmountable distance between Ada and Faraday is characterised by the different directions from which they approached science. Despite (or because of) the fact that Ada described herself with a bizarre variety as 'a Unitarian Christian . . . Swedenborgian in feelings . . . slightly Roman Catholic; & I have also my alliance with the older Rosecrucians', her approach to science was essentially pagan. She wrote of long being 'vowed to . . . the Temple of Truth, Nature, Science! And every year I take vows more strict . . . I hope to die the High-Priestess of God's works as manifested on this earth . . .' and so on. By the mid-1840s this attitude was long out of date, reminiscent as it is not only of Keats, who had died in 1821, but also of Erasmus Darwin, William Blake, even of Milton.

It suggests that Ada's ideas and metaphors are the result of over-heated book-learning, rather than of quiet reflection, something of which she may not have been fully capable.

Though taken and shaken by her vivacity and life-force, Faraday would in the long run have found little in common with Ada. She was a mathematician and he was not, having little feeling and less aptitude for mathematics; but aside from that Faraday's science grew through enquiry, observation and experiment from his measured application of a deeply rooted religious sense, rather than from an unstable mix of acquired enthusiasms, extreme intellectual ability and volatility. But although this particular tortoise and fairy were better apart, the vitality of their brief friendship confirmed to Faraday that he was still alive.

CHAPTER 22

Still, it may be True...

The brief association with Ada Lovelace drew a firm line under the part of Faraday's life that was characterised by illness, malaise, uncertainty in his science and exclusion in his religion, and gave him an impetus to look to the future. The opportunity came in October 1844 for him to look back on his career, when a journalist wrote asking him to list his many achievements. Eventually overcoming his 'feeling of extreme reluctance to do any thing that might seem to be more or less honouring myself', Faraday listed his professorships, his memberships of more than fifty learned societies all over the world, and his knighthood in the Prussian Order of Merit.[1] He was by now the most respected single individual in world science, approaching, if not having already arrived at, the position which the Astronomer Royal, Sir George Biddell Airy, would describe in 1847 as 'a universal referee or character-counsel on all matters of science'.[2]

One area in which Faraday's genius for applying scientific principles to practical problems flourished was in the improvement he made to the lighting systems of lighthouses. His association with Trinity House, for which he had been Scientific Adviser in Experiments on Light since 1836, developed in the 1840s. The extent and availability of his advice when called upon does not appear to have been greatly affected by his extended illness. Indeed, in the first few days of February 1841, when he was very firmly under doctor's – and Sarah's – orders and 'required . . . to lie bye for a twelvemonth' with mental fatigue,[3] he travelled down to the Isle of Wight to inspect the St Catherine's lighthouse near Niton. His mission was to examine the chimney that he had himself designed to carry away the smoke and moisture produced by the Argand lamps, and to devise ways of improving its efficiency. In winter the glass in front of the lamps iced up severely, dimming the light, and there were further problems caused by condensation both coming from the lamps and rising from the lighthouse tower itself. In a long report for Trinity House, written within a week of his return from the Isle of Wight, Faraday made his recommendations for improving the chimney, the lamps and the arrangement of the doors in the tower.[4]

Soon after settling the matter of the ventilation of St Catherine's Light, Faraday inspected a set of Fresnel lighthouse refractors and reported to Trinity House on their efficiency,[5] gave advice on coloured and plain glass for lenses,[6] and on the most satisfactory arrangements for the reflectors.[7] He made sure he was always available for Trinity House: safety at sea was a subject shot through with significance for the well-being of the nation as a whole, and of seamen as individuals. The ancient corporation of Trinity House, founded in 1514 to ensure safe navigation around the shores of England and Wales, was a body rich in tradition, watchfulness and care for others, overseen by experienced merchant seamen who held the ranks of Elders and referred to each other as Brethren. It is no surprise that when invited to become their adviser Faraday accepted 'with an honest sense of a duty to be performed'.[8] Although he was careful when accepting the post to say that his time was valuable to him, and he did not want to be involved in 'periodical routine attendances', the responsibilities that Trinity House carried bore deep meaning for a religious man. Indeed, beyond the fact that both had 'Elders' and 'Brethren', there are many close parallels in the activities of Trinity House and Faraday's own Sandemanian church, which begin with their respective acknowledgement of their responsibilities – the one for the care of human beings at sea, the other for human souls in the sea of faith.

As the 1840s progressed, Faraday made more visits to lighthouses – for example to South Foreland near Dover in December 1843, September 1846 and January 1847[9] – and advised on improvements to many more, including those at Bude, Lundy, Eddystone, Maplin and Start Point. His particular concern, which simple measures rapidly improved, was to better the ventilation, to increase the power of emitted light by improvements in lenses, reflectors, lamps and oil, and to safeguard lighthouses against lightning strikes. One happy recipient of an improvement was George Neale, Keeper of St Catherine's Light, who told Faraday:

> In answer to your Letter respecting the general effect of the Copper pipe fixed by your direction I feel great Pleasure to say it has realised the full anticipation you formed of its merits that is to say no damp condensing on windows no dirt shading the Lantern in every respect keeping 20 times cleaner ... Sir your Plan has driven the enemy out. I entertain not the slightest fears of him ever coming again to cause such labour as you witnessed on the 4th of Feby 1841.[10]

When he was recovering from his breakdown Faraday was drawn into major inquiries following two disastrous explosions which called on his talents as an analyst. In April 1843 the gunpowder factory at Waltham Abbey in Essex blew up with an explosion that was heard in Hyde Park, fourteen miles away. Seven men were killed.[11] Faraday was asked by the Ordnance Office – his employers in his capacity as lecturer at the Royal Military Academy at Woolwich – to report and make recommendations to prevent such an accident happening again. After visiting the site he pointed firmly in his report to the dangers caused by the grinding of the powder with marble or iron rollers, from which fragments could break off and by friction cause the gunpowder to fire.[12] The second explosion, at Haswell colliery in County Durham on 28 September 1844, caused the deaths of ninety-five men and boys.[13] The mine at Haswell, generally considered to be among the best-ventilated and best-managed in the country, had been one of those at the centre of the so-called 'Great Strike of 1844' in Durham and Northumberland, in which miners struggled with owners to improve employment conditions, wages, working hours and safety.

Humphry Davy's safety lamp, which had been introduced nearly thirty years earlier, had, through slack attitudes and incomplete training, done little to reduce explosions and deaths in coalmines. Explosions had in fact markedly increased in the intervening years as the number and depth of mines had grown, coal production had risen, and as the safety lamp gave miners a false sense of security. The Haswell explosion rapidly became a national issue, and the inquest, hurriedly called on the day of the funeral of the victims, 30 September 1844, became a political event. By the skilful manoeuvring of the Chartist lawyer William Prowting Roberts, appearing for the victims, the inquest was adjourned so that, under the recommendations of the 1835 Commons Committee report into mining disasters, the mine could be inspected by experts appointed by the Home Secretary. Roberts himself travelled to London to petition the Prime Minister, Robert Peel, who appointed Faraday and Charles Lyell. Though he was at first reluctant to take on the commission, perhaps because of his health,[14] Faraday travelled north with Lyell on 8 October, and the next day the pair were thrown straight into the inquiry. Faraday himself cross-examined the witnesses, as Lyell described, 'with as much tact, skill and self-possession as if he had been an old practitioner at the Bar'.[15] This comes as no surprise; firm but courteous cross-examination, whether of natural phenomena or of people, was Faraday's stock-in-trade. They went on to examine the mine, which remained highly unstable, and narrowly avoided injury in a rockfall.[16] It was very soon clear that the safety procedures at Haswell were shoddy, and, finding himself sitting on a bag of gunpowder while, according to one report, another man held a lighted candle, Faraday 'sprung up on his feet, and, in a most animated and expressive style, expostulated with them for their carelessness'.[17]

The inquest jury returned verdicts of accidental death, which was what the mine-owners wanted, and although in his notes Faraday remarked 'Fully agree with them,'[18] this did not mean that the two expert investigators had compromised their independence. Within a fortnight Faraday and Lyell had submitted their report.[19] It made some frank recommendations concerning the dangers posed by exploding clouds of coal dust, that fire-damp should be drawn away from the working seams in conduits, that better records of the number and names of miners in the pits should be kept, and that miners should receive better education, specifically in aspects of safety, basic chemistry and geology, and how to conduct themselves at work.[20] One point, for example, that had been made at the inquiry was that miners would expose the flame of their safety lamps to get a better light, and would even light their pipes with it. Faraday and Lyell's report set the government and the mine-owners some serious problems which could only be solved by legislation and further expenditure, and it was rapidly and skilfully shelved.

Faraday returned from Haswell hoping profoundly that he would now be able to resume his work on the liquefaction of gases. In the event, he was greeted not only by the beginning of the distracting correspondence with Ada Lovelace, but by a request from the Home Office inviting him and Lyell to go back almost immediately to Northumberland to conduct an inquiry into another coalmine explosion, this time at Coxlodge near Newcastle.[21] Their letter to the Home Office giving their initial views on the Haswell disaster, and agreeing with the verdict, had convinced the authorities that Faraday and Lyell would not rock the boat, and that they could comfortably be appointed official experts once more.[22] They turned the offer down, gently but immediately,[23] and Faraday also refused a request to analyse some samples of sea water for the Navy because he had been 'so long delayed from my own researches by investigations & inquiries not my own that I must now resume the former . . . I am now therefore resolved to shut my eyes to all but them.'[24]

He could unburden his frustrations to Schoenbein, who would understand the pressure he was under: 'I am working but I cannot get on. Work is now slow with me & one thing or another is continually occurring to prevent progress. I think I must at last entirely shut out this world for now my progress is slow & like that of a tortoise – a trifle to others stops me altogether.'[25] His 'old infirmity' as he described it to Schoenbein, loss of memory, was also plaguing him, and had made him forget some information he had meant to pass on concerning the date of the next year's British Association meeting in Cambridge: 'I cannot remember it & cannot remember where to look for it.'

Clearing the decks, Faraday got back as quickly as he could to the laboratory, where, working with ether, he found he needed a word for that '*point* of temperature & pressure at which the liquid ether & the vapourous ether are identical in *all their properties* . . . Now what am I to call it?'[26] William Whewell, to whom he wrote with a kind of sigh of relief, as if to say 'progress at last', replied promptly with encouragement and an instinctive understanding of what made Faraday tick: 'I am glad to hear that you are working, and come to a point where you want new words; for new words with you imply new things.'[27]

Whewell came up with 'vaporiscent' for the state when a liquid is virtually vapour, but prevented by pressure from being actually so; and hence 'vaporiscence' and, as an active verb, 'vaporisce', with its subtly different shade of meaning and spelling to 'vaporise'. Taking the idea further, he suggested 'disliquified' to describe the moment when the liquid state is destroyed. In the event, Faraday did not use any of the words, and replied rather apologetically to Whewell, 'It is too bad of me to give you this trouble and then not be content but the beauty of the experiment & its general results has always in my eyes been so great that I have constantly regretted we had not a word wherewith we might talk and write freely about it.'[28]

Faraday's work on the liquefaction, solidification and solubility of gases, a subject he had explored fruitfully in the 1820s, lasted for over a year, from May 1844 to the following August. The most important work of this period of renewed activity, however, was on polarised light, and the action of magnetism and electricity on light. This was in pursuit of an elusive goal in which Faraday sought a connection between the workings of light, electricity and magnetism. He knew how sound was transmitted by vibrations through the medium of the air, but did the same rules apply to light, magnetism and electricity?

Although Whewell was Faraday's prime wordsmith, Schoenbein was the man to whom he could reveal his private feelings and at the same time know that any scientific idea he floated would be discussed and appreciated on its merits. Faraday told Schoenbein of the first intimations of his new discovery, and of how he wrestled with his imagination to find words to describe it. In doing so he wrote one of the revolutionary paragraphs in the literature of the public understanding of science:

At present I have scarcely a moment to spare for any thing but work. I happen to have discovered a direct relation between magnetism & light also Electricity & light – and the field it opens is so large & I think rich that I naturally wish to look at it first . . . I actually have no time to tell you what the thing is – for I now see no one & do no thing but just work. My head became giddy & I have therefore come to this place [Brighton] but still I bring my work with me. When I can catch time I will tell you more . . . *You can hardly imagine how I am struggling to exert my poetical ideas just now for the discovery of analogies – & remote figures respecting the earth Sun*

& all sorts of things – for I think that is the true way (corrected by judgement) to work out a discovery.[29]

Faraday's experimental life had always progressed in extended bursts of activity, followed by long fallow periods – the discovery of electro-magnetic rotations in the early 1820s preceded years of drudgery on largely commissioned scientific projects; the exciting chase through more electrical discoveries in the 1830s preceded his mental breakdown. Now he was reawakening, and touching to Schoenbein on ways of using poetical ideas to lift abstract scientific constructions into the general consciousness. Language was as much Faraday's tool as were any of the pieces of apparatus in the laboratory. Coleridge wrote of how in the 1800s he attended Davy's lectures 'to increase my stock of metaphors';[30] now, in the mid-1840s, Michael Faraday was following in Davy's footsteps, trying to forge a fresh and vibrant language of analogy and metaphor which – although he did not say so – perhaps poets might also find useful.

The new experiments on light caused Faraday to bring equipment of a different cast into the laboratory. This was work of sight, sound and light – the scattering of prismatic colours, the crackle of the discharging battery, the flashing of glass – rather than of the smells, tastes, dangerous obscuring clouds and heat that characterised the work on gases. Put aside were the retorts and fragile tubes running about the benches like a Forth Bridge built out of broken spiders' legs. In their place came electro-magnets, batteries and chunky prisms.

Faraday described his discovery of an effect of magnetism on light in a paragraph as momentous as his diary entries on electro-magnetic induction in 1831:

A piece of heavy glass . . . which was 2 inches by 1.8 inches, and 0.5 of an inch thick, being a silico borate of lead, and polished on the two shortest edges, was experimented with. It gave no effects when the *same magnetic poles* or the *contrary* poles were on opposite sides (as respects the course of the polarized ray) – nor when the same poles were on the same side, either with the constant or intermitting current – *BUT*, when contrary magnetic poles were on the same side, there *was an effect produced on the polarized ray*, and thus magnetic force and light were proved to have relation to each other.

This fact will most likely prove exceedingly fertile and of great value in the investigation of both conditions of natural force.[31]

This encouraged him to upgrade his equipment and bring in a larger electro-magnet. So, with a clattering of drays, a creaking of pulleys and the heaving of large, capable men, Faraday had the new piece of equipment brought from the laboratory at the Military Academy in Woolwich to Albemarle Street:

Have now borrowed and received the Woolwich Magnet, a cylindrical Electro-magnet far more powerful than ours. When in action it holds easily a half hundredweight at each end of the core, and almost a second half hundred besides. This magnet and ours were arranged thus

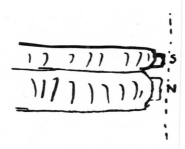

, and excited by five pairs of Grove's battery, and the poles were N for the large magnet, and S for ours.[32]

With the two magnets Faraday intended to put his discovery to the test. Over the next few weeks he worked rapidly and energetically, quickly finding that light twists through a particular angle, depending on the strength of the magnet and the direction of the electrical current. '*An excellent day's work*,' he wrote at the end of the first session with the Woolwich magnet.[33] Having shown how electricity and magnetism can affect light, he tried to discover if the phenomenon would work backwards: could light electrify or magnetise something? Could electricity be generated by the sun? Taking his equipment out of doors on a sunny October morning, he tried with a helix of wire, a magnetic needle and a galvanometer to see if any charge could be registered, but nothing came before the sun went down.[34] Faraday was approaching the problem from the wrong direction; it was not coils of wire that were needed, but a photo-electric cell, which a later generation of scientists would invent after discovering the process of photo-electricity.

Although that was a dead end, Faraday proceeded, with a new horse-shoe magnet made out of half an iron chain-link, to show that glass was diamagnetic, that is could channel magnetic lines of force through itself without itself becoming magnetic:

> The bar of heavy glass ... was suspended by cocoon silk in a glass jar ... and placed between the poles of the ... magnet. When it was arranged and had come to rest I found I *could* affect it by the Magnetic forces and give it position; thus touching dimagnetics by magnetic curves and observing a property quite independent of light, by which also we may probably trace these forces into opaque and other bodies, as the metals, etc. ... In fact the bar was under command just like a galvanometer needle, and the best way of stopping its vibrations and bringing it to a state of rest [was] to apply the force of the magnetic curves according to these laws. How well this shews a tendency to specific action, for if the air and the bar were alike, no motion of the bar would take place ... How well this shews the new Magnetic property of matter.[35]

The language Faraday uses in his laboratory diary has a mounting excitement as his powerful logic and clear procedure lead to a new conclusion. The purpose of the diary was to be Faraday's own record of the events in the laboratory. His need for a new, poetically charged language arose when he was preparing himself to face an audience, or writing a paper for publication. During his long illness, his lecturing duties had lapsed to only a small handful of lectures a year. By 1844 he was back on his feet again, and although he would never lecture as often as he did in the 1830s, he did once more use the Royal Institution audience as a forum to sound out new ideas, and they responded to him with delight. 'The Theatre was crowded to the ceiling!' Gideon Mantell wrote after a Faraday lecture in January 1845.[36]

Thus it was that on Friday, 3 April 1846 Faraday spoke on Charles Wheatstone's Electro-Magnetic Chronoscope, and after about half an hour began to change the subject and enlarge on ideas that had come to him as a result of his own light and magnetic experiments, 'matter for speculation, the vague impressions of my mind'. His lecture notes, in which he sets down a series of prompts to enlarge upon to the audience, read like this: 'Perhaps the undulations are in the *lines of force* . . . Are no limits to lines of force . . . So why may not the vibrations of light & other rays exist . . . in the lines of force that we cannot help admitting rather than in the *lines & centres* of force which are to us really suppositions.'[37]

A few days later Faraday wrote his lecture down in a letter to Richard Phillips for publication in the *Philosophical Magazine* as 'Thoughts on Ray Vibrations'.[38] There, he outlined what he had said at the Royal Institution, what is now known as the Electromagnetic Theory of Light.

> The point intended to be set forth for the consideration of the hearers was whether it was not possible that the vibrations – which in a certain theory are assumed to account for radiation and radiant phenomena – may not occur in the lines of force which connect particles, and consequently masses, of matter together – a notion which, as far as it is admitted, will dispense with the aether, which, in another view, is supposed to be the medium in which these vibrations take place.
>
> The view which I am so bold as to put forth considers, therefore, radiation as a high species of vibration in the lines of force which are known to connect particles, and also masses, of matter together. It endeavours to dismiss the aether, but not the vibrations. The kind of vibration which, I believe, can alone account for the wonderful, varied, and beautiful phenomena of polarisation is not the same as that which occurs on the surface of disturbed water or the waves of sound in gases or liquids, for the vibrations in these cases are direct, or to and from the centre of action, whereas the former are lateral . . .
>
> One thing is certain, that any hypothetical view of radiation which

is likely to be received or retained as satisfactory must not much longer comprehend alone certain phenomena of light, but must include those of heat and of actinic influence also, and even the conjoined phenomena of sensible heat and chemical power produced by them.

Faraday's 'Thoughts on Ray Vibrations' marks a watershed in his attitude to his subject and to his ways of researching and expressing it. There is a signal of this in the title he gave his paper, with its ring of vagueness which we have certainly not previously associated with Michael Faraday; indeed, he opened his published remarks by describing what he had said in his lecture as 'the vague impressions of my mind'. One of the problems he was facing was that while electricity was real, and by 1845 held few secrets for Faraday, his work in trying to find relationships between electricity, magnetism, light, the aether and later gravity was moving into areas of abstraction for which there were as yet few words and no precedent.

An equivalently abstract idea in the early twenty-first century might be the search for life in the further reaches of galaxies multi-million light years away. Such distances are difficult to grasp, though we can try. In the mid-1840s, however, when Faraday refers to the 'velocity of light through space', as he did in 'Thoughts on Ray Vibrations', as being 'about 190,000 miles a second', he is writing of a concept which he or other scientists could now show to be real, but which he knew that a layman would find very difficult, but not impossible, to comprehend. Television series such as *Star Trek*, the *Star Wars* films, science-fiction writing and the real-life journeys of spacecraft such as *Voyager*, *Galileo* and the 1999 Martian lander have brought the concept of outer space home to the early-twenty-first-century citizen, to the extent that we have become reasonably comfortable with the idea of the incomparable vastness of space: we are all 'trekkies' now. Michael Faraday, however, trying to formulate some idea of the reality of the infinite, was a space pioneer at his laboratory bench, the father of all 'trekkies'.

Having the appropriate language, quite as much as manual dexterity and the right equipment, was now becoming for Faraday a primary consideration. As well as moving glass bars, coils and magnetic needles in his laboratory, we see him sitting in his study searching for words.

The description 'magnetic field', now a perfectly ordinary epithet for a measurable natural phenomenon, was coined by Faraday at the laboratory desk in November 1845,[39] and is a piece of imagery both poetic and practical describing the widening area of physical influence set up by a magnet. But when, three and a half years later, Faraday began to look at the problem of gravity, and sought relationships between gravity, electricity and magnetism, he started his day's work (19 March 1849) not with assembling batteries and wires, but by picking up his pen and writing out his thoughts. Here, in his laboratory, science reverts to philosophy:

> *Gravity.* Surely this force must be capable of an experimental relation to Electricity, Magnetism and the other forces, so as to bind it up with them in reciprocal action and equivalent effect. Consider for a moment how to set about touching this matter by facts and trial.
>
> What in Gravity answers to the dual or antithetical nature of the forms of force in Electricity and Magnetism? Perhaps the *to* and *fro*, that is, the ceding to the force or approach of Gravitating bodies, and the effectual reversion of the force or separation of the bodies, quiescence being the neutral condition. Try the question experimentally on these grounds – then the following suppositions or suggestions arise.[40]

Faraday goes on to write in nineteen numbered paragraphs his 'suppositions and suggestions', here with confidence, there with growing doubt:

> But that a body should have less weight whilst falling and more weight whilst rising than when still or moving only horizontally, is a strange conclusion and against the general notion. Still, it may be true, for I do not see as yet that natural conditions contradict it . . .
>
> After all, there is much which renders these expectations or similar ones hopeless: for surely, if founded, there must have been some manifestation of such a condition of the power in nature. On the other hand, what wonderful and manifest conditions of natural power have escaped observation, which have been made known to us in these days.[41]

There was no assembling of batteries and wires on that day. Faraday continued with his thoughts, closing, we might say, by blinking and rubbing his eyes, and writing the concluding paragraph for which there is no precedent in Faraday, or elsewhere in nineteenth-century science:

ALL THIS IS A DREAM. Still, examine it by a few experiments. Nothing is too wonderful to be true, if it be consistent with the laws of nature, and in such things as these, experiment is the best test of such consistency.[42]

He does not appear to have returned to the laboratory for four days, but when he did he was still troubled by the abstract, and opened that day by musing once more:

Every revolving wheel – or rising or falling band – stream – etc. etc. – should then be a source of the effect or power.

If any such effect as that dreamed of, then a body should fall slower or quicker close to a wall or upright rod of metal than in free space or vacuo, for the reaction of the induction would affect it in one case, and not so much in the other.[43]

It was not until early April 1849 that Faraday began to make some experiments to find a relation between gravity and electricity. He tried dropping a loose core of non-magnetic copper through a wire helix to see if there was an effect on the galvanometer. There was nothing. He then tried to drop it from a greater height, and tried cores of glass, bismuth and shellac, but there was still no sign of a current. Undaunted, he proposed to try the experiment with an even higher descent, from the ceiling to the floor of the Royal Institution lecture room.[44]

He did not return to the subject until late August, when for six days he worked with apparatus rigged up in the laboratory, the lecture theatre (ceiling to floor) and down a staircase in the building. He considered trying the effect of a pistol or cannon shot to see if that might register an electrical charge, and contemplated also that Milton might have put his finger on something:

If there should be any truth in these vague expectations of the relation of Gravitating force, then it seems hardly possible but that there must be some extraordinary results to come out in relation to celestial mechanics – as between the earth and the moon, or the Sun and the planets, or in the great space between all gravitating bodies. Then indeed, Milton's expression of the Sun's magnetic ray would have a real meaning in addition to its poetical one.[45]

Faraday did measure some electric current – he had already coined a name for what he was looking for, 'Gravelectricity' – but, as the days progressed, it became clear that 'all the effect[s] I had heretofore obtained were due to the falling or rising loop of wire and not to any effect of Gravity'.[46]

Over the following few weeks Faraday sought gravelectricity, but it always eluded him. He refused to give the idea up, and even ten years later, when as an old man he was reaching the end of his experimental career, he continued to worry at it. Writing to a correspondent in Maidstone in June 1857, Faraday touched on the difficulties of finding acceptance for new ideas and perspectives:

I believe some [scientific men] hesitate because they do not like to have their thoughts disturbed. When Davy discovered potassium it annoyed persons who had just made their view of chemical science perfect; and when I discovered the magneto-electric spark, distaste of like kind was felt towards it, even in high places. Still science must proceed . . . It cannot, I think, for a moment be supposed that we are to go no further in the investigation [of the Conservation of Force]. What would our knowledge of light, or magnetism, or the voltaic current have been under such a restraint of the mind?[47]

Gravelectricity was one of the links in the chain of the Conservation of Forces, and Faraday pushed and pushed at the idea, writing in the laboratory diary on 10 February 1859, almost pleading with it: 'Surely the force of gravitation and its probable relation to other forms of force may be attacked by experiment. Let us try to think of some possibilities.'[48] The change in his approach, even in his philosophy, is evident in the many uses of words such as 'surely', 'suppose', 'perhaps', 'probably', 'might' and 'imagine', words which are as rare as hen's teeth in earlier volumes of the diary. As a much younger man Faraday relied on facts:

'I could trust a fact,' he wrote in 1858, reflecting on his younger self.[49] Now, it is a Coleridgean metaphor, 'my shaping spirit of Imagination',[50] that he is invoking to make an idea fly into reality:

> Let us encourage ourselves with a little more imagination prior to experiment. Atmospheric phenomena favour the idea of the convertibility of gravitating force into Electricity, and back again probably . . . If there be this supposed relation of gravity and Electricity, and the above space be chiefly or generally Negative – then we might expect that, as matter rises from the earth or moves against Gravity, it becomes Negative.
> Then we might expect a wonderful opening out of the electrical phenomena.
> So to say, even the changed force of Gravity as Electricity might travel above the earth's surface, changing its place and then becoming the equivalent of Gravity . . .
> Let the imagination go, guiding it by judgement and principle, but holding it in and directing it by *experiment*.[51]

In that moment, Faraday touched briefly on the possibility of converting the force of gravity into a motive energy for travel. He does not specify space travel, just travel 'above the earth's surface', but space is the very next step. Nearing the end of his life he is considering an idea that Sir Humphry Davy also considered in his own last years – in Davy's case it was interplanetary travel, voyaging among other worlds and other beings;[52] but Davy, unlike Faraday, had no suggestions as to where the driving force should come from.

This line of research was, for Faraday, a brave failure, but he could not shake the idea off: 'The evolution of *one* electricity would be a new and very remarkable thing. The idea throws a doubt on the whole, but still try, for who knows what is possible when dealing with gravity.'[53]

Gravelectricity did not exist within the boundaries of the physics that Faraday knew, though in quantum physics, or the physics of *Star Trek* or *Star Wars*, who knows, as Faraday himself said, 'what is possible when dealing with gravity?'

Such theoretical fancies satisfied one side of Faraday's nature and genius, the artist and poet in him, while the practicalities of his work for

Trinity House and on such matters as the Haswell accident inquiry exercised his powers of analysis and application. In the ways of the world, however, he was often at sea, frequently unhappy. He had shown extreme nervousness, amounting to panic, over the issue of his state pension, and that episode revealed his profound distaste for politics. His religion urged loyalty to Queen and country, but nonetheless the Sandemanian church did not allow its members to take any active political role. But when an issue that had scientific application rose to his attention – such as the mesmerism and table-turning craze of the early 1850s, or the question of the sewage-laden Thames in 1855 – he did not hesitate to air the matter publicly in *The Times*. Faraday's politics stood on the platform of the proper usage of science, and of the public understanding of it.

There are very few traces in his correspondence about what private party political leaning, if any, he might have had, although there may be clues in the anagrams he made, and the words he chose to make anagrams from, that he did have an attitude. The anagrams, as already discussed, may have been copied from the newspapers or have been the preserved results of family parlour games; indeed, if they were not, we might reasonably conclude that there was some kind of deeper meaning behind them. There is one group of anagrams in the Common Place Book, however, that is extremely topical, taking the names of leading radicals and turning them into anti-democratic statements that the most rabid Tory would applaud:

Sir Francis Burdett — Frantic disturber
Orator Henry Hunt — No one truth Harry
Robert Waithman — I warrant the mob
John Gale Jones — See John in gaol
William Cobbett — I'll be at it mob. W.C.[54]

Other anagrams, which pop up at irregular intervals elsewhere in the Common Place Book, as if Faraday is noting them down as he or his family think them up, include:

Revolution — To love ruin
Radical reform — Rare mad frolic
Assembly — Yes lambs[55]

But this is merely a game, and it is in the way Faraday led his life that we may more profitably look for clues to his politics. He avoided as far as he could close involvement in running institutions of science or any other organisation: he gave up the Secretaryship of the Athenaeum Club as soon as he reasonably could, refused to join the Council of the Royal Society, and twice refused invitations to become the Royal Society's President. At the Royal Institution he was an employee of the Managers. The only organisation he became active in as a leader of men and women was the Sandemanian church; and the only form of people power that he called upon was prayer.

Nonetheless, the most serious political issues do seem to squeeze their way into Faraday's correspondence, as if he was powerless to prevent their expression. In January 1837 he found himself referring in a letter to Robert Edmond Grant, a close colleague at the Royal Institution, to 'this season of universal calamity',[56] a period of deep social unrest. Two years later, as the Chartist movement was strengthening across Britain, Faraday was writing to Grant once more, telling him, 'You are a chief anchor to me in the stormy seasons of our Winter and as the tumultuous times come on I think of you with hope & comfort.'[57]

It may be, however, that this letter has no allegorical intent whatsoever, and is merely referring to winter weather, rather than to the politics of the day. But where these worries may be equivocal, Faraday revealed deeply felt anxieties about the political situation across Europe in the late 1840s. Schoenbein wrote to him in October 1848 that in spite of 'all the revolutions and commotions' of the preceding eight months, he is busying himself with research and has been 'rather industrious in my laboratory'.[58] In reply Faraday wrote one of the most heartfelt responses to a contemporary political situation that survives from his pen. He juxtaposes the delight of imagining Schoenbein 'quietly & philosophically at work in the pursuit of science', and being with his family 'amongst the pure & harmonious beauties of nature', against 'fighting amongst the crowd of black passions & motives that seem nowadays to urge men everywhere into action. What miserable scenes everywhere, what unworthy motives ruled for the moment under high sounding phrases and at the last what disgusting revolutions.'[59]

In 1849 Austria invaded northern Italy, and news of this gave Faraday personal concerns for the safety of his fellow-scientist Giovanni Majocchi, who had told him that 'he was driven from Turin & knew not what to do'.[60] It also prompted Faraday to give de la Rive a clear outline of his political attitude, which was simply one of avoidance and extreme distaste:

> For me, who never meddle in politics and who thinks very little of them as one of the games of life, it seems sad that Scientific men should be so disturbed by them and so the progress of pure undeviating unbiassed philosophy be so much & so often disturbed by the passions of men.[61]

Friends on the continent kept Faraday fairly well abreast of what was going on there, although much of the news was circumscribed and expressed in allusion. The letter from de la Rive which prompted Faraday's response contained a harrowing account of the cholera in Paris:

> I saw in Paris the sad effects of cholera; districts in which a cart collected the dead; and yet there reigned in the middle of this scourge sent by Providence an apparent indifference which made one uneasy. There was dancing and singing at one end of Paris whilst people were dying at the other. This is a courageous people, but they are not *serious*.[62]

Receipt of this letter – it was posted from Geneva on 14 June 1849 – may have prompted Faraday to write immediately to Jean-Baptiste-André Dumas, the Parisian scientist who had been keeping him informed of developments in photography and new methods of engraving images. Dumas was closely involved in French politics – he became the French Minister of Agriculture in 1850 – and Faraday may have felt that he and his family were in danger. Dumas had already written about French politics to Faraday, but had been none too clear about it, referring obliquely to France *'where one plays with fire* every day', and adding:

> You will see that the Department du Nord has just sent me to the legislative assembly. Pity me and rest assured that had it been possible to refuse this dangerous honour, I would have been anxious to do so, in order to concentrate entirely on my work. Happily there is still a peaceful corner of the world where philosophy provides a

sanctuary. You, more than any other person, were worthy that it was reserved for you.[63]

Faraday had already replied to this letter,[64] so another letter to Dumas so soon suggests fond brotherly concern on Faraday's part. 'My first thought in writing or thinking of you is are you happy,' he begins in his letter of 18 June,

for so much turns up near & about you that seems to me incompatible with your habit of mind & occupation that I mourn a little at times. What comes to pass direct from the hand of God, as the serious illness of your Son, we must indeed strive to receive with patience but that which is evolved through the tumults & passions of man does not bring with it that chastening & in some degree alleviating thought.[65]

In all these letters Faraday asserts a strong moral position, which equates the practice of science with godliness, and of politics with the worst of human passions. Over the years since his youth his outlook on the ways of the world has matured – it is now nearly thirty-five years since he had remarked, of Napoleon's escape from Elba, that 'being no politician, I did not trouble myself much about it'.[66]

CHAPTER 23

A Metallic Clatter which Effaced the
Soft Wave-Wanderings

'I have not been altogether idle but I am of necessity very slow now,' Faraday wrote in October 1855 to John Tyndall.[1] He was staying at Sydenham, with Sarah and their niece Jane Barnard,* in one of the many houses he rented for a few weeks at a time to take refuge on the edges of London from the smoke and noise of the capital. He was writing his thirtieth paper in his *Experimental Researches in Electricity*, which 'goes on slowly, but I think will be a useful contribution of facts; and may help to advance the logic of magnetism a little though not much'.

Throughout the first half of the 1850s Faraday continued to be attacked by bouts of giddiness, headaches and memory loss, and this took its toll on the quickness of his mind. His customary roll-call of ailments was now being compounded by deafness, quinsy (a form of tonsillitis), influenza, chills and face-ache, or neuralgia, which heralded the severe dental trouble that led him to have 'five teeth and a fang' pulled out in one painful session with his dentist in July 1850.[2] Reference to his illnesses in his letters becomes a litany, but he is rarely depressed about them, usually

---

* Jane Barnard was a daughter of the marriage of Faraday's sister Margaret and Sarah's brother John. Thus she was the niece of both Michael and Sarah.

jaunty about their course, and reflects every hope and sign that recovery will come soon enough.[3]

Illness kept Faraday in bed or on his couch with his legs up, and made the presentation of his lectures at the Royal Institution a hit-and-miss affair across the early years of the decade. He had to postpone two of his series of lectures on static electricity in April and May 1849,[4] while his 1853 Christmas series on voltaic electricity hung in the balance while he tried – this time successfully, for he did give the lectures – to overcome a sore throat and deafness.[5] Sarah clucked over him, asking Dr Latham during one of the bouts in 1849 if she should give her husband some wine; she was told yes, give him half a glass of sherry after dinner, and if that works 'as much or even a little more on the following day'.[6]

Despite the uncertainty of Faraday's public appearances, his audiences flocked to hear him, and welcomed him warmly. His charisma had not dimmed; if anything, prolonged absence through illness in the 1840s had sharpened the public's need for him, to the extent that 1028 people crammed into the Royal Institution lecture theatre on 11 April 1851 to hear him give a Friday Evening Discourse on Atmospheric Magnetism. This was the highest recorded figure for any of his lectures,[7] but, though exceptional, it was not much higher than the general average attendance of about eight hundred at Faraday's lectures in the late 1840s and fifties. This public rapture for science and particularly for Faraday's presentation of it was quite as great as the welcome and attention that Humphry Davy received when he was at the height of his powers as a lecturer.

Mary Ann Evans, the author George Eliot, was a member of the audience on 24 January 1851 when Faraday spoke 'On the magnetic character and relation of oxygen and nitrogen', and showed how the gases, carried in soap bubbles, behaved differently when floated into a magnetic field. She wrote afterwards: 'You must know Faraday's lectures are as fashionable an amusement as the Opera ... It always does one good to see a thoroughly enthusiastic man of science like Faraday. He told us we little knew how many hours he had spent in blowing minute soap bubbles . . .'.[8]

Another eager member of Faraday's audience in the early 1850s was Mrs Mary Robinson, a friend of Charles Babbage, a confidante of Turner, an acquaintance of the Somervilles when they lived in London, and of Ada Lovelace, the Eastlakes and Samuel Rogers and his sister Sarah. Mary Robinson was one of the bit-part players in the social scene in London from around the time of her marriage in the 1830s until her husband's death in the 1850s and her move to Richmond. Amusing, attractive and intelligent, she had coaxed some warm conversation and observations out of Turner when he came, as he seems often to have done, to dine at the Robinsons' home in Hertford Street; and for nearly twenty years, from the mid-1850s, she carried out an extended correspondence with Charles Babbage.[9] Although the nature of her part in the social scene is now obscured, Mary Robinson had enough energy and purpose towards the end of her life to write a series of nine short essays about some of the people she had met over the preceding decades and gather them together in two slim books entitled *Sunny Memories*.[10] She had a close eye for character and a clear recollection, but by the time she settled down to write her essays she had married her cousin, a Captain Lloyd, and her books were published under her new initials 'M.L.'. She had evidently taken heed of advice given to her by Sarah Rogers: 'put away your work and book, my dear, and listen to these *living* books'.[11]

One of Mary Lloyd's subjects was, as she courteously termed him, 'Professor Faraday'.[12] What struck her very particularly about Faraday was 'the charm of his character . . . the vast impression he made in what he called "this Planet, which we call our Earth"', and, most tellingly, 'his radiant face'. The image of Faraday shining in front of his audiences is one which emerges from Mary Lloyd's account, and from recollections of others, in particular the vivid account by Jane Pollock, another mature lady captivated by Faraday's public persona:

It was an irresistible eloquence which compelled attention and invited upon sympathy . . . There was a gleaming in his eyes which no painter could copy, and which no poet could describe. Their radiance seemed to send a strange light into the very heart of his congregation, and when he spoke, it was felt that the stir of his voice and the fervour of his words could belong only to the owner of those kindling eyes. His thought was rapid and made its way in new phrases . . . His enthusiasm seemed to carry him to the point of ecstasy when he expatiated on the beauties of Nature, and when he lifted the veil from her deep mysteries. His body then took motion from his mind; his hair streamed out from his head; his hands were full of nervous action; his light, lithe body seemed to quiver with its eager life. His audience took fire with him, and every face was flushed.[13]

Under the gaslight in the Royal Institution lecture theatre the face of any perspiring lecturer would shine, but in Faraday's case the charisma and respect now attached to his name and presence were such that his audience was captivated by him from the beginning, came ready to be transported by his 'clear, bright, truthful voice',[14] and ready also to see Faraday as super-human, as a prophet who told and revealed new truths. His religious beliefs and practices were by now well-known, and despite the fact that he professed to keep religion and science apart, there is clear evidence that in his later lectures he willingly failed to do so. Ada Lovelace had already spotted it, and Mary Lloyd recalled that it was 'very evident, even in his Lectures, that he had the *deepest* sense of religion', and quotes some of his words in his lecture on ozone: 'These are the *glimmerings* we have of what we are pleased to call the "*second causes*", by which the *one Great Cause* works his wonders, and governs this earth.'[15] From that meaningful flicker of spiritual expression, Faraday passed immediately, according to Mary Lloyd's account, to the practical:

We flattered ourselves we knew what air was composed of, and now we discover a *new* property, which is imponderable, and invisible, except through its *effects*, which I showed you in the last experiment; but while it fades the ribbon, it gives the glow of health to the cheek, and is just as necessary for the good of mankind, as the other parts of which air is composed.

Mary Lloyd had sufficient empathy with Faraday, and the structures he used to explain very difficult scientific concepts to lay people, that she could appreciate the 'vastness in Faraday's similes'. His manner in the lecture theatre, and the way he handled the choreographing of his experiments, appealed greatly to her; she noted

his kind manner to his valued assistant, Mr. Anderson, his good nature and patience if by chance [the experiment] failed – which was rare, and then made a reason for explaining *why* they failed –

all this left an impression on the mind which not even the aid of painting or sculpture can recall; but which will ever remain a happy remembrance to those who had the great good fortune to hear him.

The only comparable figure to Faraday in public life in the 1850s was Charles Dickens. He was at the height of his powers in 1850, the year in which he completed his seventh novel, *David Copperfield*, and in which he launched his weekly magazine *Household Words*. Dickens was famous throughout Britain as the author of enthralling and dramatic novels with plots that gained instant rapport with his readers, and narratives that spoke directly to all people in their various and vital speech-rhythms. He was also widely known by this time as an actor and dramatic reader – particularly of his own works – with a physical, passionate style that could bring an audience to tears. Where Faraday drew his private life like a mantle closely over him, Dickens's life and experiences spilt out onto the pages of his books and into personal scandals that kept his audiences agog.

The two men's similarities, however, are as arresting as their differences. Both were showmen who thrived on the excitement of public performance – their own; both relied on intense visual and aural effects to send their messages home to audiences of all ranks, abilities and ages; both had their own private stages where their audiences knew they could be found – for Faraday it was the Royal Institution, for Dickens the pages of his novels; and both wanted to teach, to reach the widest possible audience, to change society, to improve lives and to open minds.

The nature of their creativity was of a kind that took place quietly, apart. As well as being public performers they were both soloists – Dickens wrote alone, and Faraday would not be disturbed in his laboratory. For both of them these long hours on their own, accompanied by the sound of their own breathing and their scratching pen, enabled them to spring wholeheartedly out of their private offices onto a public stage when the time came. Their personal charm and magnetism was an added, perhaps an essential, ingredient for their success in the arts they practised. In Dickens his friend Carlyle had 'discerned in the inner man of him a real music of the genuine kind'.[16] The breadth of Dickens's activity, achievement and effect was great. It may have been without a trace of irony that a stage-doorman said after a performance, 'You were a great loss to the profession, Sir, when you took to writing books.'[17] The good cheer and charm of Faraday was of a less rumbustious kind than that of Dickens, but was effective and notable nevertheless. Mary Lloyd recalled Faraday's 'touching gentleness, which, together with the brilliancy of his intellect, produced a startling effect',[18] while Frederick Pollock wrote of his 'peculiar charm and fascination'.[19]

There is no record of Dickens attending a lecture by Faraday at the Royal Institution, but in May 1850, soon after Dickens had launched *Household Words*, he wrote to Faraday asking permission to reprint one of his lectures.[20] Dickens's ambition for *Household Words* was that it should campaign against social injustice, inhumane housing and working conditions, the ill-treatment and poor education of children and other radical causes. All this was set within a good-humoured, chattering framework of stories, travel writing and poetry of a kind that could be read at the breakfast table. Having Faraday as one of its contributors would be a triumph for *Household Words*, for he was a star name who would give credibility to its coverage of scientific issues, and keep interest in the magazine buoyant. In the event, Faraday sent some of his notes for the Juvenile Lecture series 'On the Chemical History of a Candle', with a letter, now lost, that seems to have told Dickens how much he enjoyed his books.[21] It was probably always Dickens's intention to edit Faraday's material to fit the light-hearted, demotic style that his magazine was adopting, and he engaged one of his regular writers, Percival Leigh, to knock Faraday's notes into shape. Within two months 'The Chemistry of a Candle' was published in *Household Words*,[22] followed by other articles either closely based on Faraday's work, or gentle parodies and variations of his manner – 'The Laboratory in the Chest', 'The Mysteries of a Tea-Kettle', 'The Chemistry of a Pint of Beer'.[23]

The *Household Words* version of 'Chemistry of a Candle' lifts the narrative away from the juvenile audience in the Royal Institution to the parlour of the Wilkinson family, somewhere in London, where young Master Harry is asking Uncle Bagges if he knows 'what you do when you put a candle out?' Master Harry has been to the Royal Institution, and he knows. With clarity and aplomb he tells Uncle Bagges everything he can remember, with a level of recall that would have left Faraday delighted. As Mrs Wilkinson explains,

'[Harry] reads a great deal about chemistry, and he attended Professor Faraday's lectures . . . on the chemical history of a candle, and has been full of it ever since.'

'Now uncle . . . we have got our candle burning. What do you see?'

'Let me put on my spectacles,' answered the uncle.

'Look down on the top of the candle around the wick. See, it is a little cup full of melted wax. The heat of the flame has melted the wax just round the wick. The cold air keeps the outside of it hard, so as to make the rim of it. The melted wax in the little cup goes up through the wick to be burnt, just as oil does in the wick of a lamp. What do you think makes it go up, uncle?'

'Why – why, the flame draws it up, doesn't it?'

'Not exactly, uncle . . .'

Master Harry, in continuing his instruction about oxygen, nitrogen, carbon, carbonic acid and the whole gamut of facts that Faraday had relayed in his lectures, is the perfect pupil and teacher, the ideal medium to spread Faraday's teaching about the candle to an audience of many more thousands than he could ever have reached at the Royal Institution. So successful was Harry that within the space of the next few weeks – by the time the next scientific article, 'The Laboratory in the Chest', was published in the 7 September 1850 edition of *Household Words* – Uncle Bagges had begun to frequent the Polytechnic Institution, had taken to 'lounging at the British Museum', and most impressively had got himself elected a member of the Royal Institution, 'which became a regular house of call to him, so that in a short time he grew to be one of the ordinary phenomena of the place'. By generating such publicity for the Institution, Dickens was continuing in the early 1850s what William Jerdan had begun twenty years earlier, in a different style but to a broadly similar audience through the *Literary Gazette*.

In his own novels, Dickens had not been deaf to the sort of talk that went on at the Royal Institution and the learned salons and meetings beyond, and he parodied something of it through the unspeakable character of Paul Dombey. *Dombey and Son*, first published in instalments in 1847 –48, opens with Dombey musing on the centrality within the universe of himself and all that is his. Here are some of Mary

Somerville's thoughts in *On the Connexions of the Physical Sciences* abused mercilessly:

> The earth was made for Dombey and Son to trade in, and the sun and the moon were made to give them light. Rivers and seas were formed to float their ships; rainbows gave them promise of fair weather; winds blew for or against their enterprises; stars and planets circled in their orbits, to preserve inviolate a system of which they were the centre.[24]

We do not know which of Dickens's novels Faraday had read, though the implication in Dickens's second letter suggests that the scientist had written some generous words about them. In these late years in Faraday's life he took to reading more and more for relaxation, as we know from two separate accounts of the period. A woman who came to know him well in the 1850s was Cornelia Crosse, the second wife of Andrew Crosse. She and Crosse had married in 1850, and one of the couple's first calls when they came to London after their marriage was on the Faradays. After Cornelia had first 'ascended the long flight of stairs leading to the Upper Chamber of that famous house in Albemarle Street', she and her husband

> were kindly greeted by Mrs Faraday, who led us through the outer sitting room, into an inner sanctum; there was Faraday himself, half reclining on a sofa – with a heap of circulating library novels round him; he had evidently rejected some, that were thrown carelessly on the floor – but his eyes were glued on the exciting pages of a third volume. 'He reads a great many novels, and it is very good for him to divert his mind,' said Mrs Faraday to us, later on.[25]

Another good friend of a generation younger than Faraday was the barrister Sir Frederick Pollock, Bart. He had studied science at Cambridge, where he was particularly inspired by the way George Airy scattered refracted and polarised sunlight around his lecture room.[26] Although his career took him into the law, Pollock and his family were habitués of the Royal Institution, and became intimate with the Faradays. In some paragraphs in his *Personal Remembrances* Pollock recalls Faraday's choice of novels:

> I like stirring ones, [Faraday told Frederick's wife Jane] with plenty of life, plenty of action, and very little philosophy. Why, I can do the philosophy for myself; but I want the novelist to supply me with incident and change of scene, and to give me an interest which takes me out of my own immediate pursuits. It does a man good to get out of his daily pursuits, and to air his thoughts a little.[27]

There had been long periods in his life when Faraday had no time to read anything other than the scriptures and 'journals and books of science, and the *Times* and *Athenaeum*'.[28] The allure of exciting, vigorous literature, however, had always lain in the background of his mind as a means to escape and 'air his thoughts a little'. With more time on his hands in the late 1840s and fifties he was able to devour books at a rate he had never been able to match since the days of his boyhood when he read everything he could find in Riebau's bindery. What we know of his choices from the circulating library and elsewhere is revealing. Pollock remembers Faraday talking about Mrs Caroline Archer Clive's sensational novel *Paul Ferroll*, published under the pseudonym 'V' in 1855. This is the story of a cultivated and wealthy man prevented, by another woman, from marrying his true love. He marries the other woman, who is violent and domineering, and later murders her. Escaping suspicion of the murder, Ferroll becomes free to marry his true love. They live happily for eighteen years, until, to save innocent men from being convicted of the murder, Ferroll confesses all to his wife. She dies of shock; their daughter is ruined. Mentioning this book, which was sending waves of excitement and disgust through literary society, Faraday calmly remarked that it had 'stir enough' in it.

Faraday's taste in literature had living strands of modernity running through it, and he no more shied from free-ranging social thought as reflected in fiction than he did from equally free-ranging thinking in science. His modernity was reflected in many spheres of his life, and would not be restrained by archaisms of either a conservative mode of thought or of a fundamentalist religion. He spoke to Frederick Pollock of *Jane Eyre* (published in 1847):

There's another modern novel I like very well too, where a man keeps his mad wife up at the top of his house, and it is very clever, and keeps you awake. Why, how good the woman's flight is across the fields; but there's a touch of mesmerism and mystery at the end, which would be better away.

That is the plot of *Jane Eyre* put by Faraday into a very small nutshell. But what his response to the novel evokes is the extent to which he is taken by strong narrative, highly coloured incident, clearly depicted landscape setting, extreme emotion, and the odd. Curiously enough, both of the novels he called to mind to the Pollocks as reading matter in the mid-1850s were about unhinged wives, deceit and second marriage.

Faraday's objection to Charlotte Brontë's *Jane Eyre* was not to the plot or narrative but to what he saw as its unfortunate references to mesmerism – although it has to be said that there is no mesmerism in *Jane Eyre*, rather thought-transference at a moment of extreme emotion. Threading through the narrative are descriptive passages and metaphors which give the kind of glancing flash that caught Faraday's breath and kept him awake. Apart from her many other traits, Jane Eyre is a painter with a pin-sharp eye who sees and depicts the natural world with clarity and detachment. Phrases and imagery slice through Brontë's narrative – 'a metallic clatter which effaced the soft wave-wanderings'; 'the grey hollow filled with rayless cells'; 'those trembling stars'; 'sky of steel'.[29] Such phrases all fly with ideas of science like banded cargo on their backs, being emphases and references that heighten the psychological tension in the story and keep the attention of a reader of Faraday's mould. Out of context, the first two images in particular have little meaning, but in their isolation they nevertheless carry as much evocative force as any number of Faraday's own diary observations. Equally, colour is everywhere in *Jane Eyre*, both in the heroine's paintbox and, seen through her eyes, in this perfect vision of England in midsummer which opens Chapter 23:

A splendid Midsummer shone over England: skies so pure, suns so radiant as were then seen in long succession, seldom favour, even singly, our wave-girt land. It was as if a band of Italian days had come from the South, like a flock of glorious passenger birds, and lighted to rest them on the cliffs of Albion. The hay was all got in; the fields round Thornfield were green and shorn; the roads white and baked; the trees were in their dark prime; hedge and wood, full-leaved and deeply tinted, contrasted well with the sunny hue of the cleared meadows between.

When Faraday travelled in the landscape it had often been in the company of a painter, George Barnard. Now, reclining on his sofa with Charlotte Brontë's novel, he is in the company of the fictional painter Jane Eyre. The heightened description of this and other of the many landscape passages in the novel gave Faraday periods of creative reflection when he was resting.

Mesmerism, the practice of inducing patients into a hypnotic state, was being revived as a medical technique in the late 1840s. Faraday had been approached by mesmerists – both medical men and cranks – enquiring after his views on the subject very soon after he had published, in 1846, his two papers 'On new magnetic actions, and on the magnetic condition of all matter',[30] that is, diamagnetism. The common thread of the letters is their authors' desire to attract Faraday's attention to mesmerism, and to try to get his approbation for it. There were some vivid descriptions of the behaviour of mesmerised patients: Benjamin Dann of Maidstone described how one of his patients saw the 'blue fire' of static electricity from an electrostatic machine run around the consulting room: '. . . it creates an atmosphere when you turn [the machine] round, spreading all around, and you are in it, and so am I – It looks like that *blue fire* that streams from your fingers when you pass them down before me.'[31]

Jane Jennings, from Cork, wrote two long letters to Faraday hoping he would become convinced by 'mesmeric phenomena', and that 'if you ever become a believer do tell me'.[32] Another correspondent, John B. Parker, an Exeter surgeon, wrote to Faraday to tell him how one of his patients behaved like a magnet when mesmerised, and 'invariably places herself with her Head to the North . . . and pulls out her Steel Hair Pins and throws them away'.[33] There is no evidence that Faraday replied to any of these letters, but an entry in a diary kept by Walter White, the Librarian of the Royal Society, records a conversation that suggests that Faraday did worry at the subject for some time:

[He] says that . . . he cannot believe in [mesmerism and the magnetic experiments of Reichenbach[34]] until their law is found to be of invariable application, until they can mesmerise inorganic matter or a baby, who cannot be supposed to be a confederate. He has lost much time in the enquiry without any satisfactory results.[35]

Table-turning, in which groups of people gathered together with a medium to try to communicate with the dead, was another aspect of scientism that plagued and irritated Faraday when he was drawn into debate about it. He managed to avoid making any public statement on mesmerism, but popular interest in table-turning became so sudden, fast and furious in 1853 that Faraday was a prime target for requests for explanations and justifications of the phenomenon. Being pestered by fanatics and enthusiasts was an uncomfortable disadvantage of being the leading and most publicly exposed scientist of the age. Less than a dozen letters to Faraday about table-moving survive, but these were the tip of the iceberg. Participants stood around a table which might move in apparent response to questions, and this craze fulfilled a public need to experience the paranormal, the unknown and unfathomable brushing up against ordered and unsatisfactory everyday life. It reached a height of popularity very soon after the national celebrations of certainty and progress in the Great Exhibition of 1851, and after the horrific scale of deaths in the cholera epidemics of the 1840s. Table-turning caught the imagination of people from all classes of society, and in many instances ran away with it. The Archdeacon of Shropshire, Revd John Allen, who might have known better, wrote to Faraday calling his attention to the phenomenon which, 'unless I am greatly deceived, will be ranked among the most astonishing discoveries of this age'.[36] William Hickson, the editor of the *Westminster Review*, demanded to know from Faraday, 'are we not on the eve of some new discovery in Dynamics? . . . which I am anxious to see our scientific men take out of the hands of Electro biologist charlatans & spirit manifesters'.[37] When Faraday replied – his letter is lost – he must have been dismissive, but Hickson was not so easily put off: 'Now, if Newton was wise in asking himself why does the apple fall, may we not, with due modesty, ask his successors, why does the hat or table turn?' He urged Faraday to come and stay with him in Kent to see the phenomenon for himself, but Faraday was too experienced an old fox to fall into that trap.

We know that there were many other letters on the subject to Faraday – he referred to the fact that 'applications to me for an opinion are so numerous'[38] – but they are likely to have been purposely destroyed by David Blaikley, a great-nephew and fellow Sandemanian, who took on the task of disposing of Faraday's papers after his death.[39] Despite Faraday's caution, and his unwillingness to engage too closely with the table-turners, he attended two seances under controlled conditions in the sensible and friendly environment of the home of Revd John Barlow, Secretary of the Royal Institution. There Faraday made up a bundle of every kind of material he could think might reasonably have been used as a means of transmission, or a preventative, to whatever forces might induce tables to turn – he listed them: 'sand-paper, millboard, glue, glass, plastic clay, tinfoil, cardboard, gutta-percha, vulcanized caoutchouc, wood and resinous cement'. With the pile under the hand of one of the participants, Faraday found that any combination of the substances, or their total absence, made no difference to the way the table turned. '[It] turned or moved exactly as if the bundle had been away, to the full satisfaction of all present. The experiment was repeated, with various substances and persons, and at various times, with constant success.'

He then made a lightweight lever, fixed to a sheet of cardboard, which he used as an indicator of the direction of the pressure the participants exerted on the table. He found that if they looked at the lever while pressing downwards the table did not move; but if they looked away motion was registered. The most valuable effect of the lever was, as Faraday pointed out, 'in the corrective power it possesses over the mind of the table-turner'. These statements are from the letter Faraday wrote to *The Times* after the session, in a clear public statement of his views on the matter: the cause of the table's movement, he said, was 'a *quasi* involuntary muscular action'. He asked for no more letters on the subject from the public, and put the lever apparatus on display at John Newman's scientific instrument shop at 122 Regent Street.

But Faraday did not leave the matter there. He had ended his letter with a peroration, a flourish amounting to a public sermon or lecture on the effects of wilful ignorance, and the error of the 'great body' of people who had been caught up in the craze:

Permit me to say, before concluding, that I have been greatly startled by the revelation which this purely physical subject has made of the condition of the public mind . . . By the great body I mean such as reject all consideration of the quality of cause and effect, who refer the results to electricity and magnetism – yet know nothing of the laws of these forces; or to the attraction – yet show no phenomena of pure attractive power; or to the rotation of the earth, as if the earth revolved around the leg of a table, or to some unrecognized physical force, without enquiring whether the known forces are not sufficient; or who even refer them to diabolical or supernatural agency, rather than suspend their judgement, or acknowledge to themselves that they are not learned enough in these matters to decide on the nature of the action. I think the system of education that could leave the mental condition of the public body in the state in which this subject has found it must have been greatly deficient in some very important principle.[40]

That was Michael Faraday at his best, fulfilling a role that he felt called to – taking a phenomenon that had shot through society like wildfire, analysing it carefully, clearly and publicly, revealing through demonstration the error it was leading to, scourging the 'great body' of the public who had been caught up with it, and suggesting a primal cause. Here Faraday was taking the role of the nation's exorciser, a Christ throwing the money-changers out of the temple, clearing away the old practices, cleansing and chastising. He was not so naïve as to think he would have complete success, however, adding in a later article in the *Athenaeum* that he could not 'undertake to answer such objections as may be made'.[41] Nevertheless he and the Royal Institution took important and timely practical steps to try to improve matters.

With Faraday's peroration in *The Times* re-echoing, the Royal Institution mounted in April and May 1854 a series of seven Lectures on Education, each by an eminent man of science, including William Whewell 'On the Influence of the History of Science upon Intellectual Education', Charles Daubney 'On the Importance of the Study of Chemistry as a Branch of Education for all Classes' and John Tyndall 'On the Importance of the Study of Physics as a Branch of Education for all Classes'. Faraday himself gave the lecture 'On Mental Education', and others covered physiology, social economy and language. The lengthy titles of the lectures, and their wide collective range, makes clear the fact that the lecturers were bidden to tackle an issue of the greatest fundamental importance for the nation.[42] The Royal Institution took the initiative to focus leading intellects and public attention onto the issue of how children and adults should be taught. The table-turning debate had been one of the catalysts, as was Faraday's crusading zeal to do something to remedy matters.

The chief guest in the audience when Faraday gave his lecture 'On Mental Education' on 6 May 1854 was Queen Victoria's consort, Prince Albert. The Prince's presence signalled the importance of this particular lecture, and the centrality of the education issue. Faraday used table-turning and table-lifting as the main illustration for his lecture, attacking the subject and showing how it ran against the laws of nature, and specifically against the principle that physical energy cannot be generated from nothing: 'If we could by the fingers draw a heavy piece of wood or stone upwards without effort, and then, letting it sink, could produce by its gravity an effort equal to its weight, that would be a creation of power, and *cannot be*.'[43]

In this lecture Faraday comes as near to using the Royal Institution lecturer's desk as his pulpit as ever he did. He spoke of the 'book of nature' as being 'written by the finger of God', and of the value to the individual of training the mind, a thing 'so wonderful that there is nothing to compare with it elsewhere in creation', to be an instrument of self-control. The following passage was so important to his message that he had it set in italics in the lecture's published form:

I will simply express my strong belief, that that point of self-education which consists in teaching the mind to resist its desires and inclinations, until they are proved to be right, is the most important of all, not only in things of natural philosophy, but in every department of daily life.[44]

With these words, '*until they are proved to be right*', scientist and preacher are united at last.

Faraday had more time on his hands while convalescing in the early 1850s, and read and reflected more. This may have provided the catalyst for him to make minor but significant changes to his way of life, and it may be that in publicly uniting his science and his religion, as he appears to have done in the Mental Education lecture, he was allowing himself to confront the dogmas of Sandemanianism, and to edge towards a variant philosophy of life that was comfortable for *him*.

There is developing evidence that although Faraday might have been reclusive in the 1830s and forties, he began to come out of his shell in the last two decades of his life. He is listed as being one of the guests at a *fête artistique* given by the opera impresario and manager of Her Majesty's Theatre, Benjamin Lumley, on 19 June 1850, the day after his return from a ten-day visit to the Sandemanian community at Old Buckenham, Norfolk.[45] The guests of honour were the French dramatist Augustin E. Scribe and his compatriot the composer F.E. Halévy, whose collaborative opera *The Tempest* had just had its first performance at Her Majesty's Theatre. The guest list reads as a roll of honour of peers, ambassadors, MPs, writers, artists and scientists – alongside Faraday in the list we see Dickens, Edwin and Charles Landseer, Clarkson Stanfield, George Cruikshank and Charles Babbage. Attendance at such a party was not the behaviour of a recluse, nor indeed is the action of 'Professor Faraday', as he is listed, in attending Royal Academy Annual Dinners in an unbroken run from 1854 to 1865. He first appears in the Academy invitation lists in 1836, but then the word 'Cannot' is written beside his name. From then until 1852 he does not seem to have been invited, and although his attendance was doubtful in 1852, from 1855 he attended with a vengeance, invariably in the company of Professor Richard Owen.[46] This is one of the roots of a remark of Silvanus Thompson: 'He did indeed dine quietly with Sir Robert Peel or Earl Russell; and of the few public dinners he attended, he enjoyed most the annual banquet of the Royal Academy of Arts.'[47]

This is also the period in which the Faradays were lent a theatre box by the banking heiress and philanthropist Angela Burdett Coutts. In a letter of thanks Faraday told her:

> We had your box once before, I remember, for a pantomime, which is always interesting to me, because of the immense concentration of means which it requires . . . you are very kind to think of our pleasures for tomorrow night . . . I mean to enjoy it, for I still have a sympathy for children, and all their thoughts and pleasures.[48]

It is possible that Faraday went to the theatre relatively often, and, if Cornelia Crosse's passing remark in quoting the above letter to Angela Burdett Coutts is any guide, he went with enthusiasm and theatrical insight. 'In later life,' Mrs Crosse observed, 'Faraday retained a taste for all scenic representation; the more curious in a man of his severely religious views. He could make very shrewd and searching criticisms on the actors of the day.'[49]

In trying to piece together the changes in the pattern of Faraday's social life outside the Sandemanian embrace in the 1850s we have rather more to go on than we did for the 1830s. 'Dining quietly' with senior statesmen Sir Robert Peel and Earl Russell cannot be passed over lightly as of no social consequence, nor can Faraday's attendance at Lumley's *fête artistique* or the Royal Academy. Other little gatherings and friendships in this decade add further evidence to the coming out of Michael Faraday. Gideon Mantell recalled a soirée at Dr John Ayrton Paris's – 'a dreadfully hot and crowded assembly; in the midst of which a few couples tried to waltz' – at which Faraday, Babbage and Brewster were present.[50] Frederick Pollock notes an 'evening at Mrs Carrick Moore's [18 April 1853] in Clarges Street. Faraday, Babbage, Lyells, Mrs Jameson, Lady Eastlake, John Murray, Sir C. Fellows etc.'[51] Their hostess, Mrs Carrick Moore, was the mother of a large, by now adult, family. The Moores were very much in the social swim of London and the western reaches of the Thames at 'their summer quarters'[52] Thames Ditton and at Hampton Court. They knew Charles Babbage well, and painters such as George Jones RA, Sir Charles Eastlake and Sir David Wilkie, and were close also to Samuel and Sarah Rogers.

A particular long-standing friend of the Moores, as we have seen, was J.M.W. Turner, who 'was seen to best advantage' with them,[53] and stayed with them at Thames Ditton regularly. During the few years after Turner's death in 1851 Harriet Moore painted the group of seven watercolours of the interior of Faraday's laboratory and apartment for which she is best known. The existence, quality and wholeness of Moore's group speaks volumes about Faraday, his attitude to science and art, and his attitude to himself. As a consciously and determinedly fabricated body of evidence, Moore's pictures are the best clue to the way Faraday wanted his image to be passed on to the future.

Faraday first had contact with a member of the Moore family when

Harriet's brother, the field geologist John Carrick Moore, was elected to membership of the Royal Institution in 1836. Faraday and John Carrick Moore had geologist friends in common – Adam Sedgwick and Charles Lyell being principal among them – and although there may have been earlier contacts it is clear that by 1850 Harriet Moore was attending lectures at the Institution. One course she attended was the six lectures given by Faraday 'on some points of domestic chemical philosophy' after Easter 1850. They soon – if they were not so already – became good friends, and a correspondence developed between them. On Faraday's side the correspondence seems stilted; his first two letters are known only in extracts published by Bence Jones, and both are rather agonised and long-winded refusals of invitations.[54] But a theme that runs through letters in both directions is Faraday and Harriet's particular enjoyment of sunsets, and their remarking upon them. Faraday tells Harriet: 'After writing, I walk out in the evening, hand-in-hand with my dear wife, to enjoy the sunset; for to me who love scenery, of all that I have seen or can see there is none surpasses that of Heaven. A glorious sunset brings with it a thousand thoughts that delight me.'[55]

Harriet later responds in kind: 'I hope you have had some fine sunsets in the north [the Faradays are at this time in Northumberland]; I always wish you were here when there is one more beautiful than usual.'[56] Two years later, in September 1853, she is moved to bring the subject up again: 'Our rooms [in Hastings] almost overhang the sea, which is to me a splendid object; on Tuesday the sunset was glorious & the moon shone upon the placid waters so beautifully that I thought how much you would have admired it.'[57]

It is not necessary to emphasise the obvious common denominator in these exchanges: the sunlit presence and influence of their mutual friend Turner.

The watercolours that Harriet Moore made for Faraday are undated, but a note in the Royal Institution General Managers' minutes states that the first two she painted, of the laboratory, were made in 1852, the year she became a member of the Institution, and the others may also date from the first half of the 1850s.[58] The laboratory watercolours, of which there are five different subjects, are full of delicious incidental detail, such as the saws hanging on the edge of the shelving in the magnetic laboratory, the rows of glass bottles, the retorts hanging to dry and the gloomy, filtering light which pervades everything. There are evocative glimpses through open doorways, reminiscent of seventeenth-century paintings of Dutch interiors, and the affectionate inclusion in one picture of Charles Anderson, who stands behind some curling rolls of magnetic field diagrams. In another Michael Faraday himself is shown pouring a tube of liquid into a retort at the far end of the Chemical Laboratory. A further laboratory subject, of a slightly different surface quality to the others, shows the short figure of Faraday leaning on the bench, and watching a taller, slimmer and older man minutely examining a piece of equipment.

The Harriet Moore watercolours of Faraday's basement kingdom are unique in their detail and clarity among the rare surviving paintings of nineteenth-century laboratories. One of the few comparable works is William Müller's watercolour, c.1840, of Thomas Morson's pharmaceutical laboratory at Hornsey.[59] Where Harriet Moore's work is outstanding, however, is in the quantity as well as the quality of her output, and its intense concentration on a single theme. Unique too is the fact that in his day-to-day research activities Faraday simply did not allow people into the laboratory unless they had a very good reason to be there. He preferred to work alone, in the silent presence of Charles Anderson, so Harriet Moore's necessarily extended presence in the basement was by permission and for a distinct purpose.

From the smiling, informal photograph taken in 1854, and from the tone of her letters to Faraday, Harriet Moore comes across as a gentle, attentive, sensitive woman, who could no doubt render herself invisible if needs be. Sitting drawing in a shadow in the corner of the laboratory, she was as well camouflaged as a mouse would have been. When she was invited upstairs to draw in Faraday's apartment, however, she made two watercolours that are as bright, open and light-filled as the laboratory series are contained and gloomy. For the greys and browns that she used on her palette downstairs, Harriet exchanges pinks, greens and blues when she climbs upstairs. Unlike the laboratory, the Faradays' apartment is shown empty of people. There is no glimpse of Michael reading a novel on his sofa, no sight of Sarah sitting sewing in a window. The drawing room, from which we see a corner of the study beyond, has a greeny-cream leaf-print wallpaper and a purple, red and green lozenge-pattern Axminster carpet. Over the white marble fireplace is a large mirror, with a narrow gold frame of rococo twists and flames, an ivory or glass tower under a tall glass dome, and one or two other glass knick-knacks on the mantelpiece. On either side of the mirror is a long green bell-pull.

The carpet in Harriet Moore's watercolour of Faraday's study also gives a character of restrained comfort to the room, a world away from the functional workshop in the basement. There is a plan or drawing chest on the left with a wide top for unrolling things, an elegant cloth-covered table with splayed legs on the right, books on shelves and in piles, and a writing desk in the window. These are subjects that are also found in Turner's large *oeuvre*, for example in the series of intimate interiors of Farnley Hall that he painted in the 1810s for his old friend Walter Fawkes; Harriet Moore's interiors of Faraday's laboratory and apartment are exercises in the same manner.

On the walls, hung from long strings, are some pictures – a portrait, perhaps a landscape or two. Most interesting among them is Harriet's rendition on the right of the far wall of what is clearly a turbulent marine storm scene with a boat in trouble, very rough, very dangerous, very Turnerian. If this is a Turnerian subject – and under the circumstances of the Faraday/Moore/Turner relationship no other serious contender springs to mind – it could either be a copy (perhaps by Harriet) or an engraving after Turner. The general layout of the picture suggests it may be based on one of two particular Turners, either *The Wreck of a Transport Ship* (c.1810, engraved by T.O. Barlow c.1854 as *Wreck of the Minotaur*) or *Snow-Storm: Steam-boat off a Harbour's Mouth*.[60] This was exhibited at the Royal Academy in 1842, and could subsequently be seen, by appointment, in Turner's gallery in Queen Anne Street West.[61] The likeliest suspect, in this very fragile identification parade, is *The Wreck of a Transport Ship*, which we know was shown in London at the British Institution in May and June 1849 and at Colnaghi's Gallery in Bond Street in March 1852, and which was much copied.[62] It was directly after the painting was exhibited at Colnaghi's that Barlow's engraving was made. It is worth mentioning that *The Wreck of a Transport Ship* had hung at Appuldurcombe, on the Isle of Wight, the home of Lord Yarborough, from about 1810 until at least the late 1840s, the years in which Michael and Sarah Faraday spent so many holidays on the island.

The notion that Michael Faraday had a marine storm scene by or after

Turner hanging in his study is very potent, and ties up a number of loose threads in his intellectual life. One of these centres around his remark to his brother-in-law George Barnard about artists' renditions of storms: 'I wonder you artists don't study the light and colour in the sky more, and try more for effect.' Barnard wrote to Bence Jones: 'I think this quality in Turner's drawings made him admire them very much.'[63] In a passing remark to the painter C.R. Leslie, Faraday revealed his private high opinion of the status of painting, referring to Leslie's 'high and intellectual pursuit'.[64]

Harriet Moore's watercolour of Faraday's study became moderately well-known from 1870 when a wood engraving was made after a pen-and-ink line drawing by Harriet from her original. She made some minor changes in this later drawing which have gone into the wood engraving: most notably, a framed landscape painting has been added to the right-hand wall, and the 'Turnerian' picture has been changed to what looks like a bosky landscape. Further, the subject of the portrait hanging over the fireplace has been changed from a woman to a man – though this may have been the engraver's fancy. A lamp has also been added to the sideboard on the right, and a plant in the window, left, and these duly appear in the wood engraving. This all means little, except that by omitting, for whatever reason, the Turnerian painting from the engraving study, Harriet Moore successfully extinguished all suspicion that Faraday might indeed have had a Turner hanging on his wall.

In enabling Harriet Moore to paint this important series of pictures, Faraday was instrumental in constructing a particular view of himself and his world for posterity. Fundamental to it is the severe divide between Faraday at work and Faraday at rest: hard, cold, manly, even primitive conditions in the basement, where men unlock the secrets of nature, contrasted with the comfort of the second-floor apartment, the realm of air, colour and light, neatly and comfortably furnished, where Faraday could enjoy the rewards of his labour, overseen by his women.

CHAPTER 24

I be Utterly Unworthy . . .

Faraday's relationships with his Sandemanian brethren encountered another watershed in the 1850s. The crises were one, possibly two, serious incidents which might have led to his second and final exclusion from the church. One error was forgivable; a second was not. The bumpy, always uncertain, ride that Faraday had with the Sandemanians coloured the last few years of his life, and brought him periods of fear and unhappiness, in extreme contrast to the adulation and unalloyed respect he had won from the wider public. Interestingly, this change runs in parallel with the apparent increase in his social activity in the 1850s and in his reading of novels.

In 1850 Faraday expressed perhaps too strongly, either in writing or in an address to other worshippers, a feeling he had that a reading of 2 Corinthians 2.6–11 would suggest that man should forgive the offender who truly repents 'lest perhaps such a one should be swallowed up with overmuch sorrow'.[1] This flew in the face of Sandemanian doctrine as expressed in a reading of Matthew 18.17, in which man is enjoined to tell his trespassing brother of the fault he has committed; and if he will not listen, take two or three witnesses; and if he still will not listen, 'tell it unto the church: but if he neglect to hear the church, let him be unto thee as a heathen man and a publican'. The key injunction here is 'hear the church', in other words the body as a whole will direct the determination of punishment and the interpretation of scriptures. This small piece of independence on Faraday's part went down very badly indeed with the Sandemanian dogma-machine, and it rapidly brought both him and Sarah great anguish.

All this blew up late in October 1850, in the months after the Faradays had made their ten-day trip to minister to the faithful at Old Buckenham. They had had a short holiday in Brighton, and Faraday was carrying out experiments into terrestrial magnetism. At three o'clock in the morning of 31 October 1850 Sarah was so frightened of the consequences of her husband's interpretation of 2 Corinthians that she was unable to sleep, and got out of bed to write to William Buchanan, 'feeling sure of your kind sympathy in my great anxiety & affliction'.[2] Clearly she and Michael had been agonising over the fact that if he were to be excluded again, that would be it, he would be out of the Sandemanian church for ever. Sarah herself was a quiet, perhaps unimaginative Sandemanian, not one to rock the boat or even to consider questioning dogma, and she wanted to hear their good friend Buchanan's view of the subject of excommunication 'from the scriptures alone'. Her husband's questioning nature was, now, going too far; it was one thing to question nature in the laboratory, quite another to question the word of God. Gripped by her fear, Sarah wrote to Buchanan not as an Elder 'but as to a dear friend & brother with whom we have had many communings & surely if his mind could be set at rest with out sowing division in the church or casting him out it will be a happy thing'.

Dominant perhaps in Sarah's mind was the fact that in the event of Michael's exclusion she would herself be torn between loyalty to her husband, and loyalty to her father, her many close relations and her church. One question that is not raised in this correspondence, but which is as solid a presence in the background as the laws of the prophets, is: would Sarah be excluded with Michael? And if she were not, would her life become intolerable as the wife of an excommunicant? The mental torment in the neat Faraday apartment at this time was evidently excruciating.

Three days later Faraday himself wrote to Buchanan:

> I am in deep distress and I write to you for my heart is full, not with any presumptious hope, but that my tears may overflow for I know that you love me both in body & spirit and I may perhaps

never write to you – more, bear with my anguish & do not refuse to sympathise a little with me by receiving this patiently though I be utterly unworthy. I may well fear that a deceived heart hath turned me aside for where my only comfort ought to be there is my sore grief & trouble.[3]

Faraday castigates himself with yet more self-inflicted wounds in this confused letter. That the great scientist, who in normal circumstances writes with such clarity and erudition, should be reduced to abject misery by this situation is pitiful to see. Clearly, in writing this letter on 'Sabbath evening' Faraday has just come home from a serious session of correction by the Elders in the chapel, and has been directed to confess the error of his ways. Faraday, who considered in the letter 'my dear wife to whom I am a snare', went over the points of his dispute with dogma. But even as he rehearses his case he is crumpling in the face of Sandemanian reality and demands to conform:

Then my mind lingers here that the command or rather instruction to separate & to restore may be alike general; that as there is no case of a second restoration so there is not of a second separation, yet the church is surely right in separating whenever the signs which our Lord of the Apostles point out occur and therefore my mind is not fully persuaded from the scriptures that we should limit the continuation of the instruction i.e. the restoration. But well may I fear for myself and hear the precept lean not unto thine own understanding. The Church is the body of Christ the pillar & ground of the truth and the Lord tells the brethren in Matt XVIII to hear the Church. I have been refusing to hear . . . Dear friend forgive me.

In her reply of thanks to William Buchanan for his advice to Michael, Sarah admits that 'we have been reasoning beyond what the Scriptures allow', and adds: 'My fear now is that his mind is quite over taxed & he seems almost as if reason would fail . . . & he again & again says "I may not be a hypocrite" he seems to me as if he could hardly take in any arguments but I hope he will get sleep & his mind be restored.'[4]

This stern, even cruel rebuke by the brotherhood of Faraday's independent thought is an unsettling example of the power that the sect held over its willing members. However firmly he held his conviction of wide bounds of forgiveness as preached by St Paul to the Corinthians, Faraday's views were as nothing compared to the strict Sandemanian line. Michael Faraday the scientist, interpreter of natural laws to the world, could be allowed no personal opinion whatsoever on the interpretation of the Bible.

After this unbending treatment, Faraday remained a firm, loyal and – we have to assume – obedient Sandemanian for the rest of his life. He and Sarah attended chapel every Sunday and Wednesday evening in St Paul's Alley and, from 1862, at a new building in Barnsbury Grove, north London. As they went in their carriage up the Caledonian Road and turned right into Offord Road, they often saw a group of small boys who Faraday recognised from the audience at his Juvenile Lectures. One of the boys, Alfred Yarrow, rose to become a great marine engineer and a baronet, and as an older man recalled his regular street-corner meetings with Michael and Sarah Faraday:

A friend of mine of the name of Walter Rutt and I were so much impressed with Faraday's personality, that it was our practice on Sundays to meet Faraday and his wife at the corner where he used to go from the Caledonian Road up the hill to the road leading to Barnsbury, where at the corner we would raise our hats to him, which salute he always graciously returned. We then ran down a side street and then one parallel to the one taken by Faraday and his wife and up another street which intersected the road which Faraday passed over, and we saluted him a second time.[5]

Yarrow and Rutt did not leave this haunting of Faraday at the pavement's edge, but followed him quietly and crept into the back of the chapel to listen to the service, 'which seemed to us very similar to a Quaker's Meeting'. Yarrow makes a final telling observation, the kind of acute insight that only an intelligent innocent could make; although it gives very little information, it does evoke something of Faraday's discomfort in the Sandemanian chapel: 'Faraday seemed much more at home at the Royal Institution than he did addressing the congregation, which devolved upon anyone who thought they should give an address.'

There is very little in the way of clues about Faraday's attitude to

Sandemanianism after the 1850 incident. He was invited in 1854 by John Barlow, in words very subtly put, to throw some light on his religion. But even Barlow, an ordained priest of the Church of England, failed to get Faraday to unbutton himself, challenging the scientist by quoting Sarah as saying that he, Barlow, '"should think your form of worship ridiculous." Now I cannot imagine any thing less possible to deride than the simplicity and earnestness of your ritual: and I am sure that it must pervade the daily life of those who are exercised by it.'[6]

In his reply Faraday simply refused to be drawn on the subject, ending his letter with the politest of refusals: 'I must pass by your observations on religion &c &c indeed must conclude in the briefest manner with our kindest wishes to you & Mrs Barlow.'[7]

So for insight into Faraday's latter relationship with Sandemanianism we are left with the result of Ada Lovelace's very direct approach, which seems to have surprised him into the frank response that the sect he belongs to is 'very small & despised'.[8]

Early in 1855 Faraday was involved in another controversy which severed the Edinburgh congregation of the sect from that in London. The issue in hand was the observance of the strict Sandemanian law that creatures that had died by strangulation may not be eaten. The reason for this was that in accordance with scriptural teaching Sandemanians could only eat the meat of animals from which all the blood has flowed at death. In a long letter of warning from the London Sandemanians, of which Faraday was a co-signatory, the scriptural references were rehearsed, the Edinburgh congregation was enjoined to 'hear the Church' and warned very severely to mend its ways.[9] This it refused to do, and the London Elders and Deacons cut them off:

From these considerations, with deep sorrow of heart, and we trust with fear for ourselves, we feel compelled to withdraw from your communion in obedience to the Divine command, Matth. 18, v.17; Rom. 16, v.17; 2 Cor. 6, v.14 &c 1 Tim 6, v.5, 2 John 9, v.11, praying that He who alone is able by His Word & Spirit to convince of sin may grant you repentance to the acknowledging of the truth.[10]

Michael Faraday was completely and wholly involved in these acts of punishment and cleansing, and with his Sandemanian mind in gear, and having signed such a letter, felt profound and absolute sadness at the route that the law had to take. The effect of the severing of relations with the Edinburgh community meant that the Faradays were forbidden to have any further contact with the Buchanans.

A revealing observation of Sandemanian practices in the 1860s was published in 1870 by J.E. Ritchie. He wrote of the Sandemanians as 'one of the expiring sects of Christendom', who 'at no time have . . . been a very powerful denomination either from their numbers, their influence or their wealth. They have never yet made their mark upon the world, nor are they likely to do so now. The late Professor Faraday was one of their elders, and for a time conferred on them a little of his world-wide reputation; but one swallow does not make a summer.'[11]

Ritchie suggests that the Sandemanians made no effort whatsoever to reveal themselves to a wider world, and indeed by the way they presented themselves appeared to be hermetic, uncommunicative and fearful. He quotes 'one of their publications' as saying: 'We are utterly against aiming to promote the cause we contend for either by creeping into private homes or by causing our voices to be heard in the streets, or by officiously obtruding our opinions upon others.' What puzzled Ritchie was the effect of the Sandemanian belief that faith is a passive grace planted in the individual by God, and for which the believer is not responsible.[12] For that reason Sandemanians kept silent in public on religious matters, and made no attempt at conversions.

Ritchie describes the Barnsbury chapel as

a neat, simple structure, of white brick, with no architectural pretensions of any kind. It only differs from other places of worship in having no board up announcing to what denomination it belongs, nor the name of the preacher, nor the hours of assembly, nor where applications for sittings are to be made, nor to whom subscriptions are to be paid. Indeed the only reference at all to an outside world seems to consist in the putting up a caution intimating that the building is under the guardianship of the police, and persons evilly disposed had better mind what they are about. Thus, and thus only, is the recognition of an outer world lying in darkness and needing true light of the Gospel in any way acknowledged.

Investigating further, Ritchie reveals:

The stranger who for the first time attends will be struck with the absence of the pulpit, instead of which he will find two large desks, one above the other, in which are seated three or four elderly persons; the attention which is paid to the reading of the Bible; the illiterate way in which those who preach and pray do so; and the length and dullness of the service. The morning service, for instance, begins at eleven, and is never over till half-past one. No wonder the Sandemanians are not a vigorous sect . . . As an outsider I should say nothing was ever more uninteresting, nothing ever more calculated to alienate from religion intelligent young people, than the services conducted by the Sandemanians. The elders and deacons, excellent men undoubtedly, are singularly deficient in oratorical ability. I think the worst sermon I ever heard in my life was preached by one of them . . . Their church seems utterly destitute of intellectual vigour; and when, as in these days, brains are beginning to rule, the piety that rejects and ignores them is in danger. There is a relation between the Bible and modern thought of which the good people who preach dull sermons and make dull prayers up in Barnsbury have no idea.

Faraday had been dead three years when that passage was published, but it reveals a thoughtful outsider's reasoned, if jaundiced, view of the sect. Equally puzzled, another theologian wrote in 1873 of 'the misty dogmas of Robert Sandeman'.[13] Contemporary accounts of Sandemanian services conflict, and to set against Ritchie's experience is Samuel Martin's report of Faraday's 'expressive reading of Holy Scripture – his exposition of the sacred writings and his fervent prayers and praises'.[14]

We are led to ask what it was in Sandemanianism that continued to attract Faraday throughout his life, and kept him faithful to its dullness. Faraday's character was to be loyal, to conform to rule and pattern, and to do his duty. Though tempted from time to time to stray from the Royal Institution and accept more lucrative employment elsewhere, he refused to do so, asserting that the Institution was his home, his family, and the object of his professional loyalty. Having been brought up in the Royal Institution, professionally born there, he knew of nothing else.

His attitude to his religion was of exactly the same kind. He had been born into a Sandemanian family, brought up in the church's teachings, married into it – married indeed high up in it, to the daughter of one of its most senior Elders – and had made his own personal confession of faith. Whether he liked it or not, he was part of it.

Ritchie was being kind when he suggested that Faraday gave Sandemanianism 'a little of his world-wide reputation'. On the contrary, his connection with the sect probably worked against it; certainly it worked against him in the world. The escaped remark about the 'very small & despised sect' seems to reflect a painful shadow of some real abuse felt by Faraday, for example the innuendo against him in government and high social circles over the pension affair; or the widespread reputation of unsociability that had gone before him for decades. Further, Sarah's comment to Barlow that the Anglican priest should think Sandemanianism ridiculous, is not an observation which suggests a serious degree of self-confidence in either of the Faradays. To survive healthily within the sect all his personal style and vigour as a public speaker, and as a public man, had to be suppressed. The Michael Faraday who stood up and exhorted the congregation was not the same man who addressed the packed Royal Institution lecture theatre on subjects of natural philosophy. The Sandemanian Faraday was a man who was deeply afraid of being 'a hypocrite in all I say and do';[15] of being thought to be 'obscure and confused';[16] of bringing 'deepest condemnation on myself' when excluded from the congregation;[17] of being a 'snare' to his wife. That boy who had been thrilled by Faraday's Juvenile Lectures put his finger securely on the problem when he noticed that Faraday was less at home at chapel than at the Royal Institution.

CHAPTER 25

The More I Look the Less I Know . . .

While the Sandemanian Faraday would conform to the wishes of the flock and attempt at all times to live an obedient and unexceptionable Christian life, the scientist Faraday had no fear of getting into scrapes and controversies in science. From the day he published his paper on electro-magnetic rotations in 1821 he was fearless of standing up for facts. In the early 1850s, the second of the two periods in which he was at his lowest ebb as a Sandemanian, Faraday continued his practice of taking firm public stands on both table-turning and mesmerism, and in the more rarefied realm of claiming priority for himself in his discovery of the magnetism of oxygen. This was in the face of counter-claims in 1850 by the French father and son chemists Antoine-César and Alexandre-Edmond Becquerel. While few Sandemanians would have known or cared about the Becquerel controversy, most will have had their views on table-turning and mesmerism, and all will have known of their brother Faraday's public pronouncements upon these and other subjects. What we do not know is whether his high public profile gave Faraday added protection and cachet within the flock, or whether it potentially weakened him as a voice of authority and caused him to stay out of sight as much as possible.

There are a number of dissonances in this part of Faraday's life and in his perception of himself. The most prominent is his attitude to the promotion of his own image, which, as we have seen, he took active steps to encourage. The last two decades of his life were also the decades in which portrait photography reached its first apogee of popularity and availability. Faraday's own pioneering work as an enabler of photography from the end of the 1830s has been discussed in Chapter 19, but it was in the 1850s and sixties that he made his own particular use of the medium as a means to create an image of himself.

Engaging some of the leading portrait photographers of the day, and the most up-to-date technology, Faraday had images created of himself alone and with colleagues that are of the same high standard as the series of painted and engraved portraits made of him from the 1820s onwards. Among the earliest photographs of Faraday, taken in the early 1840s, are a pair of posed images by an unknown photograpgher of Faraday with the inventor of the Daniell Constant Cell, John Frederic Daniell, who died in 1845. In one, Faraday, noticeably shorter than Daniell, stands on the right apparently making a stern point to his friend with an upraised finger, while Daniell, scratching his head, takes the instruction gamely. The dramatic nature of the poses is due in part to the needs of the long exposure required by photographers at that time, the subjects having to be still for as long as five or ten minutes. Thus, Faraday holds himself still by putting his left hand on the battery and his right elbow on some superstructure, while Daniell rests his elbow on a pump of some kind. In the second of this pair, Faraday, hands in pockets, looks as if he is taking instruction from Daniell.[1]

Another photograph of Faraday with a colleague must have been taken in the late 1850s, and shows him with William Brande. Faraday, a shorter man than Brande, is shown standing, steadying himself on a photographer's half-column prop, while Brande sits to the left. Looking out into the distance to the right, Faraday is clearly the dominant personality in the photograph, Brande remaining passive with heavily shaded eyes.

A third two-figure subject, taken in the early 1840s, shows Faraday seated to the right, hand on heart, and looking directly at the viewer. Sarah is standing beside him, with her hand on his shoulder, and looking down at him in some restrained adoration. Once again, it is easy to see who is the dominant figure here, and how the pose has been plotted to send out an image of a cared-for Faraday, protected and cosseted by his wife, herself well-dressed and cared-for through the fruits of Faraday's own labours, but also personifying the hard restraining hand of Sande-manianism.

Other photographers who took Faraday as their subject include Antoine Claudet, in a very sensitive head and shoulders of the early 1840s, Richard Beard, Maull & Polyblank, John and Charles Watkins, Ernest Edwards and John Mayall. Among Mayall's photographs is one which was repro-duced as a wood engraving for wide circulation, the engraving being cut by Daniel Pound, Mayall's assistant who also happened to be J.M.W. Turner's adoptive stepson.

The most telling image of Faraday lecturing is a painting by the portraitist Alexander Blaikley, a fellow Sandemanian, which shows Fara-day speaking to an audience which includes Prince Albert and the Prince of Wales in 1855.[2] There are many recognisable faces in the audience – including Harriet Moore, Sarah Faraday, John Tyndall, Frederick Pollock and Charles Lyell – and one of the accomplishments of the image is how it shows the physically diminutive Michael Faraday commanding a huge audience of the great and the good, who flow like a wave across the entire background of the work and lap up against the bottom edge of the frame in the extreme foreground. The aerial perspective cleverly isolates Faraday, and sets him in his own arena to which the audience has no access. With the smoky atmosphere of the lecture theatre well expressed, Blaikley's work gives a very clear idea of the overcrowding of the lecture theatre when Fara-day was speaking, of how he could command and silence the audience with a gesture, of how brightly his central desk could be lit by the bank of gas jets above it, and of the presence of the attentive Charles Anderson, who hovers in the background beside the fireplace.

The existence of so many posed photographs of Faraday demonstrates the depths of his concern that the image of the scientist should be associated for all time with the equipment or inventions that led to the scientific advances: thus the photograph by Maull & Polyblank of Faraday holding a bar magnet, the inclusion of the Cruikshank battery in Thomas Phillips's portrait of him, and of the electrostatic machine in Charles Turner's engraving. Further, there are a large number of photographs of him in pensive pose, or reading, which give an aura of other-worldliness and exclusion. Central also is the marble head-and-shoulders portrait bust carved *all'antica* by Matthew Noble in 1854 for the Royal Society.[3] Here, looking firmly to one side, Faraday is dressed in what is intended to be read as a Roman toga, with the far-seeing pose that was given iconic status in the early sixteenth century by Michelangelo in his bust of *Brutus*. In its distant air, the pose of Noble's bust is comparable to the pose Faraday adopted in many of the later photographs of himself.

The subject of his own image began to perplex Faraday in the mid-1850s. Schoenbein wrote to tell him that he had been writing some reminiscences of his life and friendships, as Schoenbein described it 'a sort of "quodlibet" or as the musical term runs "pot pourri" i.e. a most variegated motley of things'. He continued:

On account of its motley character I should like you could read that strange composition, but it being written in German, I am afraid its contents will never come to your knowledge . . .

In the above mentioned book there is a little chapter bearing the title 'Fachsmaenner', gallicé 'Spécialités' and anglicé perhaps – but I am unable to translate the word into your language,[4] I mean to denote by that term Men devoting their whole life and mind to one object. By no means admiring what they call universal geniuses and being convinced that it is the 'spécialités' to whom we owe every real progress in science, arts &c. I have, with a view to proving the correctness of my opinion, drawn up four slight sketches of such 'Fachsmaenner', of Berzelius, von Buch, Cuvier and of, of, but be it spoken out, of Faraday.[5]

When Faraday received Schoenbein's letter he had been sitting to Matthew Noble for the 1854 bust. It was due to be exhibited at the Royal Academy in the early summer of 1855, and this imminent wide public exposure was evidently giving him pause for thought. He deliberately delayed replying to the letter for nearly six weeks, until he and Sarah had next travelled down to Hastings, and until he had had time to reflect on his long friendship with Schoenbein. Faraday wrote to Schoenbein from Hastings on 6 April 1855, a few weeks before the Royal Academy exhibition opened, and described how time and age was taking its toll of his memory of their friendship:

I say remember it *all*, but that I cannot do; for as a fresh incident creeps dimly into view I lose sight of the old ones, and I cannot tell how many are forgotten altogether. But think kindly of your old friend; – you know that it is not willingly but of natural necessity that his impressions fade away. I cannot tell what sort of portrait you have made of me, – all I can say is, that whatever it may be I doubt whether I should be able to remember it: – indeed I may say I know I should not, for I have just been under the Sculptors hands, and I look at the Clay, & I look at the marble, and I look in the glass, & the more I look the less I know about the matter & the more uncertain I become. But it is of no great consequence; label the marble & it will do just as well as if it were like. The imperishable marble of your book will surely flatter.[6]

In trying again and again to catch it by one means or another, it seemed to Faraday that a definitive image consistently eluded him. We could describe this as vanity, but there is more to it than that. Faraday's generation of scientists was the first for whom it was possible for men and women (*vide* Mary Somerville, who was just on the cusp of this evolutionary change) to make a career in science, to become part of a scientific brotherhood. The first sprouting of this had come in the years surrounding Waterloo, when the learned societies began to be founded – the Geological Society in 1807, the Zoological Society in 1826, and, a decade later, the Botanical Society. The trend evolved into the formation of professional scientific and technological institutes and societies, the renewed form of the mediaeval guilds and companies – thus the Institutes of Civil Engineers, of Mechanical Engineers and of Electrical Engineers sprang up across the nineteenth century in the undergrowth around those ageing plants the Companies of Painter Glaziers, Barber Surgeons and Goldsmiths. From the time-honoured route of apprenticeship to a master-in-trade (something Faraday knew all about), the process of gaining experience and knowledge of a profession was beginning to be measured in terms of examination results and the award of a diploma.

As the great pioneer scientist – a pioneer both in discovery and in terms of institutionalising his profession – Faraday was aware of the importance to science as a body of a visible figurehead who would mark his particular moment, but who would all too soon have to give way to the coming generation. Christian saints had traditionally been painted with their attributes to aid recognition – the key of St Peter, the wheel of St Catherine – and with that parallel consciously or unconsciously in mind Faraday ensured that he was portrayed by Maull & Polyblank with his own attribute, the magnet. To take the argument further, and to weave an irony that would probably have been lost on Faraday, as the professional institutions grew so they promised happiness and security in this life through professional qualification and status, thus amending the picture which the Christian tradition reflects of eternal happiness and security in an afterlife.

This shift also marks the development of portrait photography into a profession of its own. There was a new clarity, immediacy and ubiquity in photography that was not available in the portrait engravings of fellow scientists that Faraday had so carefully collected for many years. In using himself as a subject for the new art and science Faraday was also quite properly marking the fact that he himself had been instrumental in disseminating knowledge of photography since 1839, and that he considered photography to be a means of image reproduction beyond compare.

While the public work that Faraday carried out in the 1820s and 1830s had centred around military and naval matters, in the 1850s and early 1860s the balance shifted to his being called to sit on official committees. In 1850 he was a member of a Great Exhibition sub-committee dealing with exhibits from the 'Vegetable kingdom',[7] and in 1851 was invited onto the jury to select exhibits for 'the Mining, Quarrying, Metallurgical Operations and Mineral Products' section. Knowing perhaps of his ill-health and the other pressures on him, Lyon Playfair, the Special Commissioner for the Great Exhibition, recommended Faraday to contribute to the Mining section 'as you would then only require to give aid as a Chemist on Metallurgical subjects & require less constant attention'.[8]

In 1853 Faraday was invited by the Select Committee of the National Gallery to advise on the problem of the cleaning of pictures on public display in the sulphurous air of London. Summoned to attend on 10 June 1853, he produced a canvas, painted with white lead which he had himself striped with layers of varnish increasing in thickness from left to right, to demonstrate that the thickest varnish was 'a perfect defender' of the original paint.[9] He described how the varnish could safely be removed by alcohol, and then he pulled another painting out of his bag. This was one of the little waterfall studies that Penry Williams had made for him in south Wales thirty-three years earlier; as he was cleaning it with the alcohol, Faraday found to his consternation that it was not an oil painting after all, but made entirely in varnish. Thus the image disappeared before his eyes until he was down to the bare canvas. What might have been a disaster Faraday turned to the advantage of science, as the accident demonstrated that particular care had to be taken in cleaning paintings which had been made with a mixture of oil and varnish. Faraday further strongly advised the committee on the importance of glazing pictures and giving them sealed backs against the ingress of dirt and dust.

Once hooked into the expert-witness circuit, other invitations came to Faraday. He examined the Elgin Marbles at the British Museum, finding them very dirty, with surfaces

> in general rough, as if corroded . . . many have a dead surface; many are honey combed, in a fine degree, more or less; or have shivered, broken surfaces, calculated to hold dirt mechanically . . . The examination made me despair the possibility of presenting the marbles in the British Museum in that state of purity and whiteness which they originally possessed, or in which . . . like marbles can be seen in Greece to this present day.[10]

Faraday blamed the damage to the marbles on the dust raised by 'the multitude of people who frequent the galleries' and on the smoky London atmosphere, and in cleaning tests tried dilute nitric acid, alkalis 'both carbonated and caustic', water and rubbing with a sponge, finger, cork or brush.

Drawn yet deeper into the management of the art world, Faraday became a member of the National Gallery Site Commission, which sat for twenty-six days in 1857 to look at various new sites for the National Gallery, either in combination with the British Museum, or in a new building at Kensington Gore. In his questioning of expert witnesses Faraday had been at pains to find out what techniques the National Gallery used to clean its paintings, pressing the Director, Sir Charles Eastlake, for information, and examining John Bentley, who had cleaned pictures in the Turner Bequest. The Commission also had a demonstration of cleaning techniques by Richard Smart, who had worked on the Royal

Academy's collection of paintings by past Academicians. Cross-examining John Ruskin on the sixteenth day, Faraday pressed Ruskin to say whether, if a painting was permanently damaged by dirt, any cleaning could restore it. 'Nothing can restore it to what it was, I think,' Ruskin replied, 'because the operation of cleaning must scrape away some of the grains of paint.'

'Therefore,' Faraday responded, 'if you have two pictures, one in a dirtier place, and one in a cleaner place, no attention will put the one in the dirtier place on a level with that in the cleaner place?'

'I think nevermore.'[11]

That gloomy assertion by Ruskin seems to represent the wide gulf in attitude to public education that separated Faraday from the most authoritative art critic of the day. In 1857 Faraday was sixty-six years old, to Ruskin's youthful thirty-eight. By now Ruskin was the author of four volumes (of an eventual five) of *Modern Painters*, his extended work of art history, art criticism, natural history, geological analysis and critical campaigning for his hero Turner. His three-volume work *The Stones of Venice* (1851–53) had also been published. There was no comparable figure in the art establishment in Britain to Ruskin, the free-lancing, but unbiddable, St George of public taste. Faraday was Ruskin's equivalent in the world of science, but, having the edge over Ruskin in terms of age and experience, he was also listened to more carefully, with greater respect and without contradiction. His religious affiliation, though baffling to the Anglican-leaning social and political establishment of Britain, was, by the 1850s, probably playing in Faraday's favour, the high, dark boundaries of Sandemanianism being observed courteously. There were for Faraday, in addition, none of the marital and sexual difficulties that had latterly affected Ruskin's public reputation. If Faraday had ever had a wild side, it was unwritten, and long forgotten.

So, in facing each other over the table at the National Gallery Site Commission meeting, John Ruskin and Michael Faraday were the twin summits of the nation's artistic and scientific expertise. How unfortunate, then, that Ruskin should overstep his mark as an art expert and tell Faraday the science consultant that, once dirtied, a painting was injured for ever. After Ruskin's assertion 'I think nevermore,' Faraday ceased his questioning for the time being, until the issue arose in the meeting of dividing the national collection into two – a 'popular' and a 'great' gallery. Ruskin was in favour of two such galleries, one sited centrally in London to house 'pictures not of great value, but of sufficient value to interest the public, and of merit enough to form the basis of early education', while 'all the precious things should be removed and put into the great Gallery, where they would be safest, irrespective altogether of accessibility'. This would be 'more or less removed' from the centre of London, where the air was polluted.[12]

This evidently divisive approach, based as it was on an ill-informed view of the cleaning of pictures, flew in the face of Faraday's profound belief in equality of educational opportunity. In proposing a hierarchy of painting, in which 'precious' works would go to the 'great Gallery' and the works 'of merit enough' to the 'popular Gallery', Ruskin is asserting his view that there are absolutes in art as in science. In the Preface to volume three of *Modern Painters* (1856) Ruskin had insisted that it took real labour and experience to be able to understand and 'judge rightly of art', invoking Faraday as he did so:

> There are . . . laws of truth and right in painting, just as fixed as those of harmony in music, or of affinity in chemistry. Those laws are perfectly ascertainable by labour and ascertainable no otherwise. It is as ridiculous for any one to speak positively about painting who has not given a great part of his life to its study, as it would be for a person who has never studied chemistry to give a lecture on affinities of elements; but it is also as ridiculous for a person to speak hesitatingly about laws of painting who has conscientiously given his time to their ascertainment, as it would be for Mr Faraday to announce in a dubious manner that iron had an affinity for oxygen, and to put the question to the vote of his audience whether it had or not.[13]

But Ruskin well knew that the certainties of art were no match for the absolutes of science, and went on in the same paragraph to say as much:

> The phrase 'I think so', or, 'it seems so to me', will be met with continually; and I pray the reader to believe that I use such expression always in seriousness, never as matter of form.

In using Faraday as his exemplar when trying to establish matching absolutes for art as for science, Ruskin was invoking a name that he knew would carry resonance with his readers. He was, however, displaying an attitude that is in stark contrast with that of Elizabeth Rigby, the authoritative author and critic who married Sir Charles Eastlake in 1849. She wrote in her diary in 1847:

> Art is like instinct, incommunicable: one age may bequeath statues and pictures to another, but it cannot bequeath knowledge. Science can be bequeathed; one fact after another is laid up. Faraday may take up where Davy left off, for science lies without the man, but art is partly within, partly without ... Each one is true and interesting for opposite reasons: Art, because it partakes of the mind, is coloured, influenced by it; Science, because it repudiates all individuality, stands free from opinion, taste or prejudice, uses the human mind to elaborate it, but shakes off all contact with it and is free.[14]

Faraday stands apart from both Ruskin's and Rigby's opposed attitudes to what art and science are and are not, and would perhaps take issue with Elizabeth Rigby on the grounds that although science may repudiate individuality, it requires individuality to divine, discover and progress it. That Ruskin failed to convince even himself absolutely may be one of the causes of his apparent disdain for Faraday, expressed at points during his later life. In *Fors Clavigera*, his series of letters 'To the Workmen and Labourers of Great Britain', Ruskin wrote in 1874 of how science had removed the joy and simplicity from myth and tradition:

> Even your simple country Queen of May, whom you once worshipped for a goddess – has not little Mr Faraday analysed her, and proved her to consist of charcoal and water ... Your once fortune-guiding stars, which used to twinkle in a mysterious manner, and to make you wonder what they were – everybody knows what they are now: only hydrogen gas, and they stink as they twinkle.[15]

In a letter to the painter George Richmond, who had drawn Faraday's portrait in 1852, and had been one of Faraday's fellow Commissioners on the National Gallery Site Commission, Ruskin most ungallantly urged him in 1874 to tell tales about Faraday:

But I'm going to have a go at Faraday! this time at Oxford. Perfectest of men, wasn't he? Domestic, Orthodox, Episcopal, Enchanting, Accurate, Infallible, Modest, Merrymaking! Well, I'm going to have a go at him for all that; but I want to know first, please, how orthodox he was? or was by *way* of being. Did he do his church regularly? – expect to go to heaven? – think Chemistry a divine operation?

It is of great importance to me to know this as accurately as I can, and I'm sure you can tell me better than anybody else.[16]

To Richmond's lost reply Ruskin retorted:

I know Faraday to be invulnerable; but he can be both evaporated and compressed; and I will do a little of both upon him, God willing. They have no God now at Oxford but Nitric acid, and Faraday is his Prophet.[17]

This persecution of Faraday should be seen in the light of the loss of faith in nature that Ruskin suffered in the early 1870s. He wrote then of 'my disgust at her barbarity – clumsiness – darkness – bitter mockery of herself . . . I am very sorry for my old nurse, but her death is ten times more horrible to me because the sky and blossoms are Dead also.'[18] In the 1850s, however, there was much more that drew Ruskin and Faraday together than drove them apart. Ruskin's lecture 'The Work of Iron, in Nature, Art and Policy',[19] given in Tunbridge Wells in 1858, is richly reminiscent of Faraday's Juvenile Lectures at the Royal Institution in the same decade. Although they expressed their priorities in different ways, Ruskin and Faraday shared an extreme conviction of the importance of widespread education; difficult facts clearly and simply expressed to all ages and levels of society. Though these are Ruskin's words, we might almost hear Faraday speaking:

You all probably know that in the mixed air we breathe, the part of it essentially needful to us is called oxygen; and that this substance is to all animals, in the most accurate sense of the word, 'breath of life'. The nervous power of life is a different thing; but the supporting element of the breath, without which the blood, and therefore the life, cannot be nourished, is this oxygen. Now it is this very same air which the iron breathes when it gets rusty. It takes the oxygen from the atmosphere as eagerly as we do, though it uses it differently. The iron keeps all that it gets; we, and other animals, part with it again . . . [20]

In 'The Chemical History of a Candle' Faraday speaks in a similar voice, but with more figures and demonstrations:

You will be astonished when I tell you what this curious play of carbon amounts to. A candle will burn some four, five, six, or seven hours. What, then, must be the daily amount of carbon going up into the air in the way of carbonic acid! What a quantity of carbon must go from each of us in respiration! What a wonderful change of carbon must take place under these circumstances of combustion or respiration! A man in twenty four hours converts as much as seven ounces of carbon into carbonic acid; a milch cow will convert seventy ounces, and a horse seventy-nine ounces, solely by the act of respiration . . . All the warm-blooded animals get their warmth in this way, by the conversion of carbon, not in a free state but in a state of combination.[21]

A further difference with Ruskin's approach is that at the close of this, the last of his six lectures 'On the Chemical History of a Candle', Faraday takes the role of the preacher exhorting his flock:

Indeed, all I can say to you at the end of these lectures . . . is to express a wish that you may, in your generation, be fit to compare to a candle; that you may, like it, shine as lights to those about you; that, in all your actions, you may justify the beauty of the taper by making your deeds honourable and effectual in the discharge of your duty to your fellow-men.[22]

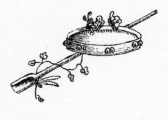

CHAPTER 26

The Body of Knowledge is, After All, But One . . .

The last ten years of Faraday's active professional life, up to about 1863 or 1864, were marked by his work as an expert adviser to committees and his own assertive interjections into public life, as much as by the scientific ideas he proposed. His Field Theory of Magnetism and his fruitless search for 'gravelectricity' move from the inspirational to the imaginative. While his magnetic field experiments proved that space had structure, he encouraged himself 'with a little more imagination' when drawing to the end of his work on 'gravelectricity'.[1] In his friendships he found comfort in the lively youthfulness of the new generation of scientists around him – John Tyndall, William Thomson, James Clerk Maxwell, William Crookes and his physician Henry Bence Jones. Attentiveness, intuition and beautiful results in scientific research were Faraday's bequests to them.

Faraday's membership of a Great Exhibition committee in 1851, and his appearance before the National Gallery Select Committees in 1853 and 1857, were by invitation. But at other times he put himself into the public eye by his own decision – the mesmerism and table-turning debates of the early 1850s, and when he wrote to *The Times* in July 1855 to bring to public attention the foul state of the River Thames in London. With graphic directness, Faraday wrote of how he had torn up pieces of white card and dropped them into the river, only to see them disappear from

sight 'before they had sunk an inch below the surface'.[2] Seeing the role
of the senior scientist to be a leader of society as much as of scientific
research, Faraday went on to say:

> I have thought it a duty to record these facts that they may be
> brought to the attention of those who exercise power or have res-
> ponsibility in relation to the condition of our river; there is nothing
> figurative in the words I have employed or any approach to exagger-
> ation; they are the simple truth . . . If we neglect this subject, we
> cannot expect to do so with impunity; nor ought we to be surprised
> if ere many years are over, a hot season give us sad proof of the
> folly of our carelessness.

There is no premonition among Faraday's surviving papers that he
would make such a dramatic entry into the problem of the disposal of
London's sewage. The letter to *The Times* was instinctive and spontaneous, the result of his happening to be on a steamboat on the river
on a hot day on the way home from the country, and being appalled at
the 'smell of the . . . opaque pale brown fluid', and at the 'feculence
[which] rolled up in clouds so dense that they were visible at the surface
even in water of this kind'.[3] In taking the action he did, Faraday must
have been reminded of the long, expensive and fruitless efforts that his
friend John Martin had gone to in the 1830s and 1840s to design embankments and sewage disposal systems for London, which lost their way in
committee and were never constructed.

By now, however, times had changed. The cholera outbreaks of 1848–
49 and 1853–54, in which twenty-five thousand people had died, forced
scientists, medical men and politicians to seek the causes of the disease.
One of these was, paradoxically, the widespread introduction of the water
closet, which now ensured that sewage was delivered down a drainage
system and emptied neatly into the river. Thus it contaminated the water
supply, rather than being left to be cleared away from local cesspools by
'nightsoil men'. But the orthodox medical view, which held until the
1860s, was that disease was not spread in drinking water but carried on
the air – Florence Nightingale believed this to be the case, as did the
influential sanitary reformer Edwin Chadwick, who claimed to a Parlia-

mentary Committee in 1846 that 'all smell is disease'.[4] Faraday too followed this accepted line, as his warning reveals: 'a hot season [may] give us sad proof of the folly of our carelessness'.

Faraday's letter to *The Times* came at a moment when political action was already being taken to establish the Metropolitan Board of Works (1856), whose responsibilities, under its Chief Engineer Joseph Bazalgette, included the construction of a system of sewers for London that would direct sewage away from the river into filter beds where it could be broken down and sold as agricultural fertiliser. In that respect, Faraday had no direct impact on the improvements, but by putting his own eminent personality into the arena he created a new focus around which public attention could gather. A cartoon in *Punch* which followed the publication of Faraday's letter[5] lifted the sewage issue from committee papers and parliamentary reports, and through the expression of his anger and impatience on the public's behalf, Faraday gave it a new impetus and urgency. 'We hope the Dirty Fellow [i.e. Father Thames] will consult the learned Professor,' urged the cartoon's caption.

Such was the power Faraday had in his sixties over public opinion and the rate of social change. Seeing science as a domain for all, he continued on a wider stage to use his influence to promote public well-being through the application of scientific principles. In November 1850 he had written to Tyndall:

> I rejoice at every addition to the facts and to the reasoning connected with the subject. It is wonderful how much good results from different persons working at the same matter; each one gives views and ideas to the rest. Where science is a republic, there it gains; and though I am no republican in other matters, I am in that.[6]

Faraday's 'republicanism' found wider boundaries when, in the early 1860s, he allowed his lectures to be taken down verbatim and published. Thus, his life came full circle, for there in the gallery of the Royal Institution lecture theatre was a scribe noting down in shorthand the speaker's every word, action and aside, just as Faraday himself had done as a boy at Davy's lectures.[7]

As a public lecturer Faraday gained in geniality as he called for change and improvement. A column in *Punch* in March 1857 published an account of his lecture 'Conservation of Forces' in the voice of young 'Mary Ann', who pointed out how 'Prince Albert was there with his star on, looking so grave and elegant . . . They set him in a great chair, you know, exactly in front of the lecturer.'[8] In linking Faraday so proudly with royalty, *Punch* was affirming his status as an oracular figure, unchallengeable, the speaker of great truths of such depth and importance that Prince Albert himself would sit at his feet and listen 'with the utmost steadiness'. 'Mary Ann' went on to say that:

> It was quite a treat to look at dear Dr Faraday's earnest face and silvery hair, not that he is an old man, far from it, and he is far more light and active than many a smoky stupid all-round collar-man that I know . . . It was a most beautiful lecture, and if anything could excel it, it was the kindness of Dr Faraday afterwards, when ladies came and asked him questions, and he did not look supercilious, or what is worse, look condescending, but he entered with evident pleasure into explanations, and did several little experiments for us . . . and if we did not understand it . . . it was the fault of the system of education you men give us, which makes us either quote like parrots, or stare like owls when philosophy comes up.

The 'Mary Ann' figure in this passage is the embodiment of women like Maria Herries, Mary Robinson and Harriet Moore whose easy attendance at Royal Institution lectures was due to Faraday's charm, clarity and the spirit of inclusiveness and welcome that his lectures always conveyed. The Faraday that 'Mary Ann' observed in action was the public figure who, if billed to lecture, would always do so if his health would possibly allow it. There are instances of members of his audience noticing he was not up to par, seemed unwell or not in control, but these are rare. A paragraph spotted by Faraday and transcribed by him in the 1850s gives an evocative insight into the troubled state of his mind, suffering as he was from exhaustion and debility. The passage quotes Talleyrand, whom Faraday had met over his electro-magnetic equipment in 1832, as saying that 'the true use of language is to conceal the thoughts', and goes on:

'This is to declare that in the present instance when I say I am not able to bear much talking it means really & without any mistake or equivocation or oblique meaning or implication or subterfuge or omission, that I am not able, being at present weak in the head & able to work no more.'[9]

Faraday's own poor state of health was exacerbated by his worry over Sarah, who in the past few years had herself deteriorated to the extent that she found walking difficult, was becoming deaf, and suffered from upset stomach and rheumatism. 'We are both changed,' Faraday wrote to de la Rive in 1854, 'my wife even more than I; for she is indeed very infirm in her limbs, nor have I much expectation that in that respect she will importantly improve.'[10]

Both Michael's and Sarah's age and tiredness were beginning to get the better of them, and as a result of the intervention of Queen Victoria they were given, in June 1858, an elegant Georgian grace-and-favour house on the Green at Hampton Court for life. They had the use of the coach-houses, greenhouse, the summerhouse and other outbuildings,[11] and even, should they want it, which they did not, 'the pew in the Chapel in the Palace which has hitherto belonged to the House'.[12]

Faraday's instinctive need to improve the efficiency of whatever piece of equipment he was using extended even in his old age to the stoves in the house 'which Her Most Gracious Majesty has been pleased recently to grant me'.[13] He wrote to the Board of Works to ask if he could 'place some fire bricks within three of the stoves . . . It is simply the introduction of so much brick instead of so much coal.' At the same time he asked for permission to take turf from the palace gardens to lay out on the kitchen garden of his house, and for Sarah to be allowed to sit in her invalid chair in the palace grounds.

Hampton Court Green was not, however, a retirement home for them, rather a permanent equivalent on the edge of London to the many and various houses they had rented on the south coast and latterly on London's rim. They still lived at the Royal Institution, but no longer had to organise, or apply to, or search for, clear-aired accommodation for respite from the London smoke. Hampton Court soon moved Faraday to verse, a habit he had fostered when he was young and in love, but had not since then had much time to indulge:

Fair Hampton Court! what pleasant hours
Have sped beneath thy fragrant Bowers
And sweet to memory are the times
We lingered near thy shadowy limes.

. . .

And while life lasts will love be there
To those who bade us freely share
In royal gift, in fair retreat,
And more than all in friendship sweet![14]

Reflecting on what was left of his physical abilities, Faraday came to the conclusion in October 1861, nearly three weeks after his seventieth birthday, that he should tender his resignation to the Managers of the Royal Institution. His letter sets out his reasons as clearly as if he were writing a report on a scientific analysis of which he was the subject:

I am not competent to perform as I wish, the delightful duty of teaching in the Theatre of the Royal Institution; and I now ask you . . . to accept my resignation of the *Juvenile lectures.* Being unwilling to give up, what has always been so kindly received and so pleasant to myself, I have tried the faculties essential for their delivery, and I know that I ought to retreat:– for the attempt to realize (in the trials) the necessary points brings with it weariness, giddiness, fear of failure and the full conviction that it is time to retire . . . And this reminds me that I ought to place in your hands the *whole* of my occupation . . . The duty of research, superintendence of the house, and the other services still remain; – but I may well believe that the natural change which incapacitates me from lecturing, may also make me unfit for some of these.[15]

In the event, the Managers only accepted his resignation as a lecturer to juveniles, and Faraday continued to manage the house and laboratories, to sign equipment out on loan and back again in a final effort of control,[16] and to give some Friday Discourses. But this was a charade, and reprieve was bound to be brief: on 20 June 1862, when talking to an audience of over eight hundred on gas furnaces, Faraday fumbled and accidentally burnt his notes – the scorch mark is still there.[17] His lecture notes show that he knew that would be his final Discourse, even before the notes caught fire, and he had prepared his farewell to the last of the audiences that had hung on his every word for thirty-six years:

> Personal explanation – years of happiness here but time of retirement. *Loss of Memory* and *physical endurance of the brain* causes *hesitation and uncertainty* of the convictions which the speaker has to urge. II. *Inability to draw* upon the mind for the treasures of knowledge it has previously received. III. *Dimness and forgetfulness* of one's former *Self-standard*, in respect of *right, dignity* and *self-respect*. IV. Strong duty of *doing justice to others* yet inability to do so. Retire.[18]

But there was still life in the old campaigning scientist, and some unfinished business to attend to. By command of the Public Schools Commission, a body that he wished most earnestly to address on the subject of the education of young people in science, Faraday drew himself out of his 'fair retreat' and took himself off on 18 November 1862 to Victoria to give evidence to the Commission in session under the chairmanship of the Earl of Clarendon. Faraday opened by deploring the fact that knowledge of the scientific advances 'given to the world in such abundance during the last fifty years . . . should remain untouched', and that no attempt was being made to convey it to young minds growing up. This, he asserted, was 'to me a matter so strange, that it is difficult to understand it'.[19] He went on to give the example that in his work for Trinity House he and the Trinity House Brethren found it difficult to find men with the aptitude to man lighthouses:

> how difficult it is to get men of ordinary intelligence with regard to anything that is out of the ordinary way. In the mere attendance on a common lamp, and of the observance of the proceedings required for security, the mere attempt to make notes of what they ought to do . . . shows such a degree of, I will not say opposition, but of ignorance. We cannot find these men. We cannot find the intelligent common man.

Lack of general scientific knowledge and its intelligent application was the root of the educational problem facing Britain, in Faraday's view, in the early 1860s. He had found the same situation when teaching at Wool-wich. These were young men at a higher level of the social scale than trainee lighthouse-keepers, but there too 'they are altogether, or nearly, unable to give me an answer to the questions which I ask them. The slightest possible examinations that I could ever give at Woolwich were very feeble and poor, in order to obtain some kind of answer; nor can I wonder at that, because they had no instruction but my lectures.'

In the twilight of his life, Faraday was as deeply concerned about public education in science as he had been in his early years as a student of John Tatum and Humphry Davy. The fifty years that he quoted as being the space across which new scientific ideas had failed to fly into schools was precisely the same span across which he himself had been working. That knowledge 'given to the world in such abundance' was the selfsame scientific advance to which Faraday and his generation of natural philos-ophers had given their lives. While natural knowledge had raced ahead during Faraday's laboratory years, it was no more, and probably less, available to the young now than it had been when he was with Tatum. This scandalous state of affairs was the one which Faraday, as a final act for society, was determined to expose. Unfortunately, however, he had entirely missed the point of the present intentions of the Public Schools Commission.

Faraday told the Commission that the first problem was to overcome the shortage of teachers:

> Such men hardly exist at present. They want the A B C of science, and not the X Y Z; they want the first elements. If I give a juvenile lecture I lecture in as plain terms as I can to children, and I simplify as far as I can the ideas, but men are not educated to do that as yet. The ordinary schoolmaster does not know it.

He was convinced that the ordinary child was receptive enough to be taught science:

> ... at my juvenile lectures at Christmas times I have never found a child too young to understand intelligently what I told him, or to come to me with questions afterwards which did not prove it ... Both boys and girls come rushing up to the table. I am under this

disadvantage in that respect, that those who like it best come first, and they so crowd round as to shut out those who do not like or care for it. I never yet found a boy who was not able to understand by simple explanation, and to enjoy the point of an experiment.

Asked which were the most important sciences for early instruction, Faraday would not be drawn, and clearly revealed the nature of his own understanding of the unity of the body of sciences:

You see they pass so thoroughly one into the other, that the body of knowledge is, after all, but one, and although we can have those of observation, such as natural history, botany, and so forth, yet, still, I never can make out the distinction between chemistry and physics.

Having only a sectional view of the breadth of the national education problem, the Chairman of the Commission, Lord Clarendon, chose Eton as the example of the typical school, and the 'upper classes' as the social spectrum with which he was here concerned. Faraday, whose own education had been on the streets of London, was taken aback and brought the generality of the issue to a head. But in doing so he revealed his own ineradicable political naïvety: 'You say you are endeavouring to consider the education as regards the upper classes; if that be all, I am saying a great deal that is all abroad, because I expected you were taking all classes.'

At this, he was brushed off and put right by the Chairman, who listed some of the nine schools with which the inquiry was concerned – Eton, Harrow, Winchester, Westminster, Rugby, Charterhouse. This gave Faraday pause, but before long he was able to counter-attack with severe criticism of 'men and women quite fit for all that you expect from education', but who were nevertheless unwilling to accept instruction. These, he implied, were the products of the public schools:

. . . they come to me and they talk to me about things that belong to natural science; about mesmerism, table turning, flying through the air, about the laws of gravity; they come to me to ask me questions, and they insist against me, who think I know a little of these laws, that I am wrong and they are right, in a manner that shows how little the ordinary course of education can teach these minds . . . They are ignorant of their ignorance at the end of all that education . . . and I say again there must be something wrong in the system of education which leaves minds, the highest taught, in such a state.

Angered by the exclusivity of what he had believed would be an inclusive examination of the education of all young Britons, Faraday gave, from this point on, brief answers to longer questions, touching on nomenclature, the value of Greek as the root language for science, and which of the sciences should be selected to be taught in preference to others. By now monosyllabic and unenthusiastic, he had had more than he could take of the Public Schools Commission. He would not give a list of preferred sciences, but turned the question round:

I think you would better indicate what knowledge ought to be obtained . . . by speaking of the subjects, the atmosphere, the waters, and the earth. I would also have a little astronomy . . . I think [chemistry] ought to come very early, as being one of the fundamental sciences, but to say that you were to pursue it to the utmost would be an error, I think.

Faraday's fury is evident. He may have been naïve in his belief that anything called the Public Schools Commission would be at all interested in the education of all classes, but believe it he did. Wanting to raise the question of poorly-educated lighthouse-keepers as a paradigm for the abject intellectual state of the vast mass of the British working population, he was reduced to a diatribe, touching on fury, about the inability of educated people to be aware, or to care, about their own ignorance. While desperate to urge Lord Clarendon's Commission to bring scientific education to all the young people represented by the boys and girls who crowded round his table after his Juvenile Lectures, Faraday seemed only to be able to impress upon the men behind the table (but probably not to convince them of) the ludicrousness of those scourges of intelligent society in the 1850s and 1860s, mesmerism, table-turning and flying through the air.

But the spirits would not let him go. The last of what survives of Faraday's commentaries on spiritualism is dated almost exactly two years after he gave his evidence to the Public Schools Commission. Replying to an unknown correspondent, he sighs:

> I am weary of the spirits – all hope of any useful result is gone but as some persons still believe in them and I continually receive letters. I must bring these communications to a close ... Whenever the spirits describe their own nature, and like honest spirits say what they can do; – or pretending as their supporters do, that they can act on ordinary matter whenever they initiate action and so make *themselves* manifest: – whenever by such like signs they come to me and ask my attention to them I will give it.
>
> But until some of these things be done, I have no more time to spare for them or their believers, or for correspondence about them.[20]

From the security of Hampton Court Faraday had the added strength to undertake further travels for Trinity House – to Birmingham in 1860 and 1861 to work on lenses with James Chance, to the lighthouses at Dover and Whitby in 1860, and to those at Dungeness and Dover in February 1863. Travel of this sort was becoming too much for him now, and from a letter to the Brethren of Trinity House we find that the sixty-nine-year-old had been 'caught in a snow storm between Ashford and Dover and nearly blocked up in the train', so that he had to return to London. A few days later he tried again, travelled to Dover and attempted to reach the lighthouse by carriage. The roads 'were still blocked up towards the lighthouse, but by climbing over hedges, walls and fields, I succeeded in getting there and making the necessary inquiries and observations'.[21]

As their lives approached completion, Michael and Sarah Faraday tended each other with care and solicitude. Theirs was a close and discreet marriage, impossible now to analyse from the outside, and as private, undisclosed and mysterious as the Sandemanian faith to which it was true. When in August 1863 Faraday went to Glasgow and Dundee to give encouragement to Sandemanians, he wrote a touching letter to Sarah: 'I long to see you, dearest, and to talk over things together ... You will have to resume your old function of being a pillow to my mind, and a rest, a happy-making wife.'[22]

By now Faraday was crumbling fast – or, as he put it in December 1863, tottering: 'My words totter, my memory totters, and now my legs have taken to tottering, I am altogether a very tottering and helpless thing.'[23] He had already written his last letter to Schoenbein, a brief and poignant farewell as his memory faded and rallied and faded again as he tried to write some sense: 'Again and again I tear up my letters, for I write nonsense. I cannot spell or write a line continuously. Whether I shall recover – this confusion – do not know. I will not write any more. My love to you.'[24]

To Auguste de la Rive he wrote another veiled farewell:

Having no science to talk to you about, a motive, which was very strong in former times, is now wanting:– but your last letter reminds me of *another motive* which I hope is stronger than Science with both of us; and that is the future life which lies before us . . . Next Sabbath day (the 22nd) I shall complete my 70th year. I can hardly think myself so old as I write to you – so much to cheerful spirit; – ease – and general health is left to me; – and if my memory fails – why it causes that I forget *troubles* as well as pleasure; and the end is, I am happy and content.[25]

Faraday's complete retirement from the superintendence of the laboratories at the Royal Institution was finally accepted in March 1865, and in May that year he retired from Trinity House. Although he continued to be taken back and forth between Hampton Court and the Royal Institution, the journeys were little more than a charade, for he had nothing more to do in Albemarle Street, and was gradually losing his mind. One member of his family wrote that in his final years Faraday was 'quite like a little child'.[26] At Hampton Court he sat under the limes, watched the sunset and the lightning when it came, standing, as Margery Reid wrote, 'at the window for hours watching the effects and enjoying the scene':[27]

I shall also always connect the sight of the hues of a brilliant sunset with him, and especially he will be present to my mind while I watch the fading of the tints into the sombre grey of night. He loved to have us with him, as he stood or sauntered on some open spot, and spoke his thoughts perhaps in the words of Gray's Elegy, which he retained in memory clearly long after many other things had faded quite away.[28]

Standing behind and slightly to the right of Faraday during his lectures at the Royal Institution had been, always, Sergeant Charles Anderson, Faraday's silent and ever-present assistant. Anderson died in January 1866, at the age of seventy-five, and Faraday was told of his death by Sir James South, who described Anderson as having been 'part and parcel' of Faraday himself.[29] South suggested to Faraday that Anderson be given a funeral and memorial at Highgate Cemetery, but Faraday dismissed the idea out of hand. He dictated his reply to Jane Barnard: 'I shall mention your goodwill to Anderson,' he said. Jane objected to that, because Anderson was dead, but still Faraday insisted that that was precisely what he meant to say, and took the pen and paper and wrote in his own wobbly hand: 'I shall mention your goodwill to Anderson.'[30] Then he asked Jane to add: 'I have told several what may be my own desire. To have a plain simple funeral, attended by none but my own relatives, followed by a gravestone of the most ordinary kind, in the simplest earthly place.'

By the summer of 1866, Faraday's creeping senility had almost wholly overcome him. He had made one of his periodical trips back to the Royal Institution apartment when Henry Roscoe, who was giving a lecture in June 1866 on the opalescence of the atmosphere, tried to find in the laboratory samples of gold film that Faraday had prepared some years before. They were nowhere to be seen, so Roscoe climbed upstairs to ask the Professor if he could remember where the gold had been put. 'Don't you remember those beautiful gold experiments that you made?' Roscoe asked Faraday. 'Oh yes,' the old man replied feebly, 'beautiful gold, beautiful gold.'[31]

During his last few years Faraday was under the care of Dr Henry Bence Jones. Jane Barnard wrote an account of a visit Bence Jones made to Hampton Court in July 1866:

My dear Uncle showed more interest & therefore more excitement at the interview than he has done at any meeting of a friend since this illness began. He remembered he said something about a book

& we knew he referred to an old copy of Shakespeare that we had been speaking of yesterday as being a suitable gift for the doctor. After a while Uncle turned to the doctor & said 'I am waiting, just waiting.' The doctor replied 'Yes, you are waiting . . .' & Uncle looking wistfully at him said 'And you? Are you waiting?' & the tears ran down his cheeks. The doctor seeing he was getting agitated tried to turn it off by saying, 'Yes, I am waiting. We are all waiting.' . . . I then told him how in the course of the week after my Uncle had repeated the first verse of the 46th Psalm he turned to me & said 'Who is Dr Bence Jones's refuge & strength?' The doctor seemed quite touched. My Uncle has spoken oftener of him than of any one . . . Now he is touchingly patient, quiet & happy, like a little child, so trusting, but shewed very little interest until this afternoon.[32]

As Faraday waited for death, sitting in his chair or up in bed, he was surrounded by the comforts and securities of his religion. Over his bed at Hampton Court he had these verses from the Book of Psalms written up on a card:

Remember me, O Lord, with the favour that thou bearest unto thy people: O visit me with thy salvation;
    That I may see the good of thy chosen, that I may rejoice in the gladness of thy nation, that I may glory with thine inheritance.
    Psalms CVI, 4, 5[33]

Bence Jones returned regularly to Hampton Court to see Faraday. In the second week of August 1867 he called as usual, and then went off on holiday to Spa in Germany. Within a fortnight, however, Faraday became noticeably weaker, he spoke little, and during the afternoon of Sunday, 25 August 1867, sitting in his chair in his study, he died.[34]

The simple funeral that he had insisted upon took place five days later. From Hampton Court Faraday's body was taken to the Royal Institution, where the carriages paused momentarily. Making their way north they crossed Oxford Street, and passed up through the Portland estates, a stone's throw from 18 Weymouth Street, where Sir Humphry Davy's carriage had once clattered up to the door. Slowly the funeral party made its way up the hill to Highgate Cemetery where a grave was waiting.

EPILOGUE

Very soon after Faraday's death, perhaps within weeks, a small cottage industry established itself to keep his memory untarnished. In his lecture 'Michael Faraday: Philosopher and Christian', given in October 1867, Revd Samuel Martin, the Congregational Minister of Westminster, dwelt on the seven 'bright points' of Faraday's character.[1] These he defined as diligence and conscientiousness; a sincere desire to live a life of godliness; supreme satisfaction in established truth; humility and modesty; patience; the high value of sure and certain knowledge; and Faraday's determination to live the life of a true Christian while engaged in the pursuits of an experimental philosopher. This is a grand model to attempt to emulate, and such stirrings of uncritical praise reached their apogee thirty years later when the poet and art critic Cosmo Monkhouse wrote a three-verse poem 'On a Portrait of Faraday', first published in 1898 as the epigraph to Silvanus Thompson's biography *Michael Faraday: His Life and Work*. The poem was later set to music by Harriet Grant; presumably an audience has heard it sung:[2]

> Was ever man so simple and so sage,
> So crowned and yet so careless of a prize!
> Great Faraday, who made the world so wise,
> And loved the labour better than the wage.

And this you say is how he looked in age,
With that strong brow and these great humble eyes
That seemed to look with reverent surprise
On all outside himself. Turn o'er the page,
Recording Angel, it is white as snow.

Ah God, a fitting messenger was he
To show Thy mysteries to us below.
Child as he came has he returned to Thee.
Would he could come but once again to show
The wonder-deep of his humility.

Where Samuel Martin seems to be advocating Faraday for a sainthood, Monkhouse goes straight for deification.

It was left to four distinguished scientists – John Tyndall (1869), Henry Bence Jones (1870), J.H. Gladstone (1872) and Silvanus Thompson (1898) – each of whom had known him well, to construct the rational picture of the Faraday which, by the turn of the twentieth century, had created the foundations of the modern understanding of him. A theme common to each of these biographies is their perception of the enduring relevance and uniqueness of the combination of Faraday's world-shaping scientific achievements with his personal qualities as a devout and not fully fathomable outsider. That is the particular combination of extremes – 'the loftiness of [his] character and the beauty of his life', as Tyndall put it[3] – that made the story of Faraday's life worth the retelling again and again in the late nineteenth century, as an uninvited exemplar of the perfect contemporary life.

Evidently, there was pressure from Faraday's extended family on the early biographers to keep the life perfect. Benjamin Abbott came out of obscurity to write two touching memoirs of his old friend, and these throw some refreshing, but hagiographic, light on Faraday's early life. But when Henry Bence Jones, in the first edition of his *Life and Letters of Michael Faraday*, was so bold as to say that the Faraday family had received charity – a loaf of bread a week during the period of famine in 1801 – he was forced to withdraw 'this error' in the second edition with an abject explanation:

I was too easily led ... by my wish to show the height of the rise of Faraday by contrasting it with the lowliness of his starting point. I ought to have been content with the few words which he wrote. 'My education was of the most ordinary description, consisting of little more than the rudiments of reading, writing, and arithmetic at a common day school.'[4]

The policing of Faraday's moral and social reputation in the first few decades after his death appears to have been tight, for not only was Bence Jones corrected so firmly, but there have been losses from Faraday's surviving papers, which suggests that they were picked over before being allowed gradually into the ownership of the Royal Institution, the Institution of Electrical Engineers and elsewhere. The drafts of Faraday's youthful, free-booting continental and Welsh journals, for example, have disappeared, and although Faraday may himself have destroyed some of them when he made his fair copy, some extracts that Bence Jones quotes came from early drafts that existed in the late 1860s, but have subsequently disappeared.[5] One cull that is known to have taken place was of papers possibly referring to mesmerism that were destroyed by David Blaikley in 1914.[6] It is remarkable that the letters from Ada Lovelace have survived, but this may be because their language of metaphor was misunderstood in the late nineteenth century.

The widowed Sarah Faraday lived in the care of the Sandemanian circle and of her nieces Jane Barnard and Margery Reid until her death in 1879. There is a crayon drawing in one of Faraday's scrapbooks of a gathering of about eight ladies sitting sewing by a window which may give a hint at how Sarah and her relations passed their time; and another, entitled 'Our sketching party, or, A gathering of busy B's', which shows a group of nine Barnard girls, each identified by her initials.[7] Her husband's ardent wish in his last days, 'I must not be afraid; you will be cared for, my wife; you will be cared for,'[8] was honoured, and Sarah was kept carefully within the Sandemanian embrace.

Faraday's scientific reputation took its own route in the world, unhampered by family pressures, and fostered by a new generation of scientists and social needs. In 1891, on the centenary of his birth, *Punch* paid homage to him with a cartoon showing Faraday with his ear to a phonograph.[9] Standing beside him is the Muse of Science, the same perhaps as the figure who had hesitated outside Tatum's lecture rooms seventy-five years earlier. 'Well, Miss Science,' Faraday says to the Muse, 'I heartily congratulate you; you have made marvellous progress since my time.'

Faraday's practice of showing, through demonstration, clear language and the selective use of exhibits, how it is that natural forces weave their effects, had become the norm in schools and universities by the beginning of the twentieth century. Indeed, when my university, the University of Birmingham, opened in 1900, it employed many teachers of the rank of Demonstrator, whose job it was to instruct their students using objects kept in no fewer than seven separate museums. This pattern, which had evolved from Faraday's teaching at the Royal Institution, was repeated throughout the country, and out into those huge parts of the wider world where British influence in education was felt. The University of Birmingham, however, may be unique in having a small stone statue of Faraday, in company with figures of eight other cultural giants, set in a frieze above the entrance to Aston Webb's main university building. Plato, Virgil, Michelangelo, Shakespeare, Newton, Beethoven, Watt and Darwin are Faraday's companions over the door through which every student and teacher at the university will pass. With his hand raised in an emphatic gesture, this stone image is just one sign that the roots of modern science, and of its teaching at school and university level, pass virtually entire through the nutritious loam of Michael Faraday's achievement.

APPENDIX 1

The Contents of Michael Faraday's 'Philosophical Miscellany', 1809–10

(Manuscript in the Archive of the Institution of Electrical
Engineers, London, SC MS 2/1/1)

The Philosophical Miscellany
being
A collection of Notices, Occurrances, Events, &c relating to the
Arts & Sciences; collected from the Public Papers, Reviews,
Magazines and other miscellaneous works. Intended to promote
both Amusement and Instruction and also to coroborate or
invalidate those theories which are continually starting into the
world of science.
Collected by M. Faraday 1809–10.
[209 pages of MS notes and extracts, with ten-page index. The
references are as given by Faraday.]

PAGE

1 Description of a Pyroneumatic Apparatus. *Ackerman's Repository*, 1809,
p.162.

4 Remarkable Property of Boiling Tar. *Ackerman's Repository*, 1809

11 Filteration [*sic*].

12 Experiments in 'the Ocular Spectra of Light & Colour' by R.W. Darwin
MD. *Ackerman's Repository*, 1809, p.252.

16 On Flies. *Ackerman's Repository*, 1809, p.175.

19 Description of a Candle Screen. *Ackerman's Repository*, 1809, p.382.

22 Lightning. *Gents Mag.*, 1795, vol. 65, pt 1, p.527

26 Electric Fish. *Gents Mag.*, 1786, vol. 56, pt 2, p.1007.

28 Ocular Spectra. *Gents Mag.*, 1786, vol. 56, pt 2, p.1098.

29 An account of the Whirlwind ... near Bury St Edmunds, Suffolk, July
    31st 1786. *Gents Mag.*, 1786, vol. 56, pt 2, p.701.

41 Sympathetic Inks. 'Hooper's Recreation', *Lady Magazine*, 1775, vol. 6,
    p.205.

50 Meteorlites [*sic*]. *Evangelical Magazine*, 1809, vol. 17, p.561.

53 Animal thermometer. *Universal Magazine*, 1763, vol. 32, p.95.

55 Extract of a Letter from Long Eckington near Southam, Warwickshire,
    Feb 28 1763.

63 Waterspouts. *Zoological Magazine* (Curiosities &c), vol. 3, p.448

65 Burning Glasses.

67 Hair of the Head. *Sturm's Reflection*, Nov 15

71 Formation of snow. *Sturm's Reflection*, Decr 5.

72 Sympathy and Antipathy. *Universal Magazine*, vol. 32, p.7.

77 To loosen glass stopples. *Lady Magazine*, 1808, p.412.

78 To convert two Liquids into a Solid. *Conversation on Chemistry*, vol. 1,
    p.110.

79 Oxygen Gas. *ditto*, vol. 1, p.147.

82 Hydrogen Gas

88 Phosphoret of lime

90 Nitric Acid

91 Carbonic Acid Gas

92 Oxy-Muriate of Potash
    Camphor

93 Ventilation. *Observer*, Feb 25, 1810.

94 Rust. *Universal Magazine*, vol. 1, 1804, p.56.
    Indian Ink. *Universal Magazine*, vol. 1, 1804, p.172.

95 Garlick
    Filtration. *Universal Magazine*, vol. 1, 1804, p.624.

96 Representations of Plants. *Universal Magazine*, vol. 12, 1809, p.231.

98 Magnet. *Universal Magazine*, vol. 12, 1809, p.318.

100 Process for preserving Pencil and Chalk Drawings. *Universal Magazine*,
    vol. 12, 1809, p.493.

101 Impressions of Leaves, Plants &c. *Universal Magazine*, vol. 12, 1809,
    p.494.

103 Lightning. *Gents Mag.*, vol. 60, pt 1, 1790, p.38.

105 Inflexion of Light. *Gents Mag.*, vol. 60, pt 2, 1790, p.614.

106 Fairy Rings. *Gents Mag.*, vol. 60, pt 2, 1790, p.1072; and *Gents Mag.*, vol.
    60, pt 2, 1790, p.1106.

110 Freezing of fish. *Gents Mag.*, vol. 77, pt 1, 1807, p.4.

113 Muriatic Acid. *Gents Mag.*, 1807, vol. 77, pt 1, p.145.

114 Coculus Indus. *The Country Magazine*, 1780, vol. 12, p.97.

117 Luminous Insect. *Gents Mag.*, 1787, vol. 57, pt 1, p.88.
    Insensibility of Pain. *Gents Mag.*, 1787, vol. 57, pt 1, p.118.

119 Electricity. *Gents Mag.*, 1787, vol. 57, pt 1, p.178.

121 To cut glass. *Gents Mag.*, 1787, vol. 57, pt 1, p.311.

122 Luminous Bottle. *Christian Observer*, 1806, vol. 5, p.120.

124 Philosophical Question concerning heat of bottom of bottle of boiling water. *London Magazine*, 1765, vol. 34, p.358.

127 Experiment for proving that Wood when impregnated with Salt is not inflammable. *London Magazine*, 1765, vol. 34, p.403.

128 Gas lights. *Christian Observer*, 1808, vol. 7, p.827.

129 Atmospherical phenomena. *Christian Observer*, 1807, vol. 6, p.398.

132 Galvanism. *Christian Observer*, 1807, p.851.

133 Fairy Rings (Mr Davy's theory, in his lecture on Vegetable Chemistry at the Royal Institution.) *Christian Observer* 1807, vol. 6, p.127.

135 Glow Worm. *Nat. Cabinet*, vol. 6, p.197.

136 Invisible Girl. *Christian Observer*, vol. 6, p.127.

140 Electricity. *Gents Mag.*, 1787, vol. 57, pt 2, p.948

142 Electricity. *Gents Mag.*, 1787, vol. 57, pt 1, p.563.

145 Lightning. *Gents Mag.*, 1787, vol. 57, pt 2, p.823.

149 Breathing of fire. *Zoological Magazine* (Curiosities), vol. 5, p.141.

150 Changes of the weather. *Zoological Magazine* (Curiosities), vol. 5, p.150.

154 Flowers in the winter. *Gardeners Magazine*, vol. 14.

155 Electricity. *Gents Mag.*, 1788, vol. 58, pt. 1, p.116.

156 Frosty ramifications of glass. *Gents Mag.*, 1788, pt 1, vol. 58, p.123.

158 Electricity. *Gents Mag.*, 1788, vol. 58, pt 1, p.220.

161 Electricity. *Gents Mag.*, 1788, vol. 58, pt 1, p.776.
Observations on Inks. *Gents Mag.*, 1788, vol. 58, pt 2, p.992.

164 Electric phenomenon. *Gents Mag.*, 1789, vol. 59, pt 1, p.338.

168 Verdigrise. *Gents Mag.*, 1789, vol. 59, pt 1, p.606

170 Atmospherical phenomena. *Gents Mag.*, 1789, vol. 59, pt 2, p.1140.

171 Pressure of the Atmosphere.
A Green Flame. *Park's Rudiments.*

172 A Red Flame. *Rudiments.*
Detonations

173 Combustion under water

175 Sudden inflammation. *Rudiments.*
Flame produced from a mixture. *Rudiments.*

176 Sudden Inflamation. *Rudiments.*
Inflamation from a mixture. *Rudiments.*
Brilliant Combustion. *Rudiments.*

177 Detonation. *Rudiments.*
Purple & Crimson flame. *Rudiments.*

178 Sympathetic Inks

179 Sudden Inflamation. *Rudiments.*

180 Combustion on Water. *Park's Rudiments.*

Luminous Water. *Rudiments.*
181 Combustion under Water. *Rudiments.*
   Sudden Inflamation.
182 Sympathetic Inks. *Rudiments.*
   Spontaneous Inflamation. *Rudiments.*
   Sympathetic Ink. *Rudiments.*
183 Spontaneous Inflamation. *Rudiments.*
184 Tooth ache cured. *London Magazine*, 1765, vol. 34, p.665.
185 Quicksilver. *Gents Mag.*, 1791, vol. 61, pt 1, p.130
186 Attraction. *Gents Mag.*, 1791, vol. 61, pt 1, p.226; 417.
193 Luminous Oyster. *Gents Mag.*, 1791, vol. 61, pt 2, p.1120.
194 Aerial phenomena. *Gents Mag.*, 1791, vol. 61, pt 2, p.1177.
196 Galvanism. *Literary Panorama*, vol. 1, p.405.
198 Electricity. *Literary Panorama*, vol. 1, 1806, p.556.
202 Galvanism. *Literary Panorama*, vol. 1, p.627.
203 Electricity. *Literary Panorama*, vol. 2, p.852.
   Exhalation. *Literary Panorama*, vol. 2, p.1298.
204 Electricity. *Literary Panorama*, vol. 4, p.793.
206 Meteor. *Literary Panorama*, vol. 4, p.1253.
207 Spontaneous ignition. *Literary Panorama*, vol. 7, p.178.

APPENDIX 2

*Declaration of faith of Edward Barnard on being admitted to
the Sandemanian Church, London, August 1760*

Written out in MS in a small red bound book, Royal Institution archive. Edward
Barnard was the grandfather of Sarah Faraday.

In conformity to the command of God by the apostle to be always ready to give
an answer to every one that asketh a reason of the hope that is in us and in
conformity to the present request I shall as faithfully as I can declare what is
the ground of my hope of acceptance before God. By the scriptures I find myself
described as abominable and filthy, as a child of wrath: and by daily experience
I find myself prone to evil. This my state deserves nothing but the curse of God
and the pains of hell forever. But blessed be God, he hath not left me ['us' in
superscript] to perish in this lost estate, but has sent his son made of a woman,
made under the law, that both Jews and Gentiles might receive the adoption of
sons, for every one that cometh unto him is accepted, for he hath said 'I will
in no wise cast them out.' This Jesus is the Prophet, Priest and King of this
Church, and as such I desire to embrace him; as a Prophet to teach and instruct
me; as a Priest to atone and intercede for me; and as a King to rule over me
knowing that in keeping his commandments there is great reward and that his
yoke is easy and his burden is light. In him and in him alone do I hope to be
accepted before God, knowing that the parable of the two debtors describes me
for I have nothing to pay and therefore can have no hope but from being freely
forgiven.

Edwd Barnard.

APPENDIX 3

Memorandum to Robert Peel, Prime Minister, putting the case for Faraday to be awarded an annual state pension, 31 March 1835   .

The signature on the copy of the document in the British Library has been fully erased. Transcribed at FJ775.

Michael Faraday, Director of the Laboratory of the Royal Institution of Great Britain, is the son of a Journeyman Blacksmith from Newcastle who died in London many years ago, leaving a widow, and four children, totally unprovided for.

After the Fathers decease, the Mother by the profits of a Lodging house in Welbeck Street, could with difficulty, keep them from absolute want.

Michael was taken as an Errand Boy by Mr Riebaud a Bookbinder, and Newspaper Vendor in Portland Street, and after 12 months service, was apprenticed to his Master for 7 years; his fellow apprentices being, Oxberry the comedian, and Fitzwilliam, the singer.

Faraday passed his leisure hours in copying out of books which he had to bind, 'anything curious'.

Whilst binding a volume of the Encyclopedia, he was much struck by reading in it, the article 'Electricity'.

Prevented by poverty from procuring in the ordinary manner, an electrical apparatus of the meanest kind, he saw in an old rag shop in Little Chesterfield Street, two bottles, which he thought would answer the purpose; the price however was beyond his means – he watched these daily; till at length able to raise six pence for the one and a penny, for the other, he converted the one into an Electrical Cylinder, and the other into a Leyden Jar – a bullet and a bit of Wire was the Conductor.

His Master allowed him to attend Tatum's Chemical Lectures delivered in

Dorset Street, Salisbury Square; of these he took copious notes, which he transcribed fairly before he went to Bed. The admission Fee to each lecture, was a shilling, and he hoarded up all the Money he got given him, to pay it.

His language being that of the most illiterate, induced Mr Magrath (the Secretary of the City Philosophical Society, and now of the Athenaeum Club,) who attended the same lectures, to devote two hours every week to his instruction; and for 7 years, did Faraday uninterruptedly receive them.

When early out of his apprenticeship he addressed a letter to Sir Joseph Banks, soliciting him, as president of the Royal Society, to place him in any scientific situation, however menial, he left the letter himself – promised to call for his answer in two or three days – he did so – repeated his call three or four times, and was at last told, that Sir Joseph had said 'the letter required no answer'. He was almost disconsolate.

Whilst his 5 quarto volumes of Manuscripts of Tatum's Lectures which he had just bound, were on his Master's Counter, Mr Dance a member of the Royal Institution coming accidentally to the Shop, looked into them – represented what he had seen to the Managers, and [gained] for him gratuitous admission to Sir Humphry Davy's lectures; and that he might take sketches of the apparatus used by Sir Humphry he, Faraday, obtained from Marquesiere [*sic*], instructions in perspective.

Of these Lectures he took Notes, which were forwarded to Davy, this led to an interview, at which Sir Humphry promised to do anything he could for him, whenever an opportunity should offer.

His apprenticeship ended, carrying with him for his exemplary conduct, not only the respect but even the love of his Master, for support, he worked as a journeyman to La Roche, the Bookbinder, his wages being 30 shillings a week. Some months after this engagement, Davy having injured his eye sight, took him as his Amanuensis. This so broke in upon La Roche's plans, that hoping to retain Faraday's services, he promised on certain conditions, to give up his business to him, and 'thus to make him a Man of Property'. The proposal however Faraday declined accepting.

The Office of Fire-lighter, Sweeper, Apparatus-cleaner and washer – or of 'Fag and Scrub' in the Institution Laboratory becoming vacant – on Davy's recommendation Faraday was appointed to it – his wages being a guinea a week.

On Sir Humphry's going to the Continent, the Managers of the Institution, authorised him to accompany him; themselves finding a locum tenens, during his absence.

On his return to England he was made 'Assistant in the Laboratory', with a salary of 70 pounds a year – the use of two rooms – with as many coals and candles as he wanted.

Now that his pecuniary circumstances were improved, he sent his younger Sister, to a boarding school; but to enable him to defray the expense, to deprive himself of dinner every other day was absolutely indispensable.

About eight years ago he was appointed Director of the Laboratory of the Royal Institution, and member of the Institution without purchase. His Salary was increased to £100 a year, and he was absolved from waiting on the Lecturers in the Theatre of the Institution.

About the year 1829, he was appointed 'Scientific Adviser to the Admiralty' – about the same time, was chosen Professor of Chemistry in the Military Academy at Woolwich, – whilst two years ago, he was nominated, by Mr Fuller, Fullerian Professor of Chemistry in the Royal Institution.

Long enrolled as a Member of almost all the Scientific Societies of the world, in 1831, the University of Oxford, did *itself* the honour, of conferring on him, an honorary degree of Doctor of Civil Law.

He has been in the Service of the Royal Institution 23 years; and for very many of them, he has toiled in the Laboratory from six in the morning till eleven or twelve, at night.

He lectures weekly, for about 3 or 4 months of the year in the Theatre of the Royal Institution, during the sitting of Parliament, and not infrequently lectures to the company there assembled.

When he first lectured – indeed till very lately – (if not till the present moment) he gave half a guinea to a professor of Elocution, to attend every one of his lectures, in order that he might inform him of any errors he might commit during the delivery of his lectures.

His Chemical, Electro-Chemical, and Magneto-Electrical Discoveries, place him by the side of Davy and Wollaston – they have conferred Glory on his Country, and have secured for him an imperishable Name.

Humblest in early life, with any, much less a liberal education, he now reads and speaks French and Italian – has a tolerable knowledge of Latin and of Elementary Mathematics. His language is good – often eloquent – always clear, to misunderstand him, is almost impossible.

His Mother yet lives, and he supports her.

Applying his Chemical or other Scientific acquirements to the wants of art – or to the comforts of social life – and guided by the most inflexible integrity, there are few, very few departments of the Government of his Country, which have not reaped important benefits from his profound knowledge.

He has never sought or followed Science, guided by sordid motives.

The Secretaryship of the Royal Society with its hundred guineas a year was refused by him, because the performance of its duties, would interfere with his original researches – whilst his salary of £100 a year granted him by the Admiralty as their Scientific Adviser, he has never claimed, because he has never been, as such, called upon to do his duty.

March 31 1835.

NOTES

ABBREVIATIONS

Ann. Phil. – Annals of Philosophy

BA – Benjamin Abbott

BA 'Jottings from Memory' – Notes by Benjamin Abbott, entitled 'Jottings from Memory' in the IEE Archive, London, SC MS 127/62

Bence Jones, 1870, 1st edn – Henry Bence Jones, The Life and Letters of Michael Faraday; 2 vols, London, 1870, 1st edn

Bence Jones, 1870, 2nd edn – Henry Bence Jones, The Life and Letters of Michael Faraday; 2 vols, London, 1870, 2nd edn

BJHS – British Journal for the History of Science

Cantor, 1991 – Geoffrey Cantor, Michael Faraday: Sandemanian and Scientist; London, 1991

Colvin, 1971 – C. Colvin (ed.), Maria Edgeworth: Letters from England 1813–44; Oxford, 1971

CPB – Michael Faraday's Common Place Book, vol. 1 (of 2), IEE Archive

Davy, Memoirs – John Davy, Memoirs of the Life of Sir Humphry Davy, Bart; 2 vols, London, 1836

Davy, Works – John Davy (ed.), The Collected Works of Sir Humphry Davy, Bart; 9 vols, London, 1839–40

Diary – Thomas Martin (ed.), Faraday's Diary, Being the Various Philosophical Notes of Experimental Investigation made by Michael Faraday DCL, FRS during the years 1820–1862 and bequeathed by him to the Royal Institution; 7 vols and index vol., London, 1932–36

DNB – Dictionary of National Biography

ERCP – Michael Faraday, Experimental Researches in Chemistry and Physics; 1859

ERE – Michael Faraday, Experimental Researches in Electricity, Series 1–39. Published in 3 vols, 1839–55

Farington's Diary – Kenneth Garlick, Angus Macintyre and Kathrine Cave (eds), The Diary of Joseph Farington RA 1793–1821; 17 vols, Yale, 1978–99

FCJ – Faraday's Continental Journal, 1813–15, IEE Archive, London. Citations are from the published edition, Brian Bowers and Lenore Symons (eds), '*Curiosity Perfectly Satisfied': Faraday's Travels in Europe 1813–1815*; IEE, London, 1991

FJ – Frank A.J.L. James (ed.), *The Correspondence of Michael Faraday*; 6 vols, London, 1991– continuing

Hamilton, 1998 – James Hamilton, *Turner and the Scientists*; London, 1998

Hamilton, 2001 – James Hamilton (ed.), *Fields of Influence: Conjunctions of Artists and Scientists 1815–60*; Birmingham, 2001

HD – Humphry Davy

IEE – Institution of Electrical Engineers, London

Lit. Gaz. – The Literary Gazette

Mantell Journal – E.C. Curwen (ed.), *The Journal of Gideon Mantell, Surgeon and Geologist, covering the Years 1818–52*; London, 1940

MF – Michael Faraday

Paris, 1831 – John Ayrton Paris, *The Life of Sir Humphry Davy*; 2 vols, London, 1831

Phil. Mag. – The Philosophical Magazine

Phil. Trans. – Philosophical Transactions of the Royal Society

Proc. RI – The Proceedings of the Royal Institution of Great Britain

QJS – Quarterly Journal of Science and the Arts

RI – Royal Institution of Great Britain, London

RI MM – Royal Institution Managers' Minutes, published in Frank Greenaway, Maurice Berman, Sophie Forgan and Donovan Chilton, *Archives of the Royal Institution, Minutes of the Managers' Meetings, 1799–1903*; 15 vols, bound in 7 vols; London, 1971–76

RI MS – Royal Institution Manuscript

RS – Royal Society, London

Somerville Papers – Papers of Mary Somerville, Somerville College, Oxford (on deposit at the Bodleian Library, Oxford)

Thompson, 1898 – Silvanus P. Thompson, *Michael Faraday: His Life and Work*; London, 1898

Tyndall, 1868 – John Tyndall, *Faraday as a Discoverer*; London, 1868

Williams, 1965 – L. Pearce Williams, *Michael Faraday*; London, 1965

Williams, 1971 – L. Pearce Williams, *The Selected Correspondence of Michael Faraday*; 2 vols, Cambridge, 1971

INTRODUCTION

1 MF, 'Observations on Mental Education', *ERCP*, p.471.

CHAPTER 1: THE PROGRESS OF GENIUS

1 *DNB* entry for Michael Faraday, written by John Tyndall, who had known Faraday in later life.
2 Thompson, 1898, p.2.
3 *ibid*.
4 Bence Jones, 1870, 1st edn, vol. 1, p.8.
5 James F. Riley, *The Hammer and the Anvil: A Background to Michael Faraday*; Dalesman Publishing, Clapham, 1954, Chapter 4.
6 MF to Margaret Faraday, 27 June 1817; FJ74.
7 Riley, *op. cit.*, Chapter 5.
8 J.M. Stratton and Jack Houghton Brown, *Agricultural Records AD220–1977*; 1969, pp.88–9.
9 C.C. Walker: *Manchester Guardian*, 27 November 1886, recalling a visit he made c.1850. Quoted Thompson, 1898, p.294.
10 Cantor, 1991. See also David Bogue and James Bennett, *History of the Dissenting Churches from the Revolution in 1688 to the Year 1808*; 4 vols, London, 1808–12, vol. 4, p.107; 'Sandemanians' in John Bellamy, *The History of All Religions. . .*; London, 1813, pp.271–3; 'The Sandemanians', in C. Maurice Davies, *Unorthodox London: Or, Phases of Religious Life in the Metropolis*; 1875 (reprinted 1969), pp.284–92; H.W.

Clark, *History of English Non-Conformity*; 1913, p.284.
11 Information from the late Mrs Molly Spiro.
12 Walter Wilson, *The History and Antiquities of Dissenting Churches and Meeting Houses*; 4 vols, 1808–11, vol. 3 (1810), pp.261–76.
13 Thompson, 1898, p.2. Marylebone rate returns show that over the period 1796–98 no rates were paid in Jacob's Mews, until they are paid by John Treble (1799–1801), John Francis (1802–05), Mrs Francis (1806–07), Executors of Maria Francis (1808–09), and Charles Cheel (1810–). See text relating to n28, below. There is no record of James Faraday paying rates in Jacob's Mews. This suggests that he rented the property from a succession of landlords.
14 W.H. Manchel, 'Marylebone and its Huguenot Connections'; *Huguenot Society Proceedings*, vol. 11 (1917), pp.58–128 (p.102). Riebau is listed in Charles Ramsden, *London Bookbinders 1780–1840*; London, 1987.
15 *DNB* entry for Richard Brothers.
16 J.F.C. Harrison, *The Second Coming: Popular Millenarianism 1780–1850*; 1979, p.223; Mary Thale (ed.), *Selections from the Papers of the London Corresponding Society, 1792–99*; 1983, pp.252, 256, 351, 469.
17 See M.B. Block, *The New Church in the New World: A Study of Swedenborgianism in America*; New York, new edn 1960.
18 See MF to G. Riebau, 5 January

1815; FJ44. MF signs himself here as 'Your [*sic*] most dutifully, Faraday.'

19 RS, MS 241.

20 'Bookbinding' entry in *Encyclopaedia Britannica*; 2nd edn, 1778–83, vol. 2, p.1244.

21 BA 'Jottings from Memory'.

22 George Riebau to an unidentified journal, October or November 1813; FJ30.

23 Maria Edgeworth to Harriet Beaufort, 5 January 1822; Colvin, 1971, p.308.

24 MF to A. de la Rive, 2 October 1858; Williams, 1971, p.691.

25 There are drawings after Hogarth, inscribed 'MF', in Faraday's Scrapbook, vol. 1, pp.71, 127; Royal Institution Archive.

26 MF to A. de la Rive, letter *cit.*

27 Emily R. Sugden, 'An Early Reader of Swedenborg'; *The New Church Review* (Boston), July 1922, pp.294–304. Patricia Fara, 'An Attractive Therapy: Animal Magnetism in Eighteenth-Century London'; *History of Science*, vol. 33 (1995), pp.127–77.

28 Marylebone rate returns, Westminster Archive Centre. The landlady appears to have been Maria Francis (d.1808). Charles Cheel, formerly of 18 Weymouth Street, moved to Jacob's Mews.

29 Quoted Thompson, 1898, p.5.

30 See n22, above.

31 Thompson, 1898, p.6.

32 Faraday's notes to John Tatum's Lectures, vol. 1, p.66; Royal Institution Archive, F4B1.

33 *ibid.*, pp.57ff.

34 *ibid.*, vol. 2, p.62.

35 Frank A.J.L. James, 'Michael Faraday, the City Philosophical Society and the Society of Arts'; *Journal of the Royal Society of Arts*, February 1992, pp.192–9.

36 Advertisement in *Phil. Mag.*, vol. 34 (1809), pp.237–8.

37 RI Archive, F4B1–4.

38 Letter from George Riebau, *cit.*, FJ30. A much later source records that Edward Magrath gave Faraday the tickets to Davy's lectures: 'Michael Faraday'; *Fraser's Magazine*, February 1836, p.244. This however is unlikely to be wholly correct, because Magrath appears never to have been a member of the RI.

39 FJ, vol. 1, Introduction, p.xxx.

40 For example, when George Dance became a Proprietor of the RI: 7 December 1807: 'George Dance Esq of Manchester Street to the share of his brother Edward Dance Esq.'

41 *Farington's Diary*, 24 May 1799.

42 *ibid.*, 21 November 1820.

43 RI. Key symbols: ⅄ Mr Wass, + Mr Lyhton [probably Leighton], ⅄ Mr Nixon, ·|· Mr Barnard, ϕ Mr Buchanan.

44 W.H. Manchel, *op. cit.*

45 R.R.M. Sée, *Masquerier and his Circle*; 1922, Chapter 8.

46 *ibid*; *Farington's Diary*, 29 September 1802, 16 April 1803, 27 March 1804, 18 December 1806, 3 November 1810.

47 *DNB*.

48 J. Constable to Revd J. Fisher, 29 August 1824; R.B. Beckett (ed.), *John Constable Correspondence*, vol. 6, 1968, *The Fishers*, p.172.

49 Bundle VIII (Masquerier Album); Dr William's Library, Gordon Square, London.
50 Thompson, 1898, p.8.
51 Bence Jones, 1870, 2nd edn, vol. 1, p.12 specifies 'Taylor's "Perspective", a 4to volume'. This is most likely to have been Brook Taylor, *Linear Perspective*, 1715–19.

CHAPTER 2: HUMPHRY DAVY

1 Davy, *Works*, vol. 1, p.128.
2 Paris, 1831, pp.90ff has an account of the early reception of HD at the RI.
3 Davy, *Works*, vol. 3, p.301.
4 *ibid.*, vol. 3, p.311. For Henry Wansey see *DNB*.
5 Davy, *Memoirs*, vol. 1, p.136.
6 *Farington's Diary*, 9 November 1806.
7 W.B. Pope (ed.), *The Diary of Benjamin Robert Haydon*, 1960, vol. 4, p.610, 5 March 1840; Lord Brougham to Mary Somerville, n.d.; Somerville Papers, dep. c.369.
8 *Farington's Diary*, 26 October 1808.
9 *ibid.*, 9 December 1807.
10 Davy, *Works*, vol. 1, p.95.
11 Paris, 1831, p.90.
12 Thomas Poole, quoting 'the ladies'; Davy, *Memoirs*, vol. 1, p.136.
13 Davy, *Works*, vol. 1, p.100.
14 Paris, 1831, vol. 1, p.295.
15 *ibid.*
16 Quoted *DNB*, entry for Jane, Lady Davy.
17 *Farington's Diary*, 2 March 1812.

18 Not William Blake the artist and poet, then poor and little-known, but William Blake the Fellow of the Royal Society, now practically forgotten.
19 *Farington's Diary*, 2 March 1812.
20 Miss Berry to anon., 30 December 1811. Quoted *North British Review*, 39 (1863), p.327. 'Sir Harry' is Sir Harry Englefield, member of the RI, *DNB*. He may have been the author of the verse.
21 Davy, *Works*, vol. 4, p.43.
22 *ibid.*, vol. 1, p.137.
23 Thompson, 1898, p.8n.
24 M. Faraday, 'Notes of Davy's 1812 Lectures'; Lecture 3, pp.183ff. RI MS F4A.
25 *ibid.*
26 Davy, *Works*, vol. 1, p.133.
27 *ibid.*, vol. 4, pp.375–6.
28 John Davy says 'almost immediately'; Davy, *Works*, vol. 1, p.158; but Paris, 1831, p.220, says that they proceeded 'immediately after the ceremony' to Sir John Sebright's mansion, and on to Scotland.
29 Davy, *Works*, vol. 1, p.158.

CHAPTER 3: A SMALL EXPLOSION IN TUNBRIDGE WELLS

1 J.M. Stratton and J.H. Brown, *Agricultural Records AD220–1977*, 1969.
2 Memorandum to Sir Robert Peel, 31 March 1835; FJ775.
3 MF to BA, 12/13 July 1812; FJ3.
4 *ibid.*
5 MF, 'Tatum's Lectures', RI.
6 MF, 'Lectures by Sir H Davy', p.363. RI. This passage is

cancelled in the original by a wavy pencil line.

7 MF to BA, 12/13 July 1812; FJ3. A reasonable case might be made for the 'unknown gentleman' being Richard Cosway, who was married to an Italian and had fruitful European contacts.

8 Samuel Johnson, *Works*; vol. 11, p.48.

9 Isaac Watts, *The Improvement of the Mind*; 1809. I may have missed it, but despite MF's assurances I cannot find any specific reference to letter writing in Watts.

10 MF to BA, 20 July 1812; FJ4.

11 MF to BA, 11 August 1812; FJ7.

12 MF to BA, 2 and 3 August 1812; FJ5.

13 MF to BA, 20, 21 and 22 July 1812; FJ4.

14 MF to BA, 11 August 1812; FJ7.

15 MF to BA, 2 and 3 August 1812; FJ5.

16 BA 'Jottings from Memory'.

17 MF to BA, 2 and 3 August 1812; FJ5.

18 *ibid*.

19 MF to BA, 20, 21 and 22 July 1812; FJ4.

20 MF to BA, 28 September 1812; FJ12.

21 MF to BA, 1 October 1812; FJ13.

22 MF to BA, 9 and 11 September 1812; FJ10.

23 MF to BA, 11 October 1812; FJ14.

24 MF to T. Huxtable, 18 October 1812; FJ15.

25 FJ30; the memorandum of 1835, FJ775, says thirty shillings.

26 Thompson, 1898, pp.9–10. See *Proc. RI*, 5 (1868), pp.199–272.

27 MF to T. Huxtable, 18 October 1812; FJ15.

28 Davy, *Works*, vol. 1, pp.158–9.

29 Anna Atkins, *Memoir of John George Children*; 1853, pp.125–7.

30 October or November 1813; FJ30.

31 MF to BA, 20 September 1812; FJ11.

32 Bence Jones, 1870, 2nd edn, vol. 1, pp.46–7. Davy's accident is also referred to in an official memorandum, written probably by Lord Ashley for the Prime Minister Sir Robert Peel more than twenty years later, in March 1835. This account of Faraday's life, providing background information in the attempt to obtain a Civil List pension for Faraday from the government (see Appendix Three), says: 'His apprenticeship ended . . . he worked as a journeyman to La Roche, the Bookbinder . . . Some months after this engagement, Davy having injured his eye sight, took him as his Amanuensis.' Memorandum, 31 March 1835; FJ775. The memorandum goes on to say that Faraday was appointed to a post in the RI, with the clear implication that this was a separate and subsequent event.

33 FJ419.

34 HD to MF, 24 December 1812; FJ17. Original bound into MF's copy of Paris, 1831. RI, Davy archive, B23.

35 RI MM, 11 May 1812.

36 Davy, *Works*, vol. 1, p.94. My description of Davy's laboratory is drawn extensively from this.

37 MF to an unknown aunt or uncle, 13 September 1813; FJ28.

38 Bence Jones, 1870, 2nd edn, vol. 1, p.39.

39 Memorandum; FJ775.

40 Bence Jones, 1870, 2nd edn, vol. 1, p.49.

41 Sir Frederick Pollock, *Personal Remembrances of Sir Frederick Pollock, Bart*; 2 vols, 1887, vol. 1, p.244.

42 RI MM, 22 February 1813.

43 If this is the date of the RI Managers' meeting, which was held in the evening, it is plausible that the late-evening visit of the carriage to Weymouth Street would have followed on immediately after the meeting had closed.

44 BA 'Jottings from Memory'.

45 Bence Jones, 1870, 2nd edn, vol. 1, p.49n.

46 MF to J.A. Paris, 23 December 1829; FJ419.

47 RI MM, 1 March 1813.

48 Davy, *Works*, vol. 1, p.84.

49 BA 'Jottings from Memory'.

50 FJ775.

51 MF to BA, 8 March 1813; FJ18.

52 See J.J. Berzelius and A. Marcet, 'Experiments on the Alcohol of Sulphur, or Sulphuret of Carbon'; *Phil. Trans.*, 103 (1813), pp.171–99.

53 MF to BA, 12 and 14 May 1813; FJ21.

54 *ibid.*

55 Margery Reid, a niece of Faraday, quoted by Bence Jones, 1870, 2nd edn, vol. 1, pp.383–4.

56 Bence Jones, 1870, 2nd edn, vol. 1, pp.59–71; also Sir George Porter and James Friday (eds), *Advice to Lecturers: An Anthology taken from the Writings of Michael Faraday and Lawrence Bragg*; RI, 1974.

57 MF to BA, 5 April 1813; FJ19.

58 MF to BA, 8 April 1813; FJ20.

59 Davy, *Works*, vol. 4, p.37.

60 MF to Robert Abbott, 6 August 1814; FJ35.

61 Paris, 1831, p.96.

62 Davy, *Works*, vol. 4, p.41.

63 *ibid.*, p.236.

64 Paris, 1831, vol. 1, p.261.

65 MF to BA, 2 or 9 October 1813; FJ29.

CHAPTER 4: THE GLORIOUS OPPORTUNITY

1 Faraday's Continental Journal, MS within the Common Place Book vol. 2, IEE. Hereafter referred to as FCJ.

2 Bence Jones, 1870, 1st and 2nd edns, vol. 1, Chapter 3. A reliable transcription of the Journal has been published as Brian Bowers and Lenore Symons (eds), *'Curiosity Perfectly Satisfied': Faraday's Travels in Europe 1813–1815*; Peter Peregrinus Ltd [IEE], 1991. References to the diary will be given as page numbers from this edition.

3 That the Welsh pages break into the continental account gives us a fairly clear date for the writing up of the first part of the 1813–15 trip, that is shortly before Faraday left for Wales in July 1819, and the rest perhaps late 1819 and 1820.

4 FCJ, 13 October 1813, p.1.

5 FCJ, 14 October 1813, p.1.

6 FCJ, 15 October 1813, p.2.

7 *ibid.*

8 FCJ, 16 October 1813, p.2.

9 FCJ, 17 October 1813, p.3.

10 FCJ, 18 October 1813, p.3.
11 *ibid.*
12 *ibid.*
13 B. Abbott, 'The Late Professor Faraday'; IEE MS 127/63.
14 FCJ, 19 October 1813, p.4.
15 *ibid.*, p.5.
16 FCJ, 20 October 1813, p.5.
17 *ibid.*
18 *ibid.*, p.6.
19 *ibid.*
20 *ibid.*
21 *ibid.*
22 FCJ, 21 October 1813, p.6.
23 *ibid.*
24 *ibid.*, p.7.
25 FCJ, 22 October 1813, p.9.
26 FCJ, 24 October 1813, p.10.
27 *ibid.*, p.11.
28 FCJ, 28 October 1813, p.14.
29 *ibid.*
30 FCJ, 24 November 1813, p.25. It is not clear if MF means that the head of the animal was let into the slab as an inlaid design, or if the head itself was a fossil. In encrina marble this would have been a starfish.
31 MF's words, quoted Davy, *Works*, vol. 1, pp.163–4.
32 FCJ, 30 October 1813, p.15.
33 Davy, *Memoirs*, vol. 1, p.147.
34 *ibid.*, p.266. There is a brief obituary of Underwood in *The Gentleman's Magazine*, vol. 4 (1835), p.446.
35 See Katharine Eustace, ' "Questa Scabrosa Missione": Canova in Paris and London in 1815', in K. Eustace (ed.), *Canova Ideal Heads*; Ashmolean Museum, Oxford, 1997.
36 FCJ, 30 October 1813, pp.14–15.
37 Paris, 1831, p.268.
38 There are five weekdays unaccounted for in the Journal for the period 1 to 11 November. MF may have been working with Davy on some of these days, but he recorded nothing of it.
39 FCJ, 1 November 1813, p.16.
40 FCJ, 4 November 1813, pp.17–18.
41 FCJ, 2 November 1813, pp.16–17.
42 MF to BA, 6 September 1814; FJ37.
43 FCJ, 7 November 1813, p.18.
44 Emily Robertson (ed.), *Letters and Papers of Andrew Robertson*; [1895], p.264.
45 FCJ, 9 November 1813, p.18. This is MF's recollection in the Journal. The original police record was destroyed during the Paris siege, 1870–71. Information from the Museum of the Prefecture of Police, Paris.
46 FCJ, 11 November 1813, p.19.
47 FCJ, 15 November 1813, p.21.
48 *ibid.*
49 Davy, *Works*, vol. 1, pp.165–9.
50 *ibid.*, p.166.
51 FJ361.

CHAPTER 5: SUBSTANCE X

1 Paris, 1831, vol. 2, p.10.
2 *ibid.*, p.270.
3 *ibid.*, p.272.
4 *ibid.*, p.269.
5 Davy, *Works*, vol. 1, pp.165–9.
6 Paris, 1831, p.274.
7 FCJ, 1 December 1813, p.27.
8 Davy, *Works*, vol. 1, p.167.
9 M. Crosland, 'Humphry Davy: An Alleged Case of Suppressed Publication'; *BJHS*, vol. 6 (1973), no. 23, pp.304–10.

10 FCJ, 11 December 1813, p.30.

11 On 20 January 1814. Pages of HD's notes are interleaved between pp.282 and 283 of MF's copy of Paris, 1831. RI, Davy archive, B23.

12 FJ31.

13 Davy, *Works*, vol. 1, pp.166–7.

14 FCJ, 14 December 1813, p.31.

15 Robertson, *op. cit.*, p.247.

16 FCJ, 16 December 1813, p.31; MF's sketch of the semaphore is reproduced.

17 FCJ, 16 December 1813, p.32.

18 FCJ, 24 December 1813, p.33.

19 FCJ, 19 December 1813, p.33.

20 FCJ, 29 December 1813, p.34.

CHAPTER 6: A POINT OF LIGHT

1 FCJ, 29 January 1813, p.34.

2 Davy, *Works*, vol. 1, pp.169–70.

3 FCJ, 31 December 1813, p.35.

4 *ibid.*

5 Davy, *Works*, vol. 1, p.178.

6 Paris, 1831, vol. 2, pp.8–9.

7 FCJ, 31 December 1813, p.35.

8 Davy, *Works*, vol. 1, pp.171–2.

9 FCJ, 5 January 1814, p.38.

10 Davy, *Works*, vol. 1, p.170.

11 FCJ, 31 January 1814, p.46.

12 FCJ, 14 January 1814, p.41.

13 FCJ, 10 January 1814, p.40.

14 FCJ, 17 January 1814, p.42.

15 *ibid.*

16 FCJ, 1 February 1814, p.46.

17 FCJ, 5 February 1814, p.47.

18 FCJ, 6 February 1814, p.47.

19 FCJ, 21 January 1814, p.44.

20 Davy, *Works*, vol. 1, pp.173–5.

21 FCJ, 7 February 1814, p.49.

22 Davy, *Works*, vol. 1, pp.175–7.

23 FCJ, 9 February 1814, p.52.

24 FCJ, 13 February 1814, p.53.

25 FCJ, 18 February 1814, pp.56–7.

26 *ibid.*

27 FCJ, 19 February 1814, p.60.

28 *ibid.*

29 FCJ, 22 February 1814, p.64.

30 MF to G. Riebau, 3 January 1815; FJ44.

31 MF to BA, 26 and 30 November 1814; FJ40.

32 FJ31; quoted from Bence Jones, 1870, 1st edn, vol. 1, pp.99–100. The original is lost.

33 MF to BA, 1 May and 24 July 1814; FJ33.

34 BA 'Jottings from Memory'.

35 FJ33.

36 FCJ, 16 March 1814, p.73.

37 FCJ, 17 March 1814, p.72.

38 FJ33.

39 FCJ, 21 March 1814, p.73.

40 FCJ, 24 March 1814, p.74.

41 *ibid.*

42 In the Journal MF writes of this experiment in the third person: 'a glass globe . . . was exhausted of air'. We can reasonably assume that the assistant who turned the pump handle was Faraday himself. See also note in 'Miscellanea', *QJS*, vol. 4 (1818), p.155.

43 FCJ, 27 March 1814, p.75.

44 FCJ, 3 April 1814, p.77.

CHAPTER 7: MR DANCE'S KINDNESS . . .

1 FCJ, 3 April 1814, p.77.

2 FCJ, 4 April 1814, p.78.

3 FCJ, 5 April 1814, p.78.

4 FCJ, 6 April 1814, p.80.

5 FCJ, 11–14 April 1814, p.84.

6 FCJ, 6 April 1814, p.79.

7 FCJ, 19 April 1814, pp.88–9.

8 *ibid.*, p.89.

9 MF writes 'Baths of Titus', but those had been largely destroyed. The Baths of Trajan are nearby.

10 FCJ, 20 April 1814, p.100.

11 MF to BA, 1 May and 24 July 1814; FJ33.

12 FCJ, 15 April 1814, p.87.

13 FCJ, 7 May 1814, p.107.

14 FCJ, 13 May 1814, p.107.

15 FCJ, 14 May 1814, p.110.

16 *ibid.*

17 MF to BA, 25 January 1815; FJ46.

18 *Consolations*, in Davy, *Works*, vol. 9, p.311.

19 FCJ, 3 June 1814, p.111.

20 FCJ, 17 June 1814, p.113.

21 Davy, *Works*, vol. 1, pp.187–8.

22 *ibid.*

23 MF to BA, 6 September 1814; FJ37.

24 *ibid.*

25 *DNB* entry for MF.

26 FCJ, 10, 11 and 12 July 1814; pp.114–15.

27 MF to Margaret Faraday, 1 July 1814; FJ34.

28 MF to Robert Abbott, 6 August 1814; FJ35.

29 MF to BA, 6 September 1814; FJ37.

30 MF to BA, 25 January 1815; FJ46.

31 Maria Edgeworth to Honora Edgeworth, n.d. [1831]; Colvin, 1971, p.513.

32 FJ37.

33 Actually, Mrs Greenwood [RI MM, 12 June 1815].

34 FJ35.

35 FJ37.

36 *ibid.*

37 MF to Margaret Faraday, 10 November 1814; FJ38.

38 MF to BA, 26 November 1814; FJ40.

39 Davy, *Works*, vol. 1, p.189.

40 FCJ, 13 October 1814, p.126.

41 FJ38.

42 *ibid.*

43 According to MF's letter to BA, FJ40; it was three days according to his letter to his mother, FJ38.

44 MF to G. Riebau, 12 January 1815; FJ44.

45 FCJ, 27 October 1814, p.128.

46 BA to MF, 20 and 22 November 1814; FJ39.

47 FJ40.

48 MF to Elizabeth Faraday, 22 December 1814; FJ41.

49 MF to Robert Abbott, 12 January 1815; FJ45.

50 FJ41.

51 5 January 1815; FJ44.

52 Mrs Udney of Hertford Street was an annual subscriber to the RI, admitted 19 March 1800. RI MM.

53 FCJ, 11 January 1815, p.140.

54 MF's Scrapbook, vol. 1, p.83. Inscribed 'Bought from Italy by MF 1814'.

55 FJ44.

56 FCJ, 24 January 1815, p.143; MF to BA, 25 January 1815; FJ46.

57 FJ46.

58 FCJ, 30 January 1815, p.152.

59 *ibid.*, p.153.

60 FJ40.

61 FJ46.

62 *ibid.*

63 MF to BA, 23 February 1815; FJ49.

64 FJ46.

65 23 February 1815; FJ49.

66 FJ46.

67 *ibid.*

68 Humphry Davy, 'Some experiments and observations on the colours used in painting by

the ancients'; *Phil. Trans.*, vol. 105 (1815), pp.97–124.

69 FJ46.

70 MF to Margaret Faraday, 13 February 1815; FJ47.

71 FCJ, 11 February 1815, p.153.

72 FJ49.

73 FCJ, 16 March 1815, p.161.

74 FJ49.

75 FCJ, 7 March 1815, p.159.

76 FCJ, 30 March 1815, p.162.

77 MF to Margaret Faraday, 16 April 1815; FJ50.

CHAPTER 8: WE HAVE SUBDUED THIS MONSTER

1 RI MM, 24 April 1815.

2 BA 'Jottings from Memory'.

3 MF to BA, 29 April 1815; FJ51.

4 RI MM, 8 May 1815.

5 RI MM, 15 May 1815.

6 MF to BA, 27 June 1815; FJ52.

7 See Ian Inkster, 'Science and Society in the Metropolis . . . 1796–1807'; *Annals of Science*, vol. 34 (1977), pp.1–32; Frederick Kurzer, 'A History of the Surrey Institution'; *Annals of Science*, vol. 57 (2000), no. 2, pp.109–41.

8 Saba Bahar, 'Jane Marcet and the Limits to Public Science'; *BJHS*, vol. 34 (2001), pp.29–49.

9 FJ40.

10 RI MM, 2 February 1818.

11 Advertisement, *QJS*, vol. 1 (1816), p.iii.

12 W.T. Brande, *A Manual of Chemistry*; 1819, pp.xi–xiii.

13 Quoted Tyndall, 1868, p.10.

14 CPB, pp.11–66, notes on Brande's six geology lectures, 27 April to 1 June 1816; p.7, notes on Brande's

lecture on burning chlorine in mercury, 30 April 1816.

15 CPB, p.7, 30 April 1816.

16 HD to MF, 3 August 1815; FJ56.

17 Paris, 1831, p.308.

18 Quoted Bence Jones, 1870, 2nd edn, vol. 1, p.361.

19 Davy, *Works*, vol. 6, p.4.

20 *ibid.*, p.9.

21 *ibid.*, p.14.

22 Interleaved in MF's copy of Paris, 1831, pp.312–13. RI, Davy archive, B23.

23 Humphry Davy, 'On the fire-damp of coal mines, and on methods of lighting the mines so as to prevent its explosion'; *Phil. Trans.*, vol. 106 (1816), pp.1–22.

24 Quoted Anne Treneer, *The Mercurial Chemist*; 1963, p.167.

25 Davy, *Works*, vol. 1, p.209.

26 Bence Jones, 1870, 2nd edn, vol. 1, p.213.

27 *ibid.*, p.361.

CHAPTER 9: THE CHIEF OF ALL THE BAND

1 Previous writers have identified the author as 'Mr Dryden' on the grounds that in the early 1820s the Society seems to have had a member called James Dryden. Thompson, 1898, p.40, records the author thus, as does Frank James, *op. cit.*, pp.192–9.

2 CPB, pp.137–58.

3 Evidently this is a different room to the one in which Tatum gave his lectures – see MF's drawing of it (in plates section).

4 *The Times*, 23 July 1814; 30 July 1814. The woman passenger is

named in unsourced cuttings, dated July and August 1814, in the Royal Aeronautical Society Library.

5 Frank James, *op cit.*, 1992, p.194.
6 Thompson, 1898, pp.40–1.
7 BA 'Jottings from Memory'.
8 See Marcus Wood, *Radical Satire and Print Culture 1790–1822*; 1994, especially Chapter 3.
9 BA 'Jottings from Memory'. A copy of *Laws of the City Philosophical Society instituted Jan 1808*, London, 1812, is in the British Library.
10 Clause XIV, Seditious Meetings Act, 1817.
11 Frank James, *op. cit.*, 1992; Ian Inkster, 'London Science and the Seditious Meetings Act of 1817'; *BJHS*, vol. 12 (1979), pp.192–6; 'Petition of John Tatum', Central London Record Office, London Peace Papers, April 1817.
12 *Parliamentary Debates*, 1817, 36, col. 83.
13 Faraday bound it with lengths of twine which had previously bound parcels of pigment, used for painting porcelain, sent from China in 1816 to Sir Joseph Banks. Presumably Humphry Davy had been given the twine at the Royal Society. Faraday relates this, and the way the twine had been made, in his first entry in the book, p.1.
14 Isaac Watts, *The Improvement of the Mind*; 1795 edn, Chapter 1, Rule 9.
15 *ibid.*, Chapter 3.
16 CPB, pp.2–5. On some pages the diagram does not correspond to the text. See Edward Hare,

'Michael Faraday's Loss of Memory'; *Proc. RI*, vol. 49 (1976), pp.33–52 (pp.47–8).
17 Feinaigle had lectured at the RI in 1811. *The Gentleman's Magazine*, September 1811.
18 Watts, *op. cit.*, Chapter 17, p.230, 'On Improving the Memory'. My emphasis. The Latin (from Pliny) translates as 'Not a day without a line'.
19 *A Memoir of Zerah Colburn Written by Himself*; Springfield, Mass., 1833, p.41. He has an entry in the *Dictionary of American Biography*.
20 HD to MF, 1 July 1816; FJ65.
21 CPB, pp.87–100.
22 Watts, *op. cit.*, Chapter 20, p.291, 'Of the sciences and their use in particular professions'.
23 *ibid.*, p.297.
24 Andrew Pyle, Introduction to *Selected Works of Isaac Watts*; 8 vols, vol. 1, pp.vii–xxiii, Thoemmes Press, Bristol, 1999.
25 MF, 'Chemistry Lectures 1816–19', p.ii. IEE, SC MS 2/1/3.
26 BA 'Jottings from Memory'.
27 CPB, p.8. From *Spectator*, no. 471.
28 *ibid.*, p.398.
29 *ibid.*, p.74; Dr Johnson, *The Rambler*, no. 137.
30 *ibid.*, p.80.
31 *ibid.*, pp.177–321.
32 Watts, *op. cit.*, Chapter 2, p.33.
33 MF to BA, 11 June 1813; FJ25.
34 CPB, pp.324ff.
35 MF, 'Chemistry Lectures 1816–19', p.10.
36 CPB, pp.324ff.
37 *ibid.*, pp.337–63.
38 See Joseph Agassi, 'An

Unpublished Paper of the Young Faraday'; *Isis*, vol. 52 (1961), pp.87–90.

39 Frank James, *op. cit.*, first traced the backgrounds of some of these men.

40 Howard Colvin, *Biographical Dictionary of British Architects 1600–1840*; Yale, 1995.

41 See his *Memoir of a Mechanic*; Boston, 1839.

42 *The Times*, 29 July 1837, p.6.

43 Letter to *The Times*, 31 July 1837; FJ1019.

44 See A.F.P. Morson, 'T.N.R. Morson and his Scientific Friends'; *Pharmaceutical History*, 1990, p.20. A trade card of 'T. Morson, Operative Chemist of 19 Southampton Row, Russell Square' is in MF's Scrapbook, vol. 1, p.45, RI Archive.

45 *DNB*.

46 *ibid.*

47 *ibid.*

48 CPB, pp.324ff.

49 *ibid.*, p.174.

50 *ibid.*, pp.171–4.

51 *ibid.*, p.335.

52 *ibid.*, p.385; *Fingal*, Book 3, para. 19.

53 *ibid.*, p.387.

54 *Penguin Dictionary of Quotations*; 1960, p.5.

55 Bence Jones, 1870, 2nd edn, vol. 2, p.475.

56 MF, 'Observations on Mental Education'; *ERCP*, p.483.

57 1 May 1816; CPB, pp.81–5.

58 10 February 1820; CPB, p.392. See also I.R. Morus, *Frankenstein's Children: Electricity, Exhibition and Experiment in Early-Nineteenth-Century London*; Princeton, 1998, pp.75ff.

59 BA 'Jottings from Memory'.

60 1 July 1818; CPB, pp.337–63.

61 BA 'Jottings from Memory'.

62 Frank James, *op. cit.*, 1992.

63 Bence Jones, 1870, 2nd edn, vol. 1, pp.50–1.

64 G.N. Rankin, *Reply to a pamphlet purporting to be a report of the Council and Committee of the City Philosophical Society*; London, 1818, p.2. Quoted Paul Weindling, 'Science and Sedition, 1795–1819'; *BJHS*, vol. 13 (1980), pp.139–53.

65 T. Claxton, *Memoir of a Mechanic*; Boston, 1839, p.34. Also T. Claxton, *Hints to Mechanics on Self-Education and Mutual Instruction*; London, 1839, p.24.

66 CPB, p.144.

67 Frank James, *op. cit.*, 1992.

CHAPTER 10: A MAN OF NATURE'S OWN FORMING

1 *QJS*, vol. 3 (1817), pp.390–3, 394–5; vol. 4 (1818), p.155.

2 MF to BA, 20 August 1816; FJ66.

3 'Analysis of the Native Caustic Lime [of Tuscany]' and 'Some Account of the Alstenia Teiformis, or Tea of Bogata'; *QJS*, vol. 1 (1816), p.261; and vol. 3 (1817), pp.92–4.

4 W.T. Brande, *A Manual of Chemistry Containing the Principal Facts of the Science . . . [as] discussed and illustrated in the Lectures at the Royal Institution of Great Britain*; London, 1819.

5 MF to BA, 9 June 1817; FJ73. But note RI MM of seven days earlier, 2 June 1817: 'Resolved that Mr Faraday be allowed leave of

absence for such time as Mr
Brande may think expedient.'

6 MF to Margaret Faraday, 27 June
1817; FJ74.

7 CPB, pp.164–6.

8 Bence Jones, 1870, 2nd edn, vol. 1,
p.378.

9 A reliable transcript, with notes,
is by Dafydd Thomos, *Michael
Faraday in Wales*; Gwasg Gee,
1972. The MS is in CPB, vol. 2.

10 *ibid.*, pp.19–20.

11 *ibid.*, p.65.

12 *ibid.*, p.61.

13 MF to J.J. Guest, 20 July 1819; FJ103.

14 Thomos, *op. cit.*, pp.44–5.

15 *ibid.*, p.32.

16 Cantor, 1991, Appendix A.

17 MF to BA, 25 July 1817; FJ75.

18 CPB, pp.73ff. Quoted in full,
Williams, 1965, pp.96–7.

19 MF to Sarah Barnard, 11 October
1819; FJ105.

20 *DNB* entry for MF.

21 MF to Sarah Barnard, 5 July 1820;
FJ115.

22 Bence Jones, 1870, 2nd edn, vol. 1,
p.278.

23 *ibid.*, p.280.

24 MF to Sarah Barnard, 8 August
1820.

25 Bence Jones, 1870, 1st and 2nd
edns, *passim*.

26 FJ126.

27 MF to Sarah Barnard, December
1820; FJ122.

28 Among MF's published articles at
this time are 'On Sirium', *QJS*,
vol. 6 (1818), pp.112–15; and
'Experimental Observations on
the Passage of Gases through
Tubes', *QJS*, vol. 7 (1810),
pp.106–10.

29 The RI Managers hired William
Greenwood 'to be employed
under the direction of Mr
Faraday to put the laboratory in
order' (6 July 1818). Allocated
rooms 19 and 20 on the second
floor instead of 26 and 28 in the
attic (RI MM, 1 November 1819).

30 HD to MF, 5 June 1818; FJ83.

31 FJ84, 87, 95, 101.

32 HD to MF, 26 June 1818; FJ84.

33 HD to MF, 9 October 1818; FJ90.

34 HD to MF, 18 February 1819; FJ95.

35 *ibid.*

36 HD to MF, October 1818; FJ91.

37 FJ89.

38 FJ94, 96, 98.

39 FJ85.

40 *QJS*, vol. 5 (1818), pp.274–80. See
also *Lit. Gaz.*, 22 August 1818,
p.537.

41 24 August 1818; FJ86.

42 William Jerdan, *An
Autobiography*; 1853, vol. 2, p.234.
See also vol. 3, p.282; vol. 4, p.338.

43 *DNB*, entry for William Jerdan.

44 MF to BA, 27 February 1818; FJ81.

45 *Phil. Mag.*, vol. 55 (1820), pp.252ff;
vol. 56 (1820), pp.455–7; vol. 57
(1821), pp.1–10; *QJS*, vol. 10 (1821),
pp.316ff; June Z. Fullmer,
'Technology, Chemistry and the
Law in Early Nineteenth-Century
England'; *Technology and Culture*,
21 (1980), pp.1–28.

46 Published 1932–36, in seven
volumes, with an index volume,
as Thomas Martin (ed.),
*Faraday's Diary, Being the Various
Philosophical Notes of
Experimental Investigation made
by Michael Faraday DCL, FRS
during the years 1820–1862 and*

bequeathed by him to the Royal Institution of Great Britain.

47 MF to BA, 27 April 1819; FJ100.

48 Quoted R.A. Hadfield, *Faraday and his Metallurgical Researches*; 1931, p.39. Williams, 1965, p.109.

49 J. Stodart and M. Faraday, 'Experiments on the Alloys of Steel, Made with a View to its Improvement'; *Phil. Mag.*, vol. 56 (1820), pp.26–35.

50 Swiss Journal, 2 August 1841, Bence Jones, 1870, 2nd edn, vol. 2, p.145.

51 See J. Stodart and M. Faraday, 'Experiments on the Alloys of Steel, Made with a View to its Improvement', *QJS*, vol. 9 (1820), pp 319–30; do. 'On the Alloys of Steel', *Phil. Trans.*, vol. 112 (1822), pp.253–70.

52 As he did; MF, 'Lettre au Prof de la Rive sur les alliages que forme l'acier avec différents métaux', *Bibliothèque Universelle*, vol. 14 (1820), pp.209–15.

53 MF to C. de la Rive, 26 June 1820; FJ114.

54 CPB, 'Iron columns', p.376, 14 December 1818.

55 MF to C. Hatchett, 15 May 1821; FJ132.

56 *Diary*, vol. 1, 14 March 1821, pp.43–4; CPB, p.392, 10 February 1820.

57 MF to William Flexman, 3 May 1818; FJ82.

58 4 September 1819; *Lit. Gaz.*

59 MF to C. de la Rive, 6 October 1818; FJ88.

60 H.C. Øersted, 'Experiments on the Effect of a Current of Electricity in the Magnetic Needle', *Ann. Phil.*, NS vol. 16 (1820), p.276. First published as *Naturvidenskabelige Skrifter . . . Scientific Papers*; 3 vols, Copenhagen, 1820.

61 Davy, *Works*, vol. 9.

62 Thompson, 1898, p.84. See also 'Historical Sketch Respecting Electro-Magnetic Rotations'; *ERE*, 2, pp.159–62.

63 FJ122.

64 St Faith-under-St Paul parish register, Guildhall Library, MS8887, p.19, no. 56. Sarah Barnard's parish was St Faith-under-St Paul, whose church, taken within the body of St Paul's Cathedral in the thirteenth century, was burnt down in 1666. St Faith's parish amalgamated with the contiguous St Augustine's, where St Faith's services were held until St Augustine's was bombed in 1941.

65 MF to Mary Reid, June 1821; FJ135.

66 MF to Sarah Barnard, 21 July 1822; FJ174.

67 BA, 'The late Professor Faraday'; IEE.

68 RI MM, 4 June 1821.

CHAPTER 11: THERE THEY GO! THERE THEY GO!

1 Anon. [MF], 'Historical Sketch of Electro-Magnetism', *Ann. Phil.*, NS vol. 2 (1821), pp.195–200 and 274–90.

2 Humphry Davy, 'On the Magnetic Phenomena Produced by Electricity'; *Ann. Phil.*, NS vol. 2 (August 1821), pp.81–8.

3 W.T. Brande, 'On the Connexion of Electric and Magnetic Phaenomena'; *QJS*, vol. 10 (1821), pp.361–4.

4 *Phil. Mag.*, vol. 57 (1821), pp.446–7 (article dated 17 May 1821).

5 R. Phillips to MF, 4 September 1821; FJ147.

6 Thompson, 1898, p.51.

7 *ibid.*

8 *Diary*, 3 September 1821, vol. 1, pp.49–50. According to Thompson, 1898, p.87, a page has been torn out here, so the account may be incomplete.

9 Thompson, 1898, p.51. Dickens describes Astley's in *Sketches by Boz* (1836–37), Chapter 11.

10 *QJS*, vol. 12 (1821), pp.74–96. The article is dated 11 September 1821.

11 *ERE*, 2, p.160.

12 MF to C.-G. de la Rive, 12 September 1821; FJ148.

13 MF to W.H. Wollaston, 30 October 1821; FJ154.

14 Bence Jones, 1870, 2nd edn, vol. 1, p.310.

15 MF to James Stodart, 8 October 1821; FJ152.

16 FJ152.

17 MF to L.W. Gilbert, 18 October 1821; FJ153.

18 MF to J.N.P. Hachette, 30 October 1821; FJ155.

19 FJ154.

20 W.H. Wollaston to MF, c.1 November 1821; FJ156.

21 *ERE*, 2, p.160.

22 Henry Warburton to MF, 8 July 1823; FJ205.

23 Davy, *Works*, vol. 6, p.262, 'On a new phenomenon of electro-magnetism', pp.257–63.

24 *Ann. Phil.*, NS vol. 5 (1823), p.304.

25 Edward Brayley, who had recorded the relevant RS proceedings in *Ann. Phil.*, later recalled that despite Sir Humphry's denial he was sure he had reported correctly. Edward Brayley to MF, c.May 1836; FJ914.

26 *Ann. Phil.*, NS vol. 3 (1822), pp.107–21.

27 FJ152.

28 MF, 'Historical Statement respecting Electro-Magnetic Rotation', *QJS*, vol. 15 (1823), pp.288–92.

29 FJ142, 144, 149.

30 J.N.P. Hachette to MF, 6 June 1821; MF139.

31 Thompson, 1898, p.89.

32 BA 'Jottings from Memory'.

33 *ibid.*

CHAPTER 12: USE THE RIGHT WORD, MY DEAR

1 Bence Jones, 1870, 2nd edn, vol. 1, p.297.

2 FJ5.

3 Cantor, 1991, p.60.

4 Walter Wilson, *The History and Antiquities of Dissenting Churches and Meeting Houses. . .*; 4 vols, 1808–14, vol. 3, p.276.

5 Anon., *The Customs of the Churches of Christ as found in the New Testament*; Edinburgh, 1908, p.13, n18. Quoted Cantor, 1991, p.60.

6 MF, 'Observations on Mental Education'; *ERCP*, p.471.

7 FJ285 (18 March 1826); FJ372 (29 August 1828).

8 MF to Sarah Barnard, 8 August 1820; FJ116.

9 MF to Sarah Faraday, 14 August 1863; FJ vol. 5.

10 Cantor, 1991, Appendix A.

11 *ibid.*, Appendix B.

12 Bence Jones, 1870, 2nd edn, vol. 1, pp.378–84.

13 *ibid.*

14 CPB, pp.171–4.

15 e.g. FJ374; 15 November 1828.

16 Cornelia Crosse, 'Science and Society in the Fifties'; *Temple Bar*, vol. 93 (1891), pp.33–51.

17 MF to J. Tyndall, 6 October 1855; FJ3027.

18 John Tyndall, *Faraday as a Discoverer*; 1868, p.37.

19 Bence Jones, 1870, 2nd edn, vol. 1, pp.378–84.

20 C. Ridolfi to MF, 16 July 1823; FJ206.

21 A.-M. Ampère to MF, 23 September 1823; FJ211.

22 FJ221, 222; *Diary*, 12 and 13 February 1824, vol. 1, pp.127–8.

23 Faraday gave verbal evidence to the Committee on 13 May and 1 June 1822. *Parliamentary Papers*; 1822 (417), vi, 180–3, 189–91. FJ171, 7 May 1822.

24 J. Stodart and M. Faraday, 'On the Alloys of Steel'; *Phil. Trans.*, vol. 112 (1822), pp.253–70; 'Experiments on the Alloys of Steel, made with a view to its improvement', *Répertoire d'Arts*, vol. 41 (1822), pp.346–59.

25 C. Pickslay to MF, 14 April 1824; FJ231.

26 Green, Pickslay & Co. to MF, c.1826; FJ278.

27 *Cambrian*, May 1822; quoted Thomos, *op. cit.*, p.149.

28 MF to Sarah Faraday, 21 July 1822; FJ174. There are five Lawrences associated with the RI around this time. Information in RI MM is not full enough to identify which Mr Lawrence it was.

29 MF to Sarah Faraday, 25 July 1822; FJ176.

30 This and previous quotations from MF to Sarah Faraday, 28 July 1822; FJ177.

31 R. Phillips and M. Faraday, 'Results of experiments made at the Hafod Works', in *Proceedings of the Subscribers of the Fund for Obviating the Inconvenience arising from smoke produced by smelting copper ores; Report of the judges. . .*; Swansea, 1823, pp.61–7; J.H. Vivian, 'Account of the Process of Copper Smelting at Hafod Copper Works, near Swansea'; *Ann. Phil.*, NS vol. 5 (1823), pp.113–24. R.R. Toomey, *Vivian & Sons 1809–1924: A Study of the Firm in the Copper and Related Industries*; Ph.D thesis, University of Wales, 1979, pp.285–6.

32 IEE Archive, 2/1/5. Paper watermarked 1821. See the transcription and commentary by David Gooding and Ryan Tweney, *Michael Faraday's 'Chemical Notes, Hints, Suggestions and Objects of Pursuit' of 1822*; 1991.

33 10 and 25 July 1822; FJ173.

34 MF to A.-M. Ampère, 3 September 1822.

35 For example Matthew 14.22–33.

36 A.-M. Ampère to MF, 23 January 1822; FJ162.

37 A.-M. Ampère to MF, 26 May 1822; FJ172.
38 A.-M. Ampère to MF, 10 July 1822; FJ173.
39 MF to A.-M. Ampère, 1 July 1823; FJ203.

CHAPTER 13: FELLOW OF THE ROYAL SOCIETY

1 Recollection of Sir Roderick Murchison, *Memorial to Faraday*, proceedings of a public meeting at the RI on 21 June 1869 to move that a subscription be raised for a public memorial to MF.
2 MF to C.-G. de la Rive, 24 March 1823; FJ189.
3 *Diary*, 19 March 1823, pp.97–9.
4 FJ189.
5 MF to T. Huxtable, 25 March 1823; FJ190.
6 MF, 'On Hydrate of Chlorine'; *QJS*, vol. 15 (1823), pp.71–4.
7 MF to R Phillips, 10 May 1836; Bence Jones, 1870, 2nd edn, vol. 1, pp.335–9. Not in FJ. The italics are Bence Jones's.
8 Paris, 1831, vol. 2, pp.209–10. The italics are mine.
9 *Lit. Gaz.*, 23 June 1827.
10 RI, Davy archive, B23, pp.394–5.
11 R. Phillips to MF, 3 May 1823; FJ195.
12 The complete list of nominators was: W.H. Wollaston, J.G. Children, W. Babington, J.F.W. Herschel, J.L. Guillemard, R. Phillips, C. Babbage, G.D. Yeats, T. Colby, W. Prout, W.D. Conybeare, H.T. de la Beche, D. Moore, J. Bostock, P.M. Roget, A.B. Granville, J.F. Pollock, R.H. Solly, G. Pearson, H. Earle, G. Blane, J. South, D. Gilbert, R. Bingley, A. Crichton, J.A. Paris, J.F. Daniell, C. Hatchett, J. Stodart.
13 Bence Jones, 1870, 2nd edn, vol. 1, pp.339–40.
14 MF to R. Phillips, 5 May 1823; FJ196.
15 MF to J.H. Vivian, 27 June 1823; FJ201.
16 *Diary*, 20 August 1823, vol. 1, pp.108–9.
17 *ibid.*
18 *ibid.*
19 Prospectus, FJ227.
20 Humphry Ward, *History of the Athenaeum 1824–1924*; 1926.
21 RI MM, 7 February 1825.
22 Faraday's lectures began on 8 February 1825; the first bricks of the Thames Tunnel were laid by the Brunels at Rotherhithe on 2 March 1825. L.T.C. Rolt, *Isambard Kingdom Brunel*; 1989 edn, p.43. See I.K. Brunel to MF, 17 January 1825; FJ250.
23 RI MM, 6 February 1826.
24 RI MM, 9 January 1826.
25 J.S. Henslow to MF, 14 May 1823; FJ197.
26 C. Ridolfi to MF, 16 July 1823; FJ206.
27 G. Cuvier to MF, 22 September 1823; FJ210.
28 A. Hartnell to MF, 19 December 1823; FJ213.
29 RI MS, F1 H and I.
30 Fully discussed by Gertrude Prescott, 'Faraday: Images of the Man and the Collector'; in David Gooding and Frank James (eds), *Faraday Rediscovered*; London, 1985, pp.15–31.

31 J.F.B. Firth, *The Velocipede: Its Past, Present and Future*; 1869; quoted Thompson, 1898, p.74. I am grateful to Scotford Lawrence for information on cycle history.

CHAPTER 14: WE LIGHT UP THE HOUSE

1 'Caoutchouc' (French) derives from the Carib 'cahuchu'. MF's ms notes of the Discourses and their programmes are in RI, F4 C–K.
2 *Diary*, vol. 1, pp.171–7, 273–9.
3 T. Hancock, *Narrative of the India-Rubber Manufacture*; 1857, esp. pp.35–48; *Mechanics Magazine*, vol. 24, pp.529ff.
4 Only male members of the RI were admitted in 1826; they paid two guineas each for the season. Women were not admitted to the Discourses until 1827.
5 M.I. Brunel to MF, 8 February 1826; FJ282.
6 Herries notebooks, IEE Archive.
7 T. Hancock, *op. cit.*, pp.23–4.
8 MF to Capt. J. Franklin, 17 May 1826; FJ292.
9 *ibid.*
10 MF to W.C. Trevelyan, 7 February 1827; FJ316.
11 6 and 7 February 1828; FJ346, 347.
12 Discourse, 29 January 1830.
13 Discourse, 19 February 1830.
14 Discourse, 12 March 1830.
15 Discourse, 23 April 1830.
16 Discourse, 7 May 1830.
17 See FJ353, 356, 358.
18 Founded 1828; not to be confused with the club of the same name.
19 *Lit. Gaz.*, 24 May 1828.

20 *Athenaeum*, 13 May 1829.
21 L.T.C. Rolt, *Isambard Kingdom Brunel*; 1989 edn, p.33.
22 *Athenaeum, loc. cit.*
23 Thompson, 1898, p.231.
24 CPB, pp.177–321.
25 Sergeant Charles Anderson, Faraday's laboratory assistant from 1827; see Chapter 15.
26 Thompson, 1898, p.231.
27 RI MM, 5 July 1824.
28 FJ292.
29 MF to D. Lardner, 6 October 1827; FJ336.
30 Thompson, 1898, p.68.
31 *Lit. Gaz.*, 24 February 1827.
32 RI MM, 21 January 1828.
33 FJ292.
34 RI MM, 26 January 1818.
35 RI MM, 21 April 1828.
36 C.R. Weld, *A History of the Royal Society, with Memoirs of the Presidents*; vol. 1, London, 1848, p.385.
37 MF to W. Jerdan, 12 March 1828; FJ353.
38 *Lit. Gaz.*, 22 March 1828.
39 FJ316.
40 MF to Prandi, 23 January 1828; FJ343.
41 W.O. Henderson (ed.), *J.C. Fischer and his Diary of Industrial England 1814–51*; 1966, pp.36–7.
42 MF to P. Berthier, 4 February 1828; FJ345.
43 MF to B. Smith, 26 March 1829; FJ395.
44 From 1826 the Friday Evenings Committee comprised Daniel Moore, Captain Edward Sabine, Captain Chapman, Mr Pilgrim, William Brande and MF. RI F4F f.6.

45 MF to W. Hosking, 5 March 1829; FJ393.

46 *Athenaeum*, 20 May 1829.

47 F. von Raumer, *England in 1835: being a series of letters written to friends in Germany, during a residence in London and excursions into the provinces*, 3 vols, 1836, p.61. Letter dated 1 May 1835.

48 MF to P. Drummond, 23 January 1830; FJ427.

49 MF to J. Marcet, 2 May 1846; FJ1873.

50 MF to A. de la Rive, 2 October 1858; Williams, 1971, no. 691.

51 RI MM, 21 January 1828. The first series was given at Christmas 1826, on Astronomy, by J. Wallis.

52 *Quarterly Review*; quoted Thompson, 1898, p.235.

53 Mrs Owen's diary, quoted Thompson, 1898, p.237.

54 F. von Raumer, *op. cit.*, p.60. Raumer's references are to the French actress Anne Françoise Mars and the German dramatist and poet Johann Ludwig Tieck.

55 F. von Raumer, 'Extracts from Letters Written in 1836', *England in 1841. . .*; 1842, p.126. Letter dated 30 April 1836.

56 21 May 1830.

57 *Athenaeum*, 7 July 1838, p.475; FJ1148, 1161. Also FJ1099, 1101, 1103.

58 *Lit. Gaz.*, 17 February 1831.

59 MF to C. Hatchett, 12 September 1826; FJ306.

60 Reported in *Lit. Gaz.*, 30 March 1833.

61 MF to John Martin, 9 November 1846; FJ1928.

62 See Justine Hopkins, 'Phenomena of Art and Science: The Paintings

and Projects of John Martin', in Hamilton, 2001, pp.51–92.

63 Accession numbers 2515 (1–104): Drawings of Prominent People 1823–49 by William Brockedon.

64 Discourse, 11 May 1827; reported *Lit. Gaz.*, 19 May 1827.

65 Discourse, 23 May 1828, 'On a new mode of projecting shot'.

66 Discourse, 14 June 1833; reported *Lit. Gaz.*, 29 June 1833.

67 13 March 1829; reported *Lit. Gaz.*, 21 March 1829.

68 MF to W. Brockedon, 1 February 1830; FJ430.

69 *Illustrated London News*, 2 September 1854, p.206. See also James Hamilton, 'Artists, Scientists and Events', in Hamilton, 2001, pp.1–30.

70 *Lit. Gaz.*, 21 March 1829.

71 MF to W. Brockedon, 22 June 1830; FJ452.

72 James Ward to Sir J. Leicester, 14 April 1824; Douglas Hall, 'The Tabley House Papers'; *Walpole Society*, vol. 38 (1960–62), p.97.

73 MF to C. Hullmandel, 12 April 1827, FJ321.

74 Bence Jones, 1870, 2nd edn, vol. 1, pp.377–8.

75 Faraday's Scrapbooks, vol. 1, p.32; RI Archive.

76 *ibid.*, pp.27, 253 and *passim*. On p.189 there is a blank invoice headed 'C. Hullmandel, 51 Great Marlborough Street'.

77 C. Hullmandel, *The Art of Drawing on Stone*; 1824, p.vii.

78 MF to W. Savage, 28 January 1825; FJ251.

CHAPTER 15: STEADINESS AND
PLACIDITY

1 HD to MF, 29 June 1823; FJ202.
2 MF later wrote these notes up in
CPB, vol. 2. They are published
in Brian Bowers and Keith
Bowers, 'Michael Faraday's
Geological Notes on the Isle of
Wight', *Notes Received, Royal
Society*, vol. 50, (1996), no. 1,
pp.65–74.
3 MF to Margaret Faraday, 25
August 1824; FJ240.
4 MF to E. Magrath, 23 July 1826;
FJ302.
5 MF to E. Barnard, 23 July 1826;
FJ303.
6 *Chemical Manipulation*; 1827,
Introduction, p.v.
7 BA 'Jottings from Memory'.
8 MF to A. de la Rive, 2 October
1858; Williams, 1971, no. 691.
9 E.R. Daniell to MF, 16 April 1827;
FJ322.
10 J.A. Paris to MF, c.May 1827; FJ323.
11 W. Henry to MF, 2 May 1827;
FJ324.
12 G. Cuvier to MF, 2 July 1827;
FJ329.
13 The *Dictionnaire Universel français
et latin* (new edn, Paris, 1771) was
known as the *Dictionnaire de
Trévoux*.
14 Anderson was forty-two in 1832;
RI Staff List, 'Helps', MS F5C, p.4.
His address is given here also.
15 *DNB* entry for MF.
16 Davy, *Works*, vol. 1, p.408.
17 MF to J.J. Masquerier, 25 June
1829; FJ401.
18 MF to J.A. Paris, 23 December
1829; FJ419.
19 FJ17.
20 MF to P. Drummond, 11 January
1830.

CHAPTER 16: FACTS ARE SUCH
STUBBORN THINGS

1 See FJ448, 5 June 1830.
2 MF to D. Gilbert, 13 May 1830;
FJ446.
3 'The Report of Mr Pond on Mr
Faraday's Telescope', 23 December
1830; Royal Society Domestic
MSS, vol. 3, f.155.
4 *Lit. Gaz.*, 29 January 1831, p.73.
5 MF to E. Magrath, 14 February
1831; FJ482.
6 *DNB*.
7 Mary Somerville's draft
autobiography, p.112–13,
Somerville Papers, dep. c.335.
Quoted Elizabeth C. Patterson,
*Mary Somerville and the
Cultivation of Science, 1815–1840*;
Boston, 1983, pp.52–3.
8 See for example letters FJ651, 652,
1001.
9 Charles Babbage, *Reflections on the
Decline of Science in England and
on Some of its Causes*; 1830, p.1.
10 G. Moll to MF, 24 December
1830; FJ472.
11 G. Moll to MF, 11 March 1831;
FJ487.
12 Nathan Reingold, 'Babbage and
Moll on the State of Science in
Great Britain: A Note on a
Document'; *BJHS*, vol. 4 (1968),
no. 13, pp.58–64.
13 J.N.P. Hachette to MF, 22 August
1830; FJ459.
14 A.-M. Ampère to MF, 10 April
1831; FJ491.

15 W. Buckland to MF, 7 December 1830; FJ469.
16 MF to W.V. Harcourt, 3 August 1831; FJ507.
17 MF to J. Rennie, 26 February 1835; FJ766.
18 Bence Jones, 1870, 2nd edn, vol. 1, pp.8–9.

CHAPTER 17: CRISPATIONS

1 *Diary*, 2 February 1831, vol. 1, p.329.
2 *Diary*, 25 June 1831, vol. 1, pp.342–3.
3 *Diary*, 17 June 1831 'and previous', vol. 1, p.336, para. 1.
4 *Diary*, para. 7.
5 *Diary*, 28 June 1831, vol. 1, p.344, para. 59.
6 *Diary*, 18 June 1831, vol. 1, pp.338–9, para. 23.
7 *Diary*, 28 June 1831, vol. 1, p.346, para. 73.
8 *Lit. Gaz.*, 18 June 1831, p.394. Paper, 'On a peculiar class of acoustical figures', read RS, 12 May 1831.
9 MF to P.M. Roget, 4 July 1831; FJ501.
10 *Diary*, 30 June and 1 July 1831, vol. 1, pp.347–50.
11 *Diary*, 30 June 1831, vol. 1, p.349, para. 91.
12 *Diary*, 18 July 1831, 'at Hastings'; vol. 1, p.358, para. 146.
13 Walter Armstrong, *Turner*; 1902, p.131.
14 MF to Capt. G. Manby, 19 April 1830; FJ442.
15 Capt. G. Manby to MF, 24 April 1830; FJ443.
16 Capt. G. Manby to D. Turner, 8 February 1831; Dawson Turner Papers, Trinity College, Cambridge. MF was not among Manby's proposers.
17 Bence Jones, 1870, 2nd edn, vol. 1, p.378.
18 James Hamilton, *Turner: A Life*; 1997, Chapter 1, *passim*.
19 John Gage, *Collected Correspondence of J.M.W. Turner*; Clarendon Press, Oxford, 1980, letters nos 242 (?20 March 1841), 269 (?late July 1844).
20 *ibid.*, no. 269.
21 Frank James, 'Harriet Moore, Michael Faraday and Moore's mid-nineteenth century watercolours of the interior of the Royal Institution'; essay in Hamilton, 2001, pp.111–28.
22 M. Arnold to M.P. Arnold, 7 March 1849; Cecil Y. Lang (ed.), *The Letters of Matthew Arnold*; vol. 1 (1829–59), University of Virginia Press, 1996, pp.139–40.
23 MF to W.T. Clark, 2 August 1831; FJ505.
24 Greater London Record Office Acc. 2558/WM/1/8/1, pp.180–1.
25 MF to J.W. Parker, 19 August 1831; FJ509.
26 MF to R. Phillips, 21 June 1831; FJ499.

CHAPTER 18: AND THAT ONE WORD WERE LIGHTNING

1 *Diary*, 29 August 1831, vol. 1, p.367, para. 2.
2 MF to E. Magrath, 2 September 1831; FJ511.
3 Richard Phillips, *A letter to Dr David Boswell Reid, Experimental*

*Assistant to Professor Hope, &c,
&c, &c., In Answer to his
Pamphlet intitled 'An Exposure of
the Misrepresentation in the
Philosophical Magazine and
Annals*'; 1831.

4 MF to R. Phillips, 23 September
1831; FJ515.

5 *Diary*, 24 September 1831, vol. 1,
p.372, paras 33–4.

6 J.W. Morrison to MF, 8 October
1831; FJ516.

7 John Craig, *The Mint: A
History. . .*; 1953, pp.304–5.

8 *Diary*, 17 October 1831, vol. 1,
p.375, para. 55.

9 *ibid.*, para. 57.

10 MF to R. Phillips, 29 November
1831; FJ522.

11 Paper read at RS in two parts, 8
and 15 December 1831.

12 This letter is lost, but in structure
it is likely to have followed FJ522,
to R. Phillips.

13 Quoted by MF in letter to W.
Jerdan, 27 March 1832; FJ560,
from *Lit. Gaz.*, 24 March 1832,
p.185.

14 'Sopra la Forza Elettromotice del
Magnetismo', *Antologia*, 44 (1831),
pp.149–61.

15 *Diary*, 1 October 1831, vol. 1, p.372,
para. 36.

16 *ibid.*, 26 December 1831, vol. 1,
p.405, para. 274.

17 *ibid.*, 10 January 1832, vol. 1,
pp.408–9, paras 293–302.

18 MF to E. Hawkins, 12 January
1832 [misdated 1831].

19 *Diary*, 12 January 1832, vol. 1,
p.410, para. 305.

20 *ibid.*, para. 307.

21 *ibid.*, para. 310.

22 *ibid.*

23 *ERE*, 2nd series, para. 190.

24 *Lit. Gaz.*, 28 January 1832, p.56.

25 *Lit. Gaz.*, 4 February 1832, p.74.

26 *Diary*, 30 August 1831, vol. 1,
p.369, para. 14.

27 Bence Jones, 1870, 2nd edn, vol. 2,
p.86.

28 MF to H.C. Øersted, 6 September
1833; FJ611.

29 Maria Edgeworth to Honora
Edgeworth, 19 February 1831;
Colvin, 1971, p.484.

30 MF to W. Whewell, 21 February
1831; FJ483.

31 MF to W. Whewell, 24 April 1834;
FJ711.

32 W. Whewell to MF, 25 April 1834;
FJ713.

33 MF to W. Whewell, 3 May 1834;
FJ714.

34 W. Whewell to MF, 5 May 1834;
FJ716.

35 MF to W. Whewell, 15 May 1834;
FJ720.

36 W. Whewell to MF, 20 May 1840;
FJ1278.

37 MF to W. Whewell, 20 May 1840;
FJ1279.

38 W. Whewell to MF, 14 October
1837; FJ1043.

39 Bence Jones, 1870, 2nd edn, vol. 2,
p.475.

40 Thomos, *op.cit.*, p.45.

41 Byron, *Childe Harold's Pilgrimage*,
Canto III, v.97; 1816.

42 Quoted Tyndall, 1868, pp.32–3n.

43 N.A. Rupke, 'Oxford's Scientific
Awakening and the Role of
Geology', in M.G. Brock and
M.C. Curthoys (eds), *The History
of the University of Oxford*; vol. 6,
1997, pp.543–62.

44 *Diary*, 19 September 1833, vol. 2, p.108, para. 722.
45 MF to G.B. Airy, 10 March 1832; FJ554.
46 MF to J.W. Lubbock, 2 November 1833; FJ686.

CHAPTER 19: CONNEXIONS

1 MF to J. Lubbock, 2 November 1833; FJ686.
2 Correspondence between MF and J. Barrow, Admiralty Secretary, December 1832, FJ631, 633–5.
3 MF to G. Penn, 2 November 1833; FJ685.
4 MF to J. Gage, 5 November 1833; FJ687.
5 MF to W.R. Hamilton, 1 October 1833; FJ681. For more about Hamilton see Katharine Eustace, *Canova Ideal Heads*; Ashmolean Museum, Oxford, 1996, *passim*.
6 'Address delivered at the Commemoration of the Centenary of the Birth of Dr. Priestley', *Phil. Mag.*, vol. II (1833), pp.390–1.
7 'Let him who has earned it bear the palm' – Lord Nelson's motto. *Lit. Gaz.*, 26 January 1833, p.57.
8 *ibid.*
9 *Diary*, 2 December 1833, vol. 2, p.177, para. 1170.
10 'On the Identity of Electricity Derived from Different Sources', *Phil. Trans.*, vol. 123 (1833), pp.23–54.
11 Anna Atkins, *Memoir of John George Children*; 1853, pp.257–8.
12 Joseph Priestley, *The History and Present State of Electricity*; 1767.
13 *ibid.*, Preface.

14 John Meurig Thomas, *Michael Faraday and the Royal Institution*; 1991, p.48.
15 *ERE*, series 7, paras 826–36.
16 Carl Woodring, *The Collected Works of Samuel Taylor Coleridge 14. Table Talk*; Princeton, vol. 1, pp.392–3.
17 Richard Holmes, *Coleridge: Darker Reflections*; London, 1998.
18 Thomas Carlyle, 'Signs of the Times'; *Edinburgh Review* (1829), 49, pp.439–59. Published in Thomas Carlyle, *Critical and Miscellaneous Essays*; vol. 2, 1899, pp.56–82.
19 Joseph Cottle, *Reminiscences*; [1837], pp.328–9; quoted Carl Woodring, *loc. cit.*, p.41n.
20 A rich source of information about these is Morus, *op. cit.*, esp. Chapter 3.
21 F. von Raumer, *England in 1835. . .*; vol. 1, p.7.
22 MF to J.F.W. Herschel, 10 November 1832; FJ623.
23 Patterson, *Mary Somerville and the Cultivation of Science, op. cit.*, p.123.
24 W. Wollaston to M. Somerville, 7 December 1828; Somerville Papers, dep. c.372.22.
25 D. Brewster to J.D. Forbes, 11 September 1829; Forbes papers, University of St Andrews Library.
26 Maria Edgeworth to her mother, 16 January 1822; Colvin, 1971, pp.321–2.
27 N. Reingold (ed.), *The Papers of Joseph Henry*; Washington DC, 1979, vol. 3, p.292.
28 MF to M. Somerville, 29 April 1848; FJ2078.

29 MF to M. Somerville, 17 January 1859; Williams, 1971, no. 695.

30 FJ684 and 732.

31 *Athenaeum*, vol. 333 (1834), pp.202–3.

32 Postscript by Margaret Herschel, in letter W. Herschel to M. Somerville, 5 January 1869; Somerville Papers, dep. c.370.

33 Hamilton, 1998, p.68 and *passim*.

34 W. Grieg to M. Somerville, 10 May 1840; Somerville Papers, dep. c.367.

35 *Mantell Journal*, pp.113–14, 16 March 1833.

36 *Lit. Gaz.*, 16 November 1833, p.730.

37 MF to F. Watkins, 25 November 1833; FJ692.

38 Cornelia A.H. Crosse, *Memorials, Scientific and Literary, of Andrew Crosse, the Electrician*; 1857, Chapter 1.

39 A full account of Crosse and the insects is in James A. Secord, 'Extraordinary Experiment: Electricity and the Creation of Life in Victorian England'; essay in D. Gooding, T. Pinch and S. Schaffer (eds), *The Uses of Experiment*; Cambridge University Press, 1989, pp.337–83.

40 Ambrose Poynter to Robert Finch, 28 October 1824; Finch Papers, Bodleian Library, Oxford.

41 *Lit. Gaz.*, 19 July 1828.

42 *Diary*, 15 January 1835; vol. 2, p.359, para. 2268. MF's doctor, P.M. Latham, detected a 'strabismus of the eye' in his patient in 1839. See E. Hare, 'Michael Faraday's Loss of Memory'; *Proc. RI*, vol. 49 (1976), pp.33–52.

43 MF to T. Hawkins, 3 May 1839; FJ1170.

44 Lord Ashley to Robert Peel, 4 April 1835; FJ777.

45 *DNB* entries for William Oxberry and Edward Fitzwilliam.

46 J. South to MF, 20 April 1835; FJ780.

47 MF to J. South, 22 April 1835; FJ782.

48 *Mantell Journal*, p.127, 24 June 1835.

49 MF to E. Magrath, 19 July 1835; FJ807.

50 S. Faraday to E. Magrath, 14 and 15 August 1841; FJ1360. This distance may have been exceptional.

51 *ibid*.

52 Bence Jones, 1870, 2nd edn, vol. 1, pp.377–8.

53 Transcript by MF of interview between him and Lord Melbourne, 26 October 1835; IEE Archive, 2/3/18/9.

54 Thompson, 1898, pp.70–2.

55 P. Ziegler, *Melbourne*; 1976, p.138.

56 Quoted *ibid*.

57 Thompson, 1898, *loc. cit.*

58 Duke of Somerset to C. Babbage, 16 December 1835. BL Add. MS 37189, f.218. Quoted Maurice Berman, *Social Change and Scientific Organization: The Royal Institution 1799–1844*; London, 1978, p.174.

59 No. 25 from Lord Melbourne, dated 2 January 1836, seems to be the final one.

60 C. Fox to MF, 22 November 1835; FJ834.

61 MF to Mary Fox, 23 November 1835; FJ835.

62 Lord Melbourne to MF, 24 November 1835; FJ837.

63 MF to Lord Melbourne, 24 November 1835; FJ838.

64 'Shewing how the Tories and the Whigs extend their patronage to science and literature', *Fraser's Magazine*, December 1835, vol. 12, pp.703–9. This appeared on the streets in late November, and an extract from the article was published in *The Times*, 28 November 1835. *Fraser's Magazine* kept the subject going in a profile article on MF, February 1836, pp.224–5.

65 Dr H. Holland to Lord Holland, 3 December 1835; FJ852.

66 Dr H. Holland to MF, 3 December 1835; FJ853.

67 MF to the Editor, *The Times*, 7 December 1835; published the following morning.

68 Sir J. South to MF, 9 December 1835; FJ860.

69 'Report of Committee of Subscribers', 22 May 1837; RI MM, vol. 8, p.487a.

70 See A.D.R. Caroe, *The House of the Royal Institution*; 1963, pp.11 and 25–6. Caroe reproduces Rocque's map of London, 1746, which suggests that there was a garden in front of the RI, between Albemarle and Grafton Streets, thus giving the new façade an open aspect. But that was nearly a hundred years earlier, and the area had been developed in the interim. See also RI MM, from May 1836, pp.422ff; and Sophie Forgan, 'Context, Image and Function: A Preliminary Enquiry into the Architecture of Scientific Societies'; *BJHS*, vol. 19 (1986), pp.89–113.

71 *Lit. Gaz.*, 2 February 1839.

72 Gertrude Prescott drew attention to the RI's priority in her essay 'Faraday: Image of the Man and Collector'; in D. Gooding and F.A.J.L. James (eds), *Faraday Rediscovered*; 1985, pp.15–31.

73 W. Havell to MF, 19 April 1839; FJ1163.

74 W. Havell to MF, 23 March 1839; FJ1154.

75 MF to J. Herschel, 18 January 1840; FJ1234. See also FJ1160.

76 A.S. Taylor to MF, 17 April 1839; FJ1160.

CHAPTER 20: THE PARABLE OF THE RAINBOW

1 MF to E. Magrath, 23 December 1839; FJ1331.

2 MF to W.R. Grove, 20 November 1839; FJ1218.

3 MF to A.F. Osler, 4 November 1839; FJ1215.

4 P.M. Latham, Casebook, vol. 1; Wellcome Library, London. Quoted E. Hare, 'Michael Faraday's Loss of Memory'; *Proc. RI*, vol. 49 (1976), pp.33–52.

5 MF to Sir M.A. Shee, 3 December 1839; FJ1220.

6 *Mantell Journal*, p.135; 31 October–3 November 1836.

7 MF and Sarah Faraday to Andrew Reid, 24 April 1840; FJ1263.

8 MF to C.F. Schoenbein, 24 February 1840; FJ1262.

9 FJ1261, 1262, 1263.

10 C.F. Schoenbein to MF, 9 July 1837; FJ1015.
11 R. Hare, 'A Letter to Prof. Faraday on Certain Theoretical Opinions'; *American Journal of Science*, 38, pp.1–11. MF to C.F. Schoenbein, 24 February 1840; FJ1261.
12 C.F. Schoenbein to MF, 4 April 1840; FJ1259.
13 MF and Sarah Faraday to Andrew Reid, 24 April 1840; FJ1263.
14 MF to A.-A. de la Rive, 24 April 1840; FJ1262.
15 RI MM, 7 December 1840.
16 MF and Sarah Faraday to A. Reid, 24 April 1840; FJ1263.
17 Bence Jones, 1870, 2nd edn, vol. 1, p.381. Margery Reid's reminiscence.
18 CPB, p.421.
19 *ibid.*, p.423.
20 In Margate they stayed at 7 Park Place (see FJ1302), and in Brighton at 56 King's Road (see FJ1344).
21 MF to C.F. Schoenbein, 27 March 1841; FJ1345.
22 C.F. Schoenbein to MF, 8 April 1841; FJ1346.
23 Bence Jones, 1870, 2nd edn, vol. 2, pp.127–60.
24 Tuesday, 13 July 1841.
25 MF to T. Andrews, 27 July 1856; Williams, 1971, no. 637.
26 Wednesday, 14 July 1841.
27 Wednesday, 21 July 1841.
28 Friday, 23 July 1841.
29 Bence Jones, 1870, 2nd edn, vol. 2, pp.141–2; Bence Jones queries his reading of 'reasoning'.
30 Monday, 2 August 1841.
31 1844, 1845 and 1847–48.
32 Particularly his *Drawing from Nature . . . with Examples from Switzerland and the Pyrenees*; 1865.
33 Thursday, 5 August 1841.
34 FCJ, 13 May 1814.
35 Tuesday, 12 August 1841.
36 MF to W. Buchanan, 29 July 1840; FJ1301. The family members MF refers to are: Edward and Mary Barnard, his parents-in-law; Jane Barnard and Elizabeth Reid, Sarah Faraday's sisters; the younger Elizabeth Reid, Sarah's niece; William Paradise, fellow Sandemanian.
37 *DNB* entry for William Buchanan.
38 FJ973, 974 and 980.
39 2 October 1840; FJ1313.
40 MF to C.F. Schoenbein, 10 August 1842; FJ1417.
41 Sermon cards RI FL8A–100, 101; Sermon notes RI FL8A, dated 29 June 1862.
42 Four of MF's exhortations are published in M. Faraday, W. Buchanan, J.M. Baxter and A. Moir, *Select Exhortations Delivered to Various Churches of Christ*; Dundee, 1910, pp.15–37.
43 See Cantor, 1991, pp.58–64.
44 Letter signed G.H. Baxter 'From the Church of Dundee to those sojourning in London', 10 December 1844. Edinburgh Meeting House MS. Private collection. Quoted Cantor, 1991, p.63.
45 Robert Cree to anon., 4 June 1845; Ferguson MS, private collection, quoted Cantor, *loc. cit.*
46 MF to C.F. Schoenbein, 12 April 1844; FJ1575.
47 MF to W. Buchanan, 21 September 1844; FJ1609.

48 M. Edgeworth to MF, 1 May 1844; FJ1583.

49 J.P. Boileau to MF, 15 February 1844; FJ1554.

50 That is Maria's favourite sister Fanny, Mrs L.P. Wilson.

51 M. Edgeworth to Mrs Edgeworth, 8 April 1844; Colvin, 1971, p.609.

CHAPTER 21: MICHAEL FARADAY AND THE BRIDE OF SCIENCE

1 There are a number of biographies of Ada, principally Doris Langley Moore, *Ada, Countess of Lovelace*, 1977; Betty A. Toole, *Ada, the Enchantress of Numbers*, 1992; Benjamin Woolley, *The Bride of Science: Romance, Reason and Byron's Daughter*, 1999.

2 A. Lovelace to MF, 16 October 1844; FJ1620.

3 *Vestiges of the Natural History of Creation*, 1844, was later revealed to have been written by Robert Chambers (1802–71).

4 J. Baillie to Mary Somerville, 25 March 1844; Somerville Papers, dep. c.369.

5 'Interpreter of God and Nature'.

6 MF to A. Lovelace, 24 October 1844; FJ1631. Quoted by permission of Laurence Pollinger Ltd and the Earl of Lytton.

7 A. Lovelace to MF, 24 October 1844; FJ1632.

8 MF to A. Lovelace, 26 October 1844; FJ1636. Quoted by permission of Laurence Pollinger Ltd and the Earl of Lytton.

9 A. Lovelace to MF, 27 October 1844; FJ1637.

10 A. Lovelace to MF, 8 November 1844; FJ1644.

11 A. Lovelace to MF, 10 November 1844; FJ1647.

12 MF to C.F. Schoenbein, 25 October 1844; FJ1633.

13 A. Lovelace to MF, 13 November 1844; FJ1649.

14 A. Lovelace to MF, 1 December 1844; FJ1655.

15 MF to A. Lovelace, n.d., November 1844; Lovelace–Byron Papers, on deposit at the Bodleian Library, Oxford, dep. 171. Quoted by permission of Laurence Pollinger Ltd and the Earl of Lytton. Not in FJ.

16 MF to A. Lovelace, 10 June 1851; FJ2434.

CHAPTER 22: STILL, IT MAY BE TRUE

1 MF to R.S. Mackenzie, October 1844; FJ1612. Mackenzie's letter is lost.

2 G.B. Airy to MF, 19 May 1847; FJ1990.

3 MF to C.F. Schoenbein, 27 March 1841; FJ1345.

4 MF to Trinity House, 10 February 1841; FJ1337.

5 MF to J. Herbert, Trinity House, 5 and 24 June 1841; FJ1350 and 1355.

6 MF to J. Herbert, Trinity House, 11 March 1842; FJ1384.

7 MF to J. Herbert, Trinity House, 13 May 1842; FJ1396.

8 MF to J.H. Pelly, Trinity House, 3 February 1836; FJ883.

9 MF to J. Herbert, Trinity House, 19 December 1843; FJ1542. 31

August 1846; FJ1908. 22 December 1846; FJ1938.

10 G. Neale to MF, 19 February 1843; FJ1473.

11 *Illustrated London News*, vol. 2 (1843), pp.275–6; *The Times*, 15 April 1843, p.5.

12 MF to Col. J.P. Cockburn, 20 June 1843; FJ1502.

13 A full account of the explosion and its aftermath is in F.A.J.L. James and M. Ray, 'Science in the Pits: Michael Faraday, Charles Lyell and the Home Office Enquiry into the Explosion at Haswell Colliery, County Durham, in 1844'; *History and Technology*, 15 (1999), pp.213–31.

14 C. Lyell to H. Bence Jones, April 1868, in C. Lyell, *Life, Letters and Journal of Sir Charles Lyell*; 2 vols, 1881, vol. 2, pp.417–22, p.418.

15 *ibid.*

16 Bence Jones, 1870, 2nd edn, vol. 2, p.181.

17 Lyell, *op. cit.*, p.419.

18 Bence Jones, *loc. cit.*

19 S.M. Phillipps to MF and C. Lyell, 25 October 1844; FJ1634.

20 C. Lyell and M. Faraday, *Report . . . on the subject of the explosion at the Haswell Collieries and on the means of preventing similar accidents*; 1844.

21 S.M. Phillipps to C. Lyell and MF, 19 October 1844; FJ1624.

22 C. Lyell and MF to S.M. Phillipps, 14 October 1844; FJ1617.

23 MF and C. Lyell to S.M. Phillips, 21 October 1844; FJ1625.

24 MF to F. Beaufort, 1 November 1844; FJ1642.

25 MF to C.F. Schoenbein, 25 October 1844; FJ1633.

26 MF to W. Whewell, 9 November 1844; FJ1646.

27 W. Whewell to MF, 12 November 1844; FJ1648.

28 MF to W. Whewell, 14 November 1844; FJ1650.

29 MF to C.F. Schoenbein, 13 November 1845; FJ1785. My italics.

30 Paris, 1831, p.92.

31 *Diary*, 13 September 1845, vol. 4, p.264, para. 7504.

32 *Diary*, 18 September 1845, vol. 4, p.267, para. 7538.

33 *ibid.*, p.277, para. 7610.

34 *Diary*, 14 October 1845, vol. 4, pp.301–2, paras 7808–21.

35 *Diary*, 4 November 1845, vol. 4, p.313, paras 7902 and 7905–7.

36 *Mantell Journal*, p.198, 27 January 1845.

37 RI MS F4G/23.

38 *Phil. Mag.*, vol. 28 (1846), pp.345–50.

39 *Diary*, 7 November 1845, vol. 4, p.322, para. 7979.

40 *Diary*, 19 March 1849, vol. 5, p.150, paras 10018–19.

41 *ibid.*, p.151, paras 10030 and 10032.

42 *ibid.*, p.152, para. 10040.

43 *Diary*, 23 March 1849, vol. 5, p.152, paras 10041 and 10043.

44 *Diary*, 6 April 1849, vol. 5, p.154, paras 10052–9.

45 *Diary*, 25 August 1849, vol. 5, p.164, para. 10112.

46 *Diary*, 30 August 1849, vol. 5, p.167, para. 10132.

47 MF to Revd E. Jones, 9 June 1857; Williams, 1971, no. 660.

48 *Diary*, 10 February 1859, vol. 7, p.334, para. 15785.

49 MF to A. de la Rive, 2 October 1858; Williams, 1971, no. 691.

50 From S.T. Coleridge, 'Dejection, An Ode'; 1802 (published 1817), verse 6.

51 *Diary*, 10 February 1859, vol. 7, pp.336–7, paras 15804, 15805 and 15809.

52 Davy, *Works*, vol. 9, *Consolations in Travel*, pp.213ff.

53 *Diary*, 10 February 1859, vol. 7, p.335, para. 15795.

54 CPB, p.434.

55 *ibid.*, pp.391, 414, 434.

56 MF to R.E. Grant, 13 January 1837; FJ965.

57 MF to R.E. Grant, 7 January 1840; FJ1230.

58 C.F. Schoenbein to MF, October 1848; FJ2109.

59 MF to C.F. Schoenbein, 15 December 1848; FJ2138.

60 MF to A. de la Rive, 9 July 1849; FJ2208.

61 *ibid.*

62 A. de la Rive to MF, 14 June 1849; FJ2199.

63 J.-B.-A. Dumas to MF, c.21 May 1849; FJ2184.

64 MF to J.-B.-A. Dumas, 5 June 1849; FJ2191.

65 MF to J.-B.-A. Dumas, 18 June 1849; FJ2200.

66 FCJ, 7 March 1815, p.159.

CHAPTER 23: A METALLIC CLATTER . . .

1 MF to J. Tyndall, 6 October 1855; FJ3027.

2 MF to B. Vincent, 25 July 1850; FJ2309.

3 More than a hundred surviving letters to and from Faraday in the period 1849 to 1855 (FJ vol. 4) refer to his health, and a further twenty-six to Sarah's health.

4 MF to J. Barlow, 8 May 1849; FJ2178 and n.

5 MF to J.H. Shaw, 19 December 1853; FJ2764 and n.

6 P.M. Latham to MF, 7 May 1849; FJ2177.

7 J. Meurig Thomas, *Michael Faraday and the Royal Institution*; Adam Hilger, Bristol, 1991, p.218.

8 George Eliot to Mr and Mrs C. Bray, 28 January 1851; G.S. Haight (ed.), *The George Eliot Letters*; 9 vols, 1954–78, vol. 1, pp.341–2.

9 Entry for Mary Lloyd in E. Joll, M. Butlin and L. Herrman (eds), *The Oxford Companion to J.M.W. Turner*; 2001.

10 M.L., *Sunny Memories*, 'Containing personal recollections of some celebrated characters'; Part 1. Printed for private circulation, London, Women's Printing Society Ltd, 1879. Part 2, 1880.

11 *ibid.*, Part 1, p.28 (essay on Samuel Rogers).

12 *ibid.*, pp.64–70.

13 [Jane Pollock], 'Michael Faraday'; *St Paul's Magazine*, vol. 6 (1870), pp.293–303. Quoted J.H.

22 MF to Sarah Faraday, 14 August 1863; FJ vol. 5.

23 MF to -?- Holzmann, 22 December 1863; FJ vol. 5.

24 MF to C.F. Schoenbein, -?- September 1862; FJ vol. 5.

25 MF to A.-A. de la Rive, 19 September 1861; Williams, 1971, no. 782.

26 S. Martin, *op. cit.*, p.39.

27 Bence Jones, 1870, 2nd edn, vol. 2, pp.474–5.

28 *ibid.*

29 J. South to MF, 12 January 1866; FJ vol. 5.

30 Bence Jones, 1870, 2nd edn, vol. 2, p.472.

31 H.E. Roscoe, *The Life and Experiences of Sir Henry Enfield Roscoe, by himself*, 1906, p.136.

32 Attr. Jane Barnard, statement dated 1 July 1866. IEE Archive, SC MS 2/3/24/5–8.

33 RI Archive, F8A.

34 J. Barnard to H. Bence Jones, 26 August 1867; FJ vol. 5.

EPILOGUE

1 Revd S. Martin, *Michael Faraday: Philosopher and Christian*; London, 1867.

2 Sheet music in the IEE Archive.

3 Tyndall, 1868, p.1.

4 Bence Jones, 1870, 2nd edn, p.v.

5 See Chapter 7.

6 See Chapter 23, n39.

7 Faraday's Scrapbook, vol. 2, pp.53 and 75.

8 Thompson, 1898, p.258.

9 *Punch*, 27 June 1891, vol. 100, p.309.

BIBLIOGRAPHY

Biographies and biographical studies of Michael Faraday, listed in chronological order of publication:

John Tyndall, *Faraday as a Discoverer*; Longmans, Green & Co., 1868

Henry Bence Jones, *The Life and Letters of Michael Faraday*; 1st and 2nd edns, Longmans, Green, 1870

John Hall Gladstone, *Michael Faraday*; 1872

Walter Jerrold, *Michael Faraday: Man of Science*; S.W. Partridge & Co., 1891

Silvanus P. Thompson, *Michael Faraday: His Life and Work*; Cassell & Co., 1898

Rollo Appleyard, *A Tribute to Michael Faraday*; 1931

James F. Riley, *The Hammer and the Anvil: A Background to Michael Faraday*; Clapham, Yorkshire, 1955

L. Pearce Williams, *Michael Faraday*; Chapman & Hall, 1965

Joseph Agassi, *Faraday as a Natural Philosopher*; Chicago University Press, 1971

Ronald King, *Michael Faraday of the Royal Institution*; Royal Institution, 1973

Brian Bowers, *Michael Faraday and the Modern World*; EPA Press, 1991

Geoffrey Cantor, *Michael Faraday: Sandemanian and Scientist*; Macmillan, 1991

Geoffrey Cantor, David Gooding and Frank A.J.L. James, *Faraday*; Macmillan, 1991

John Meurig Thomas, *Michael Faraday and the Royal Institution*; Adam Hilger, 1991

Peter Day (ed.), *The Philosopher's Tree: Michael Faraday's Life and Work in his own Words*; Institute of Physics, 1999

Collections of edited letters and scientific and other writing by or concerning Michael Faraday:

Brian Bowers and Lenore Symons (eds), *'Curiosity Perfectly Satisfied': Faraday's Travels in Europe 1813–1815*; Peter Peregrinus and the Science Museum, 1991

Howard J. Fisher, *Faraday's Experimental Researches in Electricity: A Guide to a First Reading*; Santa Fe, Green Lion Press, 2001

David Gooding and Frank A.J.L. James (eds), *Faraday Rediscovered: Essays on the Life and Work of Michael Faraday*; Stockton Press, 1985

Frank A.J.L. James, *The Correspondence of Michael Faraday*; (4 vols, continuing to 6) Institution of Electrical Engineers, 1991–

Dafydd Thomas, *Michael Faraday in Wales*; Gwasg Gee, n.d. [1972]

L. Pearce Williams, Rosemary Fitzgerald and Oliver Stallybrass, *The Selected Correspondence of Michael Faraday*; (2 vols) Cambridge, 1971

Books for general and further reading (other sources are listed in the Notes):

Maurice Berman, *Social Change and Scientific Organization: The Royal Institution 1799–1844*; Heinemann, 1978

M.P. Crosland, *Science under Control*; Cambridge University Press, 1992

A. Cunningham and N. Jardine, *Romanticism and the Sciences*; Cambridge University Press, 1990

David Gooding, Trevor Pinch and Simon Schaffer (eds), *The Uses of Experiment: Studies in the Natural Sciences*; Cambridge, 1989

Frank Greenaway, Maurice Berman, Sophie Forgan and Donovan Chilton (eds), *Archives of the Royal Institution, Minutes of the Managers' Meetings, 1799–1903*; (15 vols, bound in 7) Scolar Press, 1971–76

Mary Boas Hall, *All Scientists Now: The Royal Society in the Nineteenth Century*; Cambridge University Press, 1984

Stephen Halliday, *The Great Stink of London: Sir Joseph Bazalgette and the Cleansing of the Victorian Metropolis*; Sutton Publishing, 1999

James Hamilton, *Turner and the Scientists*; Tate Publications, 1998

James Hamilton (ed.), *Fields of Influence: Conjunctions of Artists and Scientists 1815–60*; University of Birmingham Press, 2001

Ian Inkster and Jack Morrell (eds), *Metropolis and Province: Science and British Culture, 1780–1850*; Hutchinson, 1983

David Knight, *Ideas in Chemistry*; London, Athlone, 1995

David Knight, *Humphry Davy: Science and Power*; Cambridge University Press, 2nd edn 1998

David Knight, *Science in the Romantic Era* [collected essays]; Ashgate, 1998

Jack Morrell and Arnold Thackray, *Gentlemen of Science: The Early Years of the British Association for the Advancement of Science*; Oxford University Press, 1981

Iwan Rhys Morus, *Frankenstein's Children: Electricity, Exhibition and Experiment in Early-Nineteenth-Century London*; Princeton, 1998

Elizabeth C. Patterson, *Mary Somerville and the Cultivation of Science, 1815–1840*; Martinus Nijhoff, 1983

Francis Spufford and Jenny Uglow, *Cultural Babbage: Technology, Time and Invention*; Faber, 1996

Anne Treneer, *The Mercurial Chemist: A Life of Humphry Davy*; Methuen, 1963

INDEX

Abbott, Benjamin: career, 105–6, 137;
City Philosophical Society, 128, 129,
134, 137; description of Faraday,
117; Faraday correspondence, 30–6,
39, 42, 44, 48, 50, 136, 143, 147, 153,
313; on Faraday employment, 40;
Faraday friendship, 11, 105–6,
108–9, 128, 170–1, 184; Faraday
letters from continental tour,
89–90, 91, 98, 103, 104, 113;
marriage, 171; memoirs of Faraday,
397; reading Faraday's lecture
notes, 35–6, 37; religion, 137; at
Tatum's lectures, 11, 30; tribute to
Faraday, 134
Abbott, Robert, 31, 103, 104, 105
Accademia Economico-Agraria,
Florence, 178, 194
Adare, Lord and Lady, 309
Addison, Joseph, 134
Admiralty, 223, 264, 282
African Trading Company, 151–2
Ainger, Alfred, 137, 203
Ainsworth, William, 209
Airy, Sir George Biddell, 263, 322,
348
Albemarle Street (Number 21): attic
rooms, 42, 44, 118; basement
laboratory, 272; second floor
rooms, 21, 160, 348; watercolours
of, 242, 357, 358–61
Albert, Prince Consort, 355, 372, 385
Allen, John, 352
Amiens, Peace of, 61, 64
Ampère, André-Marie: electrical
research, 158, 162, 246; Faraday
correspondence, 169, 178, 182–5,
231, 295; Faraday's discoveries, 165;
letter to Davy, 36; publications,
162; reception of Davy, 68;
'Substance X', 69, 71
Anderson, Charles: character, 221;
crispation experiments, 233; death,
394; employment, 221, 278; furnace
assistance, 221, 223, 245; lecture
assistance, 201, 344, 372;
watercolour of, 359
Annals of Electricity, 278
Annals of Philosophy, 157, 162, 169, 180
Antinori, Vincenzio, 253, 256
Antologia, 253
Apothecaries Act (1815), 122
Apreece, Jane, see Davy
Apreece, Shuckburgh, 22
Arago, Dominique, 246, 252
Arnold, Matthew, 242
Ashley, Anthony Ashley Cooper, Lord
(later 7th Earl of Shaftesbury), 280

Woodward, Charles, 137
Wordsworth, William, 21
Wright, Joseph (of Derby), 12
Wyon, William, 203, 210

Yarrow, Alfred, 365
Young, Charles Mayne, 17

Young, Thomas (Professor of
    Chemistry at the Royal
    Institution), 21, 221, 225
Young, Thomas (secretary to
    Melbourne), 285–6, 288

Ziegler, Philip, 286